The Cambridge Companion to Ballet

Ballet is a paradox: much loved but little studied. It is a beautiful fairy tale; detached from its origins and unrelated to the men and women who created it. Yet ballet has a history, little known and rarely presented. These great works have dark sides and moral ambiguities, not always nor immediately visible. The daring and challenging quality of ballet as well as its perceived 'safe' nature is not only one of its fascinations but one of the intriguing questions to be explored in this *Companion*. The essays reveal the conception, intent and underlying meaning of ballets and re-create the historical reality in which they emerged. The reader will find new and unexpected aspects of ballet, its history and its aesthetics, the evolution of plot and narrative, new insights into the reality of training, the choice of costume and the transformation of an old art in a modern world.

The Cambridge Companion to

BALLET

....

EDITED BY
Marion Kant

CAMBRIDGE
UNIVERSITY PRESS

CAMBRIDGE UNIVERSITY PRESS
Cambridge, New York, Melbourne, Madrid, Cape Town, Singapore, São Paulo

Cambridge University Press
The Edinburgh Building, Cambridge CB2 8RU, UK

Published in the United States of America by Cambridge University Press, New York

www.cambridge.org
Information on this title: www.cambridge.org/9780521539869

© Cambridge University Press 2007

First published 2007

Printed in the United Kingdom at the University Press, Cambridge

A catalogue record for this publication is available from the British Library

ISBN 978-0-521-83221-2 hardback
ISBN 978-0-521-53986-9 paperback

Contents

List of illustrations

Foreword

Ballet is a theatre art that, by virtue of its origins, is essentially and incontrovertibly European. Those origins are, in large measure, to be sought in the Italian courts of the Renaissance in the fifteenth century, where it developed as a means of displaying the splendour and power of the ruling prince. A century or so later it crossed the Alps in the marriage train, so to speak, of Catherine de' Medici, the chosen bride of King Henri II of France, becoming a dominant feature in the entertainments of the French court for more than a century until well into the reign of Louis XIV. By that time professional dancers were already being employed to add variety and brilliance through a technique that far exceeded that of even the most talented of the courtiers. However, halfway through Louis XIV's reign the court ballet went into a sudden decline, not so much on account of the king's growing corpulence as through the increasing demands on his treasury of the wars in which France then became embroiled. Providentially a far more suitable and lasting future for the ballet was then provided by the king himself in creating the Académie de Musique, which was to be the forerunner of the institution now known as the Paris Opéra. Here professional dancers found an arena from the very outset, and dance as spectacle was to play a conspicuous role in the creation of what we now recognise as the art of classical ballet. At first it took the form of an adjunct to opera, as in the opera-ballets of Rameau, but from the mid-eighteenth century it became an independent theatre art, in which the stage action was conveyed by the dancers themselves in pantomime. This was one of the great theatrical turning-points that marked the Age of the Enlightenment.

While Paris continued to be regarded as the prominent centre of this new art form, ballet soon took root elsewhere in Europe. Italy, where the infant art had been nurtured, became a fertile field as many opera houses throughout the peninsula adopted ballet as a respected adjunct to the opera. In Milan and Naples major ballets were being produced on the stages of those cities' celebrated opera houses, based upon plots that required powerful gifts of pantomime in those players responsible for the dramatic roles. By the end of the eighteenth century ballet was generally recognised throughout Europe as a significant theatre art, and one with its own philosopher in the distinguished figure of Jean-Georges Noverre, whose *Letters on Dancing* are to this day still revered as a classic.

France retained its ascendancy notwithstanding the cataclysm of the Revolution, a period that saw the emergence of the formidable figure of

Pierre Gardel, who was to dominate French ballet for some forty years. When the Revolution and the Napoleonic wars had receded into history, Paris was still regarded as the fountain-head of the theatrical dance, and it was there within the august walls of the Opéra that the conflict between the opposing trends of classicism and romanticism in the art of ballet was finally and unequivocally resolved in the latter's favour. Under the banner of romanticism the choreographers Taglioni and Perrot produced those two ballets that are treasured today as lasting classics, *La Sylphide* and *Giselle*. The Paris ballet continued to enjoy a dominance that would remain virtually unchallenged until the last decades of the nineteenth century, when the world became increasingly aware that ballet had taken root in most fertile soil in St Petersburg, underwritten by the vast wealth of the tsars but preserving nevertheless a vital French connection in the person of the Marseilles-born ballet master Marius Petipa.

In the early 1900s the first rumblings were felt of the revolution that was to come, and it was in the last few years before the outbreak of the First World War that Europe was given its first taste of the balletic riches that Russia had to offer. This came about through a privately sponsored company of dancers from the Imperial Theatres organised and directed by Serge Diaghilev that conquered Paris literally overnight in the summer of 1909, presenting not extracts from the works of Petipa, but a programme mainly produced by a younger choreographer, Mikhail Fokine. This extraordinary enterprise was continued, with a break of a few years resulting from the war, until 1929 when Diaghilev died. The consequences of his demise was to prove the permanence of the legacy left by that extraordinary company in the course of just two decades – an eye-blink in the context of history – for the disappearance of its guiding spirit let loose a younger brood of choreographers – notably Nijinska, Massine, Balanchine and Lifar – to propagate a new vision of ballet throughout Europe and America.

Not even the great conflict that then raged across the world in the mid-century would hinder this process. In many of the lands that were ravaged in those dark years, ballet provided a momentary release from the brutal consequences of aerial bombardment, invasion and occupation, gaining many converts in all ranks of society to the allurements of the dance. Such seeds have continued to bear fruit ever since, and today, more than ever before, the dance is regarded as a vital and major part of our artistic heritage. In its theatrical manifestations, most notably the great heritage of classical ballet but also in the multi-faceted complexity of freer disciplines, ballet has earned its place as a major component of the arts of spectacle in the modern world. Furthermore, it has been accepted as a subject for serious scholarship, revealing, as it does, the possibilities of human movement as a means of expression no less valid than human speech. Today a vast body of literature, recorded reminiscences, musical sources and other material of record is being assembled on the subject of dance in all its multiple forms, opening up new vistas for study and research, and requiring works of reference, such as is offered in this volume, to guide both the scholar and the devotee.

These are the rich fields over which I have been privileged to wander these past sixty years. In the beginning of my historical endeavours I luxuriated in that of Second Empire Paris, unearthing the history of a period of French ballet that had received scant attention from earlier scholars. The Library of the Paris Opéra became, for me, virtually a second home on my regular visits to Paris, and over the years my research wanderings were to lead me to other fields, some that had seen earlier harvests and others that had been more recently cultivated.

My quest to unravel the rich strands of the history of ballet has thus led me to many libraries and archives, and I have thereby become deeply conscious of my debt to the volumes of reference books which repose on open shelves as friendly guides to those in search of information. I therefore welcome – most specially, I may add, since I am a Cambridge graduate – this new companion, which I am sure will find an honoured place not only on the reference shelves of libraries, both specialised and general, but also on those of countless devotees of an art that today holds so many in its thrall.

Ivor Guest

Notes on contributors

Inge Baxmann studied romance languages and literature at the universities of Bochum and Paris. From 1981 to 1986 she was assistant professor at the Institute of French Literature of the Technical University of Berlin. In 1987 she completed her doctoral dissertation, "Die Feste der Französischen Revolution. Inszenierung von Gesellschaft als Natur". She received several post-doctoral fellowships and became a fellow of the prestigious Alexander-von-Humboldt-Stiftung. 1997 Habilitation at the Humboldt University Berlin with *Mythos Gemeinschaft. Körper- und Tanzkulturen in der Moderne*. She holds a chair for Theatre Studies at Leipzig University.

Her next book will be a study of *Cultures in Movement. Life of the Transnation. Kulturen in Bewegung: Leben in der Transnation* (Munich: Fink-Verlag).

Juliet Bellow completed her dissertation, "Clothing the Corps: How the Avant-Garde and the Ballets Russes Fashioned the Modern Body", in 2005 at the University of Pennsylvania. Her publications include "Reforming Dance: Auguste Rodin's 'Nijinsky' and Vaslav Nijinsky's 'L'Après-Midi d'un Faune'", in a special issue of the Cantor Arts Center Journal, *New Studies on Rodin*.

She teaches art history at the University of Pennsylvania in Philadelphia and at Hunter College New York.

Judith Chazin-Bennahum performed in many dance companies, including dancing with Agnes de Mille, the Robert Joffrey Ballet Company and the Metropolitan Opera Ballet Company as Principal Soloist. She also danced with the Santa Fe Opera and toured Europe with Igor Stravinsky as the conductor and was invited by George Balanchine to join the New York City Ballet. She received her Doctorate in Romance Languages at the University of New Mexico and is the author of *Dance in the Shadow of the Guillotine* (1988) a book on ballet during the French Revolution and published *The Ballets of Antony Tudor* in 1995. *The Lure of Perfection: Fashion and Ballet 1780–1830* was published by Routledge in 2004. She is preparing a volume, *Teaching Dance Studies* which will have essays on the pedagogy of teaching dance courses in a university setting.

Bennahum has choreographed for the Santa Fe Opera, the Southwest Ballet Company, the UNM Opera Studio and annually for the UNM Dance ensemble. She re-created Jean-Georges Noverre's ballet *Medea* (1780), which was filmed for video and is now being distributed by Princeton Books.

Tim Blanning teaches at Cambridge University. His research interests are focused on the history of continental Europe in the period 1660–1914. His early work concentrated on the Holy Roman Empire and the Habsburg Monarchy during the eighteenth century and he retains a strong interest in this area. During the 1980s and 1990s his focus moved westwards to France during the Revolution, especially to its foreign policy and its interaction with the rest of Europe. Most recently, he has concentrated on the high culture of Europe and its relationship to state power, which resulted in his prize-winning study *the Culture of Power and Power of Culture 1660–1789* (2002). He is currently working on why music progressed from subordinate status in the early modern period to its present position of supremacy among the creative arts. He is the general editor of *The Oxford History of Modern Europe* (2002) and of *The Short Oxford History of Europe*, editing personally the volumes on the eighteenth and nineteenth centuries in the latter series (2000). He has been a Fellow of the British Academy since 1990.

Matilde Ann Butkas holds Master of Music Degrees in piano performance and piano pedagogy from the University of Illinois, and is currently recording the complete keyboard works of Johann Mattheson on harpsichord. She is a doctoral student in musicology at the University of Oregon.

Anne Middelboe Christensen, born in Denmark, is a dance critic. She holds an MA in Danish literature and theatre history from the University of Copenhagen, on the subject of Danish dance and ballet criticism from 1771 to 1862. She also studied at York University in Toronto. She has worked as a journalist for various magazines since 1985, specialising in dance criticism and dance writing, and since 1995 writes for the daily Dagbladet Information. Since 1995 she has been assistant professor at the University of Copenhagen. She is the author of *Diversions of the Royal Danish Ballet. Interviews with the Dancers about the Bournonville Tradition* (Schønberg, Copenhagen, 2002) and *Backbone. Dansescenen, Denmark 1993–2003* (2003). She also has worked and works as a dramaturgue for choreographers Itzik Galili (Holland) and Tim Rushton (Danish Dance Theatre).

Sarah Davies Cordova. Her interdisciplinary work in French and Francophone cultures together with dance studies enables her to research texts of post-revolutionary France, and colonial and postcolonial eras which incorporate the politics of (self) representation, gender concerns, and geographical, topographical, diasporic and historical (dis)placements of persons in terms of corporeality, movement styles as well as bodily memory and traces of conforming, and resistance.

She has published *Paris Dances: Textual Choreographies of the Nineteenth-Century French Novel* (1999) and a number of articles on nineteenth-century ballet and literature; as well as on works by women authors from Guadeloupe, Haiti and Algeria. She teaches French language and literatures at Marquette University, although she is currently the resident director for the Marquette University service learning programme at the Desmond Tutu Peace Trust and in conjunction with the University of the Western Cape in Cape Town, South Africa.

Mark Franko received his Ph.D. in French from Columbia University and danced professionally before becoming a dance historian, theorist and choreographer. He has taught at Princeton University, New York University, Columbia/Barnard, Purdue University, Paris 8, the University of Nice, Montpellier 3, the Catholic University of Leuven and is currently Professor of Dance and Chair of Theatre Arts at the University of California, Santa Cruz.

He is the author of *Excursion for Miracles: Paul Sanasardo, Donya Feuer, and Studio for Dance* (1955–64), *The Work of Dance: Labor, Movement, and Identity in the 1930s* (CHOICE magazine "Outstanding Academic Title" for 2003), *Dancing Modernism/Performing Politics* (1996 de la Torre Bueno prize Special Mention), *Dance as Text: Ideologies of the Baroque Body* (1993; published in France by Editions

Kargo and forthcoming in Italy by L'Epos) and *The Dancing Body in Renaissance Choreography* (1986).

His choreography for NovAntiqua, the company he founded in 1985, has been produced at Lincoln Center Out-of-Doors Festival, the Berlin Werkstatt Festival, the Getty Center, the Montpellier Opera, Toulon Art Museum and in many national venues.

Jennifer Fisher is Assistant Professor of Dance at the University of California Irvine and teaches dance history, fieldwork, philosophy, aesthetics and criticism. She holds a master's degree in Dance from York University in Toronto and a Ph.D. in Dance History and Theory from the University of California, Riverside. A former dancer and actor, she has previously taught at York University and Pomona College. Her book, *Nutcracker Nation: How an Old World Ballet Became a Christmas Tradition in the New World*, was published by Yale University Press in 2003. She is a regular contributor of dance criticism for the *Los Angeles Times*; other publications include *Dance Research Journal*, *Women & Performance*, *Queen's Quarterly*, the *International Dictionary of Ballet*, *Stuttgarter Zeitung*, the *Encyclopedia of Homosexuality*, *Dance and Society in Canada*, and several dance periodicals. She is a contributing editor for the *Society of Dance History Scholars Newsletter* and serves on that organisation's Editorial Board (working in association with the University of Wisconsin Press). In 2003, she staged Deborah Hay's conceptual dance work, *Exit*, for students and faculty for Pomona College's spring dance concert.

Lynn Garafola is a dance critic and historian. She is the author of *Diaghilev's Ballets Russes* (1989) and the editor of several books, including *André Levinson on Dance: Writings from Paris in the Twenties* (with Joan Acocella) (1991), *The Diaries of Marius Petipa* (1992) (which she also translated), *Rethinking the Sylph: New Perspectives on the Romantic Ballet* (1997), *José Limón: An Unfinished Memoir* (1998) and most recently *The Ballets Russes and Its World* (Kurt Weill Prize 2001). She is the editor of *Studies in Dance History*, the book series published by the Society of History Scholars, and a senior editor/New York critic for *Dance Magazine*, and her essays and criticism have appeared in *The Nation*, *Ballet Review*, *Dancing Times*, *The Times Literary Supplement*, *New York Times* Book Review, *Los Angeles Times* book review, and many other publications.

She holds a Ph.D. in Comparative Literature from the Graduate Center-City University of New York and is the curator of "On Dance", a series of lectures and public programmes sponsored by the Barnard Department of Dance.

Ivor Guest is the Doyen of dance studies in the United Kingdom. He studied law at Trinity College Cambridge and worked as a solicitor for many years. He is the internationally recognised authority on nineteenth-century romantic ballet in France and England. His books *The Romantic Ballet in England* (1954) and *The Romantic Ballet in Paris* (1966) are considered standard reference works. He also wrote the official history of the Paris Opera Ballet, *Le Ballet de l'Opéra de Paris* (1976), which has been published in English in 2006. He has written many biographies of romantic ballerinas and choreographers, among others of Fanny Cerrito, Fanny Elssler, Adeline Genée, Jules Perrot and Virginia Zucchi.

An extensive bibliography is included in Guest's autobiographical *Adventures of a Ballet Historian: An Unfinished Memoir* (1982). An updated bibliography appeared in *Dance Research* (Summer 1995), an issue published in celebration of his seventy-fifth birthday.

Sandra Noll Hammond is a dancer and dance historian whose research was among the first to explore the development of ballet technique and training of the eighteenth and early nineteenth centuries. She has presented this material in many international venues, at master classes and concerts as well as lectures and articles. Recent publications include "Sor and the Ballet of his Time" in *Estudios Sobre Fernando Sor/Sor Studies* (2003) and "International Elements of Dance Training in the *Late Eighteenth Century*" in *The Grotesque Dancer on the Eighteenth-century Stage/Gennaro Magri and his World* (2005). She was co-founder and first director of the dance major at the University of Arizona and later professor and director of dance at the University of Hawaii. She studied ballet with Antony Tudor and Margaret Craske at the Juilliard School and the Metropolitan Opera Ballet, and with Arthur Mahoney and Thalia Mara at the School of Ballet Repertory. As a performer, she was a member of Pacific Ballet and Arizona Dance Theatre, and she has appeared as guest artist in concerts of baroque dance.

Thérèse Hurley holds a BM and GPD from the Peabody Conservatory of the Johns Hopkins University and an MM from Temple University. Her master's thesis "The Harp in Tchaikovsky's Ballets" examines the composer's skill at composing idiomatic music for the harp and his use of the instrument to convey the supernatural in his ballets. She is a doctoral student in musicology at the University of Oregon.

Marion Kant earned her Ph.D. in musicology in 1986 at Humboldt University in Berlin on the subject of "Romantic Ballet: An Inquiry into Gender". She has taught at German Universities, at Cambridge University, King's College London and the University of Surrey, Great Britain and was a Visiting Fellow at King's College Cambridge. She is presently teaching courses in cultural and dance history, performance criticism and the history of secularism at the University of Pennsylvania, Philadelphia. Her publications include a monograph on the German choreographer Jean Weidt (1984), several articles and books on modern German dance under Nazism: *Hitler's Dancers* appeared in 2003 with Berghahn Books Oxford and New York. An essay on *Giselle* was commissioned by the State Opera, Berlin in 2000. Her main research and subsequent publications focus on the problems of exile, on dance and music history in the nineteenth and twentieth centuries and on dance aesthetics.

Together with musicians Marshall Taylor and Samuel Hsu she has organised and presented a series of concerts commemorating *Entartete Musik*, music forbidden by the Nazis.

Erik Näslund is a dance scholar and director of the Dance Museum in Stockholm. He has written extensively on the history of the Swedish Ballet in the 1920s. He has also contributed significantly to developing methods of documenting dance and making dance collections accessible for research and scholarship.

He is the author of monographs on Birgit Cullberg and Carina Ari; from 1973 to 1981 he was the editor of the magazine *Dans*. He writes dance criticism for the *Svenska dagbladet* in Stockholm. He is engaged in the dance folklore movement of Sweden.

He recently rewrote the libretto for *The Nutcracker*, together with Pär Isberg for the Royal Swedish Ballet.

Jennifer Nevile took her undergraduate degree in music at Sydney University and wrote her doctoral dissertation at the School of Music at University of New South Wales on fifteenth-century Italian dance manuscripts. Since then she has continued her research into dance and music from the fifteenth to the seventeenth centuries.

She produced a video, *The Amiable Conqueror: Dancing at the Courts of Europe* (1999), that showcased several sixteenth-century dances and four baroque choreographies. Her research interests lie in the examination of the various dance practices in their social and intellectual contexts, that is, how the intellectual ideas current during the early modern period were transformed by the dance masters into choreographic practices. Her latest book, *The Eloquent Body: Dance and Humanist Culture in Fifteenth-Century Italy* (2004), explores dance as a physical expression of Renaissance humanism and analyses the dance practice of fifteenth-century Italy in relation to issues of economic class, education and power, as well as to the contemporary intellectual discussion on the meaning of the arts and ideas on the body, including moral concepts of eloquent movement, nobility and ethics.

She is currently investigating changes in the choreographic structure of Italian dances from the mid-fifteenth century to the first few decades of the sixteenth century.

Marina Nordera was born in Mantua and graduated in musicology at the University of Venice in 1990. Her thesis topic was on the tradition of the dialogue in *Della danza* by Luciano. From 1985 to 1994 she was a professional dancer in the following companies: Il Ballarino, Ris et Danceries, Fêtes Galantes, L'Eventail. She also performed in several dance groups specifically staging baroque dance.

Her Ph.D. thesis, written and defended at the History Department of the European University in Florence, focused on the female performer in early and modern dance: "La donna in ballo. Danza e genere nella prima età moderna."

Since 2003 she has taught dance history, aesthetics and analytical methodology of dance at the University of Nice.

Barbara Ravelhofer is a lecturer in English Literature at the University of Durham and a Research Associate of the Centre for History and Economics, King's College, Cambridge. She pursued her research at the Universities of Munich, Princeton, Bologna and Cambridge, where she was a Junior Research Fellow in Renaissance Studies.

Her latest book, *The Early Stuart Masque: Dance, Costume, and Music* (2006), studies the complex impact of movements, costumes, words, scenes, music, and special effects in English illusionistic theatre of the Renaissance. Drawing on a massive amount of documentary evidence relating to English productions as well as spectacle in France, Italy, Germany and the Ottoman Empire, the book elucidates professional ballet, theatre management and dramatic performance at the early Stuart court.

Lucia Ruprecht graduated from the Universities of Tübingen and Aix-en-Provence and completed her Ph.D. in German Literature at Cambridge. She teaches literature, thought and film on the nineteenth and twentieth centuries and on modern comparative literature at the English Faculty of the University of Cambridge. Her research to date has focused on the interaction between literature and dance, especially on questions of embodiment and subjectivity. She has a strong interest in literary and cultural theory and is co-editor of *Performance and Performativity in German Cultural Studies* (2003). She is currently working on the notion of charisma in early twentieth-century cultural theory, literature, film and dance.

Tim Scholl, associate professor of Russian at Oberlin College and the director of Oberlin's Center for Russian, East European and Central Asian Studies, is the author of *From Petipa to Balanchine: Classical Revival and the Modernization of Ballet* (1994) and *Sleeping Beauty: A Legend in Progress*, released in 2004 by Yale University Press. His perspective on the restaging of *Sleeping Beauty* is particularly intimate: he helped lead officials of the Maryinsky (formerly Kirov) Ballet of St Petersburg to some invaluable documentation of the original 1890 production's choreography. His chronicle of the reconstruction of the Maryinsky's signal work is a tale of historical sleuthing that illuminates the difficulty of interpreting historical evidence as well as the political conflict that often surrounds and shapes cultural production.

Marian Smith holds a Ph.D. degree from Yale University. She is Associate Professor of Music at the University of Oregon. She has published articles and reviews in both music and dance journals, including the *Cambridge Opera Journal*, *Dance Chronicle*, *Journal of the American Musicological Society* and *Dance Research*. She has contributed chapters to the volume *Reading Critics Reading: Opera and Ballet Criticism 1830–1848* (2001), *The Cambridge Companion to Grand Opera* and (with a co-author) *Rethinking the Sylph* (1997). Her essays on opera and ballet appear in programme books of the Royal Opera and Royal Ballet in London, and she has also presented scholarly papers in Italy, England, Germany and Denmark. Her book on the intersection of opera and ballet in nineteenth-century Paris, *Ballet and Opera in the Age of Giselle* (2000), was awarded the De la Torre Bueno Prize from the Dance Perspectives Foundation. She is currently working on projects about the historiography of nineteenth-century ballet, and the history of the *pas de deux*.

Lester Tome, a Cuban dancer, performer, dance scholar and journalist, has taught salsa, dance history, ethnography and pedagogy at Temple University, Denison University and the University of the Arts in Philadelphia. He is currently completing a Ph.D. in dance as a University Fellow at Temple. His dissertation is on Cuban ballet. As a journalist, he has published for the Chilean newspaper *El Mercurio*; in the United States, his articles and reviews have appeared in the *Durham Herald-Sun* and on *Dance magazine's* website. In Cuba he wrote for *Cuba en el Ballet*, *Evolución y Cultura*, and *CMBF-Radio Musical Nacional*. He has been a fellow of New York Times Foundation and the National Endowment for the Arts. He performed for Ally Ink and is a member of Sprezzatura, the baroque dance ensemble at Temple University. In 2003, he performed in a restaging of Paul Taylor's *Esplanade*. He also writes the notes to the programmes for Ballet de Santiago, in Chile.

Dorion Weickmann studied social and economic history and political science at the University of Hamburg, Germany. Her Ph.D. thesis focused on cultural aspects of dance and ballet history. It was published in 2002 as *Der dressierte Leib. Kulturgeschichte des Balletts (1580–1870)*. She is presently preparing a book on the history of German dance in the twentieth century. She writes for several journals, and also *Die Zeit* and *Süddeutsche Zeitung* and lives in Berlin.

Zheng Yangwen is a Research Fellow at the Asia Research Institute at the National University of Singapore. She received her Ph.D. from Cambridge University (King's College). Her Ph.D. and postdoctoral work resulted in *The Social Life of Opium in China, 1483–1999* (2005).

Chronology

1279	The Mongols conquered China.
1283	Teutonic Order completed subjection to Prussia.
1292	Dante Alighieri, *La Vita Nuova*.
1302	Bull *Unam Sanctam* pronounced highest papal claims to supremacy.
1321	Dante completed *La Divina Commedia*.
1321	Founding of minstrels' guild.
1323	Thomas Aquinas canonised.
1327	Marsillius of Padua wrote *Defensor Pacis*.
1337	Giotto (painter) died.
1347–51	Black Death devastated Europe.
1348–53	Giovanni Boccaccio, *Decamerone*.
1358	Revolt of French peasants (Jacquerie).
1362	William Langland, *Piers Plowman*.
1368	Mongul Yuan dynasty in China overthrown by national Ming dynasty.
1377	Guillaume de Machaut (composer) died.
1387–1400	Geoffrey Chaucer, *The Canterbury Tales*.
15th century	Dance treatises recorded choreographies for the first time in Western Europe and laid the structural foundations of ballet.
1415	Jan Hus burnt as a heretic in Prague.
1418	Thomas à Kempis *De Imitatione Christi*.
1421	Peking made capital of China.
1431	Joan of Arc burnt at the stake in Rouen.
1453–5	Johannes Gutenberg printed the Mazarin Bible in Mainz.
1453	The Turks conquered Constantinopol.
1455	Tristano Sforza's wedding celebrations in Milan choreographed by Domenico da Piacenza.
	Domenico da Piacenza *De arte saltandj & choreas ducendj De la arte di ballare et danzare*.
c. 1455	Antonio Cornazano *Libro dell'arte del danzare*.
1463	Guglielmo Ebreo da Pesaro *Guilielmi Hebraei pisauriensis de pratica seu arte tripudii vulgare opusculum incipit*.
1469	Letter of Filippus Bussus to Lorenzo de' Medici offering to come to Florence in order to teach Lorenzo and his siblings "some elegant, beautiful and dignified *balli* and *bassadanze*".
	Marsilio Ficino *Commentary on Plato's Symposium on Love*.
1474	William Caxton printed the first English book.
1480	Ferdinand and Isabella of Spain appointed Inquisitor against heresy.

1489	Marsilio Ficino, *De vita*.
1492	Jews expelled from Spain.
	Christopher Columbus sailed for America.
1494	The Venetian Press of Aldus Manutius issued its first book.
	Charles VIII invaded Italy and expelled the Medici.
1495–7	Leonardo da Vinci painted *The last supper*.
1503	Leonardo da Vinci painted the *Mona Lisa*.
1506	Albrecht Dürer from Milan: "I set to work to learn dancing and twice went to the school. There I had to pay the master a ducat. Nobody would make me go there again. I would have to pay out all that I earned, and at the end I still wouldn't know how to dance!"
1508–12	Michelangelo painted the ceiling of the Sistine Chapel in Rome.
1509	Henry VIII become King of England.
1512	Henry VIII celebrated epiphany with a masque.
1513	Niccolo Machiavelli, *The Prince*.
1517	Martin Luther affixed 95 Theses to the door of Wittenberg church.
1524–5	Hans Holbein the Younger painted *The Dance of Death*.
1528	Balthasar Castiglione, *The Courtier*.
1531	Thomas Elyot, *The Boke Named the Governour*.
1534	Jesuit Order founded in Paris.
1536	John Calvin went to Geneva and issued *The Institute of the Christian Religion*.
1551	Giovanni Pierluigi Palestrina appointed conductor at St Peter's in Rome.
1558	Elizabeth I Queen of England.
1570	Andrea Palladio *Treatise on Architecture*.
	Académie de Poésie et Musique founded by Jean Antoine de Baïf.
1572	St Bartholomew massacre in France.
1573	*Ballet des ambassadeurs*.
	Torquato Tasso *Aminta*.
1580	Michel Eyquem de Montaigne, *Essays*.
1581	*Balet comique de la Royne* (Allegorie of Circé).
	Fabritio Caroso, *Il Ballarino*.
1586	The war of the three Henrys in France.
end 16th c.	Emergence of *ballet de cour*.
1590	Edmund Spenser, *The Faery Queene*.
1593	Henry IV of France converted to Roman Catholicism.
1597	William Shakespeare, *Romeo and Juliet*.
1599	Opening of the Globe Theatre, London.
1600	Fabritio Caroso, *Nobiltà di dame*.
1602	Cesare Negri, *Le gratie d'amore*.
1602–4	Galileo Galilei discovered laws of gravitation.
1603	William Shakespeare, *Hamlet*.
1603	Elizabeth I died.
1605	*The Masque of Blackness*.
	Miguel de Cervantes Saavedra, *Don Quixote*.

1607	Claudio Monteverdi, *Orfeo*.
1608	*The Masque of Beauty*.
1609	*The Masque of Queens*.
1609	Johannes Kepler, *Astronomia Nova*.
1610	*Ballet de Monseigneur le Duc de Vandosme*.
1611	*Oberon*.
	William Shakespeare, *The Tempest*.
1613	*The Masque of the Inner Temple and Gray's Inn*.
1617	*Ballet de la délivrance de Renaud*.
1618–48	Thirty Years War.
1620	Puritans set up Plymouth Colony in New England.
1623	François de Lauze, *Apologie de la danse*.
1626	*Ballet de la douairière de Billebahaut*.
1629	Pierre Corneille, *Mélite*.
1632	First female professional singers in English theatre history appear in the masque *Tempe restored*.
1634	*A Masque Presented at Ludlow Castle*.
	The Triumph of Peace.
	John Milton, *Comus*.
1635	Académie Française founded by Cardinal Richelieu.
1637	Réné Descartes, *Discours de la méthode*.
1639	Nicolas Poussin appointed French court painter.
1639	Francesco Cavalli, *Le nozze di Peleo e di Teti*, Venice.
c. 1640	Stage for the *ballet de cour* is elevated.
1640	*Salmacida Spolia*.
	English Civil War broke out.
1641	*Ballet de la prosperité des armes de la France*.
1642–60	English theatres closed.
1642	Rembrandt Harmensz van Rijn, *Night Watch*.
1644	The Manchus conquered China.
1649	Charles I of England beheaded.
1650	*Il tabacco*.
1651	Thomas Hobbes, *Leviathan*.
1653	*Cupid and Death*.
	Ballet de la Nuit
1653	*Il Gridelino*.
1654	Carlo Caproli, *Le nozze di Peleo e di Teti* (*Les Noces de Pelée et Thétis*), Paris.
1654	Louis XIV crowned.
1661	Académie Royale de Danse founded in Paris.
1662	Building of Versailles begun.
1664	Molière, *Tartuffe*.
1666	Molière, *Le Misanthrope*.
1667	John Milton, *Paradise Lost*.
	Jean Racine, *Andromaque*.
1669	Académie Royale de Musique founded in Paris.

1670	Louis XIV gives up dancing in leading roles of the *ballet de cour*.
	Baruch Spinoza, *Tractatus Theologico-Politicus*.
1672	First journal for light reading: *Le Mercure galant*.
1673	William Wycherley, *The Gentleman Dancing Master*.
	Molière, *Le Malade imaginaire*.
1674	William Wycherley, *The country wife*, *The plain dealer*.
1675	*Calisto* (John Crowne).
1677	Racine, *Phèdre*.
1680	Pierre Beauchamps, second director of Académie Royale de Danse.
	Comédie française established.
	Henry Purcell, *Dido and Aeneas*.
1687	Charles Perrault, *The Age of Louis the Great*.
	Isaac Newton, *Philosophiae Naturalis Principia Mathematica*.
1688	Glorious revolution: William of Orange King of England.
1689–97	Nine years of war between England and France.
1690	John Locke, *Essay concerning human understanding*.
1695	William Congreve, *Love for Love*.
1700	Raoul Auger Feuillet, *Chorégraphie ou l'art de décrire la danse par caractères, figures et signes démonstratifs*.
1702	Charles Le Brun, *Méthode pour apprendre à dessiner les passions*.
	John Weaver, *The Tavern Bilkers*.
1702–13	War of the Spanish Succession.
1704	Jonathan Swift, *The Tale of a Tub*.
1704	Isaac Newton, *The Corpuscular Theory of Light*.
1705	Peter the Great founded Moscow University.
1706	Mr Isaac, *A Collection of Ball-Dances perform'd at Court: viz. The Richmond*.
	John Weaver, *A Small Treatise of Time and Cadence in Dancing, Reduc'd to an Easy and Exact Method, Shewing how Steps, and their Movements, agree with the Notes, and Division of Notes, in each Measure*.
	John Weaver's translation of Raoul Auger Feuillet, *Orchesography or the Art of Dancing, by Characters and Demonstrative Figures, By which any Person, who understands Dancing, may of himself easily learn all manner of Dances*.
1707	Johann Pasch, *Beschreibung wahrer Tantz-Kunst*.
1709–11	Sir Richard Steele founded *The Tatler*.
1711–14	*The Spectator*, editors Joseph Addison and Sir Richard Steele.
1712	John Weaver, *An Essay Towards an History of Dancing, In which the whole Art and its Various Excellencies are in some Measure Explain'd, containing the several sorts of Dancing, Antique and Modern, Serious, Scenical, Grotesque, etc. with the Use of it as an Exercise, Qualification, Diversion etc.*
1712	Alexander Pope, *The Rape of the Lock*.
1713	the Paris Opéra gave formal recognition to its dance constituents by establishing a permanent troupe of twenty dancers, ten women and ten men.

	Prince Eugene of Austria built the Belvedere Palace.
1717	John Weaver, *The Loves of Mars and Venus*.
1718	John Weaver, *Orpheus and Eurydice*.
1719	Claude Ballon director of Académie Royale de la Danse.
	Daniel Defoe, *Robinson Crusoe*.
1720	Christian Wolff *Rational thought on God, the world and the human soul*.
1721	John Weaver, *Anatomical and Mechanical Lectures upon Dancing, wherein Rules and Institutions for that Art are laid down and demonstrated*.
1722	Johann Sebastian Bach, *The Well-Tempered Clavier*.
1725	Pierre Rameau emphasised the vertical, balanced stance and outward turn of feet of the dancer.
	Pierre Rameau, *Le maître à danser*.
	C. Sol, *Méthode très facile et fort nécessaire, pour montrer à la jeunesse de l'un et l'autre sexe la manière de bien dancer*.
	Giovanni Battista Vico *Scienza Nuova Intorno alla Natura*.
1726	Jonathan Swift, *Gulliver's Travels*.
1728	John Weaver, *Perseus and Andromeda*.
	John Weaver, *The History of the Mimes and Pantomimes, with an Historical Account of several performers in Dancing, living in the Time of the Roman Emperors*.
	John Essex, *The Dancing-Master*, English translation of Pierre Rameau's *Le maître à danser*.
	Giambattista Dufort, *Trattato del ballo nobile*.
1729	Soame Jenyns, *The Art of Dancing. A Poem*.
1730	Johann Christoph Gottsched, *Critical art of poetry for the Germans*.
1733	John Weaver, *The Judgment of Paris, A Dramatic Entertainment in Dancing and Singing, After the Manner of the Ancient Greeks and Romans*.
	Marie Sallé in *Pygmalion*.
	Antoine François Prévost, *Manon Lescaut*.
1738	First spinning machines patented in England.
	First ballet school in Russia under Jean-Baptiste Landé.
1740	Samuel Richardson, *Pamela*.
1740s	Franz Hilverding produced dance dramas after Jean Racine's *Britannicus*, Crébillon's *Idoméneo* and Voltaire's *Alzira*.
1741	George Frederick Handel, *Messiah*.
	First German translation of a Shakespeare play (*Julius Caesar*) by von Borcke.
1743	Jean-Georges Noverre on stage for the first time in Favart's vaudeville *Le Coq du village*.
1747	Jean-Georges Noverre appointed ballet master in Marseilles, first choreography there *Les Fêtes chinoises*.
1748	First silk factory in Berlin.
	Carlo Gozzi, *Turandot*.
	Samuel Richardson, *Clarissa*.

1750	Jean-Georges Noverre *Le Jugement de Paris* (first ballet pantomime).
1751	First volume of the *Encyclopédie*, ed. Denis Diderot and Jean d'Alembert; entry on dance by Louis de Cahusac.
	Jean-Georges Noverre, *Fêtes chinoises* (Lyon).
1752	Benjamin Franklin invented lightning rod.
	Guerre des buffons.
1754	Louis de Cahusac, *La Danse ancienne et moderne ou Traité historique de la Danse.*
1754	Jean-Georges Noverre, *Fêtes chinoises* (Paris).
1755	Johann Joachim Winckelmann, *Gedanken über die Nachahmung der griechischen Werke in der Mahlerey und Bildhauer-Kunst.*
	Gotthold Ephraim Lessing, *Miss Sara Sampson.*
	Jean-Georges Noverre *Fêtes chinoises* (London).
	Samuel Johnson *Dictionary of the English language.*
1756–63	Seven Years War.
1756	Imperial Theatres as a state system founded by decree of Catherine the Great.
1757	Jean-Georges Noverre, *La Toilette de Vénus.*
1758	Jean-Georges Noverre, *La Mort d'Ajax.*
	Denis Diderot, *Entretiens sur le fils naturel.*
1759	Voltaire, *Candide.*
1760	Jean-Georges Noverre, *Lettres sur la danse, et sur les ballets,* Lyon and Stuttgart.
1760s	The *ballet d'action* arrived in Russia with Franz Hilverding and Gasparo Angiolini.
1761	Gasparo Angiolini, *Le Festin de Pierre, or Don Juan.*
	Jean-Jacques Rousseau, *La Nouvelle Héloïse.*
1762	Giovanni-Andrea Gallini, *A Treatise on the Art of Dancing.*
	Christoph Willibald Gluck, *Orfeo ed Euridice (Orphée et Eurydice).*
1763	Jean-Georges Noverre, *Jason et Médée.*
1764	James Hargreaves invented Spinning Jenny.
1765	Gasparo Angiolini, *Sémiramide.*
1766	Johann Joachim Winkelmann's *Gedanken über die Nachahmung der griechischen Werke in der Mahlerey und Bildhauer-Kunst* translated into French.
1770	Christoph Willibald Gluck, *Paride ed Elena (Pâris et Hélène).*
	Malpied, *Traité sur l'art de la danse.*
1772	Jean-Georges Noverre, *Iphigénie en Tauride.*
	Pierre Gardel refused to appear in full dress and decorative wig in the entrée of the opera-ballet *Castor et Pollux* by Jean-Philippe Rameau.
	Jacques Cazotte, *Le Diable amoureux* (novel).
1773	Johann Gottfried Herder, *Von deutscher Art und Kunst.*
	Jean-Georges Noverre, *Apelle et Campaspe.*
	Jean-Georges Noverre, *Adèle de Ponthieu.*

1774	Johann Wolfgang von Goethe, *The Sorrows of Young Werther*
	Joseph Priestley discovered oxygen.
	Gasparo Angiolini, *Thésée en Crète*.
	Jean-Georges Noverre, *Horaces et des Curiaces*.
1775	James Watt constructed first efficient steam engine.
1776	Jean-Georges Noverre, *Les Caprices de Galathée*.
	American Revolution.
	Adam Smith, *The Wealth of Nations*.
	Christoph Willibald Gluck, *Alceste*.
1778	Jean-Georges Noverre, *Les Petit Riens*.
	Jean-Georges Noverre, *Anette et Lubin*.
1779	Gennaro Magri, *Trattato teorico-prattico di ballo*.
1780	Jacques-François Deshayes appointed director of Académie Royale de la Danse.
	Jean-Georges Noverre, *Jason et Medée*.
1781	Jean-Jacques Rousseau, *Confessions*.
1784	André-Ernest-Modest Grétry, *Richard Coeur de Lion* (opera) Paris.
1785	Jacques-Louis David, *Oath of the Horatii*.
	Wolfgang Amadeus Mozart, *The Marriage of Figaro*.
1789	Abbé Emmanuel Joseph Sieyès, *Qu'est-ce que le tiers état?*
	Jean Dauberval/music arr. *La Fille mal gardée* (Bordeaux).
	French Revolution; Declaration of rights of man and of the citizen.
	Giovanni Paisiello, *Nina ou la folle par amour*.
1790	(14 July) *Fête de la Fédération* (Festival of Federation).
	Pierre Gardel, *Psyche*.
	Johann Wolfgang von Goethe, *Faust I*.
	Pierre Gardel, *Télémaque*.
1792	(30 September) Pierre Gardel, *Offrande à la Liberté* performed in Paris Opera.
1793	Pierre Gardel, *Le Judgement de Paris*.
	(10 November) *Fête de la Raison*.
1793–4	Reign of Terror instituted in France under Maximilien Robespierre.
1794	(8 June)*Fête de l'Etre Suprême*.
	Pierre Gardel, *La Réunion du 10 âout* (The reunion of 10 August)
1796	Charles Didelot/Cesare Bossi, *Flore et Zéphire* (London).
	Edward Jenner used vaccination for the first time.
1797	Johann Christian Friedrich Hölderlin, *Hyperion*.
1798	Thomas Malthus, *Essay on the Principle of Population*.
1799	Napoleon Bonaparte seized power.
1800	Pierre Gardel, *La Dansomanie* (Paris).
1803	Republication of Jean-Georges Noverre, *Lettres sur la Danse, et sur les Ballets*, St Petersburg.
1804	Pierre Gardel, *Une demi-heure de Caprice* (Paris).
	Bonaparte crowned Emperor as Napoleon I.
1807	Joseph Mallord William Turner, painting *Sun Rising in a Mist*.

	Georg Friedrich Wilhelm Hegel, *Phenomenology of the Spirit.*
1810	Walter Scott, *Lady of the Lake.*
	Johann Wolfgang von Goethe, *Colour Theory.*
	Foundation of Krupp works at Essen.
1812	Salvatore Taglioni and Louis Henry founded the school of ballet at the Teatro San Carlo in Naples.
1813	Academy of dancing established in Milan at La Scala.
	Jane Austen, *Pride and Prejudice.*
	Louis-Jacques Milon, *Nina ou la folle par amour.*
	Battle of Leipzig, Napoleon I defeated.
1814	Pierre Gardel, *Le Retour des Lys* (Paris).
	Congress of Vienna opened.
1815	Battle of Waterloo, Napoleon I finally defeated.
1816	Ernst Theodor Amadeus Hoffmann's short story *The Nutcracker and the Mouse King* published.
1818–1910	Marius Petipa.
1818	John Keats, *Endymion.*
	François Decombe Albert/Jean-Madeleine Schneitzhoeffer, *Le Séducteur du village.*
1819	Lord Gordon George Byron, *Don Juan.*
1820	Carlo Blasis, *Traité élémentaire théorique et pratique de l'art de la danse.*
1821	Carl Maria von Weber, *Der Freischütz.*
1822	Gas lighting to illuminate the stage was introduced at Paris Opéra.
	Jean Louis Aumer/Count Robert Gallenberg/Gustave Dugazon, *Alfred le grand* (Paris).
1824	Jacques-François Deshayes/Jean-Madeleine Schneitzhoeffer, *Zémire et Azor.*
	Auguste Baron, *Lettres et entretiens sur la danse.*
1825	Alexander Pushkin, *Boris Godunov.*
	Marius Petipa stage debut in Brussels.
1826	Jean Baptiste Blache/Jean-Madeleine Schneitzhoeffer, *Mars et Vénus ou Les Filets de Vulcain* (Paris).
	Felix Mendelssohn-Bartholdy, Overture to *A Midsummer Night's Dream.*
1827	Jean Louis Aumer/ Louis Joseph Ferdinand Hérold, *La Somnambule ou L'Arrivée d'un nouveau seigneur* (Paris).
	Alessandro Manzoni, *I Promessi Sposi* – first novel in Italian.
	Heinrich Heine, *The Book of Songs.*
	Franz Schubert, *The 'Trout' Quintett.*
	Vincenzo Bellini/Felice Romani, *La Somnambule* (opera) Paris.
1828	August Bournonville, *Nytaarsgave for Dandseyndere* (A New Year's Gift for Dance Lovers).
	Daniel-François-Esprit Auber, *La Muette de Portici.*
	Jean Dauberval/Louis Joseph Ferdinand Hérold, *La Fille mal gardée* (revised) (Paris).

1828–30	Carlo Blasis, *The Code of Terpsichore.*
1829	*St Matthew Passion* by Johann Sebastian Bach performed in the Singakademie Berlin on March 11, 1829 under the direction of Felix Mendelssohn-Bartholdy.
	Gioacchino Rossini *Guillaume Tell* (opera) (Paris).
	Victor Hugo, *Fantômes* (poem).
	Jean Louis Aumer/Ferdinand Hérold, *La Belle au bois dormant* (Paris).
1830	Revolutions in France and Italy.
	Adolphe Adam, *La Chatte blanche.*
	Filippo Taglioni, *Le Dieu et la bayadère.*
	Jean Louis Aumer/Fromental Halévy, *Manon Lescaut.*
	Alexander Pushkin, *Eugene Onegin.*
1830–77	August Bournonville ballet master at the Royal Danish Ballet.
1831	Dimming of house lights introduced to Paris Opéra.
	Jean Coralli/ Michel Enrico Carafo/Jean-Madeleine Schneitzhoeffer, *L'Orgie* (Paris).
	Giacomo Meyerbeer, *Robert le diable* (opera with the *Ballet of the nuns*).
1831–35	Louis Véron director of the Paris Opéra.
1832	A.E. Théleur, *Letters on dancing.*
	Filippo Taglioni/ Jean-Madeleine Schneitzhoeffer, *La Sylphide* (Paris).
	Jacques-Fromental Halévy, *La Tentation* (opera ballet) (Paris).
	Filippo Taglioni/Adalbert Gyrowetz/Michel Enrico Carafa *Nathalie, ou la Laitière Suisse* (Paris).
1833	Filippo Taglioni, *La Révolt au Sérail* (*La Révolte des femmes*) (Paris).
	André Deshayes/Adolphe Adam *Faust* (London).
1834	Jean Coralli/ Jean-Madeleine Schneitzhoeffer, *La Tempête ou l'île des génies* (Paris).
	Heinrich Heine, *De l'Allemagne.*
1835	Filippo Taglioni/Count Robert Gallenberg, *Brézilia ou la tribu des femmes* (Paris).
	Georg Büchner, *Danton's Death.*
1836	Giacomo Meyerbeer, *Les Huguenots* (opera) (Paris).
	Jean Coralli/Casimir Gide, *Le Diable boiteux.*
	August Bournonville, *La Sylphide* (Copenhagen).
	Filippo Taglioni/Adolphe Adam, *La Fille du Danube.*
1837	Carlo Blasis and his wife, Annunziata Rammaccini, directors of the Academy of dancing in Milan at La Scala.
	Nicola Guerra/Adolphe Adam, *Les Mohicans* (Paris).
1838	Therese Elssler/Casimir Gide, *La Volière ou les oiseaux de Boccace.*
1839	Joseph Mazilier/ François Benoist/ Marco Aurelio Marliani/ Ambroise Thomas, *La Gypsy.*
1839–42	The Opium War in China.

1840	Joseph Mazilier/ François Benoist/Napoléon-Henri Reber, *Le Diable amoureux.*
	Filippo Taglioni/Adolphe Adam, *Die Hamadryaden* (Berlin).
	Adolphe Adam, *L'Écumeur de mer* (St Petersburg).
1841	Gioacchino Rossini, *Moïse* (opera).
	Jean Coralli/Jules Perrot/Adolphe Adam/Frederich Burgmüller, *Giselle.*
	During a performance of *Toreadoren* August Bournonville was ordered off stage by the Danish King Christian VIII.
	Incandescent electrical light bulb patented.
1842–1911	Late Qing period in China.
1842	François Decombe Albert/Adolphe Adam, *La Jolie Fille de Gand* (Paris).
	August Bournonville, *Napoli* (Copenhagen).
1843	Richard Wagner, *The Flying Dutchman.*
	Jean Coralli/Frederich Burgmüller, *La Péri.*
	Gaetano Donizetti, *Dom Sébastien* (opera) (Paris).
1844	Joseph Mazilier/Friedrich von Flotow/Edouardo Deldevez Frederich Burgmüller, *Lady Henriette, ou La Servante de Greenwich.*
	Jean Coralli/Edouardo Deldevez, *Eucharis* (Paris).
	Arthur Saint-Léon/Cesare Pugni, *La Vivandiére* (London).
1845	Jules Perrot, *Pas de quatre* with Marie Taglioni, Carlotta Grisi, Fanny Cerrito, Lucile Grahn in London.
	Joseph Mazilier, *Le Diable à quatre* (Paris).
	François Decombe Albert/Adolphe Adam, *The Marble Maiden* (London).
1846	Joseph Mazilier/Edouardo Deldevez, *Paquita* (Paris).
1847	Charlotte Brontë, *Jane Eyre*; Emily Brontë, *Wuthering Heights.*
	Marius Petipa settled in St Petersburg.
	Carlo Blasis, *Notes Upon Dancing, Historical and Practical.*
	Jean Coralli, *Ozaï* (Paris).
	Arthur Saint-Léon/Cesare Pugni, *La Fille de marbre.*
	The sisters Elssler, *La Salamandrine* (London).
	Charles Baudelaire, *La Fanfarlo.*
1848	Revolutions all over Europe except Britain, Belgium and Russia.
	Joseph Mazilier/Adolphe Adam, *Griseldis ou les cinq senses* (Paris).
	Lucien Petipa, *Nisida ou les Amazones des Açores.*
	August Bournonville, *My Theatre Life.*
1849	Giacomo Meyerbeer, *Le Prophète* (opera) (Paris).
	Jules Perrot/Adolphe Adam, *La filleule des fées* (Paris).
	August Bournonville, *The Conservatory.*
1850	Richard Wagner, *Lohengrin.*
1850	Carlotta Grisi's debut as Giselle in Russia.
1851	August Bournonville, *The Kermesse in Bruges.*
	Giuseppe Verdi, *Rigoletto.*

	Joseph Mazilier/Jean Baptiste Tolbecque/Edouardo Delvedez, *Vert-Vert* (Paris).
1852	Coup d'Etat by Louis Napoleon Bonaparte, the French president who became Napoleon III.
	Joseph Mazilier/Adolphe Adam, *Orfa* (Paris).
1853	Giuseppe Verdi, *Il Trovatore*; Richard Wagner, *Der Ring des Nibelungen*.
1854	August Bournonville, *A Folk Tale* (Copenhagen).
	Dogma of the Immaculate Conception made an article of faith.
1854–6	Crimean War.
1855	François Henri Joseph Castil-Blaze, *L'Académie Impériale de Musique. Histoire littéraire, musicale, chorégraphique, pittoresque, morale, critique et galante de ce théâtre de 1645 à 1855*.
	August Bournonville, *Abdallah*.
	Giuseppe Verdi, *Les Vêpres siciliennes* (opera) (Paris).
1856	August Bournonville, *La Ventana*.
	Joseph Mazilier/Adolphe Adam, *Le Corsaire* (Paris).
1857	Gustave Flaubert, *Madame Bovary*.
	Marius Petipa/Ricardo Drigo/Ludwig Minkus/Cesare Pugni with a new divertissement by Delibes, *Le Corsaire*.
1858	August Bournonville, *The Flower Festival in Genzano*.
	Suez Canal Company (Compagnie Universelle du Canal Maritime de Suez) founded.
1858–9	Théophile Gautier, *Histoire de l'art dramatique en France depuis vingt-cinq ans*.
1858 and 1867	Théophile Gautier travelled to Russia (*Voyage en Russie*).
1859	Charles Darwin, *Origin of Species by means of Natural Selection*.
	France and Piedmont defeated Austria.
	Arthur Saint-Léon appointed ballet master at Imperial Theatre in Russia for eleven seasons.
	G. Léopold Adice, *Théorie de la gymnastique de la danse théâtrale*.
	Jacques Offenbach, *Orpheus in the Underworld*.
	First oil well discovered in the United States.
1860	Marie Taglioni, *Le Papillon*.
	August Bournonville, *Far from Denmark*.
1861	Victor Emanuel proclaimed King of Italy.
	Richard Wagner's *Tannhäuser* failure in Paris.
	Hans Christian Andersen completed the *Fairy Tales*.
1861–5	American Civil War.
1862	Marius Petipa, *The Daughter of Pharaoh* (St Petersburg).
1863	Arthur Saint-Léon/Cesare Pugni, *Diavolina*, Imperial Theatre St Petersburg.
1864	Arthur Saint-Léon/Cesare Pugni, *The Little Humpbacked Horse*, Imperial Theatre St Petersburg.
	Pius IX condemned all forms of liberalism in the *Syllabus of Errors*.
1866	Prussia defeated Austria and Northern Germany united.

	Arthur Saint-Léon/Leo Délibes, *La Source* (Paris).
	Fyodor Dostoyevsky, *Crime and Punishment.*
	Ambroise Thomas, *Mignon* (opera) (Paris).
1867	Giuseppe Verdi, *Don Carlos* (opera) (Paris).
	Karl Marx, *Das Kapital* I.
1868	Richard Wagner, *Die Meistersinger* (Munich).
1869	August Bournonville founded a special pension fund for dancers.
	Peter Tchaikovsky, *Undine* (opera).
	Marius Petipa/Ludwig Minkus, *Don Quixote* St Petersburg.
	After eleven years of work the Suez Canal opened in November.
1869–1903	Marius Petipa director of the Imperial Ballet in St Petersburg.
1870	Arthur Saint-Léon/Léo Délibes, *Coppélia.*
	Prussia defeated French Empire, Napoleon III captured and French Republic proclaimed.
	Dogma of Papal Infallibility declared by Vatican Council.
1871	Friedrich Nietzsche, *The Birth of Tragedy out of the Spirit of Music.*
	William I proclaimed German Emperor at Versailles.
	August Bournonville, *The King's Volunteers on Amager.*
	Charles Darwin, *Descent of Man.*
1871	First impressionist exhibition at Paris.
1872	Marius Petipa/Ludwig Minkus, *Camargo.*
1873	Severe economic crisis in Europe, America and Australia.
1875	Georges Bizet, *Carmen* (opera) Paris.
1876	August Bournonville, *From Siberia to Moscow.*
	Louis Mérante/Léo Délibes, *Sylphia ou La Nymphe de Diane* (Paris).
	Richard Wagner's Festspielhaus opened in Bayreuth.
1877	Leo Tolstoy, *Anna Karenina.*
	Pyotr Tchaikovsky/Julius Reisinger, *Swan Lake.*
	Marius Petipa/Ludwig Minkus, *La Bayadère.*
1878	André Messager, *Fleur d'oranger*, Folies Bergère.
1879	Thomas Edison perfected the electric bulb.
	André Messager, *Les Vins de France* and *Mignons et villains*, Folies Bergère.
1880	Marius Petipa, *Le Corsaire.*
	Fyodor Dostoyevsky, *The Brothers Karamazov.*
	Louis Mérante/Charles-Marie Widor, *La Korrigane* (Paris).
1881	Alexander II assassinated.
1881–99	Ivan Alexandrovich Vsevolozksy Director of Imperial Theatres.
1882	Richard Wagner, *Parsifal.*
	Monopoly of the Imperial Theatres in St Petersburg abolished, which made visits of foreign companies possible.
	Lucien Petipa/Éduard Lalo, *Namouna* (Paris).
1883	Daimler-Benz factories established in Germany.
	Friedrich Nietzsche, *Thus spake Zarathustra.*
1884	Marius Petipa/Adolphe Adam, *Giselle* (revised) St Petersburg.

1885	Edmond de Goncourt, *Chérie* (novel).
1886	Louis Mérante/André Messager, *Les Deux Pigeons* (Paris)
1888	Heinrich-Rudolf Hertz detected electro-magnetic waves.
1889	Ambroise Thomas, *La Tempête* (Paris).
	Gustave Eiffel built the Eiffel tower in Paris.
1890	Peter Tchaikovsky/Marius Petipa, *Sleeping Beauty*.
	Knut Hamsun, *Hunger*.
1891	Leo XIII issued papal encyclical *Rerum novarum* on the rights of labour.
	Henrik Ibsen, *Hedda Gabler*.
1892	Peter Tchaikovsky/Lev Ivanov/Marius Petipa, *The Nutcracker*.
1893	Giacomo Puccini, *Manon Lescaut*.
1894	Trial of Alfred Dreyfus in Paris.
1895	Emile Durkheim, *The Rules of Sociological Method*.
	Revival Pyotr Tchaikovsky/Marius Petipa/Lev Ivanov, *Swan Lake*.
	Guglielmo Marconi invented wireless telegraphy.
1895	Wilhelm Conrad Röntgen discovered X-Rays.
	Gustave le Bon, *Psychology of the Crowd*.
1898	radium discovered by Marie and Pierre Curie.
	Emile Zola, *J'accuse*.
	Marius Petipa/Alexander Glazunov, *Raymonda* (St Petersburg).
1899	Aleksandr Gorsky's production of *Sleeping Beauty* in Moscow.
	Houston Stewart Chamberlain, *Foundations of the Nineteenth Century*.
1900	Sigmund Freud, *The Interpretation of Dreams*.
c. 1900–1940	The Mountain of Truth, reform and artists colony in Ascona, Switzerland.
	Wilhelm Wundt, *Comparative Psychology*.
	Aleksandr Gorsky's production of *Don Quixote* in Moscow.
	Isadora Duncan moved to France, gave first performances in London.
1901	Aleksandr Gorsky staged *Giselle* in Moscow (and again in 1907, 1918 and 1922).
	Aleksandr Gorsky/Frédéric Chopin, *Valse fantaisie* (Moscow).
1902	Maxim Gorky, *Nights Lodging*.
	Aleksandr Gorsky, *Don Quixote* (restaging of Petipa's ballet at Imperial Theatre).
1903	George Bernard Shaw, *Man and Superman*.
	Introduction of ballet to China by Yu Ronglin.
	Wright brothers flew the first aeroplane.
	Marius Petipa, *The Magic Mirror*, St Petersburg, a failure.
1903–4	The Imperial Ballet ballet employed 122 female and 92 male dancers.
1904	Russo-Japanese War.
	Isadora Duncan's first tour of Russia.
1904–83	George Balanchine.

1905	Revolution in Russia.
	Herbert George Wells, *Modern Utopia*.
	Richard Strauss, *Salome*.
	Albert Einstein, *Special Theory of Relativity*.
	Michel Fokine, *Acis and Galatea*.
	Isadora Duncan established her school of modern dance in Berlin.
1907	Shell Oil Trust founded.
	Henri Bergson, *L'Evolution créatrice*.
	Michel Fokine/Camille Saint-Saëns, *The Swan* for Anna Pavlova.
	Michel Fokine, *Pavillon d'Armide*.
	Rainer Maria Rilke, *New Poems*.
	Michel Fokine/Frédéric Chopin, *Chopiniana* (St Petersburg).
1908	Pablo Picasso and Georges Braque founded cubism.
1909	Serge Diaghilev presented Russian dancers in five ballets in his *Saisons russes* in Paris.
	Michel Fokine/Frédéric Chopin, *Les Sylphides*, Ballets Russes (Paris).
	Filippo Tommaso Marinetti published the *Founding and Manifesto of Futurism*.
	Arnold Schøenberg, *Three Piano Pieces*.
	Vasily Kandinsky announced absolute painting.
1910	Michel Fokine, *Schéhérazade* and *Firebird*, Ballets Russes.
1911	Michel Fokine, *Le Spectre de la rose* and *Petrushka*, Ballets Russes.
	Nationalist Revolution in China.
	Vasily Kandinsky, *Concerning the Spiritual In Art*.
	Richard Strauss, *Der Rosenkavalier*.
1912	China declared republic.
	Thomas Mann, *Der Tod in Venedig* (Death in Venice).
1912–13	The three Balkan wars.
1913	Edmund Husserl, *Phenomenology*.
1913	Vaclav Nijinsky/Igor Stravinsky, *Le Sacre du printemps*, Ballets Russes (Paris).
1913–14	Mikhail Fokine in Stockholm.
1913–18	Rudolf von Laban lived in Ascona, on the Mountain of Truth and founded Modern German Dance there.
1914	(July) Michel Fokine's manifesto of the new ballet first appeared in *The Times*.
1914	(28 June) Archduke Franz Ferdinand assassinated in Sarajevo.
1914	Heinrich Mann, *Der Untertan*.
1914–18	First World War.
1915	First use of poison gas by German army.
1915	(February – December) Battle of Verdun.
1915	Denishawn dance school in Los Angeles founded.
1917	Germany proclaimed unrestricted submarine warfare.
	Filippo Tommaso Marinetti, *Manifesto on Futurist Dance*.

Jean Cocteau/Pablo Picasso/Eric Satie, *Parade*, Ballets Russes (Paris).

(November) Bolshevik Revolution in Russia.

United States declared war on Germany and the Austro-Hungarian Empire.

1918   President Woodrow Wilson issued *The 14 Points* (programme for a just peace).

William II abdicated, Germany declared a republic.

(November) armistice ended the First World War, revolution in Germany and other European countries.

1919   Peace Conference began at Versailles.

Bauhaus founded in Germany.

Alexander Sacharoff, *Au temps du grand siècle/Pavane royale*.

Sociedad Pro-Arte Musical founded in Havana.

1920   Léonide Massine, *Pulcinella*.

Vaclav Nijinsky/Claude Debussy, *Jeux*, Jean Börlin/Isaac Albeniz, *Iberia*, Jean Börlin/Alfvén, *La Nuit de Saint-Jean*, Jean Börlin/Alexander Glazunov, *Derviches*.

Jean Börlin, *La Maison de fous*, Jean Cocteau/Darius Milhaud, *Le Boeuf sur le toit*, Ballets Suédois (Paris).

1920–5   The Ballets Suédois in Paris.

1921   Jean Börlin/Jean Cocteau/Les Six, *Les Mariés de la Tour Eiffel*, Jean Börlin/Darius Milhaud, *L'Homme et son désir*.

Agrippina Vaganova began teaching career at the Leningrad State Choreographic School.

1922   Anna Pavlova brought *The Dying Swan* to Shanghai.

Jean Börlin, *Skating Rink*, Ballets Suédois (Paris).

Oskar Schlemmer, *Triadic ballet* (*Triadisches Ballett*) (Stuttgart).

Benito Mussolini and Fascists came to power in Italy.

1922–3   Hyper-inflation in Germany and Austria.

1923   Bronislava Nijinska, *Les Noces* (Paris).

Rudolf von Laban began his Kammertanz Theatre in Hamburg.

Adolf Hitler and Nazis attempted coup d'état in Munich.

Fyodor Lopukhov/Ludwig van Beethoven dance-symphony, *Magnificence of the Universe*.

Jean Börlin/Darius Milhaud, *La Création du monde*, Jean Börlin/Cole Porter, *Within the Quota*, Ballets Suédois (Paris).

1924   Death of Vladimir I. Lenin, leader of Russian Bolshevik Revolution.

Bronislava Nijinska, *Les Fâcheux*.

Ballets Suédois last evening: Jean Börlin/Francis Picabia/Eric Satie, *Relâche*, Jean Börlin/Arthur Honegger/Fernand Léger, *Skating Rink*, Jean Börlin/Darius Milhaud, *La Création du monde*.

1925   Fyodor Lopukhov, *Paths of a Ballet-master*.

Léo Staats/Léo Delibes, *Soir de fête*.

Kasyan Goleizovsky, *The Legend of Joseph the Beautiful* (Moscow).

1926	George Balanchine, *La Pastorale*.
	George Balanchine, *The Triumph of Neptune*.
	Marie Rambert founded the Marie Rambert Dancers, later called the Ballet Club, Ballet Rambert (1935–87) and finally Rambert Dance Company.
	Martha Graham gave her first New York performance.
	Fritz Lang, *Metropolis* (film).
1927	George Balanchine, *La Chatte*.
	Isadora Duncan, A*utobiography*.
	Kasyan Goleizovsky, *The Whirlwind*, led to his resignation.
	Death of Isadora Duncan.
	Lev Lashchilin, Vasili Tikhomirov/Reinhold Glière, *The Red Poppy*, Bolshoi Theatre Moscow.
1928	George Balanchine/Igor Stravinsky, *Apollon musagète*.
1928	Ninette de Valois engaged as director of Sadlers Well's Ballet (VicWells Ballet); Sadler's Wells Theatre Ballet eventually split in 1956 into the Covent Garden's Royal Ballet and Birmingham Royal Ballet.
1929	Kurt Jooss, *Pavane on the Death of an Infanta*.
	George Balanchine, *Le Bal*.
	George Balanchine, *Le Fils prodigue*.
	(May) Soviet Union adopted first Five-Year-Plan.
	(October) US stock market crashed on Black Friday; world depression began.
1931	Several Austrian and German banks collapsed.
	Ninette de Valois, *Job*, Camargo Society (London).
	(September)Japan invaded Manchuria.
1932	Kurt Jooss/Fritz Cohen, *The Green Table* (Paris).
	The Ballets Russes de Monte Carlo founded as a fusion of the Ballets de l'Opéra de Monte Carlo and the Ballet de l'Opéra Russe à Paris, with Colonel de Basil as director and René Blum as artistic director.
	Vasily Vainonen/Boris Asafiev, *The Flame of Paris*, Kirov Theatre (Leningrad).
1933	(January) Adolf Hitler chancellor of Germany – Nazi seizure of power.
	(March) Franklin D. Roosevelt inaugurated as President of the United States; banks closed for three days throughout the country.
	George Balanchine arrived in New York.
1934	The School of American Ballet officially opened.
	The Nutcracker (Tchaikovsky) staged at Vic-Wells in London with help of Nikolay Sergeyev.
	Rostislav Zakharov/Boris Asafiev, *The Fountain of Bakhchisarai*.
	George Balanchine/Pyotr Tchaikovsky, *Serenade* (New York).
1935	Martha Graham, *Imperial Gesture*.
	Wu Xiaobang choreographed first modern ballet in China.

1936	Broadway musical, *On Your Toes* (Rodgers/Hart), choreography George Balanchine.
	Spanish Civil War.
	The Ballets de Monte Carlo, founded by René Blum.
1937	George Balanchine/Igor Stravinsky, *Apollo, Le Baiser de la fée, Jeu de Carte* (New York).
1938	The Ballet Russe de Monte Carlo (a descendant of René Blum's Ballets de Monte Carlo) opened in 1938 and lasted into the 1950s. Léonide Massine artistic director.
	Ivo Váňa Psota/Sergey Prokofiev, *Romeo and Juliet* premiere in Brno, Czechoslovakia.
	(November) 'Kristallnacht' – violent anti-semitic pogrom organised by Nazi party.
1939	Valborg Borchsenius/ Harald Lander, *La Sylphide*.
	(September) Britain and France declared war on Germany, beginning of the Second World War.
1940	First retrospective exhibition of Cuban art at the University of Havana.
	Leonid Lavrovsky/Sergey Prokofiev, *Romeo and Juliet* (Moscow).
	Alexandra Federova's version of *The Nutcracker* (Tchaikovsky) for the Ballet Russe de Monte Carlo tour in South America.
	Walt Disney film *Fantasia* (with music from Tchaikovsky's *Nutcracker*).
1941	(June) Germany invaded the Soviet Union.
	Japanese aircraft destroyed US American fleet at Pearl Harbor, United States entered the Second World War.
1942	Nazi state agreed on "Final Solution of the Jewish Question".
	US Navy defeated Imperial Japanese navy at Battle of Midway.
1942–1943	(September – February) Soviet Red Army defeated the German Wehrmacht in Battle of Stalingrad; German retreat from Russian territory began.
1943	Alicia Alonso danced Giselle in a performance of the Ballet Theatre in New York.
1944	Broadway musical *Song of Norway* (Robert Wright/George Forrest), choreography George Balanchine.
	(June) Allied landings on beaches of Normandy.
	First *Nutcracker* production in the United States by Willem Christensen in San Francisco.
1945	(8 May) German armed forces surrendered to allied forces unconditionally.
	(June) Charter of the United Nations signed.
	(August) first atomic bomb dropped on Hiroshima.
	(August) Imperial Japan surrendered to allied forces unconditionally.
	George Orwell, *Animal Farm*.

1946	Ballet Society, a subscription only company founded by George Balanchine and Lincoln Kirstein.
	George Balanchine/Paul Hindemith, *The Four Temperaments* (New York).
1947–52	Marshall Plan or European Recovery Program.
1947–89	The Cold War in Europe.
1948	William Shockley invented transistor radio.
	Ballet Society became New York City Ballet, first season: *Concerto Barocco, Orpheus* and *Symphony in C.*
	Alicia Alonso founded the Ballet Alicia Alonso in Havana; staged *Giselle* for it.
1949	Roland Petit, *Carmen.*
	José Limón, *The Moor's Pavane.*
	Peoples Republic of China declared.
	George Balanchine/Igor Stravinsky, *Fire Bird* (New York).
1950	National School of Ballet Alicia Alonso opened (Harana).
1953	Harald Lander, *La Sylphide* Grand Ballet du Marquis de Cuevas.
	Death of Joseph Stalin.
1954	Beijing Academy of Dance founded.
	George Balanchine/Pyotr Tchaikovsky, *The Nutcracker* New York (performed annually ever since).
1955	Maurice Béjart/Pierre Henry and Pierre Schaeffer, *Symphonie pour un homme seul.*
	Frederick Ashton/Sergey Prokofiev, *Romeo and Juliet*, the Royal Danish Ballet.
	Serge Lifar/Sergey Prokofiev, *Romeo and Juliet* (Paris).
1956	Bolshoi Ballet in London with *Romeo and Juliet.*
	Leonid Jacobson/Aram Khatchaturian *Spartacus*, Kirov Theatre (Leningrad).
1957	George Balanchine, *Square Dance* (Antonio Vivaldi/Arcangelo Corelli), *Gounod Symphony, Stars and Stripes* (Philip Sousa), *Agon* (Igor Stravinsky).
	Treaty of Rome established European Economic Community.
1958	John Cranko, *Romeo and Juliet* (Milan).
	Alvin Ailey founded American Dance Theatre.
1959	Fidel Castro Prime Minister of Cuba.
	George Balanchine/Martha Graham/Anton von Webern, *Episodes.*
1960	Frederick Ashton/John Lanchberry arr. Hérold, *La Fille mal gardée*, Royal Ballet.
	Elsa Marianne von Rosen, *La Sylphide* (Stockholm).
	Maurice Béjart founded the *Ballet de XXe siècle.*
	George Balanchine, *Donizetti Variations*, New York City Ballet.
1961	Frederick Ashton/Edouardo Deldevez, *Les deux pigeons*, Royal Ballet (London).
	(13 August) East Germany sealed off Berlin by Wall.

1962	Cuban Missile Crisis.
	George Balanchine/Felix Mendelssohn-Bartholdy, *A Midsummer Night's Dream*.
	New City Ballet tour to Soviet Union.
1963	George Balanchine/Igor Stravinsky, *Movements for Piano and Orchestra*.
1963–75	Vietnam War.
1964	*Hongse Nianzijun* or *Red Girl's Regiment* performed in Bejing.
1965	*White Haired Girl* performed at Shanghai Academy of Dance.
	Kenneth MacMillan, *Romeo and Juliet*, Royal Ballet with Margot Fonteyn and Rudolf Nureyev.
	George Balanchine/ Nicolas Nabokov, *Don Quixote* (New York).
	Yvonne Rainer, *Parts of some sextets*.
1966–76	Culture Revolution in China.
1967	Hans Brenaa, *La Sylphide* (Copenhagen).
	George Balanchine/Gabriel Fauré/Igor Stravinsky/Pyotr Tchaikovsky, *Jewels*.
	Maurice Béjart, *Messe pour les temps presents*, text: Buddha, Song of songs, Friedrich Nietzsche, music: Pierre Henry, military marches, traditional Indian and Japanese music.
1968	George Balanchine/Leo Délibes, *La Source*, New York City Ballet.
	Yury Grigorovich/Aram Khachaturian, *Spartacus*, Bolshoi Theatre (Moscow).
	Student Revolution in Paris.
	Prague Spring (Czechoslovakia dismantled Stalinist Regime).
	Warsaw forces suppressed Czechoslovak liberal regime.
1969	Leonid Jacobson, *Vestris*.
1970	George Balanchine/George Gershwin, *Who Cares?*
1971	Elsa Marianne von Rosen and Allan Fridericia, *Napoli*, Gothenburg Ballet, Kirov Ballet in St Petersburg and the Royal Swedish Ballet in Stockholm.
1972	Alicia Alonso's *Giselle* production staged at the Paris Opéra.
1974	Kenneth MacMillan, *Manon*, Royal Ballet, Covent Garden.
1975	Kenneth MacMillan, *The Four Seasons*, Royal Ballet.
1976	*New York Baroque Dance Company* founded by Catherine Turocy and Ann Jacobi.
1977	Rudolf Nureyev, *Romeo and Juliet*, London Festival Ballet.
1978	Jiří Kylián, *Symphony of Psalms*.
1979	First Bournonville Festival in Copenhagen.
	Peter Schaufuss, *La Sylphide*, London Festival Ballet.
	Maurice Béjart, *Un instant dans la vie d'autrui*.
1980	*Ris et danceries* founded by Francine Lancelot.
1980s	Francine Lancelot decodes Raoul Anger Feuillet's dance notation.
1981	George Balanchine/Tchaikovsky, *Mozartiana* (revised).
1983	*L'Eclat des Muses* founded by Christine Bayle.

1984	William Forsythe director of Ballett Frankfurt; *Artifact*.
	Flemming Flindt, *La Sylphide*, Dallas Ballet.
1985	Mikhail Gorbachev became General Secretary of the Communist Party of the Soviet Union.
	L'autre pas founded by Klaus Abromeit.
	Toni Lander and Bruce Marks reconstruction of *Abdallah* by August Bournonville.
1986	Mark Franko, *Le Marbre tremble*.
1987	*Atys* by Lully (baroque revival by *Arts Florissants*).
1988	Henning Kronstam, *La Sylphide* (Copenhagen).
	François Raffinot, *Caprice*.
	Guy Debord, *Society of the Spectacle*.
1989	Ayatollah Khomeini issued Fatwa demanding execution of Salman Rushdie, author of the *Satanic Verses*.
	Mark Morris, *Dido and Aeneas*.
	Berlin Wall fell, disintegration of Eastern European Socialist bloc.
1990	Maurice Béjart/Richard Wagner, *Ring um den Ring*.
	Federal Republic of Germany absorbed German Democratic Republic.
	World Wide Web originated at CERN, European Organisation for Nuclear Research.
1991	Jiří Kylián, *Petite Mort*.
	Frank Andersen, *A Folk Tale* (together with Anne Marie Vessel Schlüter).
1992	Second Bournonville Festival in Copenhagen.
	Dinna Bjørn and Frank Andersen, *Napoli*, Royal Danish Ballet (also 1998, 2005).
1993	*Fêtes Galantes* founded by Beatrice Massin.
1994	The ZIP drive with removable computer storage developed.
	Maurice Béjart, *Le Ballet des mots*.
1995	William Forsythe, *Eidos Tellos*.
1997	Dinna Bjørn, *La Sylphide* (Copenhagen).
	DVD went on sale for first time.
1998	Maurice Béjart, *Nutcracker*.
1999	Soviet Union abolished.
	Frank Andersen, *La Sylphide*, Chinese National Ballet, Inoue Ballet and the Royal Swedish Ballet.
	Beatrice Massin, *Le Roi danse*.
2003	Tim Rushton *Napoli – den nye by* (Napoli – The New Town) New Danish Dance Theatre, Copenhagen.
	Nikolaj Hübbe, *La Sylphide* (Copenhagen).
	Hans van Manen/Johann Sebastian Bach, *Monologue, Dialogue*.
2004	Thomas Lund and Johan Holten, *En anden akt* (Another Act) Copenhagen International Ballet, Bellevue Teatret.
	Jiří Kylián/Dirk Haubrich, *Sleepless* for Nederlands Dans Theater II.

2005	Jiří Kylián/Dirk Haubrich, *Toss of a Dice* for Nederlands Dans Theater I.
	Dinna Bjørn and Frank Anderson, *Napoli* Finnish National Ballet.
	Third Bournonville Festival at the Royal Theatre in Copenhagen.
	Ulrik Wivel, *Jeg Dig Elsker* (I love you) (film on *La Sylphide*).
	Dinna Bjørn and Frank Andersen, *Napoli* Finnish National Ballet in 2005.
2006	Peoples Republic of China declared Ghengis Khan Chinese.

Introduction

MARION KANT

Another ballet book?

Not exactly. A Companion, a book to accompany you when you go to see ballet or when you want to know something, find a name, a date, a work; it is a book to read and a book to consult, not on everything in ballet, not a complete book, not even a complete history. A book with essays that revisit aspects of this beloved and detested art form, a book that is needed as much as ballet is needed. Yes, "needed", as we need our bodies. Ballet shows us what the trained human body can do to make flesh become art. Ballet, the art of the body, puts our physical presence into form, into fantasy and into a deeper reality. "Needed" because in the nineteenth century ballet became a uniquely feminine enterprise, and to an extent it has retained this aspect in the twenty-first century. The great ballerina floats before us, telling us something about ourselves, our genders, our fears, hopes and, above all, prejudices. The artificiality and conventions of ballet protect our nervous sensibilities but also indirectly assault them.

Ballet is part of our history and our heritage and if we deny our past we will not comprehend the present nor grasp the future. Either in life or in dance. Ballet has a history, which reflects and refracts the social order in which it arises. A courtly society demands an art form in which the king can dance and his court revolve around him. A revolutionary society proclaims its ideals in dance; a conservative one does the same. Ballet, adored and reviled often for similar reasons, belongs to our contemporary cultural landscape as much as any other performance art. Ballet tells us about ourselves and the world we inhabit; it holds up a mirror and projects wishes and desires; it expresses our ideals and mocks our vanities; it demolishes certainties and tests limits; it creates values and sets standards; it invents the past as much as the future.

Constant reflection, introspection and evaluation are part of a process which helps us assess critically where we are and how we got there; then we can make choices for the future and think about alternatives. Such a process of thinking must never end; it is a vital component of our artistic consciousness. Thinking about ballet poses special problems because it creates its meanings without words. It literally "embodies" meaning. It lets us know in its own way what being human, having arms and legs, a gait, a posture, a gesture, means or could mean. Ballet has changed but never gave up its history, its link to the past: the invention of the "white ballet" in the nineteenth century revolutionised and transformed a courtier's code into the "woman question". Every time a "classical" ballet is performed, it reminds us that the "woman question" still has no satisfactory answer. But the shape in which it is presented has significantly been transformed. Those new and old forms transport new and old philosophical questions alike.

The authors gathered together in this book come from many parts of the world; they stand for a truly international crowd, as international as ballet itself. The methods with which they work reflect different attitudes in research and highlight the fact that ballet is not one homogenous thing but a flexible art as well as a serious academic research subject. Many of the contributors combine practice and theory of dance and ballet and can thus offer a wide range of experience.

This *Companion to Ballet* consists of twenty-four chapters gathered in four parts on various aspects of the art form's historical evolution and on its aesthetic properties. They consider the most important developmental stages since its "origins" in the fifteenth century and travel to the end of the twentieth century, sometimes stopping to consider a particular movement, sometimes to contemplate a specific moment of importance, sometimes to review a particular artist's contribution or a specific choreography.

All the essays consider an art of the highest public interest and discuss ballet as an expression of "modern" ideas at various times. We never intended to provide a complete history or a full theoretical framework of aesthetic ideas. Instead we offer an impression of the most important elements, which demonstrate continuity and gradual evolution as well as those which mark sudden changes of artistic direction. This Companion is not a history book in the strict sense; yet it cannot ignore the importance of historical developments. Thus it has been organised along historical axes, for ballet is an art form, which has grown over time and peculiarly and intimately symbolises the age in which it arises.

In the first chapter we begin our journey in northern Italy to which Jennifer Nevile takes us and introduces us to the dance manuals of the fifteenth century, their philosophical ideas and the structure of an art form which they describe. We then make a leap to France and England and their royal courts. The genres of the *ballet de cour* and the masque took up the challenge of the ballet that was born a couple of centuries before in free city states and had been modified to celebrate the glory of emperors and empresses. Marina Nordera and Barbara Ravelhofer present court ballet as an integral part of a social order. Mark Franko introduces the "baroque body" – a concept through which a historical moment is preserved today; a corporeal reality we can no longer recall but have to imagine and invent in order to understand the past.

In the second part we follow the transformation of court ballet to a bourgeois public expression. The modernisation of ballet in the eighteenth century lay in its opening up of spaces and its new approach to the human body and human movement. Dorion Weickmann supplies an overview of the concept of the *ballet d'action* and Sandra Noll Hammond explains the training principles that led to a complete professionalisation of dance. Tim Blanning and Judith Chazin-Bennahum write about two important and innovative choreographers and dance theoreticians: John Weaver and Jean-Georges Noverre. We leave the eighteenth century with the French Revolution, the event that changed all European societies and countries for the next 200 years. With its radical conceptions of a "new man" it also redefined the place, the order, the structure and aesthetics of human movement.

The third part looks at Europe and Russia after the French Revolution. Romanticism had descended upon France and Germany and quickly spread. Sarah Davies Cordova and Anne Middleboe Christensen evoke romantic representations in France and Denmark and the emergence of the ballerina as the ultimate embodiment of romantic ideas. Marian Smith reminds us of the close interaction between music and dance and recalls the often forgotten practices of composing for ballet. Lynn Garafola and Thérèse Hurley take us to Russia where the Italian-French Marius Petipa dominated ballet for two generations and together with the composer Tchaikovsky created ballets that belong to the canon of the art form today. Lucia Ruprecht argues that ballet as an art form in the public sphere very much depended on the critic; ballet entered the consciousness of the bourgeois audience through its written reflections in news-papers and journals as much as through its nightly performances. The critic was then, as now, an institution – an advocate for or against, a propagandist who used ballet to advance more than only a personal opinion. The chapter ends with my investigation of the ballet costume, especially skirts and shoes, in their cultural context. I interpret their formal properties and meaning: the full white skirt and the pointe shoes still symbolise ballet and the power of the female dancer.

The last and most extensive part examines the twentieth century. Ballet had become a well-established art form, no longer accessible only to an elite but to many – high and low. It also carried historical baggage with it, had over the centuries modernised and reinvented itself several times. With choreographies and performance styles, dance philosophies had developed. Dance had been "done" but also written; it had become memory of physicality and incarnation and had entered the intellectual sphere of European culture. By the early twentieth century ballet had to cope with its own history and the stereotypes and tropes it had created. With the Russian and Swedish

Ballets of the early twentieth century – both companies as well as aesthetic principles – Tim Scholl and Erik Näslund recall important instances of another modernisation process in ballet. The Russian as well as the Swedish Ballet soon were regarded as revolutionary breaks with tradition, yet both were also firmly connected with ballet's tradition as well as to other social and artistic developments of the time. The Russian Revolution of 1917, very much like its French predecessor, fundamentally shaped the European landscape and also affected ballet. From post-revolutionary Russia came the man who is synonymous with ballet – George Balanchine. Matilde Butkas traces Balanchine's career from Russia to Paris and eventually to the United States, whereas Juliet Bellow pauses in Paris to show how Balanchine broke down the notion of classicism in the 1930s before reinstating it in the 1960s. Jennifer Fisher focuses on one ballet – *The Nutcracker* – and describes how it was transformed from near failure to the most successful and most often performed piece of our contemporary era. Every small company can today realise its ambitions by staging a *Nutcracker* and integrate references to regional politics, cater to local tastes and satisfy the native community's demands. With the chapters by Zheng Yangwen on ballet in China and Lester Tome on Alicia Alonso's Cuban *Giselle* we see ballet in its worldwide context and understand the politics of internationalisation. Ballet from its very beginning had been an international affair. In the first century of its existence it had crossed the European continent and when the colonial powers spread their cultural ideals they took with them their value systems. Ballet too suited the needs of these powers to proclaim their ideas of rule and order. But it was neither a simple nor a one-sided relationship. Ballet, as other arts, is never just a tool in the hands of a regime to control nor a means to suppress indigenous interests. Thus for Zheng Yangwen ballet, like opium or communism, offered itself as a vehicle to translate contradictory beliefs in a society in full transformation. In China and in Cuba this initially foreign artistic articulation offered itself as an agent to formulate those national principles which it was supposed to help replace. My chapter ends the part by revisiting the ideological challenges of the entire century. I too emphasise that art and ballet have never been static but served the diverse needs of those who took up the challenge of expressing through movement the problems and tensions of their contemporary world.

The division in the twentieth century between ballet and modern dance has produced two very different types of movement art, often fiercely and destructively hostile to each other. The final chapter in Part IV tells the story of modern dance as a counterpoint to ballet in the same period. It is to be hoped that in due course modern dance will be granted the full treatment which it deserves in a Companion of its own. As editor I had to take another, difficult decision: did Martha Graham, Merce Cunningham or Siobhan Davies belong in this book? I decided that these three as all other modernists certainly played an important part in the story of theatrical dance in the twentieth century but that they represent a different genre of dance. Their motivations in dance, their philosophies, movement codes, structural and formal features have to be treated independently from ballet.

The Companion does not provide a guide to becoming a ballet dancer. Problems of professional training, anatomical requirements and medical advice for dancers or nutritional questions have deliberately been excluded. Neither has the history of companies and theatre institutions, nor the rich history of ballet design been observed. Many names will not appear and many works are only mentioned in passing. But the omissions should make you, the reader, want to find out more, search for that volume which will solve your question and lead you to the next level of understanding. This collection of chapters should whet your appetite and rouse your curiosity. We hope the Companion will live up to its name – that it will accompany you as a useful guide and open up the complex, fascinating world of theatre and ballet. We hope that it will be a friendly and reliable escort during a first encounter with ballet as well as a good interpreter during future visits. My fondest wish is that at some future performance you, the reader, will remember a fact, a name or an evolution of technique that you first read in this book and now see on stage. If the pleasure of recognition or the application of information sharpens your enjoyment of the work before you, the Companion will have done its job.

PART I

From the Renaissance to the baroque: royal power and worldly display

1 The early dance manuals and the structure of ballet: a basis for Italian, French and English ballet

JENNIFER NEVILE

In the dance treatises of the fifteenth century choreographies were first recorded in Western Europe: dance became literary and philosophical as well as a physical skill and oral tradition. These treatises laid the foundation for the future structure of European dance. The main dance genres recorded in the treatises, *ballo, bassadanza*, and *basse danse* in the fifteenth century, *pavane, galliard, branle, almain, balletto, bassa, brando* and *cascarda* in the sixteenth century, were the dances of the upper levels of society: the courtiers and nobility, those who wielded power, as well as the wealthy merchants and trading families. Important state occasions, marriage celebrations, official visits by neighbouring rulers or ambassadors, annual religious festivities and theatrical events were all marked by formal balls or dancing at which members of the elite performed. Often these dance events took place in public spaces, on a stage erected in the main piazza in front of thousands of spectators. At other times the space in which the dancing was conducted was more private, being the main hall of a palace. But even on these occasions the dances performed were part of the official ceremonies and rituals, contributing to the presentation of the image of a ruler as a powerful and magnificent prince, whose authority could not be challenged. When a ruler and the leading members of his court danced in public before his subjects he was displaying his magnificence, and in doing so he was displaying his power. The Italians in particular were obsessed with protocol and ceremony, and one of the chief means of indicating rank was by spatial relationships among people. Thus dance, an art form with spatial relationships as its basis, was a significant tool in this presentation of power and rank through rituals and ceremonies.

The dances recorded in the treatises are overwhelmingly for both male and female performers (see Fig. 1). Many of the dances are for one or two couples, or for three performers, two men and one woman or vice versa. Some dance genres were processional in nature, for example the *basse danse, pavane* and *almain*, during which a line of couples paraded around the hall, exhibiting not only their skill at dancing, but also their sumptuous clothes, hairstyles and jewellery. Other genres chronicled the social

Figure 1 Maestro dei Tornei di Santa Croce, cassone panel, *La magnanimità di Scipione*, 1460. London, Victoria and Albert Museum, Inventory No: 5804.1859.

interactions between the men and women. The choreographic sequences and floor patterns of the Italian *balli*, for example, emphasised typical interactions that occurred on a daily basis at court. Some of the *balli* enact themes of fidelity, fickleness or jealousy. *Sobria* is a *ballo* for one woman and five men where the sole woman remains faithful to her partner despite the advances and pleading of the other four unattached men. *Merçantia*, for one woman and three men, presents the opposite scenario, as the woman is all too ready to abandon her partner and flirt with the other two men. *Gelosia* (jealousy), a *ballo* for three couples, is a dance in which the men constantly change partners, thereby providing many opportunities for the display of this emotion. In the sixteenth century the confrontation between the sexes became more explicit with dances entitled *Barriera*, *La Battaglia* and *Torneo Amoroso*. Often these dances started with two lines of men and women who advanced and retreated before clashing (often striking hands that echoed swords hitting shields) and the final reconciliation. Other dance genres such as the *galliard* were explicitly choreographed for a display of virtuosity and athleticism, especially on the part of the man, who was expected to perform sequences of complicated variations that could involve kicks, leaps and turns in the air. Hundreds of these variations were recorded in the dance treatises, and competent dancers were expected to memorise many of them, to be used at will during a performance. By the sixteenth century the necessity for a courtier to be skilled in the art of dance was without question. The ability to perform gracefully, seemingly without any effort, was one of the distinguishing marks of a courtier and the absence of this ability exposed a gentleman or lady to ridicule and derision from colleagues.

The dance treatises from the fifteenth and sixteenth centuries (often dedicated to members of the leading families) contain hundreds of choreographies – a substantial body of material. Perhaps the most obvious contribution of these treatises to European dance practice is the idea of a choreography as a unique arrangement of steps, floor patterns and music. Dances such as the *pavane*, in which a simple sequence of steps was repeated until the end of the music, continued throughout this period, but the vast majority of dances recorded in the treatises were individual choreographies. A dance was therefore a specific creation: it needed a creator – usually a dance master – who also often wrote or arranged the music to fit the step sequences of each dance. The fifteenth-century Italian dance master Guglielmo Ebreo recognised dancing as an innate, natural human activity.

> [I]f eight or ten people are dancing without music, [but] with steps that are harmonised and measured together, then it is a natural thing. And when a musician plays and those dancing harmonise and measure their steps to the music, then it is an acquired skill.[1]

But when music was played and the dancers adjusted their steps to fit the music, then dance became an art, a product of human ingenuity and skill. In this latter scenario the "natural" product of dance was ordered and perfected by the addition of human application and skill, and training and education in the dance.

Each new dance was a unique combination of steps drawn from the existing step vocabulary. The number of different steps available to the choreographer increased dramatically in the sixteenth century. The step vocabulary of the fifteenth-century Italian *ballo* and *bassadanza* were nine "natural" steps and three "accidental" steps, with variety obtained from performing the steps of one *misura* (a specific combination of metre and speed) to the music of a second *misura*, and from adding the quick "accidental" steps to the "natural" steps.[2] By contrast, the late sixteenth-century Italian dance treatises of Fabritio Caroso contain descriptions of fifty-eight different steps (*Il Ballarino*, 1581) and seventy-four (*Nobiltà di dame*, 1600) respectively. Cesare Negri in *Le gratie d'amore* (1602) describes fifty-one widely used steps, as well as forty-two variants on the galliard *cinque passi* and thirty-four different galliard *mutanze*, twenty-seven *salti* (jumps), thirty *capriole*, and ten *zurli* (spinning turns).[3] With this many steps the possibilities for new combinations of step sequences were vast, even without the addition of improvised passages and added ornamental steps.[4]

The structure of these individually choreographed dances enhanced the importance of memory in European ballet, and led to the requirement for sustained rehearsal. A good memory was crucial for anyone who wished to perform in public, as one had to commit to memory each different choreography. Dances were subject to fashionable trends, and those in the elite level of society had no wish to be seen performing last year's dances, let alone those of five or ten years ago, which had now filtered down to a lower level of society. Therefore, new dances had to be continually learnt and mastered. For example, in 1469 the dance master Filippus Bussus wrote to Lorenzo de' Medici offering to come to Florence in order to teach Lorenzo and his siblings "some elegant, beautiful and dignified *balli* and *bassadanze*". According to Bussus, the performance of such new and elegant dances would bring "honour and fame" to Lorenzo and his family.[5] The letter from Bussus highlights the need for rehearsal before these dances were performed in public. Thus dance education began at an early age for the children of the nobility. Ippolita Sforza was only ten when she danced at Tristano Sforza's wedding celebrations in Milan in 1455, while Isabella d'Este started her public performances from the age of six.

A high level of skill was needed in order to perform gracefully in public, without error. A dancer had to be able to learn the correct carriage of the body, to master the steps and their variants and to memorise the choreographies. Furthermore, he or she had to possess a thorough understanding of the interaction between the dance and the music, the ability to adapt the patterns of each dance to the available space, the wit and invention to subtly vary each step so that it was not performed the same way several times in a row, a knowledge of the gestures and movements of the body which accompanied the steps, an awareness of the phrasing of each step as well as the agility to cope with the speed changes in the choreographies. An example of the difficulty of mastering the mechanics of the dance practice as an adult, let alone its subtleties, is illustrated by a letter from the German painter Albrecht Dürer. Dürer, while on a visit to Venice in 1506, wished to improve his social standing. Apart from buying new and luxurious clothes, Dürer also enrolled in a dancing class. He found this part of the process of social ascension much more difficult than just purchasing expensive clothes, as the somewhat complaining tone of his letter reveals. "I set to work to learn dancing and twice went to the school. There I had to pay the master a ducat. Nobody would make me go there again. I would have to pay out all that I earned, and at the end I still wouldn't know how to dance!"[6]

Dürer's letter vividly illustrates that dancing was a social marker, a means of distinguishing those who belonged to an elite group from those who did not. In the thirteenth and fourteenth centuries dance had always been regarded as a normal aristocratic pastime. But from the fifteenth century onwards the art of dance as described in the dance treatises became a sign of membership in the upper levels of society. The rules and postural codes as taught by the dance masters were part of the mechanism by which the court made itself appear superior and inaccessible to the rest of society. The courtiers believed that their superiority should be demonstrated to the rest of society by the different way in which they moved, walked, danced and even stood in repose. Their carriage and demeanour when on the dance floor did not change once they finished dancing: it remained with them as it became their normal posture. Thus the instruction the young children received from the dance masters was extremely important socially and ethically, as it not only allowed them to obtain approbation when they exhibited their skills in the dance, but it also trained them in the patterns of behaviour and deportment essential for membership in the social elite. If you moved ungracefully you immediately demonstrated to others that you did not belong to the right class of society, as you could not perform the movement patterns appropriate to that class. Dancing taught the chosen members of society control over their body and over all their actions, both when dancing and in day-to-day interactions with their colleagues and superiors. It was visible evidence that a person was capable of appearing in public without making an exhibition of herself or himself. If a person could control his or her outward bodily movements, then they were capable of controlling their inner emotions as well. Dancing, therefore, functioned as a social marker, as one of the ways a certain group in society defined itself and excluded others. A stark example of how dance was used to define the elite in society comes from Nuremberg in 1521. In this year those who held political power wished to limit further the numbers of citizens entitled to vote. Therefore they designated the voting elite as "those families who used to dance in the *Rathaus* in the olden days, and who still dance there".[7] In Nuremberg it was the ability to dance that was used as a tool to exclude people from the group who exercised political power.

Dance as an elite activity was strengthened in the Renaissance because it became a form of consumption: a consumption of both time and money. The dance practice recorded in the treatises needed many hours of teaching and practice from a young age, and only those who were wealthy enough to have the leisure time to devote to this activity were able to participate.

The fifteenth-century Italian dance treatises were more than just a compilation of choreographies.[8] These manuscripts also contained a theoretical section in which the steps were briefly described, rules for the mastery of the dance were given, as well as the essential principles of the art and its philosophical basis. In their treatises the dance masters argued for dance to be included among the liberal arts. The authors of the treatises, Domenico da Piacenza, Antonio Cornazano and Guglielmo Ebreo, were fully aware that for dance to be included in the liberal arts through its association with music, it had to be understood both on a physical and intellectual level. If dance was a liberal art it could then lay claim to be a demonstration of eternal truths, and a path to understanding the nature of God and the universe. The dance masters, especially Domenico, devoted a great deal of attention to setting out the philosophical basis of the art of dance that had the same numerical basis as the other mathematical arts of the quadrivium. These numerical proportions that were believed to order the cosmos found expression in the ratios of the relative speeds of the four *misure* – *bassadanza, quaternaria, saltarello* and *piva misura* – out of which the *balli* were constructed.[9]

Dance masters were also concerned with eloquent movement. Ever since the late fourteenth century, Italian humanists had been passionately concerned with eloquence in spoken and written text. The humanists' professional activity was the use of words, and so the production of elegant prose or poetry was one of the chief aims. The professional métier of the dance masters was movement of the human body, and this was where they strove to inculcate eloquence. For Domenico and his colleagues a person's gestures, deportment, facial expressions and manner of walking were a silent language that carried a rich treasury of meaning.

Given the concern of the dance masters with the performance of elegant patterns of movement, it is not surprising that a large part of the specialised technical vocabulary developed in their treatises dealt with nuances of these eloquent movements. *Maniera, aiere, gratia* (grace), *ondeggiare, campeggiare*[10] and *fantasmata*[11] were all terms developed by the dance masters in their attempts to describe elegant movements, all of which involved a fluidity and flexibility in the dancer's body. For movements to be eloquent they also had to be in harmony with the gestures and steps performed (a constant refrain in Guglielmo's treatise), as well as with the clothes worn by the dancer. Movements that would look dignified and seemly when dancing in a long garment would appear slightly ridiculous when dancing in a short tunic. Similarly, the jumps, turns and flourishes that appear elegant when wearing a short garment would have the opposite effect if observed on a dancer in a long tunic. Elegant movements, therefore, were not always slow or stately. They could be vigorous and lively when appropriate.

The engagement of the dance masters with contemporary intellectual concerns continued in the sixteenth century. From the mid-sixteenth century onwards the intellectual climate in both continental Europe and England fostered an interest in symbols. Indeed, the "manipulation and interpretation of symbols became a popular intellectual sport in the sixteenth century".[12] Symbols were seen as a great force both to draw heavenly power down to earth, and to help raise human understanding closer to a knowledge of the divine. Marsilio Ficino, in his treatise *De vita* (1489) is explicit on the power of "figures" (*figurae*) to influence human activity. And these "figures", or magical symbols that contained a hidden power, included music, people's gestures, facial expressions, movements and dance.[13] Ficino's writings were very popular in France in the sixteenth century, not only *De vita*, but also his *Commentary on Plato's Symposium on Love*, which influenced many poets including Ronsard and Baïf, both of whom were involved in the danced spectacles at the French court. In Ronsard's own writings he says that dance is divine and has the power to bring those divine effects down to the earthly sphere to transform those who perform and watch it.[14]

> The evening that Love enticed you down into the ballroom to dance with skill, the wonderful dance of Love ... The dance was divine ... now it was circular, now long and then narrow, now pointed, as a triangle ... I mistake myself; you did not dance, but rather your foot touched the summits of the earth; and your body was transformed, for that night, into a divine nature.[15]

The aim of the dance master when choreographing a dance for a masque or fête was to present to their educated audience of the court a series of symbols and images that communicated messages to the viewers just as did the spoken or sung portions of the spectacle. To them dance was a language analogous to writing, a form of "moving script" and the geometric figures created by the physical bodies of the dancers were the equivalent of the words and sentences of a spoken or written text. Thus choreographers built the dance around a series of discrete geometric figures or patterns that continually changed over the course of the dance. Each different rearrangement of the geometric shapes of a circle, square, triangle, or symbol such as a cross, produced a new dance figure with a different meaning. Dance masters saw themselves as architects responsible for the design of a dance, in geometric and proportional terms, and for these choreographers the true beauty of their dances resided in the geometric figures. Geometrically patterned choreographies were one way in which cosmic influences could be magically (that is, in a hidden or occult manner) transported to earth and, once there, could induce the same cosmic harmony to operate on earth.[16] Dance was seen as a form of alchemy: an alchemy that acted upon performers and viewers, refining and transforming them into a purer state, closer to that of the divine nature. Therefore the notebook of a French dancing master who worked in Brussels *c.*1614–19 does not contain written descriptions of steps as do the treatises of Caroso, Negri and Arbeau, but rather over 450 drawings of figures for five to sixteen dancers.[17] Many of the figures are simple geometric shapes – squares, circles, triangles, pyramids and lozenges – as well as composite figures in which discrete geometric figures are combined to form larger figures. Other named shapes are alchemical images: the salamander, serpent, tortoise, dart, sun, moon and star.[18]

Thus the interest in images and symbols that prevailed in society in general affected the choreographic structure of the theatrical dances in the late

1500s in France and England. By this time alchemical images and emblem books circulated widely, and by the beginning of the seventeenth century the language, images and metaphors of alchemy "were available to anyone who cared to read or listen".[19] It is inarguable that the texts of the masques and the French fêtes were written by the leading poets of the time, all of whom would certainly have been well aware of alchemical ideas and images, but the choreographers would also have had access to this imagery through the large number of printed books available on the subject, as alchemical books were part of the staple literature of the reading public.[20] By the end of the sixteenth century the corporeal rhetoric and eloquent movement of the previous century had given way to a language of symbols – alchemical and mystical – that spoke directly to those watching who had the intelligence to comprehend and interpret what they saw.

A further contribution of the early dance manuals to European ballet was the ideal of dance as morally virtuous behaviour. In *quattrocento* Italy it was a commonly held belief that movements of the body were an outward manifestation of the movements of a person's soul.[21] This belief was part of the reason for the dance masters' cultivation of, and insistence on, elegant movements, and the distancing of their choreographies from the dances of the peasants. Thus those who moved in an ungraceful and inelegant manner in public exposed their inner nature for all to see. There was more at stake than momentary ridicule for one's clumsiness. Vulgar movements that were not eloquent would be a clear sign that a person's soul was not virtuous. Dancers could move those who saw their performance to sorrow, anger, happiness or laughter, as the emotions of the dancers were made visible through the movements of their body. This gave them both a tremendous power and responsibility: a power to affect the emotions of those who watched, and the responsibility to represent only morally edifying emotions.

Thus dance had the ability to teach ethical behaviour. A virtuous person when dancing would be imitating in his or her movements various positive ethical states, these would then be recognised by the spectators, who could themselves learn to imitate these virtues in their own lives. Naturally, the reverse position was also true; that is, a dancer's movements could represent negative emotional states. Guglielmo did not seek to deny that the art of dance could be abused and used for immoral or improper purposes. But he also argued that when used by virtuous, noble and moral men, it could have a positive ethical effect on its practitioners and on those who observed it. Even though Guglielmo devoted an entire chapter on the behaviour and demeanour expected of young women of gentle birth, which he said had to be more moderate and virtuous than that expected of young men, he was not excusing a low level of behaviour from the latter. They still were expected to exhibit courteous and virtuous behaviour. Therefore, the dance masters had an interest in promoting the moral virtues of the art of dance, and in emphasising its benefits for society as a whole, as is illustrated by the following passage from Guglielmo's treatise:

> But when it is practised by noble, virtuous and honest men, I say that this science and art is good, virtuous and worthy of commendation and praise. And moreover not only does it turn virtuous and upright men into noble and refined persons, but it also makes those men who are ill-mannered and boorish and born into a low station into a sufficiently noble person. The character of everyone is made known by the dance.[22]

In the sixteenth century the ability of dance to teach moral truths was carried further by northern European writers. The status of dance as a medium of moral instruction was elevated by the publication of such works as Thomas Elyot's *The Boke Named the Governour* (London, 1531). Elyot's book was an educational treatise for young boys who were destined for careers in the country's administration. According to Elyot, dance was a noble and virtuous pastime, as it provided both recreation and a means to learn and comprehend the virtues necessary for adult life. Through the study and practice of the *basse danse* children could learn the important moral truths, as each step of the *basse danse* signified a different aspect of prudence.[23] For example, the reverence that begins every *basse danse* signified the honour due to God that is the basis of prudence, and which should be the starting point for all of mankind's actions.[24]

The *written* history of Western European ballet begins in the fifteenth century with the production of the dance treatises. These manuscripts document a dance practice many of whose characteristics continued in the ballet of later centuries. Each dance was individually choreographed: a unique arrangement of steps, floor patterns and music. The treatises record hundreds of individual dances, as well as describing a large and sophisticated step vocabulary. These dances required a creator, or choreographer, and their complexity demanded that dancers learn, memorise and rehearse them before performing in public.

The choreographies were performed by members of the aristocracy, those who participated in the government and wielded power. These performances were often part of official state ceremonies and festivities, as well as for private entertainment. Dance was part of the display of wealth and power of the elite, as its practice involved the consumption of leisure time and money. The dance practice as described in the treatises, with its specific movement patterns, gestures and carriage of the body, acted as a social marker, identifying those who belonged to the elite level of society.

The dances that are recorded in the treatises are overwhelmingly chore-ographed for both men and women, rather than for one sex only. Thus the dances served as a means of expressing common social interactions and relationships between men and women. The dances also embodied societal norms, such as the need to control the movements of one's physical body and inner emotions. The dances performed by the elite in society were also seen as teaching ethical behaviour to those who watched through the external representation of moral virtues.

Most importantly, the dance practice as described in the treatises was part of the contemporary intellectual culture. The choreographers, either through the corporeal eloquence of the dancers' movements, or through the figures and symbols formed by groups of dancers, communicated important truths to the viewers who had the knowledge to comprehend what they were seeing. Dance was a liberal art, and as such was one path towards understanding the nature of God.

2 *Ballet de cour*

MARINA NORDERA

The *ballet de cour* is a type of composite theatre performance, made up of instrumental and vocal music, texts declaimed in verse and prose, stage design, scenic accessories, costumes, masks and, not least, dance. Its "potentially chaotic"[1] structure includes a series of successive entries, variable in number and type, divided into acts and culminating in a final *grand ballet*. The term "ballet" is used, therefore, to indicate both the whole piece as an entity as well as the danced portions of it. The definition *ballet de cour* was coined only in the nineteenth-century historiography[2] in order to legitimate – although that was not explicitly expressed – classical ballet by associating it with the noble context in which it had allegedly been born.

The *ballet de cour* was born and developed at the French court in the last decades of the sixteenth century and lasted – with a variety of ups and downs, among which was a crisis of popularity during the regency of Anne of Austria – right to the end of the seventeenth century. Its evolution tracked the parallel consolidation of the French monarchy from the first Valois king, Henry III, through the Bourbons Henry IV and Louis XIII. It reached its apogee at the beginning of the reign of Louis XIV (1638–1715) in the years after 1643 when he became king. Louis, who until 1670 regularly danced leading roles himself, attracted the attention of his courtiers, both French and those from foreign courts, to the *ballet de cour*. The progressive decline of the form began when the king retired from active performance but also as a consequence of altered conditions in court politics and in the relations between the crown and society as a whole.

The evidence by which we can reconstruct the *ballet de cour* comes from a variety of types of sources; among them are libretti, with the poetic texts or the subject matter, the musical scores and the many printed illustrations, which reproduce the staging and costumes, and descriptions that are contained either in official chronicles or private documents. As a result we can state that the corpus of works so documented runs to hundreds of ballets,[3] which in spite of their great variety and differences, display certain common features.

The narrative plot of the *ballet de cour* is simple and schematic, drawn from the mythological universe or medieval romances. It is built with the rhetorical tropes of allegory and metaphor. From the dramaturgical point of view, within the vast, authenticated repertory, there are some more and some less coherent examples. Where some *ballets de cour* contain presentation, development, resolution and conclusion of an intrigue or plot, others reduce themselves to a series of episodes linked by a pretext.[4] Each *ballet de cour* has its origin in a celebration of a specific event or occasion in the life of the court and in particular the royal family or a military victory[5] or notable success in international relations. Most are secular but occasionally we find that a piece has a religious pretext. The allegorical and mythological narratives are elaborated in such a way as to convey the significant elements which recall the precise social or political events. As a consequence the themes chosen, though masked by a rhetorical apparatus or sometimes by irony or the primacy of pure spectacle, always reveal a direct, immediate and easily recognisable relation to actuality.[6] While in the major part of the cases, the intent, well understood in such coded signs, is to serve the propaganda of the sovereign power, there are often ironic nuances, touches of self-criticism and even subversion.

The *ballet de cour* took place in the chambers of the royal palace, in various royal residences in Paris and in the provinces. The public sat on three sides. The sovereign took the central position on a raised throne above the stage level on which the ballet unfolded. At the conclusion of the *grand ballet*, as the final episode, the public took the stage following a practice which had begun to be popular during the sixteenth century. There they joined the dancers on the stage to execute a variety of social dances like the *branle*. The final bal united the public and the stage dancers on the same plane "in an ambiguous area between participation and presentation".[7] In fact, one or more members of the royal family often danced in the production, joined by members of the court entourage, generally male, and from time to time accompanied by professional dancers or tumblers who took particularly complicated or special roles. So called "hommes de qualité", privileged courtiers, were not supposed to measure their abilities against the technique and virtuosity of the dance masters, as François De Lauze made explicit in his chapter on the *courante*, a dance considered especially noble, in his treatise on dance for the gentlemen and ladies of court:

> n'aymerois point qu'ils meslassent parmy leurs compositions des pas qui sentissent son baladin, comme fleurets, frisoteries, ou branslements de pieds, piroüetes (j'entens à plusieurs tours violens ou forcez), caprioles, pas mesmes des demy caprioles, si ce n'est en tournant ou finissant, et tout plain d'autres petites actions ennemies du vray air qu'on y doit observer.

> ([I] do not want them to include in their compositions any steps that evoke a clown, like *fleurets*, *frisoteries*, or shaking of feet, *pirouettes* (I mean those with violent or unnatural turns), *caprioles*, not even half-*caprioles*, except if turning or finishing, and many other little movements that go against the gracious appearance one must respect).[8]

Thanks to the involvement of real members of the court, the ballet acted as a mirror set between spectators and dancers in which court society staged itself, its particular worries and political projections. The role assigned to each performer, as indeed the role assigned to, and occupied by, each spectator, embodied a precise meaning in the order of society. Allegory transposed that mirroring into the relationship between the individual and the universe in which the social order became symbolised as cosmic reality and at the same time the universal stood for the social. In the game of symmetry, which kept the balance between the realisation of the work on stage and the realisation of the pattern of court society, the *ballet de cour* became a way to consolidate a consensus in society, which reflected it and on which it reflected.

The *ordonnateur des plaisirs royales* furnished the theme and coordinated the diverse trades and crafts needed in the production of a *ballet de cour*. In some cases the *ordonnateur* had at his side or occupied himself the position called by de Pure *Poëte*, who incorporated the functions of "autheur, inventeur, dessinateur, entrepreneur",[9] a notion of the poet, which seems to return to the original Greek meaning of the word *poiein* (to make).

Court artisans carried out the staging of the scenes, the operation of the theatrical machinery and the realisation of the accessories, costumes and masks. Many of them were Italians, who had come to Paris either in the retinue of Catherine de' Medici or were summoned on commission by her. They contributed to the transmission of technical skills in the field of theatre elaborated for decades in the Italian courts, especially those in Florence. The scenic dressing of the stage of the *ballet de cour* in their hands aimed at pure spectacle, made up of the ingredients of surprise, of the marvellous and exotic. For example, in the *Ballet de la délivrance de Renaud* of 1617, the Italian stage designer Tommaso Francini provided four changes of scene, renewing the perspective in the Italian manner while the audience watched. When the economic situation permitted it, the sovereign would place huge sums of money at the disposal of his stage designers in order to meet such challenges as would exalt his magnificent lavishness. In periods of austerity, sets and costumes would be reused or readapted for the most disparate thematic contexts and varied narratives.[10]

The costumes and accessories formed a combination that identified the characters, but they became overloaded symbolic indicators that reached the level of the absurd and achieved an "overkill" of meaning, so to speak. One example of such overbearing symbols was the female giant who appeared in the entrée of the music fairie (from the French *féerie*) in the *Ballet des fées de la forêt de Saint-Germain* of 1625, portrayed in a drawing by Daniel Rabel:[11] she carries a director's baton and a musical score; she wears as hairdo a fiddle; lutes and theorbos are attached to her skirt, a triangle serves as an earring and

Figure 2 Guillemine la Quinteuse, Fée de la musique. *Ballet des fées de la forêt de Saint-Germain* (1625), drawing by Daniel Rabel, Musée du Louvre, Inv. 32 604.

small cymbals as ornaments of her corset (see Fig. 2). Another Rabel drawing portrays hermaphrodites in the *Ballet de la douairière de Billebahaut* of 1626. Their bodies, seen from the front, are divided vertically in two parts. The right-hand side from the spectator's point of view is feminine. The bosom is uncovered, the hair is long, the figure wears a skirt and holds a spindle in her hand. The left side is masculine. The leg is exposed and muscular, he has a moustache, a plumed hat and a sword in hand.[12] (see Fig. 3). All the characters – grotesque or not – always wear masks which accentuate the characterisation of the individual or render a group entirely homogeneous. The masks according to de Pure serve to beautify and ornament the character but above all to render it recognisable as such for the public. The mask must eradicate the personal identity of the dancer in such a way that the spectator sees in it only the character which he or she incarnates.

In spite of the collaboration of the various artistic authorities, the principal role in the production of a *ballet de cour* remains that of the poet, which confirms the dominance of the text in the hierarchy of the arts. The most prolific poet who produced *ballets de cour* and whose career covered thirty years (1651–81) was Isaac de Benserade, a member of the Académie Française from 1674, holder of pensions from Richelieu and Mazarin and author of successful libretti in the second half of the seventeenth century. Benserade was admired for his ability to let the real figures of the courtiers of the epoch and actual episodes from their world shine through the actions of allegorical or mythological characters who appeared on stage.

Figure 3 Androgynes, *Ballet de la douairière de Billebahaut* (1626), drawing by Daniel Rabel, Musée du Louvre, Inv. 32 692.

As to the form, structure, themes and modes of representation, the *ballet de cour* continued the tradition of the Italian *intermedii* and the French *masquerades*,[13] divertissements that were more or less extemporaneous and which delighted the private and public social life of the court beginning at the end of the sixteenth century. It continued through the entire seventeenth century and into the eighteenth.[14] The elements of that inheritance were reorganised in order to adhere to a coherent theoretical system put forward by the Académie de Poésie et Musique, founded in 1570 by Jean Antoine de Baïf. He was a poet and member of the Pléiade, a group of poets who had come together for the common purpose to give new life to French poetic art. The Académie intended to restore the unity and synthesis of the arts of the ancient Greek drama. Poetry, music, dance and song were to be subordinate to the same aesthetic principles and the same rhythmic and melodic laws. The model created for dance was that of choral movement based at the same time on the spatial geometry, which organised the evolution of the groups on the stage and on the expressiveness of gestures capable of rendering a wide range of meanings not expressible in words. In spite of the attention dedicated to the stage arts, for the Academicians the poetic text remained the principal motor of the action and the main ingredient of the aesthetic synthesis.

This first attempt to provide norms for the ballet failed to impose a system of rigid rules based on the unity of time, place and action or subdivisions into acts derived from Aristotle and frequently imposed on the other forms of theatrical performance. Its flexible forms lent themselves easily to various types of experiment.[15] Seventeenth-century theorists – de Pure, Ménestrier and Saint-Hubert[16] – limited themselves to description of the characteristics of the ballet without codifying precise rules. Indeed Michel de Pure insisted on emphasising the advantages brought to the ballet by the very absence of codes and rules:

> Soit que jusqu'icy les Loix du Balet n'ayent pas esté publiées, ou que le Ciel et sa bonne fortune l'ayent préservé des chicaneuses et ridicules inquiétudes des Maistres-ez-arts, il n'est tenu que de plaire aux yeux, de leur fournir des objets agréables et dont l'apparence et le dehors impriment dans l'esprit des fortes et de belles images.

> (Whether it is that up until now the Laws of Ballet have not been published, or that the benevolence of Heaven has preserved it from the ridiculous and petty concerns of the masters of arts, Ballet must only please the eyes, it must provide them with pleasant objects whose appearance and forms imprint strong and beautiful images in the mind.)[17]

De Pure was a court intellectual and "aumonier du roi" (king's chaplain). He was an assiduous spectator of performances at court and was writing at a time when the *ballet de cour* was at its height. The long chapter which he dedicated to this type of performance contains descriptions and critical observations of current practices and another attempt to systematise the art. After a definition of the word "ballet", he examines the elements which come together in its creation and realisation: subject, title, subdivisions in parts and entrées, music, texts in prose and poetry, instruments, dancers, costumes, masks and above all *le pas de balet*, the true, proper choreography of the piece. Dance therefore joins together with all the other arts in the constitution of the *ballet de cour* and, even though it gives its name to the entire composite performance, it is not dominant: song, declamation, surprises in staging and scenery join the choreography on equal terms. The choreutic vocabulary used is the same as that in social dances, even if the technical level varies according to the competence of the interpreters and the type of dance. In the *ballet de cour*, in fact, diverse forms of choreography coexisted and alternated: figured dance, dances drawn from the repertory of society, pantomime, solos of great virtuosity, masked processions and dressing-up.

Some social dances were integrated into the *ballet de cour* because of their expressive or functional value, for example, the *pavane* was used for royal entries or divine interventions, or some *branles* offered the basic structures for group dances. An example is given in one of the entrées of the ballet *La Douairière de Billebahaut*:

> Les Donzelles qui la suivent luy marchent sur les tallons cherchant et ne trouvant pas la cadence des Bransles de Bocan; et leurs pas plutost de balle

que de ballets tesmoignent qu'elles ont grand tort de venir estudier dans la
Salle du Louvre pour aller danser ailleurs.

(The women who follow him step on their heels attempting in vain to find
the rhythm of Bocan's *branles*; and their steps, more proper to a ball than a
ballet, testify to the fact that they were very wrong to come and study in the
Salle du Louvre in order to dance elsewhere.)[18]

This passage would seem to indicate the ironic deformation of a pre-existing
branle that had been composed by Bocan, a famous ballet master of the
epoch. In the solos, great importance was given to the symbolic significance
of the character, produced by the richness of the costume and the social rank
of the interpreter, which concentrated the attention on him or her, as in the
case of *ballet de cour*, in which the sovereign himself took part. In the *Ballet
de la nuit*, presented in the Hall of the Petit Bourbon on 23 February 1653,
with music by the young Jean-Baptiste Lully, Louis himself played the rising
sun. In the following year *Le nozze di Peleo e di Teti*[19] became a political
event of fundamental importance after the Fronde crisis. Louis XIV, the
son of Louis XIII and Anne of Austria, was crowned in 1654 but prevented
by rebellion, the so-called two *frondes*, one the *fronde* of the nobles, the
other *fronde* of the parliamentarians, from assuming the full powers of the
crown. The young Louis XIV danced the role of Apollo and appeared as
the victor, pacifier and central figure of re-established, political harmony.
The use of expressive dance for such ends was documented by theoretical
texts and the iconography of the time. When gods or allegorical figures were
set in the dance, such elevated figures drew their gestures and moves from
the declamatory arts and rhetoric, which young nobles had learned at the
Jesuit colleges. In the case of grotesque or burlesque characters, the skills
of acrobats and of comedians furnished a vast range of gags or acrobatic
jests. Finally, in addition to every sort of armed combat, certain types of
"professional" moves and gestures were choreographed as in the case of
gardeners, carpenters and wood-cutters who utilised the tools of their trades
in cadence and in fantastic formations.

In the so called "figured dance", sometimes called "horizontal", dancers
took positions to create geometric designs, letters of the alphabet or symbols,
all legible only by the spectator who saw them from above and from a central
position relative to the stage. The king, his family and the dignitaries closest
to them were among the few privileged spectators who would have been in a
position to decipher the message correctly. No source reveals to us the rules
of composition for the "figured dance". The descriptive elements which have
survived to our day come from libretti distributed before the show, from
celebratory texts edited afterwards and from contemporary descriptions.
Some of these libretti contain the geometrical figures which the choreographic compositions intended to "design" (possibly because on stage such

Figure 4 Faun from Lully's *Le Triomphe de l'amour*, 1681.

figures were not really legible). The figures that were composed of knights in the final ballet of the *Ballet de Monseigneur le Duc de Vandosme* (1610) represented letters drawn from an ancient druidic alphabet, which is written out and illustrated in the libretto. Each figure represents a concept: "pouvoir supreme, verité connue, peine agréable, ambitieux désir" ("supreme power, known truth, sweet sorrow, ambitious desire") and so on. The succession of the figures on stage constructs the phrasing of an abstract, verbal discourse, transmitted in code to those who were in a position to decipher it (and openly revealed to readers of the libretto!). The degree of comprehension of the message depended on the position which the spectator occupied in the hierarchical organisation of space. The figures in the dance could be static or in movement. The transition from one figure to another occurred in a kind of internal fluctuation of the dance or in passages apparently neutral. Mark Franko indicates that in these transitions of spaces an independence from the text of the body emerges, which "loses its human resonance when it becomes a marker of geometrical position",[20] and hence achieves its own political autonomy. The body acquires in this way a strong power to evoke abstract concepts, cosmic and astral movements, which overcome its corporality. A dialectical game begins as a consequence between the autonomy of the dancing body and the text, in which the body, itself in process of becoming text, assumes its own political significance that is independent of the text and sometimes in open contradiction to it.[21] Around 1640, under the influence of Italian staging practices, the stage became elevated and it was no longer possible to perceive such figures, which therefore disappeared progressively from the compositions.

De Pure noted in 1660 with a certain irony that the "figured dance" had established itself to show certain courtiers who could not do more than walk in time to the music in a good light and called that practice a technical short cut, which showed clearly that the art of ballet had degenerated. For de Pure, the practice of dancing was not unbecoming to a "homme de qualité" who therefore should apply himself with greater commitment. By acquiring greater technical and expressive competence the amateur interpreters of *ballet de cour* would be able to execute the complex compositions proposed by dance masters.[22] A distinction seemed to emerge thus between "simple dance" and ballet. This was neatly expressed by Claude-François Ménestrier, a Jesuit historian, who published two works on ancient and modern theatrical ideas:

> Et cela nous apprend la différance qu'il y a entre les Ballets, et que la simple danse est un mouvement qui n'exprime rien, et observe seulement une juste cadence avec le son des instruments par des pas et des passages simples ou figurés, au lieu que le Ballet exprime selon Aristotle les actions des hommes, leurs mœurs, et leurs passions.

> (And that teaches us the difference that there is between ballets and simple dance: that simple dance is a movement that expresses nothing and observes only an exact rhythm with the sounds of instruments, by steps and simple passages or step sequences, whereas the ballet according to Aristotle expresses the actions of human beings, their customs and their passions.)[23]

Though there was a common vocabulary between social dance and ballet, the mode of executing both varied. The production of a *ballet de cour* required the presence of two professional figures, whom we would nowadays describe with the anachronistic terms director and choreographer. These observations make us grasp how the quantity and quality of dance contained in a *ballet de cour* depended on the type of interpreters who staged it, on the type of dance employed and on the notion of dance which it implied. Unfortunately, the scarcity of specific sources does not permit us to define exactly the nature and range of these differences.

The *ballet de cour*, and in particular the *Balet comique de la Royne*, a piece which has been described as the ancestor of the genre by current historiography, is one of the most extensively studied episodes in the history of dance.[24] The reasons for such particular interest are manifold: above all, the qualitative and quantitative wealth of sources which document it has allowed the reconstruction of various aspects and of the salient episodes in its development. In addition, its evolution coincides with the political apogee of the French court, an object of many studies because of the important place which the Sun King and his entourage occupy in French history, also serving as a model to lesser courts in Germany and other European countries. Finally, the *ballet de cour* represents a key moment in the historiographical project, which claims that the noble origins of classical ballet legitimate it as the highest form of dance. This legitimisation operates at the same time in aesthetic-literary and political terms. The "mythical" origins are made to go back, in fact, to the century in which the literary codification of theatrical genres took place and when the will of enlightened and powerful sovereigns used this form of performance not only as entertainment and as an end in itself but also for their political and personal self-promotion.

The *ballet de cour* enjoyed great success beyond the confines of the Parisian court, in particular in the form of the English masque and in Piedmont at the Savoy court, where it developed a particular form thanks to the activity of cavaliere Filippo d'Aglié, the younger son of a distinguished family, who became secret councillor to Christine, daughter of the French King Henry IV and Maria de' Medici, when she married the Duke of Piedmont Vittorio Amedeo I. Our knowledge of the ducal repertory is derived from a rich collection of sources. There are reports of historians and chroniclers, libretti, engravings and paintings but, above all, several codices conserved in the Royal Library and the National Library in Turin. These volumes were written in the hand of the ducal secretary Tommaso Borgonio who, in addition to the texts, reproduced stage scenes and costumes in priceless images. Altogether, the collection represents an incomparable corpus of documentation by comparison to what remains on the Parisian *ballet de cour*.

As in Paris, the ballets were interpreted by court nobility but the grotesque characters required the employment of professional dancers and actors, frequently people from the *commedia dell'arte*, who are, however, not named in the documents. D'Aglié took on the composition of the ballets as far as the themes, the development, the characters, the stage design and the music were concerned. The structure of the entries, the thematic choices and the procedures for conveying meaning were similar to those in Paris but with a preference for demonstrative stage effects and surprises in costumes and accessories. Usually, after an initial entry, which presented the theme, the remaining entries followed in a crescendo of ever more spectacular effects. For example, *Il tabacco* (1650), whose theme was suggested by the recent legalisation of the tobacco leaf, displayed the natives of the island of Tobago, who praised the virtues of the tobacco. Successive scenes presented smokers, ancient and modern, from all the nations. *Il Gridelino* of 1653 celebrated the *gris-de-lin* (literally grey linen) in a series of entrées; this grey was the favourite colour of Madame Christine and symbol of "constant and persevering love". After the God of Love has chosen *gris-de-lin* among all the colours presented to him by Iris, gardeners alternate in presenting flowers and plants of that colour; weavers then present this colour in cloth and so on through a series of entrées on the set theme – grey linen. Taking account of what happened outside the French court and following the parallel trail to Savoy and England helps to reposition correctly the *ballet de cour* in the historiographical panorama of Europe in the eighteenth century.

Balet comique de la Royne or *Allegorie de Circé*, was staged at the court of Henry III, Valois-Angoulême King of France, for the marriage of his favourite Monsieur Anne d'Arcques, Duke of Joyeuse, to the sister of the queen, Mademoiselle de Vaudemont, Marguerite de Lorraine. It was performed in Paris on 15 October 1581. We are accustomed to consider it as the very first *ballet de cour* in history, which it was not: we have much evidence that before this work other performances of the same type had been staged in France and Italy, but they were not called "ballet".[25] The historic relevance given to the *Balet comique de la Royne* is closely linked to the importance of the event which it celebrated and hence the fact that it motivated the production of a rich documentation, which has survived to our time: most importantly the libretto, which was written by Balthasar de Beaujoyeux[26] and published roughly four months after the performance; secondly, the music, then the printed illustrations, which portray the staging, costumes, the fixed and movable scenic elements, the plan of the hall in which the production was staged and finally official and unofficial chronicles of the occasion. The libretto through which the *Balet comique de la Royne* is transmitted to us is a unique example of its kind. The great majority of *ballets de cour* lack such documentation. The rich documentation of the promotional apparatus of the *Balet comique de la Royne* forces itself on the attention of the historian who has to keep alert to make a correct exegesis of the material, peeling off the thick layers of rhetoric and bombast. The libretto provides exaggerated data, which makes it necessary to check every fact. As an example of this exaggeration, we are told that the number of spectators was between 9,000 and 10,000, while we know in fact that the hall could only accommodate 500.[27] We have therefore to read the sources carefully, and the weaving in of other sources can give more accurate dimensions of this type of show.

For example, analysis of the contribution of the various arts in the *Balet comique* refutes the declaration of Beaujoyeux that he had given the central role to dance: "I'ay toutefois donné le premier tiltre & honneur à la dance, & le second à la substance, que i'ay inscrite Comique" (I have always given the first role and honour to dance and the second to substance, which I inscribed in Comique). Beaujoyeux actually used the word *balet* for only two choreographic scenes that the piece contained. He described them as "n'estant à la verité que des meslanges geometriques de plusieurs personnes dansan ensemble sous une diverse harmonie de plusieurs instruments" (being, in truth, no more than the geometrical groupings of people dancing together, accompanied by the varied harmony of several instruments).[28] Sparti has remarked justly that "this oversimplified definition of 'balet' hardly sounds like the words of a choreographer, even one writing for a 'non-specialised' audience. One would think that Beaujoyeux as choreographer would have wanted to impress, explicitly, the spectators-readers with the importance of his dances by alerting them to their complexity, significance and worth."[29] It is legitimate here to ask why that theatrical production should have been called *ballet* in the first place. To pose such a question opens more general issues about the corpus of work which we habitually call by that name. Indeed, the fact that successive studies have from time to time assigned diverse chronological limits to the *ballet de cour* shows how definitions of the genre can fluctuate. Lacroix presented the *Ballets et mascarades de cour* that were staged between 1581 and 1652; Prunières, who intended to illuminate the Italian origins of the genre, studied the phase preceding the "classical" and "French" epoch of Benserade and Lully (see Fig. 4); McGowan's treatment begins with 1581, which she considers as the date of the "first effort that constructs a ballet that realises all the aspirations of the theoreticians" and the period for her ends in 1643, which corresponds with the death of Richelieu and Louis XIII and marks the introduction of *gusto italiano* by Mazarin. Mark Franko broadens the thematic and chronological span of his research, which extends from 1573 (the first known work of Beaujoyeux, the *Ballet des ambassadeurs polonnais*) to 1670 and the ultimate *comédie ballet*, *Le Malade imaginaire*. In this way, Franko overthrows the conventional definition of *ballet de cour*, which is both improper and invented, and proposes a much wider idea of *ballet*, which would comprehend the proper, true *ballet de cour*, the *ballet burlesque* and the *comédie ballet*.[30] The historiographical approach proposed by Mark Franko abandons the assumption of a long-standing critical tradition that presupposes a continuity between *ballet de cour* and classical ballet and argues that the seventeenth-century composite form had more in common with the performance art of the twentieth century than with the evolution of the ballerina in the tutu.[31]

This brief historiographical excursion shows how the *ballet de cour*, by its multiform heterogeneity, by its capacity to renew itself and by the strategies adopted to plant itself in its time, naturally lends itself to successive exploration and leads us to pose questions of much greater scope about the relationship between sources, history and historiographical work.

Translation Jonathan Steinberg
Translation from Old French Kristin Stromberg Childers
and Roger Chartier

3 English masques

BARBARA RAVELHOFER

English masques were allegorical entertainments with dance and music, costumes, songs and speeches, and festive scenery. As a protean phenomenon, which flourished in the sixteenth and seventeenth centuries, masques might assume the character of a low-key countryside event, a civic festivity, a high-profile state occasion, a university romp or a jollification at the Inns of Court in London. Plays of the early modern period often treated their audiences with a masque *en miniature*: silent dancing highlighted pivotal moments in the action and added to the suspense.[1] Shakespeare's *The Tempest* includes a wedding masque whose "graceful dance" of nymphs and reapers "in country footing"[2] is dangerously interrupted by invaders. In Restoration operas, masques showcased magical characters and dazzled spectators with spectacular ballet and scene transformations.[3] Masques fused English traditions with foreign performance practices. With their abundance of danced pantomime, they represent an important precursor to John Weaver's balletic drama in the eighteenth century. This chapter will provide a brief history of this multifarious genre, and explore in greater depth the impact of continental balletic forms on masques performed in London during the early seventeenth century.

Masque-like mummeries had been popular since at least the early Tudor period. Henry VIII is said to have introduced disguisings in Italian style to the English court. In 1512, the king and his courtiers celebrated epiphany

> disguised, after the maner of Italie, called a maske, a thyng not seen afore in Englande, thei were appareled in garmentes long and brode, wrought all with gold, with visers and cappes of gold, & after the banket doen, these Makers came in, with six gentlemen disguised in silke bearyng staffe torches, and desired the ladies to daunce, some were content, and some that knewe the fashion of it refused, because it was not a thyng commonly seen. And after thei daunced and commoned together, as the fashion of the Maskes is, thei toke their leaue and departed, and so did the Quene, and all the ladies.[4]

Audience participation remained a crucial element in "masks". As the Milanese ambassador reported about nightly revels in 1514, the king was dancing "in his shirt and without shoes" with the ladies, and leaping "like a stag".[5]

Elizabeth I inherited the passion for Italian entertainment culture. In her youth, the French ambassador De Maisse recounted that the queen "danced very well, and composed measures and music, and had played them herself and danced them ... without doubt she is a mistress of the art, having learnt in the Italian manner to dance high ... they called her 'the Florentine.'"[6] De Maisse not only alluded to Elizabeth's well-known enthusiasm for Italian dancing (she also employed at least one Italian professional, Jasper Gaffoyne) – he even suggested that she composed music *and* choreographies (one meaning of "measure" at the time).[7] Entertainments in honour of Elizabeth sought to please her with artistic feats by foreign professionals. At Kenilworth in 1575, an eyewitness was bowled over by an Italian tumbler who showed off his bravura technique:

> feats of agilitee, in goings, turnings, tumblings, castings, hops, iumps, leaps, skips, springs, gambauds, soomersauts, caprettyez & flyghts: forward, backward, sydewyze, doownward, vpward, and with such wyndyngs gyrings & circumflexions: al so lightly and wyth such eazyness, az by me in feaw woords it iz not expressibl [*sic*] by pen or speech.[8]

The tumbler's athletic prowess recalls the manifold leaps and capers described in Italian dance manuals of the period (see Chapter 1). Doubtless it pleased a queen who herself took pleasure in "dancing high". Skilful jumping seems to have remained a benchmark for fine dancers in the years following Elizabeth's reign. In a reception in 1604, Prince Henry Stuart danced before a Spanish visitor. As the guest observed, he performed "with great ease, yet dignified restraint" and mastered "some capriols".[9] It has been suggested that Henry acquired these skills from perusing Cesare Negri's *Nuove inventioni di balli* (1604), and that both this work and Fabritio Caroso's famous *Nobiltà di dame* (1600) were available at court during Henry's lifetime – a hypothesis worth considering.[10] Given the eminence of Italian festival culture at the time, dancing styles as practised in Florence, Rome or Milan must have had an impact on the early Jacobean court. Prince Henry repeatedly asked for Florentine festival books.[11]

After the accession of the Stuarts in 1603, entertainment culture developed a new professional dimension. Under James I and Anna of Denmark, and Charles I and Henrietta Maria, lavish masques were performed at Whitehall between 1604 and 1640. These so-called "court masques" celebrated the monarchy before a specially invited audience of diplomats, courtiers and citizens.[12] Given their excellent documentation (stage and costume designs, texts and bills survive), court masques prove particularly attractive for dance and performance research.

The best poets of the day composed the songs and speeches for masques, among them Samuel Daniel, George Chapman, Thomas Carew and William

Davenant. The artistic partnership of the poet Ben Jonson and the architect Inigo Jones – who was responsible for stage and costume designs – led to such legendary productions as *The Masque of Blackness* (1605), *The Masque of Queens* (1609) and *Oberon* (1611).

While masques stunned the senses by the combined impact of words, music and visual effects, it is fair to say that no other form of theatre in early modern England placed greater emphasis on dancing. As the poet Thomas Middleton remarked, masques consisted in "one houres words, the rest in Songs & Dances".[13] Much of the action evolved within a specially constructed dancing area which separated the stage from the auditorium; court records mention a wooden floor covered with green fabric to muffle the noise.[14] There, participants exerted themselves for long hours. As the courtier Thomas Roby reported about one of Henrietta Maria's dancing nights, "ye Mask...on Sunday last begann at Tw[e]lve at night and was not done till almost fyve".[15] Not surprisingly, balletic expertise was in great demand. Masques thus encouraged the rise of the dance professional in early modern England.

Professional dancers were highly mobile and contributed to the cultural interchange between different countries. English artists ventured to the continent. In 1608, William Pedel, a pantomimist skilled in "dauncing & vaulting", travelled to Leyden where he exhibited "beautiful and chaste performances with his body, without using any words".[16] Caleb Hasset served the Landgrave of Hesse-Kassel in the 1630s, and George Bentley worked in Dresden in the 1650s.[17] Continental artists and dancers settled in early Stuart London. The Tuscan designer Constantino de' Servi provided settings for Thomas Campion's *The Somerset Masque* (1613). The renowned violinist and choreographer Jacques Cordier (also known as Bocan) served both the French and English courts, where he was involved in Campion's *Lords' Masque* (1613) and probably Carew's *Coelum Britannicum* (1634) (see Figs. 5 and 6).

Structurally, court masques often fell into three parts with distinct kinds of dancing. They started with a mimic display of the forces of chaos and misrule; then royal and aristocratic performers restored order by their formal ballet; and finally audience and performers joined for dances and refreshments. The first part (called "antemasque" by Daniel and Middleton, "antimasque" by Jonson, and also known as "antic masque" or "entry/entrée") abounded in grotesque, amusing roles (such as nymphs, satyrs or drunkards), which were commonly taken by professional actors and dancers either in group or solo performances. Although the movements must often have seemed spontaneous or erratic to the onlookers, they were tightly choreographed, which can be deduced from the carefully cued changes of rhythm in surviving music and the references to choreographers in masque texts.

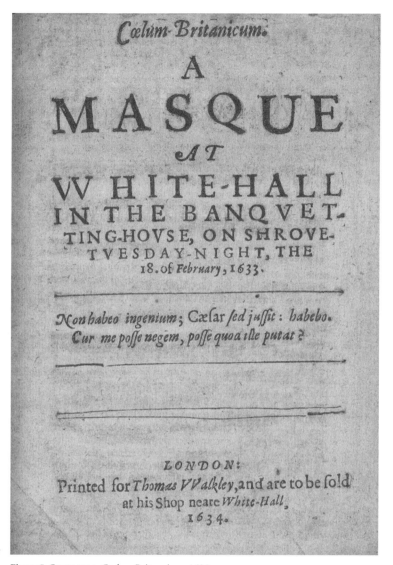

Figure 5 Cover page, *Coelum Britannicum* 1634.

Thus in *The Masque of Queens* (1609), male dancers erupted onto the stage in the guise of witches:

> with a strange and sudden music, they fell into a magical dance, full of preposterous change and gesticulation, but most applying to their property [i.e. habits], who, at their meetings do all things contrary to the custom of men, dancing back to back, hip to hip, their hands joined, and making their circles backward to the left hand, with strange fantastic motions of their heads and bodies. All which were excellently imitated by the maker of the dance, Master Jerome Herne, whose right it is here to be named.[18]

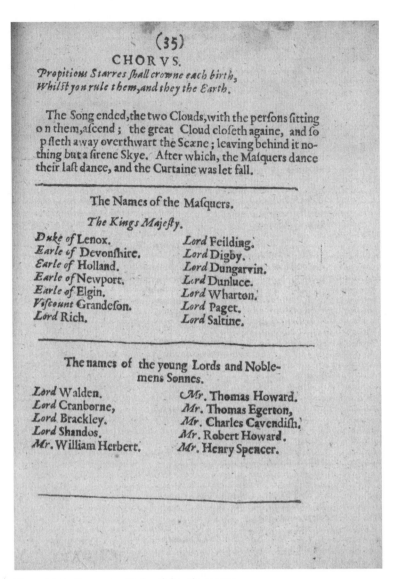

Figure 6 List of masquers, *Coelum Britannicum* 1634.

James I loved antimasques and often asked for an encore. In Francis Beaumont's *The Masque of the Inner Temple and Gray's Inn* (1613), dancing statues, servants, baboons and other droll figures won "perpetual laughter and applause":

> the dancers, or rather actors, expressed every one their part so naturally and aptly, as when a man's eye was caught with the one, and then passed on to the other, he could not satisfy himself which did best. It pleased his Majesty to call for it again at the end, as he did likewise for the first anti-masque, but one of the Statues by that time was undressed.[19]

With the years, these "antic" performances increased in number, partly thanks to popular success, partly a consequence of French tastes at Whitehall. French *ballet de cour* favoured serial entrées and allowed courtiers to perform as "low" characters. Most English court masques maintained a distinction between "professional" and "aristocratic" dancers in the casting of roles.[20] Yet events on a smaller scale, especially those performed in private residences in the countryside, were less rigid in their divisions of rank. Thus, the francophile Duke of Buckingham danced as a pickpocketing gipsy in 1621.[21] With the arrival of Henrietta Maria, a French princess, at the English court, continental customs became even more fashionable. Henrietta Maria was an accomplished dancer and singer who had performed in ballets since her childhood. French kings mingled with the bourgeoisie in public ballet events[22] – unthinkable for Charles I, a monarch obsessed with protocol. Henrietta Maria, however, felt at ease in venues outside the court. Invited to a performance of *The Triumph of Peace* (1634) in the Merchant Taylors' Hall, the queen was carried away when she danced before the citizens: "The Queene dancing at the Lord Maiors, strained her foote & was like to haue taken much hurt."[23] The anecdote is emblematic for the increasing strain on both royal effort and civic goodwill. *Salmacida Spolia* (1640) – the last court masque staged before the Civil War – anxiously exhorted spectators to preserve peace under a benevolent Stuart monarchy. The event boasted an inflated number of twenty antimasques, which indicates how desperate the king and queen were by then to entertain their audience.

The theatrical part of a masquing night culminated in the main masque (or "masque proper"). Here an ensemble of splendid aristocratic performers engaged in silent dancing. As in the antimasque, the movements were specially choreographed; but now they emphasised formality in a grand ballet. Masquers traced geometric patterns or alphabetic letters, which was common practice in Italian theatre repertoire of the period and the *grand ballet* in French *ballet de cour*. Typically, *The Masque of Beauty* (1608) saw nymphs performing "squares and rounds" and "a most curious dance full of excellent device and change", which ended "in the figure of a diamond".[24] Geometric circles and squares projected to all sides of an auditorium.[25] In masques they would have been equally visible from any of the seats which surrounded the dancing space on three sides. Choreographies with such figures were clearly intended to please as many viewers as possible and thus challenge the current view that formal dances were intended for the ruler's eye only. Yet the association of early Stuart courtly repertoire with absolutism cannot be dismissed. In a politically motivated inversion of masquing conventions, Milton's *A Masque Presented at Ludlow Castle* [*Comus*] (1634) elevated country dances – usually the domain of the antimasque or the revels – to the "masque proper" section. The upright simplicity of these dances ("without duck or nod") contrasted with the "ill-managed merriment" of Comus and his "glistering", beast-like courtiers, caricatures of Cavalier revellers. By privileging local festive traditions, Milton offered a poignant critique of what he perceived as a centralised court culture of excess under Charles and Henrietta Maria.[26]

While antimasque characters were always impersonated by men, the main masque was open to women: Queen Anne and her ladies gave daring (in the view of some English courtiers, too daring) performances as black daughters of the River Niger or Amazonian queens. Henrietta Maria pioneered speaking and singing roles for women, as they had long been practised on the continent. Her court masque *Tempe Restored* (1632) featured the first female professional singers in English theatre history.

In the final part of a masque, the "revels", select members of the audience joined the masquers for yet more dancing.[27] The revels drew upon a pre-existing pool of social dances. Contemporary accounts mention, for example, country dances, *branles*, or "measures".[28] The latter may, in this case, allude to a repertoire taught in English dancing schools since Elizabethan times.[29] The choice of dances and participants would have been pre-established; even so, revels or revellers enjoyed themselves. Queen Anne's masquing nights reveal a sense of merry abandon:

> for galliards and corantoes they [Anne and her ladies] went by discretion, and the young prince [probably Henry] was tossed from hand to hand like a tennis ball. The Lady Bedford and Lady Susan [de Vere] took out the two ambassadors and they bestirred themselves very lively, especially the Spaniard, for his Spanish galliard shewed himself a lusty old reveller. The goddesses they danced with did their parts, and the rest were nothing behindhand when it came to their turns; but of all for good grace and good footmanship Pallas [Anne] bore the bell away.[30]

Revels repertoire was probably easier to perform than the preceding theatrical parts and thus facilitated audience participation, as shown by the Spanish guest's vigorous contribution. Dancing immersed a heterogeneous audience in the total experience of a masquing night. It rendered the event more inclusive, creating a "corporate and festive identity".[31]

Unfortunately all choreographies for the great court masques are lost, and their nature must be inferred from circumstantial evidence, such as eyewitness accounts of masque texts. Two dance sources are directly connected with masque performers: François de Lauze's *Apologie de la danse* (1623) and Barthélemy de Montagut's *Louange de la danse* (before 1623), both dedicated to the Duke of Buckingham, a famous dancer and sponsor of masques. But they describe social, not theatrical dance repertoire. Their new emphasis on gliding steps and *pliés* suggests an affinity to French *danse noble.*[32] There is no evidence that de Lauze ever worked in England; in later years he danced in French *ballet de cour*. Montagut, on the other hand, taught Buckingham and orchestrated entertainments for him; he later became Charles's dance instructor, performed in at least two court masques, and was a well-remunerated member of Henrietta Maria's household. In seventeenth-century England, reading and learning by doing offered parallel access routes to dance repertoire. The lawyer Justinian Pagitt noted, "write the marks for the stepps in every daunce under the notes of the tune, as the words are in songs".[33] A few manuscripts containing social dances may indicate the dissemination of repertoire by manuscript circulation; a collection of eleven country dances entitled *Chorea*, for instance, contains errors as they typically occur in the process of copying another document.[34] Persuasive evidence for learning dances from a written source derives from John Playford's country dance collection *The English Dancing Master* (1651, subsequently expanded, eighteen editions until 1728). Yet, as far as early Stuart masques are concerned, the absence of any choreographies is striking, especially given the wealth of surviving masque music.

One exceptional source shows how a masque dance could have been fixed to paper. In about 1650, the merchant clerk Robert Bargrave penned an entertainment for the wedding of the English ambassador's daughter at Istanbul. His diary records the masque poetry next to music scores and verbalised choreographies. This unassuming document may well contain the first surviving theatre choreographies in English drama. Bargrave uses one-letter abbreviations for performers, and very basic floor patterns such as squares and triangles. His notes represent memoirs rather than an instruction for dancing – in the case of one dance, Bargrave writes "figure forgotten".[35]

The choreographies consist of four seasonal dances (a popular topic in English masques) and an antic dance. The seasonal dances are relatively simple; their terminology is reminiscent of that used for contemporary country dances, as in this typical passage:

> Chace one another forward, then backward & so fall thus:
>
> > a[utumn]   w[inter]
> > s[ummer?]   s[pring?]
>
> 2:^d time :So: & Sp: face W :&: A: then Au: & So: separat from W: & Sp: then back & fall into a ranke :2.^d part Hay till each comes into his Place: 2.^d time salute each other, & the Company, & go off.-[36]

The final "antic" dance, a pantomime, involves four "men", two "boys" and one "woman" (probably played by a man, given the graphic nature of the performance). Accompanied by a "ranting" tune, the performers tumble over each other, fight a mock battle, and beat the "woman". Then the action proceeds to a mock marriage, and finally the "woman" gives birth, onstage, to two boys:

> First part; Men bring in W. great Bellied, hiding two naked boyes under her coats :2:ᵈ time :B. doune on all fower, A kneeling behind him (to resemble a Chaire) C. & D. make her sitt downe :2.ᵈ part She sets her selfe in travell, & they officiat :2.ᵈ time, the two boyes runn out from under her: – then the :4: daunce round the W. who nurses the boyes at each breast, & so runn all In:- (p. 98)

Bargrave's simple devices are the work of an enthusiastic amateur, not a professional but they show an imaginative sense of humour. It is a pity that they were never performed, as the wedding was cancelled.

Back in England, James Shirley's *Cupid and Death* (1653) pessimistically declared about the gentry that "their dancing days" were "done".[37] Yet masques continued to be performed: Henry Purcell's *Dido and Aeneas* (two versions, pub. 1698, 1700) is variously called "masque" and "opera", and John Dryden composed a *Secular Masque* as late as 1700. Charles II briefly considered reviving sumptuous court masques as they had been practised before the Civil War. John Crowne's *Calisto* (1675), the magnificent result of such deliberations, borrowed its five-act structure from the French *comédie-ballet*. *Calisto* was an Anglo-French choreographic co-production. Josias Priest, later responsible for *Dido and Aeneas*, collaborated with eight French professionals, including Mr St-André, a member of the Académie Royale de Danse at Paris. Preparations extended over six months, involving a cast of ninety-one (with Princess Mary in the leading role).[38] In contrast to Caroline spectacle, the spoken parts were taken by courtiers, while most dances were performed by professionals.[39] Had theatrical repertoire become too difficult for courtiers? It is tempting to think of Michel de Pure, a critic writing about Paris theatre in the 1660s. For de Pure, the "stupidity of most great lords and persons of quality" affected the choreographies in opera productions. These noble amateurs were

> not capable of anything, and constrain in this manner the neatest and most famous masters to restrain the force of their steps, the speed of movement, and other graceful elements of the dance, so as not to cripple an entry by the discrepancy in step and action [. . . the *pas de balet*] must be more expressive and vigorous than that of common dancing, as applied in the balls and those ordinary and domestic dances which the women proudly boast of doing as well as the men . . . it needs to have something faster and more vivacious.[40]

Yet in London, the cast succeeded so splendidly that the poet Crowne apologised for daring to put their achievement into words. A self-effacing preface to *Calisto* states that such efforts must be eclipsed by the actual performance:

> Reader, If you were ever a Spectator of this following Entertainment, when it was Represented in its Glory, you will come (if you come at all) with very dull Appetite, to this cold, lean Carkass of it [i.e. Crowne's printed account]. The Dancing, Singing, Musick, which were all in the highest Perfection, the most graceful Action, incomparable Beauty, and rich and splendid Habit of the Princesses ... must needs have afforded you a delight so extraordinary, that this will appear very insipid.[41]

Calisto afforded a short-lived epiphany of royal splendour. Fostering the *comédie-ballet*, Charles II emulated Louis XIV in France, the absolutist sun king since his legendary appearance in the *Ballet royal de la nuit* (1653).[42] Harking back to Caroline court masques he sought to capture once more Stuart magnificence. Charles I and Henrietta Maria made universal "motion cease and time stand still" when they traced their noble figures on the dancefloor: "good is here so perfect, as no worth / Is left for after-ages to bring forth", gushed the lyrics of *Coelum Britannicum* (1634).[43] *Calisto* belonged to an "after-age". The gods of the Restoration stage granted at most, as Crowne's modest libretto knew, "the small dominion of a Star".[44]

4 The baroque body

MARK FRANKO

Baroque dance developed from the late sixteenth-century and early seventeenth-century court ballet, *ballet de cour*, and survived into eighteenth-century opera ballet until it was eventually displaced by the dramatic innovations of Marie Sallé and Jean-Georges Noverre.[1] Although it disappeared entirely from European stages with the emergence of the nineteenth-century romantic ballet, the baroque made a return in the twentieth century through a series of "baroquisms" in modern dance and ballet, as well as through historical reconstructions of a scholarly and theatrical nature. There is evidence of a serious attempt to reconstruct baroque dance as early as 1910 in Germany.[2] The creation of original or speculative baroque movement languages, however, was more prevalent until mid-century. Modern dancer Alexander Sacharoff, for example, choreographed and performed solos such as *Au temps du grand siècle/Pavane royale* in 1919, and Kurt Jooss choreographed *Pavane on the Death of an Infanta* in 1929.[3] Oskar Schlemmer was influenced by early seventeenth-century burlesque ballet costume design in his experimental *Triadic Ballet* (1922). Bronislava Nijinska choreographed *Les Fâcheux* for the Ballets de Monte Carlo in 1924 and danced the male lead herself.[4] Martha Graham choreographed *Imperial Gesture* in 1935 and José Limón choreographed *The Moor's Pavane*, based on *Othello* with a Henry Purcell score, in 1949. In all of these cases, something understood as the marker of period style was incorporated into a twentieth-century concept of dance modernism.

The baroque could easily seem the natural domain of classical ballet even if choreographers had no specific knowledge of historical dance; for example, the Stuttgart Ballet's *Sleeping Beauty* in the 1970s skilfully used the contrast between seventeenth- and nineteenth-century ballet costume to convey the two worlds of the narrative. George Balanchine's *Agon* (1957) was inspired by François De Lauze's 1623 dance treatise *Apologie de la danse*; I have seen performances of *Agon* where the early seventeenth-century influence is indicated explicitly by period bows performed in intervals to the main dances. But, for the most part, the baroque body is not visible in *Agon*, although doubtless still present by virtue of musical reference.[5]

Baroque dance can also seem the domain of modern dance in that it preceded and was radically different from classical ballet. Unlike classical ballet, the legs are never lifted high in the air, and the foot is often flexed at the ankle rather than pointed. The arms do not trace airy, expansive *port de bras* above the head but contained half circles in front of the chest and not higher than shoulder level. Supple hand rotations starting at the wrist ornament these circular arm movements. Jumps do not soar through the air but are more like hops. In general, one could say that baroque dance blurs the distinction between classical ballet and modern dance while remaining a historical style in its own right. As the polarity between classical and modern softened by the latter half of the twentieth century, baroque dance became more visible as a viable contemporary performance option. No matter what technical skills the dancer starts with, baroque dance technique is not easily mastered. Being highly cerebral, musically complex and often counter-intuitive, it demands special study.

Although full-length seventeenth-century ballets are rarely, if ever, integrated into the repertories of major ballet companies and modern dance companies present only historical reconstructions of twentieth-century choreographers, by the mid- to late twentieth century baroque dance technique became the domain of dancers specialising in period style. Such specialisation was possible because of dances surviving in the period notation of Raoul Auger Feuillet and Pierre Rameau.[6] In the United States, Wendy Hilton analysed the notation and translated it into performative terms.[7] In 1976 Catherine Turocy and Ann Jacoby formed the New York Baroque Dance Company, which staged full-scale productions of the eighteenth century and brought baroque dance to a worldwide audience (see Fig. 7). In the 1980s, French dance scholar Francine Lancelot also cracked the code of Feuillet notation. Her dance company Ris et danceries, founded in 1980, also toured internationally.[8] Lancelot taught this material to modern dancers and ballet dancers who incorporated aspects of it into contemporary choreography. Former company member Christine Bayle founded L'Eclat des Muses in 1983, and Beatrice Massin's Fêtes Galantes was founded in 1993. Both companies, based in Paris, as well as the New York Baroque Dance Company, still perform today, as does Marie-Geneviève Massé's Compagnie L'Eventail.

The specificities and peculiarities of baroque dance technique gained greater public exposure when Lancelot staged her baroque-derived choreography, such as *Quelques pas graves de Baptiste* (1985), for the Ballet de l'Opéra de Paris. Similar exposure for the idea of reinvention occurred when Mikhail Baryshnikov danced Leonid Jacobson's *Vestris* (1969) or when Beatrice Massin choreographed for the film *Le Roi danse* (1999). Other dancers currently working with baroque reconstruction and reinvention on the concert stage include Linda Tomko, Sarah Edgar and Patricia Beaman. While reconstruction attempts faithfully to reconstitute the original choreography, reinvention takes liberties with the historical sources.[9]

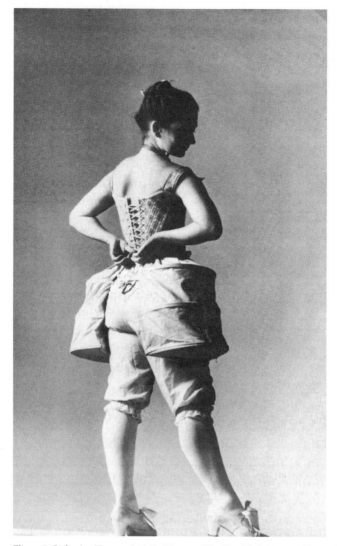

Figure 7 Catherine Turocy, Artistic Director, The New York Baroque Dance Company.

Another important aspect of twentieth-century choreographic creativity is research into early modern performance practices.[10] Baroque gesture is a key area of such research; the technique of baroque gesture is not identical to the arm and hand movements of baroque dance, nor is it the pantomime of nineteenth-century ballet, but rather a form of dramatic action that bridges theatre, dance and opera and has links to rhetorical delivery. The scholarly presentations of baroque dance reconstruction at conferences such as the Congress on Research in Dance and the Society of Dance History Scholars frequently focus on variants in notated dances. Such presentations are in their way extremely erudite and aimed at specialists. In some cases, the knowledge required to stage responsible reconstructions makes

Figure 8 Mark Franko in *Le Marbre tremble*.

demonstrations appear to be a strictly academic exercise. Reinvention, on the other hand, treats historical materials – technique, music, costume and scenarios – as springboards for the development of new work that can speak to a contemporary public but is also anti-modernist. Klaus Abromeit's L'autre pas company in Berlin has experimented with the juxtaposition of baroque and everyday movement. The commitments of pedestrian movement of the late 1950s and 1960s are here transformed into a historicisation or historical relativisation of contemporary experience. Works by François Raffinot such as *Caprice* (1988) bring baroque technique into contexts that are wholly reinvented, thus implying that the creative premises of another era apply to contemporary experience. Mark Franko's *Le Marbre tremble* (1986) for his company Novantiqua set in motion the caryatids of Pierre Puget through choreographic interpretation and photographic projection (see Fig. 8). The idea behind the piece was that of a baroque slave figure – Puget's models were galley slaves – exploring physical suffering by applying baroque visual art to dance. Recently members of Catherine Turocy's New York Baroque Dance Company presented experimental works ("post-modern baroque") based on the baroque technique and theatrical conventions contrasted with their contemporary analogues. Choreographic reinvention is the outcome of the authenticity debates that also took place in musicological circles during the 1980s.[11] According to these debates, despite rigorous efforts to determine what was "historically correct", no one interpretation could ultimately be authoritative. Unlike the modernist adoption of the baroque, these works are post-modern in that they reflect critically their own means and ends.

Scholars who have conducted important research into the aesthetics and politics of baroque dance include Françoise Christout, Margaret M. McGowan, Rudolf zur Lippe and Mark Franko.[12] In the background of these and other studies lies the link between court ballet aesthetics, rituals of state and early modern subjectivity. Court ballets were created for specific state occasions and were thus imbued with allegory, diplomacy and intrigue. Research has shown how baroque dance enables a reflection on spectacle and power, the early modern performance of gender and the relation of self-fashioning to political absolutism. Giovanni Careri has given special attention to the relation of the numerous seventeenth-century ballets based on Tasso and the development of modern subjectivity and affectivity.[13] These topics, like choreographic reinvention, create a bridge between seventeenth-century ballet and contemporary cultural criticism. Spectacle during the reign of Louis XIV, for example, was an extension of his political power; thus the notion of the spectacular in itself continues to suggest power relations. In some ways, vanguard scholarship has been more influential on baroquist reinvention than on academic reconstruction. William Forsythe's *Artifact* (1984), largely inspired by baroque dance, was among other things a conscious attempt to create a hyperbolically spectacular ballet through choreographic geometries.[14] At the same time, the spoken word in this piece was used to explore the theme of the fold, which clearly suggests and refers to Gilles Deleuze's[15] influential theory of the baroque based on an analysis of the writings of German philosopher Gottfried Wilhelm Leibnitz. The early modern engineering of state power as a spectacle – an idea whose relevance to contemporary life has been demonstrated by Guy Debord's *Society of the Spectacle*[16] – has also been the subject of important research on representation and power by Louis Marin, Stephen Orgel and Jean-Marie Apostolidès.[17] The antipathy for expression in post-structuralist theory and a concomitant interest in surface finds its analogue in the baroque's rejection of psychological depth. From the perspective of aesthetics, a renewal of interest in allegory in the 1980s also brought baroque aesthetics to the fore in a number of areas.[18]

An interesting focus of recent scholarship to emerge from this trend is the dancing king's body itself: the cross-dressed king and the king in the role of the hermaphrodite extends thought on the performativity of power to the realm of sexuality, gender and dance in the early modern setting.[19] How can the king, who represents patriarchal authority in the body politic, represent sexual ambiguity on stage? Again, one can note the contemporary resonance of baroque dance, not just because it suggests pastiche or the post-modern recycling of historical styles, but also because it pre-dates psychological motivation in the performance of unconventional sexualities and transgression, thus bypassing bourgeois morality while remaining fundamentally anti-modernist.[20] Mark Morris's *Dido and Aeneas* (1989), performed to the music of Henry Purcell's opera, is a good example of modern dance riding the wave of the baroque music revival while evoking the story of love and death in the context of the HIV/AIDS pandemic.[21] Morris himself played the cross-dressed roles of Dido and the Witch. While the choreography does not reflect early modern performance practices, it is a baroquist work. It is unusual in that the most interesting choreographic passages are performed to the *recitatif* that was usually reserved for a more rhetorical presentation, while the set pieces traditionally reserved for dancing are markedly less interesting. That is, the dancing invades the domain of gesture and Morris uses deaf-mute sign language as his methodology.

The desire to find an alternative to the narrative embedded in psychological motivation that has characterised much modern dance and contemporary ballet since the 1940s, as well as an alternative to post-modernist formalist abstraction since the 1960s, has transformed our view of baroque and baroquist work from a specialised historical exercise to a provocative theatrical experiment. The non-modern became appealing and fascinating and we might call it the post-modern archaic. This is a different gesture from that of assimilating tradition in the interest of overcoming subjectivism as, for instance, in the works of T.S. Eliot. However, the baroque revival also complicates facile notions of the post-modern by rethinking modernism through the lens of the early modern. In this sense, the return of the baroque in the twentieth century could be considered a modernist project.

German artist Oskar Schlemmer's interest in dance developed out of his enthusiasm for the tradition of classical ballet and his belief that baroque costume design counteracted two trends of early twentieth-century dance modernism: nudity and the fluttery veils of the ballerina. Schlemmer sought formal innovation in choreographic movement based on a re-conceptualisation of the human form that led him to the idea of the *Kunstfigur*, the art-figure or artificial figure. This idea was largely influenced by early seventeenth-century French costume drawings. Court ballet, for Schlemmer, was "free of constraints and thus predestined to furnish time and again the starting point for a theatrical Renaissance".[22] Schlemmer was perhaps the most influential artist to assimilate baroque stylistics to the modernist project of aesthetic innovation. Interestingly, he is now considered a progenitor of post-modern performance art. Thus, one can say that the baroque is a cultural space of cohabitation between modernism and the post-modern. All this would not be possible without the substantial preliminary research on court ballet prior to the twentieth century. In the mid-nineteenth century Paul Lacroix and Victor Fournel collected and published many court ballet libretti, which contain accounts of the action of the song lyrics (*récits*).[23] The music for much of this song repertory survives in the *Philidor* collection,[24] but the dance music, for the most part, does not. The baroque music revival can be traced back to the Bach revival of the early and mid-nineteenth century; the most important event was surely the performance of the *St Matthew Passion* by Johann Sebastian Bach in the Singakademie Berlin on 11 March 1829 under the direction of Felix Mendelssohn-Bartholdy. The Bach revival may have awakened a similar curiosity of bibliographers and theatre historians for the nineteenth-century research into court ballet texts.[25] But the cultural production of the late Renaissance and early seventeenth century, which is often thought of as pre-baroque but no longer Renaissance, remained largely hidden. Musicologists had long neglected the music of this earlier period.[26] French court ballet was also characterised by an extravagant costume culture from the workshops of Daniel Rabel in the early seventeenth century and Jean Berain in the later seventeenth century.[27] The interdisciplinary nature of performances and their elaborate production values conspire to make court ballet a challenging form to revive in the contemporary dance world. This is perhaps why the work of reconstruction began with the dance technique itself.

Along with a vogue for historical reconstruction from other periods of dance history and the revival of baroque music in the 1980s through an intense concentration on period instrument performance, the performance of baroque dance was internationally well received during that decade. The apogee of the baroque revival is said to be the lavish Arts Florissants production of Lully's *Atys* (1987), perhaps because the economic resources expended on this production evoked the riches available to court performance in the baroque period itself. It would be hard to duplicate such production values in further work. (In reality there was not a lot of baroque dancing in the production; the high point was Jean-Christophe Paré's solo as Morpheus.) Possibly for this reason, the baroque music revival has continued to flourish because it does not depend on production values that are so onerous to sustain. If dance, on the other hand, is to progress beyond what it has already demonstrated about vocabulary and performance style to work as persuasively with the reconstruction and/or reinvention of the entire stage space, enormous resources will have to be dedicated to it. As scarce resources are currently devoted to work that is most obviously new and innovative, this is a difficult proposition to sustain.

Nevertheless, baroque dance, art and music catalysed experimental choreography during the 1980s, the decade of twentieth-century dance that should be called "baroque". Baroquist aesthetics and its offshoots resonated with the post-modern recycling of historical styles. Yet, it was really not about random sampling or an equalisation of choreographic languages, but instead a way to reflect allegorically on movement and identity. But, coming after the dance boom of the 1960s and 1970s, interest in baroque dance also reflected a greater sophistication about the history of dance itself in the Western tradition. This was due in part to reconstructions of historical modern dance starting with the work of Isadora Duncan that began to take place in the early 1970s. Although there is always the possibility that it can be read as anti-democratic royalist nostalgia it also has the effect of revealing an unusual arsenal of theatrical movements, costume and make-up. It has a sociological connection to the financial excess and irresponsibility of the Reagan era, a time when even dance believed itself to be a big business. The powers of defamiliarisation in baroque dance rival its historical connotations. The idea of the baroque as a brand of post-modernism, an anti-modernist gesture without a classical model or an extension of modernism through the absorption of the past in the generation of new forms, was prevalent in the visual arts as well as in dance of the 1980s. Connections of the baroque to anti-normative or non-classical aesthetics made it a cultural rendez-vous of 1980s choreographic culture throughout Europe and America. One of its appealing effects was an assumed artificiality that counteracted high seriousness without falling into the other extreme of indifference.

The vogue for the baroque did not extend much beyond the 1980s and early 1990s, however, and allusions to this style are now less frequent on the ballet and modern dance stage. As French choreographers came of age during the 1990s, baroque or baroquist choreography may have become perceived in France as less relevant to the contemporary focus as a sine qua non of choreographic creativity. Once the interest in the baroque was characterised as antiquarian, its pertinence decreased and its venues dwindled. Also, with the funding crisis of the early 1990s, which particularly affected dance, resources on both sides of the Atlantic have been consecrated to preservation over performance. Paradoxically, the emphasis on heritage preservation in the dance world as a result of decreased funding has served to displace the role of historical reconstruction in live performance. International dance festivals seem less eager to programme dance reconstructions of any period. It is also likely that the baroque project as a whole missed its true mission as an anti-normative response both to classical ballet and to high modernism. As such, both reconstruction and reinvention remain unfinished projects. The baroque body is by definition a phantasm.

PART II

The eighteenth century: revolutions in technique and spirit

5 Choreography and narrative: the *ballet d'action* of the eighteenth century

DORION WEICKMANN

The *ballet d'action*, a narrative ballet, was an invention of the eighteenth century. It replaced the pompous *grands ballets* of baroque absolutism that had evolved out of the Italian Renaissance *intermedii*. Both court entertainments, *grands ballets* and *intermedii* or divertissements, had primarily represented and glorified the sovereign; the *ballet d'action*, on the other hand, was supposed to tell stories that followed their own narrative logic and lay beyond princely power fantasies.

The emergence of the *ballet d'action* relied on three factors: first, enlightenment ideas had spread to dance theory. Hence it became possible to introduce the notion that dance could and should be independent from the other arts. Secondly, the academic ballet of the eighteenth century strove towards a technical refinement that aristocratic amateurs practising dance could no longer fulfil. Thirdly, theatre as a cultural institution underwent a process of professionalisation in which the performer and the observer began to be separated from each other.

Critical contributions for a ballet reform came from France and the French *danse d'école*. Paris, the Mecca of the art of dance, housed the Académie Royale de la Danse, founded by Louis XIV in 1661, the institution that had overseen dance and had created a style that reached far beyond Paris or France into Europe. Students of the Académie had been celebrated as virtuosi. Increasingly, though, the empty pompousness of the absolutist court ballets and the rococo divertissements aroused more and more criticism. Louis de Cahusac, librettist, Secretary of the Comte de Clermont and also contributor to the *Encyclopédie*, was one of those critics who initiated a change. In 1754 he declared the *grand ballet* a means simply to achieve hollow effects and wrote that "Everything that is without action is unworthy of the theatre; all of it becomes an ornament without taste and without warmth".[1] Choreographer Jean-Georges Noverre, with whom the invention of the *ballet d'action* is still associated today, aimed at something similar. In 1760 he published his fifteen *Lettres sur la danse, et sur les ballets*[2] and introduced, at least theoretically, a new understanding of theatrical dance: the *ballet de cour*, the courtly ballet and the divertissements, were to be replaced by a dramaturgically conceived ballet with action and concept.

Despite Noverre's intervention in dance history through his famous letters and his claim to have been the first to do so, the course of ballet had
changed much earlier, at least half a century before Noverre, in England.
The English dancing master John Weaver had published his *Essay towards a
History of Dancing* in 1712[3] in which he assessed the status quo of the dance
very critically. Dancing, Weaver emphasised, had turned into a "ridiculous,
unskilful movement"[4] and sunk to a low level. The prototype of emptiness of form and content, Weaver remarked sarcastically, could be studied
nowhere better than in Paris at the Opéra. One of the soloists there, Jean
Ballon, "pretended to nothing more than a graceful Motion, with strong and
nimble Risings, and [by] casting his Body into several [perhaps] agreeable
Postures: But for expressing anything in Nature but modulated Motion,
it was never in his Head: The Imitation of the Manners and Passions of
Mankind he never knew anything of, nor even therefore pretended to shew
us."[5] The French, according to Weaver, were always making "a confus'd
chaos of steps ... which they indifferently apply'd, with any Design, to all
Characters".[6]

Weaver suggested a revival of the ancient pantomime as counter-model
to the French boring mess. In his opinion imitation of passionate emotions
and actions through gesture without words was to be much preferred to the
stilted and overblown spectacles of the *danse d'école*. For Weaver, the real
weakness of contemporary dance lay in the demand for sensational caprioles.
Instead of learning "what is natural, fit, or proper"[7] dancers were taught
merely to please. He recognised that "Stage Dancing was at first design'd
for Imitation; to explain Things conceiv'd in the Mind, by the gestures
and Motions of the Body, and plainly and intelligibly representing Actions,
Manners and Passions; so that the Spectator might perfectly understand the
Performer by these Motions, tho' he say no word".[8]

As ideal there emerged a mime-style dance language that orientated itself
along ancient examples, managed to exist without words and offered a realistic expression of human passions. Weaver tried to realise this ideal in his
own dances on stage, for instance in *The Loves of Mars and Venus; A Dramatick entertainment of Dancing, Attempted in Imitation of the Pantomimes
of the Ancient Greeks and Romans,*[9] conceived for the Drury Lane Theatre
in London. Yet despite all his good intentions Weaver did not manage to
work without accommodating public taste. He could not omit declaiming
or singing; he could not forgo extensive comments explaining his intentions
in programme notes. His audience, he knew only too well, was not prepared
to follow his "dance event" that was made out of one consistent action.

On the other side of the channel the audience was even less willing to
accept a new view on and new interpretation of dance. The *grand ballet* that
still dominated France had reflected the autocratic make-up of the French

state on several levels: in the self-disciplined and deferential attitude of the dancing courtiers, in the geometrical design that always led to the king as the centre, and on the discursive level of the content of the story told. Gods and ancient heroes, forces of nature and mythical creatures lived in this cosmos, its focus always the ruler. The *grand ballet*, composed of dance, declamation, song and illumination, impressed with its anti-Aristotelian qualities, with colourful changes from entrées to divertissements, with its intoxicating colours and shapes. The dramaturgy followed ceremonial formulas; only occasionally would these formulas contain an exposition, a development and a finale, as, for instance, in the *Balet comique de la Royne* of 1581. The *grand ballet* completely lacked "individual expressivity".[10] The individual dancer remained nothing but a tiny wheel in a gigantic machinery that aimed at praising the king.

It was this state of affairs that French ballet theorists of the eighteenth century criticised; they began to imagine a different practice of ballet. They intended to supply the dance with an unmistakable and autonomous poetics instead of understanding it as a hybrid form of poetry, music and painting. Against the absolutist demand of servitude the French writers defined form, function and content of ballet in a new way and harmonised all these new components. Instead of presenting mere virtuosity and conceptual emptiness, dance was supposed to translate human emotions and affects. Instead of simply confirming power relationships, dance was now to show "la belle nature" itself, that is, the beauty of the human condition, of human temperaments and characteristics. Dance literature from the mid-eighteenth century onwards followed this motif of a new sensibility.

The problem of action, of the plot, had occupied a central position after 1715, during the Regency. The mythological, allegorical and heroic themes of the absolutist period never disappeared completely during the eighteenth century and even survived into the post-revolutionary phase in France. At the high point of absolutism every figure pointed to the monarch's power. His right to represent the state was manifest by being transfigured – personally or symbolically – into a god or legendary hero. Though the figures of the Hellenic myths still populated the stages, their bodies told different stories. Monarchical glory and grandeur disappeared and were replaced by human conflicts, sentiments and souls.

Most theorists who thought about the future of ballet did not consider bodily codification or dance notation any more, as Raoul Auger Feuillet had still done in 1700 in his *Chorégraphie ou l'art de décrire la danse*.[11] They turned their attention to historical and dramaturgical problems. This tendency became obvious in Louis de Cahusac's three volumes called *La Danse ancienne et moderne ou Traité historique de la danse* that was printed in

Paris in 1754. Cahusac judged the stage practices of his time very critically. In his opinion, the poverty of action of the court ballets and divertissements destroyed the aesthetics as well as the function of theatrical dance: "L'Opinion commune est que la Danse doit se réduire à un developpment des belles proportions du corps, à une grande précision dans l'exécution des airs, à beaucoup de grace dans le déployment des bras, à une légerté extrême dans la formation des pas."[12] (Common opinion assumes that dance can be reduced to the development of beautiful physical proportions, great precision in execution of airs, graceful deployment of the arms and an extreme lightness in making steps.) Yet that was not enough in itself because it would often only mean mechanical repetition.

Cahusac demanded that ballet abandon empty entertainment pieces and replace them with stories in which the protagonists truly express their spiritual situations. Cahusac therefore pleaded for a "danse en action", a dance in action that substituted the art of storytelling that would reach the heart and soul of the audience for pure bodily technique. "La Danse en action a sur la Danse simple la supériorité qu'a un beau tableau d'historique sur des écoupures de fleurs. Un arrangement méchanique fait tout le mérite de la seconde. Le génie ordonne, distribue, compose la premiere."[13] (Dance in action is as superior to the simple dance as a beautiful historic tableau is to a bunch of cut flowers. A mechanical arrangement represents the entire value of the second but genius orders, distributes and composes the first.) Cahusac not only demanded that absolute spectacle be replaced by narrative composition but also suggested a dramaturgical structure for all ballets: they were to follow an Aristotelian three-part organisation in which the exposition of the dramatic conflict was followed by its development and its dissolution. Cahusac hoped that clarification of the subject in turn would lead to a revival of ballet.

Jean-Georges Noverre in his *Lettres sur la danse, et sur les ballets* wrote down a series of revolutionary views which, unfortunately, he could not always carry out in practice. After he had received his education with Louis Dupré, one of the most famous dancers of his time, Noverre made his debut at the Paris Opéra-Comique in 1743. Later he joined the company as its ballet master and staged his first full-length works there. His *Les Fêtes chinoises* of 1754 received ovations. Because Noverre could not immediately launch his career at the bigger rival, the Paris Opéra, in 1760 he went as ballet master to Stuttgart. As one of the favourite courtiers of the Wurttemberg Duke Carl Eugene, Noverre celebrated one triumph after the other. Nevertheless, he moved to the Viennese Royal Opera in 1767 where he remained in the position of ballet master until 1774. During the years in Vienna Noverre engaged in a violent controversy with his colleague Gasparo Angiolini, in which both sharpened their views on meaning, form and intention of the art of ballet. In 1775, at last, Noverre received the long-awaited position at the Paris Opéra but he failed there as a result of intrigue and envy. In 1781 he capitulated and settled in London where he spent his last years as a choreographer at the King's Theatre. Noverre returned to France in 1796 and died in October 1810.

In spite of his professional reverses, his *Letters on Dance* were republished several times in amended form. He argued that ballet had to go beyond entertainment. Most choreographers neglected the beauty of naive and graceful sentiments and presented instead symmetrical dances, mechanical repetition and spectacles without content or message. Noverre's first rule stated that the choreographer had to break the custom of symmetry and evenness. Noverre used arguments of the Encyclopedists to substantiate his claims: nature knew no symmetrical movements and human beings had different, not identical temperaments. Therefore the theatre should make these unmistakable differences clearly visible in every scene, in every drawing of a character. As real ballet was nothing but the imitation of "belle nature" – a view Noverre and many of his contemporaries firmly believed in – it had to resist the temptation of dull symmetry.

Noverre articulated the spirit of a new age: the symmetrical design that centred on the monarch had outlived its time. The Enlightenment with Rousseau's demand "back to nature" had changed civilised societies' understanding of values; it had pervaded notions of right and wrong and left its mark on political and aesthetic paradigms; it had also influenced dance theory. For Cahusac or Noverre, representation no longer meant the glorification of the king but the imitation and illustration of human passions and sentiments. The audience wished to see not the godly ruler but itself; it wanted to confront its own feelings, desires and needs.

The moral mission of ballet shifted to the foreground with the ability to move the observer. All dramaturgical means had to submit to this demand. The classical division of acts and scenes should be mirrored in the texture of its individual parts – every particular scene within an act should have an exposition, a middle and an end. The structure of the piece as a whole should be mirrored in all its parts. The corps de ballet had to come out of the shadow that the soloists had cast on it and shed its merely decorative function. All members should be able to turn into acting individuals, though they should never interfere with the soloists.

Noverre asserted that any situation could be turned into dance. For instance, Racine, Corneille, Voltaire or Crébillon could be adapted to make a ballet. In principle "il faut qu'un Maitre de Ballets connoisse les beautés & les imperfections de la nature. Cette étude le determinera toujours a en faire un bon choix: ces peintures d'ailleurs pouvant être tour-à-tour historique, poétiques, critiques, allegoriques & morales, il ne peut se dispenser

Figure 9 *Jason et Medée* by Jean-Georges Noverre, music by Jean-Joseph Rodolphe 1781. Gaëtan Vestris as Jason.

de prendre des modèles dans tous les rangs, dans tout les états, dans tout les conditions."[14] (It is necessary that the ballet master understand the beauties and imperfections of nature. That study will always help him to make a good choice of them: these paintings in addition can be in turn historical, poetical, critical, allegorical and moral. He cannot avoid taking some models from all ranks, all estates and all conditions.)

Noverre also tried hard to get rid of the overloaded costumes and wigs the dancers were forced to wear. Everything that hindered natural appearance, covered up the figure of the dancer or concealed movement impeded the newly developing art form. He demanded that all the actors on stage had to be free, free to move. The face, above all, had to be laid bare and made visible because it formed the centre of the silent scene, it conveyed emotions to the audience (see Fig. 9).

Expressivity demanded the trained human body. To portray "nature" required rigorous exercises and physical control. Like Proteus, the dancer was supposed to slip into any figure and express any sentiment that the plot of the ballet demanded. The body turned into a tool, a finely tuned instrument. In Noverre's theory the body characterised the genre as well as the dramatis personae. Previous authors like Weaver had touched upon the problem, yet it was Noverre who systematically defined the body in relation to plot and action. He initially distinguished between three areas of dance: firstly, the serious, heroic and noble – *danse noble* or *sérieux*, secondly, character dance – *danse demi-caractère* and thirdly, comic dance – *danse comique*. Physical traits classified the dancer's place within the dance genres: height and looks determined whether a dancer was a beautiful hero, a tender lover or a comic fool. Such interweaving of genre and bodily qualities pointed to the identity of content and form which became one of the most important criteria of the neoclassical theory of art to which Noverre belonged.

The heart of his reform Noverre described in the following way: "il faut s'écarter avec grace des règles étroites de l'Ecole, pour suivre les impressions de la nature & donner à la Danse l'âme, & l'Action qu'elle doit avoir pour intéresser"[15] (It is necessary to put aside in a gracious manner the narrow academic rules in order to follow the impressions of nature and give to dance the soul and the action which it must have to be interesting). Noverre hated the mechanical perfection of many contemporary dancers; in his view they were unable to perform dance in action. Action was the magic word. So what about plot? "L'Action en matière de Danse est l'Art de faire l'expression vraie de nos movements, de nos gestes & nos passions dans l'âme des Spectateurs. L'Action n'est donc autre chose que la Pantomime."[16] (Action with respect to dance is the art of evoking a true expression of our movements, our gestures and our passions in the soul of the spectator. Action is therefore nothing but pantomime.) Hence dance and mime melted into one dramatic plot that would be conveyed through gestures, steps and figures. The difference between this and the model of antiquity consisted in the elimination of language and singing. In Noverre's ballet the body alone reigned – without words, without arias or explanatory slogans. In practice, Noverre never got rid of the symmetrical figurations on the stage. His *Fêtes chinoises*, first performed at the Opéra-Comique in 1754, ran through a set of variations on Far Eastern themes and *La Toilette de Vénus* of 1757 never had a consistent plot though it was called a *ballet d'action*. Noverre had a weakness for elaborate sets and costumes that were hardly less opulent than those absolutist ones he accused of excess.

This is why Noverre clashed so violently with Gasparo Angiolini, Noverre's predecessor at the Viennese Opera; the controversy between both was carried out directly and personally, in memoranda, programme notes or public correspondence. Angiolini insisted on a clean structure based on Aristotelian unity of place, time and plot. He objected to the fact that Noverre's ballets did not achieve a dramaturgical climax and instead contained scenes superfluous to the action. For Angiolini drama with its strict rules provided the real standard for dance. Therefore, he sought inspiration and subject matter in works of contemporary playwrights, which he in turn adapted to the ballet stage. Noverre, on the other hand, at least when staging his own ballets, believed in following the principle of *ut pictura*, the painterly effect that the work should attain. He flatly refused to follow any pre-set rules just as much as he rejected the idea of notating dance. In his view such practice would inevitably lead to stagnation. The application of notation, he predicted, would invite simple, standardised reproductions and replications of once original works, in addition to which, only professional notators would be able to decode complicated sign systems. Angiolini envisioned the opposite: written signs would stabilise the ephemeral art of dance by turning it into a very specific tradition and thus make it part of a greater cultural heritage.

Angiolini and Noverre never agreed on the place of music. Angiolini, who also composed music and advised other choreographers and ballet masters to do the same, treated music and dance as two separate components that the dancer had to unite within his own body. Noverre disagreed and declared that a musical score would pre-set and manipulate the actions and movements of the performer. The protagonist was supposed to translate music into gesture, make its meaning transparent.

Angiolini represented a moderate modernisation in the development of dance; he intended to hold on to tradition as a secure guideline. He energetically demanded a consistent dramaturgy that would structure dance and movement according to spoken theatre. Noverre wanted freedom – freedom to invent and freedom to display sensibilities. For him Angiolini symbolised narrow-minded dogmatism and a stubborn adherence to principles; in his view Angiolini missed the essence of the new art: true copying of nature. Angiolini, though, had a point when he accused Noverre of proclaiming himself the genius-inventor of the *ballet d'action*. That he certainly was not. But in true romantic fashion Noverre swept away all such considerations. Angiolini declared that his teacher Franz Hilverding had already fused dance and mime elements in order to make them convey a dramatic action. Angiolini, his protégé, had carried on from there. With his *Don Juan* of 1761 and his *Semiramide* of 1765 he had staged an action ballet, a dramatic entity conveyed solely through dance and movements. The dancer Marie Sallé, one of the visionaries of her day, had done away with spoken and sung language in a *Pygmalion* performance in 1733 in London and thus had, in practice, staged a *ballet d'action*.

Noverre would have none of that and refused to acknowledge a gradual evolution of 'his' new genre.

Even without Noverre's prodding, the age of heavy wigs and ornate costumes was coming to an end. Then, in 1772, Pierre Gardel refused to appear on stage in full dress and decorative wig in the entrée of the opera-ballet

Figure 10 Dancers from the Australian Ballet as hens in *La Fille mal gardée*, 1970s.

Castor et Pollux. The audience greeted his bare head with thunderous applause – the dam had broken. The new trend produced its first real triumph in *La Fille mal gardée*, first performed on the eve of the French Revolution in 1789 in Bordeaux. Libretto and choreography had been written and developed by Jean Bercher (called Dauberval), who had been a pupil of Noverre but had parted acrimoniously from his teacher.

Dauberval told a love story, in a rural setting: Lisa, daughter of a female landowner, is to be married to the clumsy Alain, also the child of wealthy peasants. But the girl loves Colin, a poor farmer. In order to get her beloved she has to battle with her cunning and unscrupulous mother, but eventually succeeds and wins the man of her own choice. *La Fille mal gardée*, still in the repertories of our ballet companies today, was the first ballet to unite all of Noverre's requirements: a dramatically consistent narrative with character portraits and a clear subject, a piece that was totally different from court affectation and allegorical plots full of myths and gods. Dance alone told the story. What Weaver, Hilverding, Angiolini and Noverre had begun, Dauberval completed – a narrative ballet that really deserved its name – a *ballet d'action* (see Fig. 10). Apart from the feeling of saturation experienced by the theatre-going public with exalted absolutist hymns of praise, there were other dynamic relationships working in the eighteenth century to produce the desire for reform.

In addition, ballet technique evolved during the eighteenth century beyond the amateur's ability to execute it on stage. The absolutist *grand ballet* could recruit its performers from talented courtiers; their education included dancing as well as fencing, riding or playing music. The foundation of the Académie de la Danse as a certified institution separated stage and stalls, performer and observer. The Académie professionalised dance by regulating dance training and promoted professional dancers to replace courtiers. In 1713 the *Ecole de danse*, part of the academy, had no other object than to produce professional dancers.

The eighteenth century also generated the phenomenon of the *étoiles*, the star performers at the Paris opera, who vied for the admiration of the audience. Marie Sallé, Anne Cupis de Camargo, Marie Madeleine Guimard, Jean Pierre Aumer, Pierre and Maximilien Gardel, Gaëtan Vestris and his son Auguste enchanted the public and received unprecedented ovations. Their brilliant performances made ballet an art of technical perfection. At the same time the Paris opera house employed a corps de ballet, a group of well-prepared yet badly paid professional dancers, men and women from the poor quarters of Paris. As technique improved, the world back stage expanded. That world turned into a complex artistic cosmos in which the rise and fall, the glamour and wealth of the soloists was intricately inter-woven with the misery of the poverty-stricken members of the ensemble. Professionalisation of dance also meant that social dance and stage dance, up to the early eighteenth century inextricably linked to one another, gradually moved apart. The routine of accepted dance forms such as *musette, tambourine, chaconne* or *passepied* or other popular dances with a set of elaborate steps or movement sequences were replaced. The eighteenth-century books describing body and dance techniques show just how much over a relatively short period of time the movement and step vocabulary changed, advanced and increased. Raoul Auger Feuillet had been one of the first dance masters who attempted to write a grammar of dance and to notate dance by fixing positions of feet and legs as well as by designing spatial patterns. Positions of arms, later called *port de bras*, were more or less completely absent. But by 1725 Pierre Rameau's *Maître à danser*, published in Paris by Jean Villete, offered a supplement to the sequences Feuillet had compiled and now also included arm movements and new combinations with turns, *pirouettes*. In 1770 a dance master called Malpied,[17] who had set up shop near the Paris opera, presented a complete codification of arm positions. Just as the feet had been placed in five agreed positions (positions that had turned into part of an authoritative technique since the seventeenth century), so the arms and hands of the dancer now also had to be used according to a set of rules. The neoclassical demand to harmonise content and appearance had taken hold of the entire body. It had to be shaped and moulded according to a powerful superior will towards form that fixed the beginning and end point of every movement. The *danse d'école* drove form and technique to new heights. But such excellence and precision in execution called for strict self-control; it was far beyond the means of a non-professional to be able to fulfil such technical demands.

Authors of scholarly books now focused on training future dancers and not on pleasing amateurs. Social dance hence was only dealt with in passing. The last dance notation of the eighteenth century was written by Gennaro Magri who had made a name for himself at the opera houses in Naples, Vienna and Venice. His *Trattato di ballo* from 1779 clearly demonstrates how complicated the movement sequences had become over the last eighty years. Since the beginning of the century, since Feuillet's *Chorégraphie*, the repertory of steps, figures, turns and jumps had been augmented by about one third.[18] The professionalisation and academisation of dance had made progress and began to pay off. Quantitative as well as qualitative changes emerged: movement patterns had become complicated, combinations diverse, difficult passages were woven into one another rather than set apart; the obligatory arm movements demanded skilful coordination. Several steps and *pirouettes*, often composed of challenging variations, could be accomplished only by professionals. All this brought about the division between stage and social dancing.

The departure of stage from social dance had another cause: the organisational and public structure of the opera house had undergone dynamic development. Though this phenomenon still needs to be studied far more extensively, several contemporary sources indicate that the aristocracy was increasingly losing its privileges. Boxes and stalls were being sold to the emerging bourgeoisie, not given away to favoured courtiers. That development had begun very gradually in the era of Jean-Baptiste Lully, the composer who had been opera director under Louis XIV. Lully moved the opera from its location at court to a separate building, the Palais Royal, and opened it to the interested public.[19] In the first half of the eighteenth century the opera house was already frequented by the aspiring bourgeoisie who mixed with the king and his court. The French bourgeoisie, divided into representatives of trading and banking, factory owners, non-aristocratic notables and professionals such as doctors, engineers and lawyers, climbed the social ladder, whereas the disenfranchised, impoverished or disowned aristocrats from the royal court increasingly lost their once influential positions. But the landowner who also kept a little artisan workshop in the city, the speculator, the journalist, the doctor, the notary, the barrister or solicitor all cultivated aristocratic habits. They went to the opera in order to amuse themselves and copied those customs that they had or should have criticised as aristocratic evils, above all sloth. Instead of acting they often only re-acted or re-enacted. Their ambiguous judgement of opera, and even more so of ballet, reflected a tendency to preserve a "bourgeois Versailles", but without absolutist commitments. On the one hand, the bourgeois audience saw

Figure 11 'Modern grace, – or – the operatical finale to the ballet of Alonzo e Caro' (Rose Didelot; Charles Louis Didelot; Madame Parisot) by James Gillray, 1796.

theatre as the embodiment of moral decay and sin, as the perpetuation of those gallant ways now repudiated. On the other the theatres, the opera houses became places of merrymaking, temples of amusement where the factory owners and merchants forgot about their money troubles.

The growing demand for amusement had its dark side also in that it forced the artists to provide enjoyment. If the enlightened bourgeois wanted to see light-hearted pieces, then the theatre or opera house had to offer that illusion of graceful distraction; if the bourgeois wanted it together with a little historical instruction and moral edification, then again, the theatre had to oblige. Only one thing was out of the question: nothing was allowed to resemble the *grands ballets*. The answer the choreographers had at hand was the *ballet d'action*. It seemed an ideal, flexible vehicle that made it possible to find endlessly new variants of human experience. What Jean-Georges Noverre had foreseen and proclaimed in the mid-eighteenth century was never forgotten: "Rien n'interesse si fort l'humanité que l'humanité même"[20] (Nothing interests humanity as strongly as humanity itself). This sentence contains the secret motto of the *ballet d'action*, it summarises its ideological credo and comprises its aesthetic programme (see Fig. 11).

Translation Marion Kant

6 The rise of ballet technique and training: the professionalisation of an art form

SANDRA NOLL HAMMOND

On any given morning of the year, if you were to ask a ballet dancer, "What are you going to do today?" the answer most probably would be, "First, I'll take class." "Taking class" means the daily regimen of formalised exercises to refine, strengthen, maintain, and prepare the dancer's body for performance. This is the *leçon* or lesson – a process based on a codified, although ever-evolving, academic theatrical dance technique, done under the supervision of a ballet instructor. This chapter will discuss early ballet technique and training, with particular focus on developments in the eighteenth century, when the codification, the instruction, the academies and the performing companies – the professionalisation of ballet – became well established, setting the tone for decades to come and influencing the art into our own day.

At the outset, it is important to acknowledge that the historical traces of the development of ballet technique and training, as well as of ballet repertoire, are relatively rare. Unlike its sister arts, music and drama, ballet did not develop a comprehensive and universally accepted way to leave written or notated records capable of reflecting the complexities of its technique and choreographies, although in the early eighteenth century there was one valiant attempt at notation. Prior to the early nineteenth century, there were no detailed accounts of systematised training practices for professional dancers, although there are many tangential sources about training exercises from earlier periods and many later sources for corroborative material.

The complexities of ballet's highly codified technique required a methodical and formal approach to the training of dancers; dancers were not self-taught; they studied with master teachers who had acquired certain credentials and attained a necessary level of competence. Gradually, this led to the formation of schools or academies of dance. Thus, a common definition of ballet is "A form of Western academic theatrical dance based on the technique known as *danse d'école* (the classical school)".[1] Although certain individuals have had important influences on the development of ballet technique and training, and certainly on stylistic and choreographic trends, any one dancer's contributions must be seen as part of a continuum in this highly institutionalised art form. An important early institution to legitimise dance in the Western world, "as a discipline with both artistic and scholarly lineage – its establishment as an art rather than a guild-regulated craft", was the Académie Royale de Danse, founded in Paris in 1661.[2] The young King Louis XIV, already an avid patron of ballet productions and a skilled performer in court ballets, signed the letters of patent for the founding of the academy. The documents themselves were the result of efforts by thirteen young dancing masters "to explore new directions of dance technique, to go beyond the mastery of their fathers and other dancing masters".[3] These mid-seventeenth-century dancers were requesting autonomy from the minstrels' guild, which, from its founding in 1321, had "supervised the training of dancers throughout France, granting them the mastership that allowed them to teach".[4] This tradition had ensured that those who taught dancing were perforce also musicians, and the violin, typically played by the dancing master himself, came to be the instrument used to accompany dance classes.

Having been granted independence from the musician's guild, the new academicians now could instruct classes of aspiring dance teachers, approve or reject new choreographies, and confer teaching credentials on their students – all this without having to pay the customary fees to the musicians' guild or relying on its approval.[5] The new academicians did not, however, sever the close association between music and dancing; dance masters still were expected to play a violin to accompany their classes, and many also continued to compose and to arrange dance music. The dancer and dance master Pierre Beauchamps composed dance tunes as well as creating choreographies for productions with both the composer Jean-Baptiste Lully and the playwright Molière. Beauchamps, who counted Louis XIV among his private pupils, became the second director, in 1680, of the Académie Royale de Danse. Beauchamps moved the academy from its headquarters in the Louvre to his own home, where free dance classes were given each Thursday for professional dancers as well as for noble amateurs.[6] By the articles outlining the formation of the academy, the academicians could hold their meetings at a place of their choosing and rented at their own expense. Beauchamps probably offered his house in an effort to be economically efficient; thereafter the academy met at the house of the subsequent heads of the academy.

The stated purposes of the academy, "to restore the art of dancing to its original perfection and to improve it as much as possible",[7] seem to have been taken to heart by Beauchamps, for, as acknowledged by other dance masters and writers, Beauchamps is credited with the codification of the five basic positions of the feet (all ballet steps, movements, and poses relate in some way to one or more of these positions) and for the regulation

LA DANCE.

Des bonnes Positions.

LEs bonnes Positions font au nombre de cinq.

La premiere eft lors que les deux pieds font joints enfemble, les deux talons l'un contre l'autre.

Premiere Position.

La deuxiéme, quand les deux pieds font ouverts fur une même ligne, de la diftance de la longueur du pied, entre les deux talons.

Seconde Position.

La troifiéme, lorfque le talon d'un pied eft emboëté contte la cheville de l'autre.

Troifiéme Position.

La quatriéme, quand les deux pieds font l'un devant l'autre, éloignez de la diftance de la longueur du pied entre les deux talons qui font fur une même ligne.

Quatriéme Position.

La cinquiéme, lorfque les deux pieds font croifez l'un fur l'autre, de maniere que le talon d'un pied foit droit vis-à-vis la pointe de l'autre.

Cinquiéme Position.

Figure 12 The five positions of the feet, as depicted by Feuillet in his *Chorégraphie*, 1700.

of the movements and positions of the arms.[8] These are the rules that have formed the foundation of ballet technique (Fig. 12).

Around 1680, Beauchamps also began to develop a system of dance notation, but it was another choreographer, Raoul Auger Feuillet, who, in 1700, was the first to succeed in publishing a revolutionary new system of recording dance by means of abstract symbols.[9] *Chorégraphie*, as the Feuillet system was called, could indicate positions, steps and the seven basic movements of the dance – *plié* (bend), *élevé* (rise), *sauté* (jump), *cabriole* (beat of the legs while jumping), *tombé* (fall), *glissé* (glide or slide) and *tourné* (turn). The notation symbols, which could be augmented with additional signs to indicate more complex movements, were aligned along

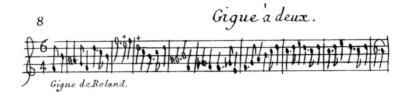

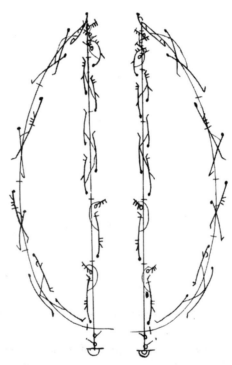

Figure 13 An example of the opening phrase of a theatrical duet, as notated by Feuillet in his *Recueil de Dances*, 1700. The woman is on the right side, the man on the left.

the choreographic figure or pattern of each dance. The accompanying music was written at the top of each page of the dance notation, and a small line drawn across the dance pattern indicated each corresponding musical measure (see Fig. 13).

A collection of social dances and a collection of theatrical dances were published with the first edition of *Chorégraphie*.[10] Feuillet's notation system proved to be popular, and for the next twenty-two years annual publications of notated dances were eagerly sought by those wishing to study the latest choreographies from Paris.

By the early eighteenth century, France, and specifically Paris, was the acknowledged leader in the art of both social and theatrical dance in Europe. Throughout the century, study with a French dancing master, either in France or with one of the many teachers who had emigrated to other European courts or to English and American cities, was considered essential for an aspiring dancer. Ballet terminology was, and remains today, in the French language. This did not mean that there was only one style of theatrical dance in eighteenth-century France or elsewhere. Leading soloists typically were assigned to one of the three, sometimes four, stylistic genres: the serious (or heroic, noble) style, the demi-caractère (or gallant) style, the comic and/or grotesque style. These genres called for different body types; the serious/heroic style was best suited for a tall, statuesque dancer, whereas the comic or grotesque categories required a dancer with a more muscular, compact build. More importantly, the different genres were associated with the portrayal of different types of characters in a ballet. This in turn determined the types of costumes worn as well as the choice of certain movements and the manner in which steps and body positions ("attitudes") were performed. A dancer's training, although steeped in the basic fundamentals of ballet technique, would require emphasis not only on the technical but also on the stylistic needs of the genre appropriate to the individual. Individual training, studying privately with a dancing master, was widespread, but early in the century an official school was established for the training of professional dancers.

Dance training

In 1713, the Paris Opéra gave formal recognition to its dance constituents by establishing a permanent troupe of twenty dancers, ten women and ten men,[11] and by establishing a school of dance for the purpose of "training performers suitable to replace those who are found lacking".[12] Classes were to be free of charge, but limited to those already employed in the ranks of the opera dancers in order to perfect their technique. By all contemporary accounts, dance training continued to be largely at private studios and must have begun at a very early age. In 1707 Johann Pasch advises that lessons for a would-be dancing master should start at the age of six and consist of at least three to four hours of daily practice.[13] Prodigious child performers were commonplace in the eighteenth century. The dancer and choreographer Marie Sallé, for instance, made her first recorded appearance at about ten in London. Her partner was her older brother, aged twelve. Dance instruction was a necessity, not only for children and youth, but also for seasoned performers who wished to enhance their technique.

Dancers often came from families who were associated with the performing arts; they trained with their parents or with relatives who were professional dancers. François Ballon, a Parisian dancing master, was the father of the celebrated Opéra dancer, teacher and choreographer Claude Ballon, who in 1719 became head of the Académie Royale de Danse. Sallé, the daughter of an actor-tumbler, was a member of a large family of entertainers at the Parisian fairs. It was with these itinerant artists that she had her first training. Then, according to her London publicity, she and her brother had become "scholars of M. Ballon (that would be Claude), lately arrived from the Opéra at Paris".[14] These are examples of the familial dance lineage so prevalent in the eighteenth century, and they underscore the very personal handing down of ballet technique from one generation to the next that has always been and continues to be a feature of ballet training.

Information on the dance studio where François Ballon taught, found among contracts and other legal documents of professional dancers, describes it as containing two large mirrors and a small one, two armchairs, a gilded wooden plaque, a small crystal chandelier and four brocaded benches.[15] Dance masters from the period mention the importance of mirrors for checking one's form when practising alone: "I would advise you to stand before a glass and move your arms as I have directed, and if you have any taste you will perceive your faults, and by consequence mend."[16] Mirrors remain a feature of ballet classrooms. Importantly, a main feature of Ballon's studio was empty space, a wooden floor on which his students could practise, first learning the fundamentals of ballet and then eventually studying the steps of virtuosity and the nuances of individual expression so necessary for career advancement and public acclaim.

Ballet technique: basic principles

Even more fundamental to ballet technique than the five positions of the feet was and is the vertical, balanced stance of the dancer. In the words of dance master Pierre Rameau in 1725, "The head must be upright, without being stiff, the shoulders falling back, which extends the breath, and gives greater grace to the body... the waist steady, the legs extended, and the feet turned outwards"[17] – a posture that reflected the elegant bearing of the nobility. Basic to that elegant and graceful bearing was the turnout or outward rotation of the legs from the hip joint. This "handsome carriage of the leg",[18] was displayed on the ballroom floor as well as on the fencing field, and it was incorporated into the training of dancers for the stage, where it was found to be a more efficient and visibly legible way for dancers to move quickly while facing an audience seated "out front".

"In order to dance well, Sir, nothing is so important as the turning out-wards of the thigh," wrote ballet master Jean-Georges Noverre,[19] and, as stipulated by earlier authors, such as Giambattista Dufort in 1728, both legs should be rotated to the same degree so that the toes are equally turned out.[20] To be turned out "*tout à fait*",[21] or absolutely, was seemingly contrary to nature, but could be accomplished by regular practice of specified exercises.

The structure of the lesson

Typically, the first exercises, then as now, were the *pliés*, the bending and then straightening of the knees while standing in the basic positions of the feet. Rameau noted the fundamental importance of these movements, even for the amateur: "dancing is no more than to know how to sink and rise properly".[22] The rise also could be onto the balls of the feet (*sur les pointes* was the usual phrase) in order to make the insteps both strong and flexible.

These and other "premiers Exercices",[23] could be practised while holding onto the hands of the dancing master, then later by lightly holding onto the back of a chair and then finally without support.[24] Each exercise had a particular purpose. "In order to be well turned outwards [in the legs]", Noverre, in 1760, advocated the "moderate but regular exercise" of *ronds de jambes en dehors* and *en dedans*, and *grands battements tendus* "working from the hip".[25] The *ronds de jambe* are circling motions of the leg; the large *battements*, or beats, are straight (*tendu*), forceful lifts of the leg, followed by a firm closing to fifth position. To the "height of the hip" eventually became typical for the execution of *grands battements*, although virtuoso dancers such as the *grotteschi* would routinely execute higher lifts of the leg. In 1779 Gennaro Magri, a skilled performer in the grotesque category, suggested that the large *battements* go "at least as high as the shoulder", but he also advised the student "to keep the supporting leg very steady". Otherwise, he warned, careless practice could result in injuries, and he gave some vivid examples.[26]

Small beats and circles of the lower leg were important to practise, because they frequently were used to embellish steps, jumps and turns. Students were advised to start these exercises slowly and then gradually to increase the speed. Many repetitions were important. In discussing a particular *battement* exercise, Magri said to repeat the beating action as many times as possible and with the greatest possible speed in order that the movements may be used with ease when dancing. Besides, he argued, the quicker the action, the more beautiful.[27]

It was important first to practise these preliminary exercises by holding onto a chair or rail and finally without any support. Then the lesson continued with a series of movements that emphasised balance, control and harmony of design. By the early nineteenth century, these exercises had coalesced into well-defined combinations of movements designated by names such as the *tems de courante*, the *coupés*, the *attitudes*, the *grands fouettés*, and so on.[28] The names as well as the movements themselves were derived from those used in the training of dancers in the eighteenth century, and they in turn had originated as steps or step sequences used in dances. As classroom exercises emphasising aplomb, these combinations became quite lengthy, progressing from simple to complex, adding turns and higher lifts of the leg, as well as increases in speed.

Training included the practice of a variety of turns (*pirouettes*), steps (*pas*), and combinations (*enchaînements*) linking several different steps. Some steps could be executed close to the ground (the *temps terre à terre*); others required high elevation (the *temps de vigueur*) and many were embellished with beats and quick *ronds de jambe*. Thus far the lesson embodied what Noverre termed "the mechanism of the dance". By that he meant the "steps, the ease and brilliancy of their combination, equilibrium, stability, speed, lightness, precision, the opposition of the arms with the legs".[29]

The making of a professional dancer

Ultimately, however, the dancer, to be successful, needed to cultivate a variety of expression in his movements. In order for this to happen, Noverre wrote, it was necessary for the dancing master "to arrange *entrées*" in which the student "would have many passions to represent".[30] Moreover, individuality was important. Giovanni-Andrea Gallini, a dancer, choreographer and theatre impresario contemporary with Noverre, wrote in 1762 that "a dancer, like a writer, should have a stile of his own, an original stile".[31] Echoing this sentiment many years later, G. Léopold Adice, a dancer and teacher at the Paris Opéra, recalled ballet classes during his youth in the early 1800s. To finish the class, he said, students would perform sequences of intricate steps

> designated by the name of *entrée de ronds de jambe, entrée de fouettés*, etc., and from them each dancer chose the one that seemed fitting to his inclinations. He gave particular attention to the task of perfecting it in order thus to create for himself a kind of dance and execution of it that were uniquely his.[32]

Magri, too, stressed the importance of inventing "new, surprising and pleasing things" in order to "make an excellent *ballerino*". He also revealed that in the *chaconne* "for the most part, all the solos are danced impromptu", meaning the dancer invented or improvised his solo.[33] This was no small assignment, inasmuch as the *chaconne* was one of the most intricate and lengthy of the dance forms.

Individuality and invention were prized in performers; it is not surprising that Noverre would declare "undoubtedly, one of the essential points in a ballet is variety".[34] He deplored the excessive use of "*caprioles, entrechats*, and over-complicated steps" at the expense of expression and sensitive interpretation of the character and style of the ballet. This, then, was the challenge facing dancers and ballet masters in the eighteenth century – how to embrace both virtuosity and expression.

There were individuals who succeeded in early attempts at this fusion and in crossing the boundaries associated with the customary genres. One was the versatile English dancer Hester Santlow, who was also an accomplished actress in both tragic and comic roles. Her repertoire as a leading dancer at Drury Lane Theatre included serious minuets and *passacailles* as well as Harlequin dances and diverse characters in the new type of pantomime ballets by John Weaver. Seven of Santlow's vast repertory of dances survive in Feuillet notation.

Italian dancers were especially fond of and skilled at swift movements that marked the virtuoso dancer – multiple beats while jumping ("capers") and high elevation both in jumping and in leg extensions. The clearest account of this style from a dancing master comes from Magri in Naples in 1779. Early in his treatise Magri wrote about how "we moderns" differ from "the ancients". One of those ways was by putting "more steps into one bar" of music. Where three *battements* had been done, now "up to eight or ten *battements* are repeated".[35] But even earlier in the century movements requiring great virtuosity were well known, as cited in German texts by dancing masters Louis Bonin (1712) and Gottfried Taubert (1717) who described *cabrioles* (beats of one leg against the other) where the feet were raised to the height of the hips.[36] And, interestingly, Bonin was discussing the "serious dance", where apparently all was not *terre à terre*.

French dancers were noted and admired for their grace and elegance in the serious or noble style, especially at the Paris Opéra, but even there, and certainly at other French theatres, dancers in the demi-caractère and comic genres gained accolades for their virtuosity. Antoine-Bonaventure Pitrot, a dancer and ballet master, worked in London, Warsaw, Dresden, St Petersburg and in many Italian venues as well as in Paris at the Opéra and the Comédie Italienne, where he also directed diverse productions – serious, pastorale, comic. Magri acknowledged Pitrot's strength and virtuosity as "incomparable" and admired his superb "aplomb", describing how Pitrot balanced "on the tip of his big toe" so that his entire leg from thigh to foot was in "one perpendicular line".[37] This, of course, is the stance of a ballerina today on pointe.

Although there seem to be no accounts of female dancers clearly dancing on full point in the eighteenth century, there are illustrations and descriptions from 1801 and soon after depicting female dancers on full point. Such accomplishments, in the un-reinforced shoes of the time, would have required considerable prior training and practice. In the eighteenth century, dancers certainly were rising higher and higher onto the tips of their feet, as indicated by contemporary accounts of Giovanna Baccelli "standing on the toe of her foot" and "alighting, standing and pirouetting on the toe".[38] In any case, eighteenth-century *danseuses* clearly were capable of great virtuosity. One vivid example is Marie Camargo, whose brilliant twenty-five-year career, beginning in Rouen and then as a star of the Paris Opéra Ballet, had significant influence on eighteenth-century Western theatrical dance. Noverre recalled Camargo's dancing as "quick, light, full of gaiety and brilliancy. She could perform with extreme facility *jetés battus*, the royale, cleanly cut *entrechats*."[39] Steps such as these usually had been the prerogative of male dancers, but Camargo challenged these and other norms, paving the way for other female dancers. Not long after her debut at the Opéra in 1726, Camargo grabbed her opportunity for achieving notoriety and acclaim. When Dumoulin, a leading *danseur*, failed to appear for his solo entrance, Camargo quickly took his place, "improvising the part of the absentee dancer, under showers of applause".[40]

Undoubtedly the century's most accomplished technician, its greatest virtuoso, the dancer whose performing range encompassed aspects of all three genres – serious, demi-caractère and comic – was Auguste Vestris. A child prodigy, who received his early training from his father, the illustrious noble dancer Gaëtan Vestris, twelve-year-old Auguste first appeared on stage at the Paris Opéra in 1772 and soon after was admitted there as a pupil. Four years later he was a soloist. He was especially noted for his prodigious elevation, rapid *pirouettes*, the lightness and precision of his *cabrioles*, and the multiplicity of his *entrechats*. These and other tours de force were performed with an ease and grace and artistry hitherto unseen. As he matured, Vestris developed "a dramatic talent that seemed to grow with every new rôle he undertook in the ballet-pantomimes that were becoming so popular".[41] Vestris not only succeeded in embracing both virtuosity and expression, he also "mixed together elements from all the styles ... to the point where a new and unique composite style of dance came into being".[42] His career as a dancer lasted some forty years, but his influence continued long after as one of the leading teachers of the Paris Opéra, where he helped "prepare dancers for the demands of the new style".[43]

By the end of the eighteenth century, the dance form that had begun to flourish in the court of Louis XIV could boast of a theatrical dance technique with a language, a step vocabulary and rules of movement for the arms, legs and torso in a system of training that was international in the Western world. A great many of its leading dancers, instructors and choreographers were truly international in their careers, going from theatre to theatre, city to city and country to country. Ironically, at the Opéra in Paris, where so much influence had emanated, its School of Dance, by the 1770s, still "did not yet play a very prominent part in training soloists, or sujets, as they were called".[44] Most of them apparently studied privately. But, as ballet became a more important component of productions at the Opéra, and as the popularity grew for the newer dance-pantomimes or *ballets d'action*, the number of Opéra dancers was increased and new performance standards were demanded for even the lower ranks, the *choeur de la danse* (later called the corps de ballet). These changes required reorganisation of the school so that it could supply well-trained dancers at all levels for the company. In 1780, Jacques-François Deshayes, a dancer and later ballet master at the Comédie-Française, was appointed director of the school, a position he held until his death in 1798. Under Deshayes's able leadership the school began to set a higher standard for ballet training. At the time, two full-time teachers were the norm at the Opéra; a number of private teachers were "attached to the Opéra but not on its regular payroll".[45] The 1799 regulations state that classes would be daily, taken alternately with the two masters, "as the fundamentals are unchanging and uniform". From 1805 until around 1827, the regulations stipulate that only three regular classes per week were required, the boys studying on Mondays, Wednesdays and Fridays while the girls were taught on Tuesdays, Thursdays and Saturdays. The regulations of 1807 mention two levels of classes, *première* or elementary and *supérieure* or advanced. Upon graduation, usually at the age of sixteen, students would continue to study privately, at their own expense, in order to perfect their technique.

Vestris and other teachers, notably Jean-François Coulon, instilled more rigorous classes, attracting talented dancers of the next generation, such as August Bournonville and Jules Perrot, both outstanding dancers and later important choreographers; Geneviève Gosselin, an early exponent of point work; M. Albert (the professional name of François Decombe), considered the last of the great noble dancers; and Fanny Elssler and Marie Taglioni, who were to become stars of the romantic ballet. Elsewhere, other important schools were established, guided by innovative teachers, many of whom had received their training in Paris. Salvatore Taglioni and Louis Henry, both

Figure 14 From Carlo Blasis, *The Code of Terpsichore*, 1828, showing that the raised foot is in a "position of a pirouette on the instep". The dancer is not quite on a full pointe, and the arms are carried very low.

students of Coulon, founded the school of ballet at the Teatro San Carlo in Naples in 1812. The next year an academy of dancing was established in Milan at La Scala in order to provide a corps de ballet for its opera. Carlo Blasis and his wife, Annunziata Rammaccini, became the school's directors in 1837. In his *Notes Upon Dancing, Historical and Practical*, Blasis discusses the staff, admission requirements, school regulations, dress code and the two "spacious rooms" for lessons at the academy, where the floors were "laid with a descent [raked], like the stage itself, to accustom the pupils to dance upon an inclined plane",[46] which was the reality in most theatres at the time. As we know from his other books, the Blasis system of instruction was rigorous indeed. But, as Blasis was quick to admit in his first publication in 1820, his instructions emanated "from the schools of leading masters who have contributed immensely to the progress and beauty of modern dancing".[47] He, of course, was referring to the tradition of training that had begun over a century before and had been handed down to him.

In summing up the goals of ballet training, Blasis lists "ease, freedom, lightness, life, vigour and the power of leaping (*sbalzo*)", all the while being "ever mindful that the strictest harmony should exist between the music and every motion". He reaffirms the eighteenth-century notion that a dancer's "attitudes, movements, gestures and positions" should emulate the ideals found in painting and sculpture (see Fig. 14). And, finally, in a clear echo of Noverre's sentiments, Blasis writes that "dancers both male and female, should execute their dances with appropriate feeling and expression, adapted to the part they perform; their action ought not only to satisfy the eye, but it should also say something to the heart and the imagination – it should be the poetry of motion".[48]

7 The making of history: John Weaver and the Enlightenment

TIM BLANNING

Weaver's life

Weaver was born on 21 July 1673 at Shrewsbury in the county of Shropshire, where his father (also called John) was a dancing master. The family moved to Oxford shortly after John junior's birth. It is probable that he was sent back to Shrewsbury at about the age of ten to attend the eponymous school. He followed in his father's footsteps as a dancing master in the town until 1700 when he moved to London to work as a dancer in the theatres of the capital. Two years later he staged *The Tavern Bilkers* at Drury Lane Theatre, claiming later that it was "the first Entertainment that appeared on the English Stage, where the Representation and Story was carried on by Dancing, Action and Motion only".[1] He also worked closely with Queen Anne's dancing master, known simply as Mr Isaac, in notating the dances devised by the latter for court occasions. He enjoyed a mutually supportive relationship with the other major metropolitan dancing master of the period, Thomas Caverley. Important for his career as a writer was his friendship with Sir Richard Steele the Irish-born journalist and playwright who with Joseph Addison edited *The Spectator* (1711–14). Steele commissioned several articles on dancing for his periodical from Weaver, gave helpful publicity to his history of dancing (1712) and may also have had a hand in getting the book published in the first place. In 1707 Weaver had returned to Shrewsbury, where his wife Catherine, whom he had married in 1696, died in childbirth in 1712. After marrying a fifteen-year-old girl, Susanna, in 1716, he moved back to London, again finding employment at Drury Lane Theatre, where Steele had become manager in 1714. Although his best-known ballet, *The Loves of Mars and Venus*, was given a good reception when premiered in 1717, he was never able to establish himself permanently in the capital's theatrical world. As the anonymous author of *The Dancing-Master. A Satyr* jeered:

> W— –r has Understanding, Parts and Sense,
> And knows right well to gather up the Pence
> . . .
> But him, as others, Stars malignant rule.
> Tho' always rubbing off, still runs a Score,
> Tho' always getting, he is always poor.

By 1720 he was back in Shrewsbury, earning a living as a dancing master, although still making the occasional foray to London. He retired formally from the stage in 1721 to devote himself to the theory and science of his art. However, it appears that economic necessity forced him to tread the boards again in 1728 at the ripe old age of fifty-five as a comic dancer. Even a second retirement the following year did not prove to be final, as he returned to Drury Lane for another production of *The Judgment of Paris, A Dramatic Entertainment in Dancing and Singing, After the Manner of the Ancient Greeks and Romans* in 1733. He spent the rest of his exceptionally long life back in his home town, concentrating on the running of his boarding school. According to the distinguished musicologist Charles Burney, who was educated at Shrewsbury School in the 1730s, Weaver's establishment enjoyed a great reputation. With the help of the beautiful Mrs Weaver he continued to run it until the end of his days.

Theoretical works and choreographies

Although Weaver was a prolific writer, he has three main claims to posterity's attention in the literary department. The first was his translation of Raoul Auger Feuillet's *Chorégraphie ou l'art de décrire la danse par caractères, figures et signes démonstratifs* (Paris, 1700), which he published in 1706 with the title *Orchesography or the Art of Dancing, by Characters and Demonstrative Figures, By which any Person, who understands Dancing, may of himself easily learn all manner of Dances*, and dedicated to Mr Isaac. As the leading modern authority on Weaver, Richard Ralph, observes, Weaver took great pains to find appropriate English equivalents for the technical terms, consulting widely among his fellow dancing masters, many of whom returned the compliment by subscribing to the finished product. In the same year he translated a second, shorter work by Feuillet entitled *A Small Treatise of Time and Cadence in Dancing, Reduc'd to an Easy and Exact Method, Shewing how Steps, and their Movements, agree with the Notes, and Division of Notes, in each Measure*, and thus became "the first of his profession to make a system of rules relating to time in dancing available in English".[2] The most important work of his own was *An Essay Towards an History of Dancing, In which the whole Art and its Various Excellencies are in some Measure Explain'd, containing the several sorts of Dancing, Antique and Modern, Serious, Scenical, Grotesque, etc. with the Use of it as an Exercise, Qualification, Diversion etc.*, which appeared in 1712 dedicated to Thomas Caverley, whose school he hailed as "a Nursery of Virtue and Good-Breeding".[3] For all too long, he argued, exponents of dancing had been content to communicate the secrets of their art by word of mouth, with the result that "an undeserved Contempt has been cast unwarily on the Art, as Low and Mechanick".[4] It was his mission to demonstrate that "it is an Art both Noble and Useful, and not unworthy the Encouragement of all Lovers of Elegance and Decorum; without which Gentlemen and Ladies, are but half accomplish'd".[5] Consequently, much of the book reads more like a manifesto than a history, with a good part of the volume devoted to showing how "beneficial and delightful" dancing is and to defending it against the charges of the Fathers of the Church that it was an "Effeminate, Lascivious, Amorous, Lust-exciting and dangerous Incendiary of Lust", and an Occasion of and Preparative to "Whoring, Adultery, Wantonness, and all Effeminate Lewdness".[6] *The History of the Mimes and Pantomimes, with an Historical Account of several performers in Dancing, living in the Time of the Roman Emperors* of 1728 is essentially just a reprint of chapter 6 of *An Essay Towards an History of Dancing*, with a number of amendments and additions. Thirdly, in 1721 Weaver published a treatise entitled *Anatomical and Mechanical Lectures upon Dancing, wherein Rules and Institutions for that Art are laid down and demonstrated*, acclaimed as "the first scientific treatise to relate the kinetic workings of the human body to a technical analysis of classical ballet positions and steps".[7]

Intellectual and artistic influence of Weaver

Weaver's translation of Feuillet's book was greatly superior to other English versions, not least on account of its prolific illustrations. The standardised system of dance notation allowed dancing masters across the length and breadth of the country to be confident that they were following faithfully the latest metropolitan fashions. In *The Art of Dancing. A Poem*, published in 1729, Soame Jenyns lamented that dancing had for long been "unfix'd and free" and so each master taught differently, with the result that every new dance died with its creator. Now, however, the new system of notation meant that:

> Hence o'er the World this pleasing Art shall spread,
> And ev'ry Dance in ev'ry Clime be read;
> By distant Masters shall each Step be seen,
> Though Mountains rise, and Oceans roar between.
> Hence with her Sister-Arts shall Dancing claim
> An equal Right to Universal Fame
> And Isaac's Rigadoon shall last as long
> As Raphael's Painting, or as Virgil's Song.[8]

The previous year John Essex had written in the preface to *The Dancing-Master* that the profession was obliged to Weaver "for the Many Proofs of his Knowledge, that are so many Helps to our Art, which in Reality he has rather made a Science".[9] Weaver's influence long outlasted even his long life. In 1802 Charles Burney wrote of *Orchesography*, "we remember it in general use even in the country, among the professors of the Art".[10] Also of enduring influence was his history of dancing, even if subsequent authors did not always acknowledge the source of their information and insights. As Richard Ralph dryly comments, *An Essay Towards an History of Dancing* has been used as "a source of silent borrowings"[11] by English writers on dancing until the present day. Less durable were Weaver's productions for the stage. Next to nothing is known about the trail-blazing *The Tavern Bilkers* apart from its attempt to reintegrate mime and dancing into the story and focus on its presentation through motion. It might have had a poor public reception at the time but dance scholars today see this piece as one of the earliest and most important expressions of a new ballet type, the *ballet d'action*, which was to transform the ballet stage for several centuries to come.[12] He did publish detailed accounts of *The Loves of Mars and Venus* (1717), *Orpheus and Eurydice* (1718), *Perseus and Andromeda* (1728) and *Judgment of Paris* (1733) but they found few if any imitators. London audiences seem to have preferred the coarser fare offered by John Rich at the rival Lincoln's Inn Fields Theatre, including parodies of Weaver's serious ballets. Significantly, although his last work *The Judgment of Paris* was claimed to be "A DRAMATIC ENTERTAINMENT of dancing after the Manner of the ancient Pantomimes", it had a libretto by William Congreve[13] set to music by Seedo (the German expatriate Sidow).

Weaver's significance in historical context

Weaver epitomises the cultural advantages and disadvantages of London, which during his lifetime (and for long thereafter) was the greatest metropolis in the world in terms of size, wealth, commercialism and variety. Its population had more than trebled in the course of the seventeenth century, reaching *c*.675,000 by 1700 and still rising at an accelerating pace to pass the three quarters of a million mark by the time Weaver died. This was at a time when only nine other European cities had populations in excess of 100,000. Moreover, the city's stout resistance to Stuart attempts to establish an authoritarian regime ensured that it was also exceptionally liberal, de facto if not de iure, rivalled in this regard only by Amsterdam. Consequently, it also boasted the largest and most developed "public sphere", that space in which private individuals meet to exchange information, ideas and criticism and thus to form a whole greater than the sum of their parts. An early sign of its cultural implications was the emergence of public concerts towards the end of the seventeenth century. If a public concert can be defined as a musical performance, at which there is a clear distinction between performers and audience and to which the anonymous public is admitted on payment of an entrance fee, then the first took place in London in 1672 when *The London Gazette* printed an advertisement for "Musick performed by excellent Masters . . . at Mr. John Banister's house (now called the Musick School) over against the George Tavern in Whyte Fryers".[14] By the time John Weaver reached London in the first year of the new century, there was a thriving concert scene in several different locations, from inns to theatres.

It was just this sort of commercial opportunity that took him to the capital in the first place. As Roger North complained, "mercenary teachers, chiefly 'forreiners' had discovered 'the Grand Secret', that the English would follow Musick & drop their pence freely, of which some advantage hath bin since made".[15] *Mutatis mutandis*, the same applied to the closely related art of dancing. The regularity with which Parliament convened after the "Glorious Revolution" of 1688 meant that the country's landed elites now gathered in the capital each year and so a proper season developed. A prominent feature of the elite's social gatherings was, of course, dancing and so the demand for dancing masters increased correspondingly. If their status was low, their influence on their pupils was believed to be great. The Marquess of Halifax observed caustically in *Advice to a Daughter* that a coquette would adopt virtue "if she had her Dancing Master's Word that it was practis'd at Court".[16]

As this comment suggests, Weaver's career also demonstrated that London's public sphere was not so developed that the court did not matter. St James's was not Versailles, but it still set the tone for polite society. Mr Isaac enjoyed his acknowledged supremacy in his profession because he was dancing master by appointment to the court. He published the dances he devised for official occasions, so that they could then be copied at balls in the capital and provinces. In 1706, for example, he published *A Collection of Ball-Dances perform'd at Court: viz. The Richmond*, the *Rondeau*, the *Rigadoon*, the *Favorite*, the *Spanheim*, and the *Britannia*, all notated by Weaver. The latter also notated a dance created the following year by Isaac called *The Union* to mark the union of the kingdoms of England and Scotland. London may not have been a residential city in the manner of Versailles or Vienna, whose economies were shaped by and depended on the presence of the court, but its tradesmen were well aware of the advantages it conferred. So they petitioned the Vice-Chamberlain to encourage the queen to give "dancings and balls at Court on her birth night and other public occasions . . . for a Ball at Court . . . is . . . the cause of hundreds of balls among the quality in the City and all over England".[17] As this demonstrates, it is misleading to postulate too sharp a contrast between the culture of the public sphere and the culture of the court.

The court may have set the tone for the rest of the kingdom, but its sponsorship of dancing was confined to balls. This was in stark contrast to contemporary France, where Louis XIV not only appeared as a dancer in ballets (for the first time at the tender age of fourteen), but lavished a great deal of time and money on the art. Most crucially, he gave it an institutional basis in the Académie Royale de Danse, founded in 1661 and arguably the world's first ballet school. With Molière and Beauchamps as choreographers and Lully in charge of the music, Louis's patronage secured for France a hegemonic position in the world of dance, which was to endure for the best part of two centuries. Yet Weaver does not even mention Louis XIV in his *Essay Towards an History of Dancing*, despite devoting a substantial chapter (number VII) to "Modern Dancing". He grudgingly concedes "It must be allowed that the French excel in this kind of dancing"[18] (i.e. ballet) but otherwise he only mentions them to damn with faint praise or to condemn outright. Even the repertoire of the best French dancers "who have been seen with so much Applause, and follow'd with so great an Infatuation"[19] consists of nothing more than motion, figure and measure. The most famous of them, Claude Balon, confined himself to trying to move gracefully, leap nimbly and assume what he thought to be agreeable postures, "but for expressing any thing in Nature but modulated Motion, it was never in his head".[20]

In Weaver's eyes, it was the English who had achieved most among the moderns: "The Dancing so much esteem'd among us, and so necessary a Qualification for Gentlemen and Ladies, whether taught privately or publickly, I shall call common Dancing, and in which the English do not only excel the Ancients, but also all Europe, in the Beauty of their Address, the Gentleness and Agreeableness of their Carriage, and a certain Elegancy in every Part." This was thanks to the fact that "there are not better Masters for instructing Scholars in a genteel Movement and Address, than the English".[21] He singled out Isaac and Caverley for special praise, modestly neglecting to mention his own services to the art. English supremacy in this all-important social dancing was no accident but derived from the country's especially fortunate political and social culture. In "this free nation of England",[22] there was no great divide between the classes and consequently none of that uncouthness to be found in less favoured nations. In *Mimes and Pantomimes* too, the English had shown themselves to be superior to the degenerate Italians by getting closer to the Roman originals than any other national group. Such complacency was the stock-in-trade of many if not most English contemporaries, whose sense of superiority was based securely on what seemed to them to be the mutually supportive tripod of liberty, prosperity and Protestantism. No true culture could flourish in the barren soil of despotic, impoverished and Papist France. It was the English who had invented country dancing which – mutated into *contre danses* – now dominated dancing on the continent. If this seems absurdly insular, it should be borne in mind that Weaver's long life coincided with three episodes of the Second Hundred Years War between England and France: the Nine Years War (1689–97), the War of the Spanish Succession (1702–13) and the Seven Years War (1756–63). Isaac's Court Dance for 1705 was christened *Marlborough* to commemorate the eponymous duke's crushing defeat of the French the previous year at Blenheim and that for 1706 was *Britannia*. Although he was happy to make his reputation by translating Feuillet's treatise, Weaver had only contempt for "our French Pretenders to Dancing",[23] as he dubbed them. It is one of the clichés of historical writing that the Age of Reason was also an age of cosmopolitanism; in reality, the nationalism of Weaver and Isaac was much more representative of contemporary attitudes.

In the battle of the time between the Ancients and the Moderns, which began when Charles Perrault read his poem *The Age of Louis the Great* to the Académie française in 1687, Weaver should probably be numbered among the Ancients. He relied heavily on Lucian's Greek dialogue *Peri Orcheseos* when writing his history of dancing, taking it at face value and clearly not sharing some modern commentators' doubts about Lucian's sincerity. What Weaver admired most about the classical world's attitude to dancing was its seriousness: "It began in Religion, and was, in the politer Times of the Greeks and the Romans, the necessary Qualification of a Hero."[24] Anticipating none other than the German composer Richard Wagner, he was especially attracted by the Greek combination of dancing with music and poetry to form a total work of art. He concluded: "It must indeed be granted, that our Modern Dancing, in several Particulars of Beauty, falls infinitely short of that of the Greeks and Romans, if we may believe Eye-witnesses of its Perfection, and admirable Effects."[25] Together with his remarks about the degeneracy of so much of the contemporary scene, this verdict seems to place Weaver unequivocally among the Ancients. However, he immediately added a qualifier: "Yet this must be said, that as to Dancing in its Fundamentals and Expediency, Modern Dancing is of equal Desert, as will appear hereafter."[26] In fact, what followed did not show that at all, only that what Weaver, Isaac, Caverley and the other London dancing masters were achieving was of a high order of distinction. It is reasonable to compromise by claiming Weaver as an early exponent of neoclassicism in the definition offered by Charles Rosen in his analysis *The Classical Style*, namely: "I have used 'neoclassicism' in a narrow sense of a return to the assumed simplicity of Nature through the imitation of the ancients."[27] Weaver's ambitions for dancing corresponded very closely to the more celebrated demand made for art by his contemporary, Anthony Ashley Cooper, Third Earl of Shaftesbury, namely that it should be "chaste, severe, just and accurate".[28] Like Weaver, Shaftesbury believed that the Glorious Revolution had ushered in an era of gentlemanly rule and gentlemanly culture and it was this which both men sought to foster. A free state, they held, was both supported by and helped to create a true culture: "the high Spirit of Tragedy can ill subsist where the Spirit of Liberty is wanting".[29] Those last words stem from Shaftesbury but they might just as well have come from Weaver, with the word "dancing" substituted for "tragedy".

If, as is often the case, Voltaire is thought to be the personification of the European Enlightenment, then Weaver must be denied enlightened status. It was Voltaire, after all, who believed that the cultural history of Europe could be divided into peaks and troughs, the former being Ancient Greece, Augustan Rome, Renaissance Italy and Louis XIV's France. In a more general sense, however, he does merit inclusion, not least because of his insistence on the need for standardisation, uniformity and the "accuracy" demanded by Shaftesbury. The great problem in the past, Weaver maintained, was that the practitioners of dancing had passed their art from one to another and from one generation to another orally ("like the Druids").[30] The result had been analogous to Chinese Whispers: distortion, misrepresentation, fragmentation, decadence. What was needed was a clear, rational, and, above all, universal system of notation. In *A Small Treatise of Time and Cadence in Dancing, Reduc'd to an Easy and Exact Method, Shewing how Steps, and their Movements, agree with the Notes, and Division of Notes, in each Measure*, published in 1706, Weaver stressed: "The best and only Method of finding the Cadence or Time of each Step, is to know its just Value in the same manner as the Notes of Musick; after which all the Steps in a Measure, are to be reduc'd to an equal Time or Length, as the Notes in the Measure of the Tune."[31] His translation of Feuillet's system of notation was a massive step in the desired direction of uniformity.

Weaver also appreciated that anarchy in the dancing world had had a detrimental effect on the status of those who taught and practised the art. When priests were its leaders, he observed, it had enjoyed high prestige as part of a total work of art that was also worship. But when it fell into the hands of men who understood just the steps and taught it simply as a means of social recreation, it slumped to become nothing more than an "amusing Trifle".[32] Indeed, the status of the dancing master at the turn of the eighteenth century appears to have been low, the stereotype condemned as both effeminate and lascivious. It is not known whether Weaver attended a performance of William Wycherley's contemporary comedy *The Gentleman Dancing Master*, but he would not have enjoyed the experience. This intensely Francophobe play (which also features a renegade Englishman "Mr. Paris, or Monsieur de Paris, a vain coxcomb, and rich city heir, newly returned from France, and mightily affected with the French language and fashions")[33] is centred on the attempt by a true gentleman to gain access to his beloved Hippolita by pretending to be her dancing master. As she says: "A dancing-school in half an hour will furnish you with terms of the art." But the father is not deceived: "Nay, nay, dancing-masters look like gentlemen enough, sister: but he's no dancing master, by drawing a sword so briskly. Those tripping outsides of gentlemen are like gentlemen enough in everything but in drawing a sword; and since he is a gentleman, he shall die by mine ... Your dancing masters and barbers are such finical, smooth-tongued, tattling fellows; and if you set 'em once a-talking, they'll ne'er a-done, no more than when you set 'em a-fiddling: indeed, all that deal with fiddles are given to impertinency."[34] Yet Weaver believed himself to be a gentleman and not the least of his numerous achievements was to raise the station of his profession by his demonstration that it was possible to be both a dancing master and an intellectual, thus anticipating Sir Joshua Reynolds's celebrated advice to painters later in the century.[35]

8 Jean-Georges Noverre: dance and reform

JUDITH CHAZIN-BENNAHUM

Noverre's life

Jean-Georges Noverre was born in Paris on 27 April 1727 and died in Saint-Germain-en-Laye on 19 October 1810. He had an abrupt and demanding temperament, made many enemies and stirred up a variety of fierce artistic controversies during his long career. More than any other choreographer before him, he turned ballet into an independent art form and means of expression. Diderot called him "le génie", the one who would save dance, and Voltaire named him "Prométhée de la danse".

Noverre's mother, Marie Anne de la Grange, is thought to have been born in Lausanne, although P. J. S. Richardson suggested that she was born in Picardy. His father, Jean Louys, was a Swiss soldier. Like Rousseau, Noverre's Swiss origins created suspicion about his loyalty to France, although he always considered himself a Frenchman. His father expected him to be a soldier, but the boy insisted on dancing and eventually followed his own instincts. Still a child, he went to Paris to study with M. Marcel and then with the famous Louis Dupré. His critical eye quickly led him to question why the arms had such a circumscribed use, and to wonder why masks, high heels, panniers and over-blown wigs were popular in ballets as they constrained all movements of the head, arms, legs and face.

Noverre's first dancing probably occurred at Jean Monnet's Opéra-Comique at the Foire Saint Laurent on 8 June 1743 in Favart's vaudeville *Le Coq du village*. There, in that free environment, he detected other ways of using gesture and movement. He learned much by observing the Italian comedians with their emphasis on physical and improvisational theatre. At the age of fifteen he appeared at the court at Fontainbleau. With his "copains", Campanini and Lany as well as his teacher Dupré, Noverre was recruited to dance in Berlin before the young Frederick II and his brother Prince Henry of Prussia. It was the first of his many trips outside Paris. Still in his teens, he performed in Dresden, Strasburg and again at the Opéra-Comique. At the age of twenty, Noverre became ballet master in Marseilles and created what became a well-known piece, *Les Fêtes chinoises*. There it is thought that he met his wife, the actress Marie-Louise Sauveur. In 1750 he became Principal Dancer in Lyons and partnered the celebrated Marie Camargo. In addition, he made his first ballet pantomime, *Le Jugement de Paris*. He then moved from Lyons to Strasburg in 1754 for one year, and then returned to Paris and the Opéra-Comique. There he created ballets which organised the elements of a production into beautifully arranged pictures. From 1755 to 1756 he and his company went to London to work with the famous David Garrick at the Drury Lane Theatre. Like Samuel Johnson, the writer, with whom he had gone to school in Lichfield, "Davy" Garrick was a poor boy making it in the new commercial market for theatre and books in London, then one of the richest and least censored cities in the world. He performed Shakespeare with notable brilliance and gained a reputation for eloquent and expressive gestures in his performances and for the consummate taste of all his theatrical productions. Noverre, who received handsome fees from Garrick, was able take his new wife and sister with him.

The London period introduced Noverre to different conceptions of theatrical style. Garrick belonged with Rousseau and others in the middle of the eighteenth century to the school of "natural" theatre. In 1752 the arrival of an Italian opera company in Paris, which performed *opera buffa* by Pergolesi, Alessandro Scarlatti and other composers, triggered a fierce debate between proponents and opponents of that new natural style, which emphasised melody over harmony. Jean-Jacques Rousseau made his name in a famous attack on Jean-Philippe Rameau, the most prominent court composer at the time. This *guerre des buffons* (the war of the *opera buffa*) raised the same issues that had begun to occupy Noverre. Like Rousseau, he rejected artificiality, the use of masks and statuesque formalities and thought that art had to achieve "truth". In order for theatre to be true, pantomime must be used, which aroused the intelligence of the viewers by engaging them in the emotions of those on stage and thus presenting human dramas to be considered. While working in Drury Lane, Noverre became acquainted with Eva Weigel, Garrick's Austrian wife. She had studied ballet with the innovative Franz Hilverding in Vienna, who also experimented with what would become known as the *ballet d'action*. As early as 1740 Hilverding produced such dance dramas for the Viennese court as Jean Racine's *Britannicus*, Crébillon's *Idoméneo* and Voltaire's *Alzira*. These tragedies had proper plots and portrayed human emotions. Noverre adopted that model. The true ballet was not defined by the steps but the sentiments and nuances that were enacted by the dancer to create the real dramatic effect.

In spite of his progressive views, he ran into political trouble in London. In 1756 a war between Britain and France broke out, which was part of a worldwide conflict on the continent that was known as the Seven Years War but in North America as "The French and Indian War". The English audience rioted at the performance of Noverre's *Fêtes chinoises*; they were incensed by the way the French had stirred up Indian tribes to massacre English settlers. Both the French, whose colonial economy rested less on settlement than trade in forest products, and the Indians, who found English pioneers cutting homesteads from their forests, had a common enemy. Noverre had to leave London in 1757. He wanted to work at the Paris Opéra, but quickly realised that he would be swimming against the prevailing currents of courtly dance. He returned to the provinces and to Lyons where he created new and very different ballets based on his newly found expressive movement. He worked with the seductive and distinguished Mlle Guimard in an anacreontic ballet, *Les Caprices de Galathée*. He garbed the fauns in tiger skins, shoes that looked like tree bark and leg stockings the colour of carnation for the forest inhabitants. The nymphs' material was speckled with flowers and greenery. All of these features associated Noverre with the new naturalist attitude towards costume and put him in the mainstream of the culture of the French Enlightenment. One of his enduring successes centred on his work *La Mort d'Ajax*, a tragic ballet that permitted him to portray strong emotions that touched and moved his audiences.

Noverre always had a knack for sensing which way the artistic wind was blowing. The year 1760 was ideal for publishing his *Lettres sur la danse, et sur les ballets* and he managed to find both a French and a German publisher respectively in Lyons and in Stuttgart. His ideas on dancing and performance fitted the new culture in Germany based on the so-called *Affektenlehre*, the doctrine of emotions or "sensibility". Lyons had been good to him but an invitation to serve at the court of the Duke Carl Eugene of Wurttemberg could not be resisted. Carl Eugene, who ruled his principality for more than forty years, may have been the most extravagant, luxurious and irresponsible of the substantial German princes, a group notorious for conspicuous consumption. He built six huge palaces on the model of Versailles on the taxes of his 600,000 groaning subjects. In Stuttgart, Noverre had a 350-seat theatre for his ballets, the services of the distinguished scene designer Servandoni, the costume designer Louis-René Boquet and composers Nicolò Jommelli, and Jean Joseph Rudolph (Rodolphe) who composed his most famous ballet *Jason et Médée* in 1763. Since the duke never cared how expensive his artists and architects were, Noverre staged ballets on the grandest scale imaginable. He created at least twenty new works and built his reputation. As the author of a serious treatise on choreography and ballet, he had the ideal setting to put his ideas into practice. He attracted remarkable dancers such as Gaëtan Vestris ("the god of dance") who played Jason, Anna Heinl who is credited with having invented the double *pirouette*, Le Picq and the extraordinary Dauberval who went on to create the famous *La Fille mal gardée* (1789) in Bordeaux.

When Noverre launched *Jason et Médée* in Stuttgart, he borrowed ideas explored in Vienna by Hilverding, Christoph Willibald Gluck and the librettist Raniero di Calzibigi. They too were seeking a deeper definition of, and credibility for, ballet and opera. Noverre knew that where the ideas of the French Enlightenment had spread, important patrons emerged; in such areas his doctrine of natural dance, his work on gesture and expression would find a favourable reception. And patronage was the name of the game in the eighteenth century. For after all, Noverre was like Samuel Johnson and David Garrick, a poor boy without class. Johnson could write in his great dictionary of 1755 that "a patron is a wretch who supports with insolence and is paid in flattery",[1] but he could get away with it because London had a huge commercial printing and publishing business and his dictionary easily found a market. Johnson never needed a patron. Neither did David Garrick with his commercial Theatre Royal in Drury Lane. But nobody could buy tickets to Duke Carl Eugene's theatre. Noverre worked on the continent where royalty still controlled the arts. Hence Noverre had to choose his patrons with extreme care. Though he wanted to return to the Drury Lane in London, the British victory in the French and Indian war had not yet calmed anti-French sentiments. He decided to try his luck in Vienna, the capital of the Holy Roman Empire, the most important city of the German-speaking world, and the place where the young Emperor Joseph II, to the irritation of his mother, Maria Theresa, the reigning queen (a woman could not hold the imperial title), made serious attempts to impose the culture of the Enlightenment on the huge, polyglot realm. As always, Noverre had guessed shrewdly. He found royal patronage and managed to stage nearly thirty-eight new ballets. He also revived earlier works and created dances for operas that were great successes, such as Gluck's *Pâris et Hélène*, *Orphée et Eurydice* and *Alceste*. Noverre knew what historians tend to forget: in the *Ancien Régime* no artist could succeed without very wealthy protectors, and in Vienna he secured the highest possible patroness, the Queen Maria Theresa herself. He became *maître de danse* for the twelve-year-old Marie-Antoinette, the queen's favourite daughter, and remained her close friend and confidant until she was guillotined during the French Revolution in 1793. He knew he only had to wait until she came of age to do as he liked. With the composer Franz Aspelmayer he created *Iphigénie et Tauride* (1772), *Apelle et Campaspe* (1773) and with Joseph Starzer *Adèle de Ponthieu* (1773). With *Horaces et des Curiaces* (1774) Noverre deployed a frightening and moving scene of ancient Roman history, a combat between brothers and also a grand military parade with extraordinary pomp and splendour. Unfortunately, his use of a theme of the great French playwright Corneille went too far. It must have annoyed the very conservative Maria Theresa, who presumably ceased to protect him. In any case, the production cost him his job. In 1774 he decided to move to the Teatro Regio Ducale in Milan, which was the capital of Austrian Lombardy and by far the richest Italian city, the sort of place that could afford a Noverre. Here

unfortunately his ambition collided with reality. The Milanese did not take
kindly to Noverre, and many reviews of his ballets cast aspersions on him,
criticising the fact that his works were slow moving, "With long stretches of
pure mime, and boring".[2] He grew despondent at his lack of success. Italians
were used to spectacular and exciting grotesque dancing that included jumps
and virtuosic moves and, besides, Italian national sentiment had begun to
stir. As in Germany in the 1770s, so in Italy, young, influential intellectuals
no longer looked to France for their artistic models. After only two years, he
returned to Vienna to manage their Kärntnertor Theatre. Finally, in 1776,
after a thirty-three-year journey throughout Western Europe, his long-term
investment in royal patronage paid a big dividend. In 1770 his former pupil
Marie Antoinette had married the Dauphin Louis, grandson of the King
of France, Louis XV and who thus had the prospect of becoming queen
of the richest, most powerful and most populous state in Europe. Paris
alone had more inhabitants than the entire Duchy of Wurttemberg. In 1774
King Louis XV died, and Marie-Antoinette became Queen of France. His
esteemed friend Marie Antoinette had not forgotten her dancing master.
She ordered his return and secured his appointment at the Paris Opéra.
His ambition had now been fulfilled. Noverre, poor, provincial, without
class or breeding, had managed his patronage so adroitly that now he could
rule the world of dance. But the loyalty and support of royalty can shift.
Other geniuses had access and the fate of a low-born subject mattered little
especially to the frivolous and casual queen. Noverre got into trouble with
Mozart, who had composed *Les Petits Riens*, a bagatelle performed at the
Paris Opéra in 1778. Noverre constructed a slight and charming theme to
Mozart's music: the famed Vestris pursued with a net L'Amour (Mlle Allard)
disguised as a bird. Mlle Guimard captured the bird and, in a happy ending
the bird escaped. Dauberval played a character role in the piece. Apparently
Mozart was disappointed with the ballet's production and that was serious since Mozart already enjoyed the reputation of musical genius. Noverre
with his usual arrogance must have assumed that with the queen as patron
nobody could touch him. But Dauberval and the ambitious Maximilien
Gardel enlisted a cabal against Noverre. They called him egotistical, overly
serious and, what is more, they did not like his pantomime pieces. Mlle
Guimard also rebelled against his authority and poisoned many prominent
people against him. He was unseated and, in 1779, wrote a seventeen-page
memorandum describing the difficulties of his reign. His felicitous effect
on the Paris ballet world was perpetuated by his later staging of his tragic
ballet *Jason et Médée* (1780) that created a sensation, as did his ideas on costume and his thoughts on ballet pantomime, which were dutifully carried
through by Pierre Gardel, who inherited the throne and the running of the
Paris Opéra in 1787.

Noverre returned to his beloved London and the King's Theatre where he had a brilliant season in 1781, and staged many of his successful ballets from Stuttgart and Vienna. He also returned to Lyons from 1782 until 1787 to recreate many of his old works. There was a poetic justice in this happier golden era of his later years. Again from 1787 to 1788 he redid older works in London, many of which did not conform to his loftier, youthful aesthetic pronouncements, but were much appreciated by London audiences.

The French Revolution broke out in the summer of 1789 and Noverrre, in spite of his lowly birth, had depended on royal patronage for much of his career and saw earlier than most that France would be an uncomfortable place for royalists. He hid for a while in the remote area of Triel in France, and managed to get to London, where he spent two years from 1791 to 1793. When the "Terror" and the executions of "enemies of the people" finally ended in July 1794 with the fall of Robespierre and the Jacobins, the fanatics of the revolutionary era gave way to the less puritan and less devoutly republican regime of the Directory.

In 1795 Noverre could safely return to his home in Saint-Germain-en-Laye, in front of the Château, near the Hôtel de Noailles where Mozart had been received. Noverre was nearly destitute because of his association with the old regime and had lost his funds from the Opéra. He returned to visit its studios and stages where young talents were nurtured. He attended rehearsals where he gave advice to young dancers, "and deplores that no male dancers are being formed, with the result that the danseuses now exceed the danseurs in numbers".[3] He republished in 1803 his *Lettres* in St Petersburg, amended with the benefit of many years of disappointment and experience. His ballets, however, continued to be revived on the major European stages. He died in Saint-Germain-en-Laye on 19 October 1810 at the age of eighty-three.

The intellectual and aesthetic world of the young Noverre

The art of dance paralleled other developments in theatre and performance in the eighteenth century. Its reliance on carefully patterned steps and an extremely stylised approach to movement, gesture and emotion associated with the absolutist style of the seventeenth century came under criticism. "The real meaning of dance movement was lost in the flash of twinkling feet, in the curve of voluptuous arms, in the coquettish empty glance."[4] A new emphasis on the expressionistic possibilities of plot and movement enlarged the emotional opportunities for dancers, especially if a ballet had its own beginning, middle and end, and was not merely a divertissement in an opera. Several aestheticians in the early eighteenth century had already expressed interest in a modern form of dance. P. J. Burette (1719) and Abbé du Bos (1719) cited Plato and Aristotle as well as the contemporary Italian actors as advocates of gesture with meaning. Pantomime became an important topic since pantomimes in antiquity were of high repute. In addition, the idea of a ballet with a plot or the *ballet d'action* also took root. In 1741 Rémond de Saint Mard objected to the uniformity and passionless quality of the contemporary ballet. Five years later, Charles Batteux saw the possibility of dance as an independent art form and wrote copiously about its lack of variety and interest. Louis de Cahusac, a librettist, also wrote eloquently about ballet. He was responsible for several articles on dance in the *Encyclopédie* and in 1752 agreed with Batteux about ballet's enormous unfulfilled potential. "Sur nos théâtres nous avons des pieds excellents, des jambes brillantes, des bras admirables. Quel dommage que l'art de la danse nous manque."[5] (In our theatres we have excellent foot work, brilliant leg work and admirable arms. What a shame that the art of dance is missing!) But the most celebrated heroes of this discussion were the philosophers of the Enlightenment. Denis Diderot, who edited the *Encyclopédie*, wrote extensively on many of the arts including painting and theatre. He also took notice of the ballet and in his *Entretiens sur le fils naturel* (1758), emphasised the goal of imitating nature as had the Ancients. He felt that ballet needed a genius, a writer who would bring down to earth those magical and enchanted regions.[6]

Jean Jacques Rousseau in *La Nouvelle Héloïse* (1761) included a brief exposition of ballet's decadence in his diatribe. He noted that dances were thoughtlessly thrown onto the stage without any dramatic reason. "The priests dance, the soldiers dance, the gods dance, the devils dance; people dance into their graves and everyone dances no matter for what reason. Dance continually interrupts the plot or finds itself on stage for no reason, really imitating nothing."[7]

Noverre's dispute with Gasparo Angiolini

Franz Hilverding's dance dramas profoundly affected Italian ballet through the activities of his pupil Gasparo Angiolini and most dance historians believe that pantomimic dancing was well established in Italy in the 1740s. Written scenarios or libretti were necessary accompaniments to performances of ballet pantomimes, since the gestures and plots were not always clear to the audiences. The ballet's scenes and plots needed a structure, laid out on paper, just as the plot and the scenes of a play were written. These well-written libretti became the occasion for a passionate conflict between Angiolini and Noverre. In his *Lettres*, Noverre had urged the use of the libretti and the importance of a tight and moving plot without subplots and silly scenes, but instead libretti founded on logic and simplicity. Not only was Angiolini infuriated for his mentor Hilverding's sake by Noverre's claims to have invented the ballet pantomime, but he was appalled that Noverre had to depend upon a written crutch for the success of his ballets. Using his *aviso* or preface to his ballet *Le Festin de Pierre, ou Don Juan* (1761) and *Sémiramide* (1765) as forums for a debate, Angiolini quarrelled with Noverre's statements that ballets must be developed like plays. After all, plays lasted as long as three hours, while a ballet would not normally endure for more than one and a half hours. In 1773, Angiolini published a pamphlet, in which he criticised Noverre's use of overly long and detailed libretti. One year later, in the *aviso* to *Thésée en Crète* (Vienna 1774) Angiolini argued that programmes were an abuse. "If the ballets were unintelligible without the printed scenarios, the movements of the ballet should clarify the plot."[8] The bitter dialogue continued; but history tells us who won this debate. It was Noverre, as fairly lengthy and descriptive ballet programmes continued to be used throughout the nineteenth and twentieth centuries.

The letters on dancing and ballet

Noverre's greatest claim to influence in the history of ballet rests on his famous *Lettres*. Shortly after their publication, Noverre sent Voltaire a copy of the book and must have been delighted by Voltaire's response in October 1763: "The title of your book may only indicate dance, but you shed a great deal of light on all the arts. Your style is as elegant as your ballets have imagination." After expressing his sorrow at being unable to see one of Noverre's ballets, Voltaire added: "I think that your talent will be much appreciated in England, since they love the truths of nature. But where will you find the actors capable of executing your ideas? You are a Prometheus and you must create men and then animate them."[9] Six months later Voltaire reaffirmed his high opinion of Noverre: "I find that all you do is full of poetry; painters and poets will argue with one another as to whether you are a painter or a poet."[10] This praise from Europe's most prominent thinker encouraged Noverre to pursue his grand programme.

Like the Encyclopedists, Noverre was never content to make observations on a level of abstract criticism. He expected his ideas to yield practical results and from 1757 began writing a discourse that was inspired by practical experience. His own ballets, particularly *Fêtes chinoises*, presented in Lyons in 1751, Paris in 1754 and London in 1755, had already demonstrated his desire to go beyond traditional entrées and create an integrated cohesive presentation.

The writings of the philosophers confirmed his own thoughts. The first edition of the *Lettres* of 1760 criticised contemporary ballet and enthusiastically proposed reforms. Later he added letters to defend both his principles and his innovations in technique. In the final editions, those of St Petersburg, 1803, and Paris, 1807, he evaluated his previous attitudes, explaining why he had changed or modified certain ideas and expressing displeasure with current trends, some of which directly contradicted his basic tenets.

Noverre dedicated the first publication of his *Lettres* to the Duke of Wurttemberg who, as we have seen, allowed him to spread his wings and practise his newly found artistic principles. Following prevailing eighteenth-century aesthetics, Noverre insisted on truth, simplicity, harmony and the imitation of nature. He usually linked the word nature with "belle" and maintained that the artist must make choices in order to correct the defects of nature and embellish his subject sufficiently to arrive at a noble or picturesque effect. The artist must avoid servile reproduction, rejecting details that are confusing, useless or that delay action: the art was to disguise the effort.[11]

The letters discuss their subjects in a question and answer format; they address an imaginary intelligent, genteel and educated reader. Though most letters begin with a specific problem, they quickly move to general observations and to the demands for reform that Noverre made. Noverre regularly attacked colleagues, ballet masters and dancers alike, which made him many enemies. But the polemics always lead back to his grand and unified vision of a new ballet aesthetic, which he explains over and over again. Noverre accepted the theory that the art of pantomime had its origins in antiquity and found this a convenient justification for his own innovations. Later he discovered that pantomime was not as effective as he had hoped, and he looked to the future of ballet by championing the dancing of his contemporaries. They offered more variety, more sophistication and truth in their simulation of natural sentiments.

Like Diderot, Noverre refused to limit his canvas to mythological and heroic subjects. He advocated unlimited choice and urged *maîtres de ballets* to be alert to subjects taken from daily life in the country and the city. They were not to preach but never to forget the moral purpose of art. "How many varied pictures will he not find amongst working men and artisans! Each has different attitudes born of the positions and movements which his work imposes. This stance, this deportment, this way of moving, always common to his trade and always pleasing, must be suggested by the choreographer" (*Letters*, p. 73). Indeed Noverre put peasants on stage in *Annette et Lubin* and in *Adelaïde ou la Bergère des Alpes* taken from Marmontel.

In spite of his claims to represent real life, he really preferred the depth and sublimity of tragedy. He showed in his grand historical works that tragedy could work in a ballet (*Letters*, p. 85). The term historical here embraced historical, mythological and religious themes. He criticised the use of arbitrary, abstract, exaggerated allegory (*Letters*, p. 143), but accepted that it could be instructive as well as entertaining when used with circumspection to depict human virtue (*Letters*, pp. 279-83).

Noverre understood that the audience might be dazzled by virtuosic dancing, but he believed that ballet could not achieve its full potential if brilliant mechanical execution lacked warmth and feeling. He proposed a reorientation in purpose: dancers needed to understand that ballet was a composition of passions and that their souls spoke through their eyes (*Letters*, p. 94). For this reason dancers should sacrifice complicated steps, which detract from the natural. He advised them to learn the art of pantomime in order to hide the effort of dance and to evoke the passions being represented (*Letters*, p. 35).

Noverre assumed that facial expressions could be more expressive than words because words, which have to be arranged in sequences over time, can never have an immediate effect. Since the language of pantomime came from the soul of the performer, it went directly to the heart of the viewer (*Letters*, p. 140). He had watched Garrick as the best possible representative of this technique. Noverre rejected the use of masks, because they destroyed the true proportions between the head and the body, and prevented the communication of sensitive facial expressions. He compared wearing masks to giving a performance from behind an un-raised stage curtain (*Letters*, pp. 20–4).

Noverre associated ballet with all the arts, but especially with painting, either in detail of execution, or in overall effect: "A ballet is a painting, the scene is the canvas, the mechanical movements of the dancers are the colours, their facial expressions are the paintbrush. Thus the whole ensemble, the vivacity of each scene, the musical voice, the decoration and the costume comprise the subtle colorations – and finally the choreographer is the painter" (*Letters*, p. 88). Of all the arts, he saw dance as the highest expression because of its dynamic portrayal of a series of ideas or emotions in time. However, he expressed regret that dance was ephemeral and that time, energy and talent expended for a moment of beauty would disappear so quickly (*Letters*, p. 324).

Noverre's methodology for the training of dancers paved the way for many future treatises, especially Carlo Blasis's ground-breaking 1820 work *An Elementary Treatise upon the Theory and Practice of the Art of Dancing*. Noverre understood that human anatomy was paramount. In Letters 11 and 12 Noverre analysed why knowledge of the muscles, bones and nerves of the body was essential to the dancing master. How could a teacher ask the student to turn out at the knees if the knee was incapable of turning out? It could only bend and straighten. Each student had particular difficulties with the ballet technique and the teacher had therefore to take them into consideration when giving corrections.

Noverre, never a modest man, announced that he single-handedly intended to transform the entire art of dance. He spoke about pulling the dance out of its lethargy and languor. He alone had the courage to struggle against deeply engrained prejudices and habits. If something went wrong, he quickly found someone else to blame: he was either successful or misunderstood and therefore less successful. But his conclusions in 1803 swept away all uncertainties: "The glory of my art, my age and my numerous brilliant successes, permit me to state that I have achieved a revolution in dancing, as striking and as lasting as that achieved by Gluck in the realm of music. The successes even by imitators today are the greatest testimony to the value of the principles which I have laid down in my work" (*Letters*, p. 2).

9 The French Revolution and its spectacles

INGE BAXMANN

Revolutionary festivities and cultural disruption

During the French Revolution of 1789 a deep change in the representation of social communication and interaction took place. The spectrum of the new sociability reached from refashioning the national costume that replaced the old dress codes of the guild and social hierarchies to the republican, informal way of addressing each other, from imitating Roman slave haircuts to rituals of fraternisation, from frugal banquets in the open to name-giving ceremonies of newborn babies (Brutus was one of the preferred choices), from the revolutionary catechism that spread ancient Roman models of virtue to the introduction of a new, republican calendar. All these measures were intended to mark a break not only with the *Ancien Régime* before 1789 but with history as it had been known.

The French Revolution understood itself as a "regeneration", a return to a social order that was close to nature. A stable political order was the goal and certainly not a permanent revolution. But the Revolution, particularly after the execution of the king, had become a threatening crisis. To the horror of many politicians, post-revolutionary France proved extremely mobile and unsettled. The movement cultures and body performances of this time can be seen as an attempt to contain the "too much" of social movement by controlling the individual body within the mass. Hence the painter David and the choreographer Gardel saw themselves confronted with the problem of convincing passionate crowds to move within ordered forms, to make a moving, yet manageable, organised, yet innocuous, collective body out of an unruly mass that threatened to explode at any moment. The revolutionary fête was to construct the *citoyen*, the citizen of the new republic. The movement culture of the Revolution strictly rejected the court ballets of Louis XVI, their "seductive culture" and elitist claims. In their place something new was to be practised on and off stage. Inside and outside the theatre the actors sang republican hymns together with the audience.

The *Fête de la Fédération* (Festival of Federation) began on 14 July 1790 when actors, musicians, singers and dancers from several Parisian theatres gathered in Notre Dame cathedral and imitated the fall of the Bastille, the signal that had begun the Revolution. The next day a procession marched through Paris; in the evening the people danced in front

Figure 15 *Festival of Federation*, 14 July 1790; copper engraving by Paul Jakob Laminit, no date.

of the Bastille; the whole square had been converted into a dance space (Fig. 15).

The revolutionary fêtes endeavoured to transfer enlightenment ideals into political practice. The construction of a "natural body" with "natural movements" and as part of a "natural way of life" belonged to such an endeavour. So-called "codes of naturalness" were to initiate the restructuring of French civil society. Old, aristocratic norms were to be banished. Instead, a new net of social responsibilities was to anchor "natural" human sentiments as moral behaviour and make unequivocally clear the universal and unchangeable truths of the Enlightenment and the Revolution. The restructuring of movement culture therefore must be understood as part of a fundamental change of social codes and moral sentiments.

The French Revolution put the people on stage. At court festivities the people stood outside as observers, but revolutionary festivities invited the people to join in. They could act out new roles in folk dances such as the *Carmagnole*, a round dance, in "banquets fraternels" (fraternal banquets), or in processions and orchestrated eruptions of emotions like, for instance, the "cris d'allegresse" (lighthearted cries) or the "pas joyeux" (jumps of joy). Everyday life during the French Revolution had to be aestheticised, because reality had not yet caught up with the ideal. New forms of life had to be practised in the pedagogic sense of the word. The theatre and the revolutionary festivals were a means of instruction, aimed at forming a republican sensibility. On 30 September 1792 the Opéra in Paris performed the *Offrande à la Liberté*, a lyrical divertissement or interlude that reproduced the events of the Revolution as an opera. It was a tremendous success. The music had been composed by François-Joseph Gossec and the scenario had been written by Pierre Gardel. The *Marseillaise*, the revolutionary national anthem, was sung on stage. Groups of women, children and soldiers marched towards a "Temple of Freedom", where they worshipped the goddess of freedom, danced in her honour and promised to use their weapons in her defence. The festivities expressed an "image dynamique de rassemblement" (dynamic image of gatherings) in dances, ritual activities and collective gestures.

The new movement ideal: the "natural body" opposed to the "artful body"

Dances like the *Carmagnole* deliberately used the ecstatic energies of the masses. In the *Carmagnole* the dancers formed enormous circles. While singing they slowly turned, stamped their feet and accelerated their movements during the refrain. Pierre Gardel's choreography for *La Réunion du 10 âout* (The reunion of 10 August), performed on 5 April 1794 also contained market scenes and village people. This was a complete novelty. In addition, Gardel integrated everyday movements into the dances and let the people appear in their real clothes.[1] Contemporary commentators felt threatened by such popular dances and accused them of being ecstatically disordered and chaotic. Such rejection is easily explained. An audience in the 1790s could easily recall the display of disciplined bodies and aristocratic movement styles of court ballet. Dances like the *Carmagnole* were provocations, particularly if they were put on stage. They created a counter-model to court style: ecstatic chaos versus geometric movements. The court culture of the *Ancien Régime* was based on a particular power model that relied on perfect interaction of the performance of political representation and forms of sociability, together expressed in the ideal of the "honnête homme". This ideal incorporated the concept of the "artful body", which demanded constant practice; the nuanced gestures, movements and complex step sequences had to be inscribed on the body. The "natural gracefulness" of the aristocracy had to appear effortless. Only by perfect staging could the aristocratic elite advance its claim to leadership. The fencing and riding or dancing exercises that occupied the elite of the *Ancien Régime* were thus much more than simply a pleasant way to pass time. For this reason, the court ballets of Louis XIV have been described as "seductive".[2] A collective sensibility emerged in the process of forging the "honnête" ideal of the body.

Only someone who could master the techniques of the body would have a chance to survive the power struggles within the elite. Manuals and rituals of court behaviour as well as court dances were directed towards one goal: control of the affects and sensibilities that guaranteed promotion at court.

Gracefulness in dance and aptness on the battlefield formed this collective body. The *danse noble* and the "artful body" presented an image of noble perfection. The ballets drew symmetrical, linear and elegant lines around an invisible central axis, the symbolic body of the king. The "artful body" expressed a refined sociability that justified a claim to leadership. The nation was symbolically represented through the body of the king and the artfully arranged bodies of his courtiers.

The enlightened counter-model established the "natural body" as an expression of universal human feelings. It was free of masquerade, affectation, disguise or learned rules of behaviour. "Nature" versus "artifice" became a fundamental dichotomy of enlightened thinking. Within the enlightened model "natural" gestures and "natural" bodies opposed the "artificial" movement style of the *Ancien Régime*. Long before the French Revolution, these gradual transitions had prepared the emergence of new codes and cultures in all the arts from hierarchical, guild and class-orientated social distinctions to a broader communication among social groups. In the theatre the melodrama, the "drame bourgeois", and in the fine arts the discovery of antiquity in neoclassical paintings marked stages in the transition. Artists such as Jacques-Louis David or the genre painter Greuze, or in dance the *ballet d'action* of Jean-Georges Noverre point to the evolution of a new model of social interaction and communication.[3] The *ballet d'action* expressed "sentiments". The goal of dance, according to Noverre, was to express natural feelings through movement and touch the soul of the observer. Instead of the court ballet with its elegant movement patterns around a central spatial axis, the audience now could follow the performance of natural human passions and conflicts.

Thus elements of the new revolutionary art had emerged before 1789. After the outbreak of the Revolution, Maximilien and Pierre Gardel developed a movement aesthetic and a choreographical concept derived from Noverre's dance theory and Diderot's theory of drama. Gardel used them for the revolutionary festivals and the choreographies at the opera. In both genres movement emerged as an expression of natural human feelings. He adopted the *ballet d'action* as a formal model to organise dramatic conflict and eliminated elaborate movement techniques. Gesture and style came close to mime. Costumes changed: corsets, heavy wigs and weighty brocade disappeared and were replaced by lighter costumes. Dancers wore tunic-like frocks made of light material and sandals or slim shoes, designed after Roman models. Another model with revolutionary connotation was the everyday-dress worn by the *Sansculottes*, the radical, working-class Jacobins. Their distinctive costume, the *pantalon* (long trousers) replaced the *culotte* (silk breeches) worn by the upper classes. New clothes made new movements in both senses of the word visible. Higher jumps, dancing on demi-point and new dramatic expression appeared on stage as did the equivalent figures represented in the new dress.

Antiquity as utopian past

It proved much simpler to abolish all the *Ancien Régime's* signs of social distinction in dress, codes of behaviour and communication styles, than to put something new in its place. The term "nature", from the beginning of the Enlightenment, served as a collective concept for very different ideas of change. The concept indicated that "return to nature" was a call to arms against the old regime. It pointed to revolutionary social utopias. After 1789 all this could be traced in the self-representations of the new order, from collective symbols to republican festivities, from movement cultures to dress and everyday rituals.

The "civil republic" needed new norms of behaviour that rested on universal moral values. Since the Enlightenment had turned antiquity into a utopian past, the revolutionaries hoped to draw new patterns from it. The social changes constructed by the Enlightenment were a "regeneration", a return to an earlier stage of social equality and freedom. Jacques-Louis David as a painter and Pierre Gardel as a choreographer had both been representatives of the neoclassical style even before the French Revolution; both had therefore the same aesthetic ideal. Pierre Gardel's choreographies, though following the neoclassical tradition embraced by the new order, were compatible with certain aspects of the *Ancien Régime*, which in its own way had a vested interest in classicism. Court ballets, after all, also acted out antique myths and stories. Gardel's ballets were called *Le Jugement de Paris* or *Psyche* or *Télémaque*, whereas his revolutionary productions (including those repeated on the theatrical stage) combined neoclassical style with political content, as for instance in his *L'Offrande à Liberté*. If we want to look for something new in Gardel's ballets, we must look not merely at the integration of classical antiquity into ballets.

The Enlightenment had generally interpreted antiquity in a special way. Johann Joachim Winckelmann's *History of Ancient Art* had been translated into French in 1766. In it he described Greek antiquity as model for a democratic society. Based on the surviving artefacts, he pictured a culture that encouraged human development. Antiquity as unifying cultural model, typified in neoclassicism, seemed to offer a consensus for a new cultural policy that the elite of the Revolution needed. From an enlightened perspective, antiquity realised the unity of human nature and society. Ancient heroes of the Roman republic could be converted into incarnations of republican state virtues. But this involved a fundamental shift in the perception of antiquity: it was to serve not as cultural legitimisation of royal claims to power, but instead as a model for an egalitarian society.

Jacques-Louis David in his *Oath of the Horatii* of 1785 had already interpreted antiquity with enlightened concepts as a backdrop. This picture, more than any other, moulded the self-conception and self-representation of the French revolutionaries. In a celebration organised by David and Robespierre, participants re-enacted the oath. The picture functioned as a kind of emblematic summary of imperturbable loyalty to the new state, a reference which contemporaries at the time understood without any knowledge of the complex history of ancient Roman reality. The emotional fracture of the family is another important theme in the painting, and with it gender dualities and gender ethics. The scene stems, as mentioned, from Roman history; it showed the battle between Rome and Alba, which represented different, rival concepts of the state. The Horatii swore to fight the Curatii even though they were related by marriage. The moral strength of the men (the father who holds the sword and the three sons who swear the oath) manifested itself in gesture and body stance. The firm gaze, the energetic way of holding their heads, the tense leg muscles and the outstretched arms mark the men in the centre of the picture, while the group of women and children sit on the right-hand side. Helpless and resigned, the mother of the Horatii and her two daughters Sabina and Camilla have their eyes half closed and pose in a weak, effete way. Within such republican display of values and ideals femininity was reduced to an object and mirror of manly virtue and will to power. The painting was re-enacted in revolutionary celebrations as well as on stage.

The constitution of 1792 demanded that every active citizen swear the "serment civique" (the civil oath) to the constitution and its core idea, the rights of man. The oaths were also part of festive rituals; men would swear that they were willing to defend the republic whereas women swore that they would only marry a republican.

Fraternal space and the natural order of society

Revolutionary notions regarding space are reflected in many contemporary debates; there was a great need to define the new order spatially and at the same time justify it as based on natural laws. Hence the preferred topographical forms were circles, globes and spheres, all considered natural, harmonious and tested in ancient times. These spatial constellations would ensure the opening up of a previously restricted space. The opening up of space, making it public, signified the attempt to abolish social barriers.

The sphere represented an egalitarian model of power; in one such model, a design for a tombstone honouring Isaac Newton, Etienne-Louis Boullée argued in 1784: "Tout les points de son surface sont également distans de son centre ... Il [le corps sphérique] réunit l'exacte symétrie, la régularité la plus parfaite, la variété la plus grande; il a le plus grand développement, sa forme est la plus simple, sa figure est dessinée par le contours le plus agréable"[4] (All points of its surface are equally distant from its centre ... It [the spherical body] combines the most exact symmetry, the most perfect regularity with the greatest variety; it is the greatest development, its shape is most simple, its form is designed according to the most agreeable contours). Hence it was no coincidence that the Abbé Sieyès used just such an image to describe the social contract in his treatise *What is the third estate*?: "Je me figure la loi au centre d'un globe immense; tout les citoyens sans exception sont à la même distance sur la circonférance et n'y occupant que des place égales; tout dependent également de la loi, tous lui offrent leur liberté et leur propriété à protéger; et c'est ce que j'appelle les *droit communs* de citoyens, par où ils se ressemblent tous" (I picture the law as being in the centre of a huge globe; all citizens, without exception, stand equidistant from it on the surface and occupy equal positions there; all are equally dependent on the law, all present it with their liberty and their property to be protected; and this is what I call the *common rights* of citizens, the rights in respect of which they are all alike).[5]

This image expressed the problem of planning social relationships among equals without introducing anything that could be associated with anarchy, violence or chaos. Rounded shapes when applied to demarcate a public space, like the amphitheatre, made possible the presence of the faceless masses with their tendency towards chaos as citizens, individuals in a non-hierarchical order, but held in check by the architecture of republican space. In such "fraternal spaces" the citizen could envisage himself in a newly unified society that was based on natural principles and he could explain his relationship to other individuals as one within the "grande famille humaine" (the great human family). The view was to be open so the gaze could roam freely; the ideal example would show a society that seamlessly merged into external nature – landscape, mountains, forests, rivers – and at the same time reflected it. The representation of social order as an analogy with the harmonic order of the cosmos would displace history and make rules unequivocally universal and eternal. Conversely, the eternal laws of nature would certify everlasting social principles. Hence circular spatial forms confirmed a natural, cosmic order, which would channel anxieties about the future in the right direction.

Contemporary iconography tells us that the caesura created by the Revolution meant a new beginning for humankind but one mixed with fear of the future, of violence and anarchy. The revolutionaries had crossed an important boundary: they had abolished the necessity of hierarchy and had suggested equality. But that raised the question of how it would be possible to maintain order if, at the same time, those in power questioned hierarchical order and eradicated difference. Hence revolutionary visions of equality themselves came dangerously close to chaos and disorder because they could only be achieved through violent change. This deep-seated anxiety found its representation through the paradigm of femininity. *The Contrast*, a lithograph, shows "British Liberty" as a seated woman wearing a Bonnet Rouge and classical robes, in her left hand the Magna Carta and in her right hand scales. At her feet sits a lion, in the background we see a ship, the symbol of trade. Opposite her, on the torso of a decapitated figure, stands "French Liberty", in a threatening posture and with her face distorted by aggression. In her left hand she holds a spear which has pierced through a decapitated head, dripping with blood, in her right hand – ready to fight – a sword. Her face and her arms look mannish; on her Gorgon's head snakes grow instead of hair and the belt around her torn frock is also a snake. In the background hanged bodies, wearing aristocratic garments, dangle from the gallows and clouds of smoke rise. The concept of equality appears as a contradiction of natural order and as a perversion of known gender characteristics. This version of the Revolution was not only that of foreign counter-revolutionaries but also resonated in the collective anxieties of those in France scared of "confusion". The republic was founded on an act of violence. From the point of view of the revolutionaries it was justified, yet they too feared further acts of violence. This fear has to be recalled if we wish to understand the pedantic attention to detail in staging revolutionary celebrations. In all directives on celebration the emphasis lay on the danger of "confusion". If participants did not keep to their assigned places or social roles the worst had to be feared. The "bad" citizen and the counter-revolutionary would immediately take advantage of such slippage. Movement patterns in the new public spaces, in pageants and ritual festivities followed the model of "natural" order that relied on "natural" differences and necessitated clearly demarcated spaces and movement orders. The inherent conflict between the ecstatic, "chaotic" moment of general fraternisation, which every celebration demanded, and the urge to represent the Revolution as structured and ordered was not easily reconciled. The tension between mobility and order proved to be fundamental for revolutionary politics. As one of the politicians pointed out: "Il nous a fallu être révolutionnaire pour fonder la

Révolution, mais pour la conserver il faut cesser de l'être"[6] (We have had to be revolutionary to establish the Revolution, but to conserve it, we have to cease to be revolutionary).

Gardel directed several choric dance dramas that interpreted episodes from the revolution in a patriotic spirit, for instance, *La Réunion du Dix Août* at the Paris Opéra, where the *Fête de la Régénération* (the festival of regeneration) of 10 August 1793 had to be contained within a theatrical and orderly dramatic action. The phases of the celebrations were copied onto the stage; the Revolution appeared as liberation of the poor and innocent from slavery. One of the last festivities was called the *Fête de la Raison* (festival of reason), held on 10 November 1793; it coerced the not very cooperative singers and dancers of the Opéra into participating.[7]

The contemporary aesthetic debate in the fine arts, particularly in painting, and dramatic theatre established the cultural codes that the organisers of revolutionary festivities needed. In their presentations and performances they searched for the typical and constant in human nature, for instance, for the expression of passion in all sorts of situations. The organisers focused on the universal and the unchangeable in thought, feeling and taste. The goal of aesthetic representation could not be found in the empirical, the real example, but in the idealised form of beautiful nature. The festivals had a double task; they were supposed to form the interior while representing the ideal exterior. A successful celebration could prove itself as a useful contribution towards a republican education. The aesthetic conception of self-representation in revolutionary celebrations corresponded to contemporary knowledge of human perception. And that suggested that the soul of the viewer or participant could be touched above all through the eye, through images. Hence J. B. Gence conceived of the festival parade as a "Tableau mouvant". Every group within the procession was to express one particular idea and therefore should be noticed as a separate, isolated event. "It would be ideal neither to mix nor to disperse the artefacts, neither to isolate nor to muddle ideas and perceptions of every group." In addition it would also be good if the movement of the pageant were to be "uniform and rather slow so the eye has time to catch the story line and learn the lessons and keep them well in mind".[8]

During the *Fête de l'Etre Suprême* (Festival of the Supreme Being) in Nancy, one wagon was decorated as "Char du Bon Ménage" (cart of the good marriage); it showed a mother bent over the cot and a father teaching the child on his knees to read. A third child embraced both parents and a fourth crowned them with laurel. In this "tableau vivant de la morale et du patriotisme" the principles of Greuze's moralistic painting as well as the literary theory of the Enlightenment guided the conception. Greuze, as Diderot had in his theory of drama, considered the tableau an emphatic climax of a scene that immediately became contained. The unifying principle of the tableau made it possible to move away from history towards the anthropological constants of human nature and to make visible the ethics of that nature. In comments on the festive events one can often find comparisons with paintings. One critic compared the *Fête de la Fédération* (1790) with a "tableau d'ordonnance romaine". The participants were mostly characterised according to natural biology; they were separated by gender and age. Figures from the ancient republican repertoire of state representation were added, such as the "magistrat". The simplification of social relationships through stylisation in the tableau made social interaction direct, transparent and graspable as a new social policy. "Familialism", the principle of seeing society naturally as a family, brought together the masses into manageable blocs. In enlightened philosophy and state legal doctrine, the family was universally accepted as a kind of *Ur*– or original – model of human interaction. The metaphor of family hence could be used as the model for social relationships as such, though their interpretation shifted during the time of the Revolution. In its first phase, aristocrats and the wealthy remained part of the family if they could be purified through education. A characteristic feature of celebratory representation excluded the acknowledgement of social antagonisms; as taboos they were banned from the social family. The harmonious order of society included a strict spatial division among its individuals according to their "nature": men and women occupied separate spaces. The *Fête de l'Etre Suprême*, organised by David and Gardel on the Champ de la Réunion, choreographed the bloc of marching men and the elderly descending from the right of the hill whereas women, mothers and young girls were grouped on the left hand side. "Battalions of the Young Men" encircled the hills and the "national representatives" were placed on the top of the hill. Each group wore banderoles on their sleeves with mottos that summarised the ideals they embodied. Their spatial position emphasised their distinct social place and divided the groups from one another[9] (Fig. 16.) Commissioners, responsible for keeping order, oversaw the pageants so that there would be no danger of "confusion". "Each occupies his post. Each holds a green twig, flower or corn ear in his hand. There were as many commissioners as groups to control movement. The bad citizens and the immoral are recognisable in that they try to introduce disarray and turmoil into this honourable event."[10]

The costumes and props also denoted roles: women wore white frocks cut to match antique patterns and braided hair (associated with the ancient republics and chastity), whereas the men and boys carried swords as a symbol of readiness to fight.

Not only were the modes of behaviour and movements of the specific variants of human nature applied to individual groups of participants in

Figure 16 *The Festival of the Supreme Being*, 8 June 1794 at the Champs de Mars in Paris, painting by (Pierre) Antoine Demachy, no date.

the festivals but also the different codes of expressions of emotion found in painting and theatre were used (for example from Charles Le Brun's *Méthode pour apprendre à dessiner les passions* of 1702). All these expressions were distinguished by age and gender. Tears of deep emotion, "cris d'allegresse" (shrieks of joy) as well "pas joyeux" belonged to the repertoire of gestures and movements, which made externally visible the appropriately felt emotions.

The French Revolution imposed a clear differentiation of male and female and turned them into decisive patterns of order. Gender roles were pushed to the top of the agenda because they could be used to combat the "crisis of difference", a crisis that was concerned with the invalidation of traditional hierarchies and the implicit fear of loss of order and ensuing chaos.

A new-found equilibrium

Movement threatened the unstable balance between nature and history. Revolutionary celebrations confirmed exactly those values that constructed their own social utopias and new behaviour had to be practised in order to introduce a new, acceptable French reality. "Equilibrium" instead of mobility was advocated as the future social ideal. One hymn that was sung in the celebrations asserted: "May a free people emerge out of your midst. May you love the new people, love one another – that is the happy pillar of your equilibrium."[11]

Because the Revolution destroyed the old equilibrium, organisers of revolutionary festivities attempted to create a new one. Movements, minutely arranged and defined in gestures and grand rituals, "performed" social order. Through repetition, order was to inscribe itself in the physical and psychological body. Revolutionary spectacle turned from nature to order. When the egalitarian-democratic myth of state self-representation broke down during the 9th Thermidor (27 July 1794) and Robespierre and the Jacobin leadership were sent to the guillotine, society after the "Great Terror" needed to find a new stability. Many of the old conflicts and antagonisms emerged. The harmonious vision of society was unmasked as a fiction. Revolutionary celebrations degenerated into military parades and mass entertainments. During the Directory (1795–9) a clear division of state and society was proclaimed and the absolute ruler as symbol of representation reintroduced. The established forms and scenarios of state representation that the earlier periods of the French Revolution had developed were still used but gradually stripped of their utopian potential. The people, the masses, were once again observers at the spectacles.

Translation by Marion Kant

PART III

Romantic ballet: ballet is a woman

10 Romantic ballet in France: 1830–1850

SARAH DAVIES CORDOVA

PREMIERE OF *GISELLE OU LES WILIS*
MONDAY 28 JUNE 1841
BALLET-PANTOMIME IN 2 ACTS AT THE ACADÉMIE ROYALE DE MUSIQUE

The first chords of Rossini's music announcing the beginning of the third act of the opera *Moïse* can be heard faintly by the spectators who, uninterested in the 1827 opera chestnut, still wander about the Opéra's foyer as its prominent clock strikes eight. They have at least another hour before the curtain rises to reveal the long-awaited and much talked about new ballet, *Giselle*. Others – men, dressed in black tailcoats and top hats, asserting their privileged status derived from their associations with the worlds of business, of politics and the intelligentsia – have paid for the entitlement of entering the *foyer de la danse* to chat with the dancers. Aglow with the excitement of opening night, the dancers warm up and mark out their steps before the foyer's full-length mirrors. Or, in their dressing-rooms, they look to their make-up, jewels, last-minute fitting of their villagers' costumes; many lay out their calf-length white dresses of layered gauze and crowns of flowers for the ballet's second act peopled with wilis, those enchanting dancing ghosts of maidens who, having died before their wedding day, lure each passing man into a dance that only ceases with his death from exhaustion and their diurnal fade-out. As is customary at the Paris Opéra, the evening will last three to four hours, almost until midnight.

Despite recurring postponements of the premiere due to the leading dancer Carlotta Grisi's slow recovery from her accident in May, then due to the tumour François Antoine Habeneck, the conductor, was fighting, and to safety issues facing the machinists and stage hands, frequent press releases succeeded in keeping interest in this momentous production alive. Since the Opéra could not bank on a memorable midsummer night, the on-stage dress rehearsal on Saturday 26 June had been closed to the press and on Sunday, further rehearsals had kept dancers, stage hands and musicians at the Opéra for most of the day in order to ensure Monday's commercial and artistic success.

After the performance, before setting off home or going on to the Café anglais, or to Tortoni for an ice-cream, bedazzled, and some tear-stained, patrons of the Opéra linger in the foyer, under the covered arches, on the steps, where they await their coachman, or a hackney carriage. They chatter enthusiastically about the new ballet.

— Why did Giselle die? From a broken heart? Why did Hilarion denounce Loys and reveal him to be duke Albert?

— Didn't you read the libretto? Weren't you paying attention? You'll have to wait for the newspaper reviews. They always recount the story in great detail.

— Giselle's mother, Berthe was so concerned! And Myrtha, queen of the wilis, what determination! Why do the wilis not kill Albert?

Punctuating discussions of the plot, exclamatory praise for Ciceri's decor abounds, especially about the contrasts between the first act in a sun-drenched autumnal German wine-producing valley and the second on the grassy bank of a northern European pond in a dark forest with its vaporous moon-like lighting, and the wilis' shadowy figures with diaphanous wings before the final sunrise.

"Carlotta Grisi" falls from everyone's lips. The ballerina from Italy con-joins in her incarnation of Giselle both the everyday young girl and the otherworldly evanescent feminine figure. Her character's tragic transfor-mation from disobedient, self-centred dancing villager madly in love with Loys into generous, self-sacrificing, yet still insubordinate wili caught the collective imagination. Her exuberant yet lilting execution of the waltzes in the first act contrasted with her ensuing dance of death, which in turn was echoed by Loys/Albert's exhaustion as the wilis slipped back into the tufts of flowers and tall grasses at daybreak. Impudent and dar-ing, Grisi remained delicate and chaste all the while standing up for the love of her life and her passion for dance. She performed the mime and movement needs of the role with precision and clarity without over-emphasising them. The hybridity of her performance combined pan-tomime to portray the stereotypical naiveté of the peasant and her inten-sive single-mindedness as a wili with sharp, precise seemingly effortless pointe work and flowing *port-de-bras* arms and torso for the demanding adagio work during the demure yet defiant second-act solos and *pas de deux* (see Fig. 17).

Jules Perrot's emotive choreography and attention to Giselle and Albert's partnering pleased many. Their duets delineated both their separate des-tinies and the clear demarcation between male and female ballet vocabu-laries. Lucien Petipa, whose pantomime matched Grisi's with its graceful despair and touching passion, partnered her expressively and garnered his share of praise for his role as duc Albert, initially disguised as Loys, her fellow peasant. Appealing to the spectators' melodramatic verve, the final guilt-free reintegration of Albert into his own social milieu also played out the recognisable romantic hero's plot.

Figure 17 Carlotta Grisi as Giselle, Paris 1841 from *Les Beautés de l'opéra, ou Chefs-d'oeuvre lyriques, illustrés par les premiers artistes de Paris et de Londres sous la direction de Giraldon...* (Paris: Soulié, 1845).

The second act lingered on in the audience's mind's eye since the wilis, shimmering in white gauze during their nightly outing, recalled the *ballet des nonnes* of the convent scene in *Robert le diable* (1831) with the white-clad dancing lapsed nuns, the woods in *La Sylphide* (1831) peopled with flying ethereal, translucent sylphs, and the underwater scene in *La Fille du Danube* (1836) with its female water-sprites, the *undines*. *Giselle* reiterated these successful antecedents with its troupe of alluring wispy wilis, hauntingly illuminated by the ghostly, other-worldly effects of the developing lighting technology.[1] As the latest incarnation of these two-act ballets, which would become synonymous with the "ballet blanc" (the white ballet or the ballet in white) as one constitutive element of the romantic ballet, the inspiration for this box-office success derived from the German author Heinrich Heine's *De l'Allemagne*, and Victor Hugo's poem *Fantômes*.

Wilis referred to those girls "who loved to dance too much", and who, it was imputed, died "on their wedding's eve, at the height of unconsummated sexual arousal".[2] This deathly notion associated with dancing too much holds for much of the nineteenth century as can be seen in Edmond de Goncourt's 1885 novel *Chérie*. For some, loving to dance too much connoted sexual promiscuity, while dying from dancing signified orgasm as in "la petite mort". The French poet, novelist and journalist Théophile Gautier, a fervent admirer of Victor Hugo and partisan of romanticism, first worked these sources into a ballet, which the prolific librettist Jules-Henri Vernoy de Saint-Georges then translated into a ballet libretto, one palatable to the Opéra's management. Indeed since the 1820s, popular male literati were often called upon to write the libretti as against an earlier practice according to which the dancing master (who would later be known as choreographer) both devised the story and the dancing. Some, such as Filippo Taglioni, however, took exception to the new practice. During the 1830s,[3] he often occupied both positions as he worked to ensure that his daughter Marie Taglioni had the stylistic vehicle to sustain her supremacy on the European stage.

The alterations Saint Georges brought to Gautier's manuscript included a major rewriting and resetting of the first act in a realistic yet seemingly anachronistic village, as well as the determination of two key (melodramatic) elements in romantic stories, the marriage plot[4] and the love triangle,[5] whereby Giselle is pursued by Hilarion and by Albert disguised as Loys, who in turn is already engaged to Bathilde, the daughter of a prince. Adolphe Adam, one of the regular composers of the Opéra, arranged the expressive music over a two-month period, so that it followed referentially and mimetically the characters' actions, gestures and mimed (and therefore silent) dialogues. Jean Coralli, who admitted that Jules Perrot had contributed significantly to Giselle's *pas*, was credited with the overall choreography wherein each clearly defined character performed steps and mime sequences which adhered quite literally to the scripted plot.

The audience pouring out of the Salle Lepelletier of the Académie royale de musique's theatre, otherwise known as the Opéra, on 28 June 1841 experienced a very different performance from a comparable night at the beginning of the twenty-first century at the Opéra Garnier, in Paris. Priorities and expectations have altered considerably the shape, content, form and melodrama of ballet-pantomimes or what have since been categorised as romantic ballets. Yet the theatre managements in both epochs reach for similar goals. As is borne out by their respective media resources, they seek to amaze and fascinate. Over the course of the nineteenth century, posters became part of the urban landscape and the Paris Opéra utilised the medium to its advantage for advance sales, while the newspapers both announced and reviewed theatrical events as well as developed gossip columns. Special volumes printed on fine paper about the theatrical world and its members, which often included revised versions or reprints of press reviews and a series of illustrations – portraits of dancers, actresses, and opera divas both in costume and in street-wear as well as drawings of key scenes from the popular ballets and operas – furthered the theatre's publicity campaigns and the individuals' renown. Much of what we can now understand about performances in the 1830s and 1840s relies upon these descriptive sources and in some cases on rehearsal notes (*répétiteurs*), which circulated abroad to such cities as Brussels, London, St Petersburg, and among the provincial theatres where these ballets were staged.[6]

Clearly, the evening's entertainment aroused delight and appealed to the spectators' senses. As at most performances during the July Monarchy, a cross-section of Parisians attended, including members of the government who often cut short their political discussions in order not to miss the ballet. The curtain went up somewhere between seven and eight and finally came down well into the night since, as in the case of *Giselle*'s premiere, the design of the programme invariably included a cross-genre double bill and several intermissions. When the full-length work being performed was a ballet, the evening generally opened with a one-act opera, or a favourite act from a full-length opera, with or without a danced scene which lasted about an hour. The reverse occurred when a full-length opera played. Such a programme catered to all tastes and reminds twenty-first century audiences that the two genres – ballet and opera – cohabitated closely under the same theatrical roof, with ballet as at least the equal, if not the predominant, partner of opera. Indeed dancers often performed in the course of a single evening in both a ballet and an opera, in which the danced sections and especially the title roles in such often repeated operas as *La Muette de Portici* (Auber, 1828), *Le Dieu et la bayadère* (Auber, 1830) and *La Tentation* (Halévy, 1832) were as demanding as in the ballets (see Fig. 18).

Apart from the patrons with their own boxes who came and went as they pleased during the evening and often only watched one act – they actually complained when the main ballet act came too early and prevented them from enjoying a leisurely dinner – most spectators witnessed two genres of spectacles. Both required similar skills to decipher the codes at play in the plots' staging. Romantic ballet's storylines incorporated complicated twists with intricate mimed passages, which proved difficult to understand without the help of the published libretti. These often translated the mimed sections into verbalised dialogue, and during the July Monarchy, some members of the press corps quipped that people read more than they watched at the Opéra. Mime generally played as large a part as the dancing in the romantic ballets for it advanced the characters' emotional state and developed the intricacies of the plot's evolution. Its affective intensity was echoed by the accompanying music, which was shaped by the libretto's necessities and expressed by analogy the location(s) and the period of the story. Together they sentimentalised dramatically the story's circumstances.

Figure 18 Mademoiselle Marquet in *Le Dieu et la Bayadère*, opera-ballet 1830.

Giselle perhaps best epitomises the *ballet blanc* of romantic ballet. Its enduring popularity stems in part from the way it uses dance as a medium for exploring the interconnectedness of human interaction. Indeed the dancing seemed naturally induced: the logic of the plot itself called for dancing to celebrate in Act I the harvest, and in Act II the arrival of the new wili. Grisi as Giselle conjugated two character types and styles into one, since she shifted from earth- to spirit-bound as she moved from the first to the second act. "Christian ethereality" and "pagan earthliness", qualitative characteristics which Gautier applied to Grisi's two antecedent rivals, Marie Taglioni and Fanny Elssler respectively, fleshed out an opposition which highlighted the two ballerinas' contrasting dancing styles. Giselle combined the distinctive traits taken from their signature roles: Taglioni as eponymous sylph in *La Sylphide* (1831) and Elssler as Florinde in *Le Diable boiteux* (1836); or from the sylphide (Taglioni) and Effie (Lise Noblet), the two opposite (aerial and earthly) characters in *La Sylphide* itself. Grisi embodied and rearranged the two to figure as Christian earthliness in Act I with her *terre-à-terre* dancing and as pagan ethereality in Act II with her seemingly aerial pointe work and diaphanous fleetingness. As both, she upheld a social role, which cohered with the ballerina's own life and created the balletic realisation of the nineteenth-century poetic muse.

Giselle, like so many romantic ballets developed between 1830 and 1850,[7] can be read allegorically. As the numerous exegeses divulge, and as its various adaptations make manifest, the ambivalence of *Giselle*'s messages layers its appeal.[8] During its first run, its legibility depended upon its spatial and temporal structures, which referred both to the artists involved in its creation and to their own socio-historical epoch: the July Monarchy. While the fury of the wilis' abhorrence of men contrasted with the gentility of Giselle's resolve to save Albert from Queen Myrtha's revenge, Berthe's motherly protective determination prefigured her daughter's forgiving gesture, which reunited the earth-bound, non-dancing Bathilde with the divided forsworn Loys/Albert. This array of single women – the cohort of wilis and their queen, mother, daughter, fiancée – participated in the period's discourse about women in the public and private spheres: their assigned roles, their contestation about choices, the acknowledgement of their availability, together with society's indecision about the role of the Church within post-revolutionary France.[9] *Giselle*'s themes of impossible love and of love that kills demonstrate that the union of the protagonists is unrealisable because of the ideological codes at work during the period. As saviour, Giselle exemplified perfectability by enacting the feminine values of a patriarchal society; as covert witch, she troubled the prevailing social mores. Sexual desire was performed under the cover of modernity's aesthetic. The ballet brilliantly repressed the erotics of the body's staging even as it participated in the commodification of the object of desire: the dancer herself and romantic ballet.

Romantic ballet changed the way Europeans, in particular, danced and the way they looked at dance. The requirements of its technique ensconced the separation of social and theatrical dance so characteristic now of Western societies. The paradigm shift, which occurred as ballet abandoned its use of spoken language, resulted in romantic ballet's exclusive reliance on nonverbal movements. Carefully coordinated musical illustration, iconic and objective props such as a portrait or a royal accoutrement, occasional written signposts indicating location, a character's gravestone, and constructed machine-dependent effects which created the illusion of flying, all complemented the bodies' pantomime and movement to convey ballet's stories. Even as it evoked the social within its own performance, romantic ballet set

Figure 19 Cut-out paper dolls, depicting Marie Taglioni and Fanny Elssler in contemporary fashionable frocks, 1830s.

itself apart from the traditions of French courtly dancing and demarcated social dancing from theatrical dance, the social event from the spectacle.

As the French romantic movement shifted from its aristocratic leanings to address the social problems of the workings classes, ballet asserted, through its disciplined and decorous corporeal expressiveness, the harmonious disjunction of its modes of moving. It incorporated the *danse d'école* as formalised by the dancing masters serving at the Académie Royale de Musique since its inception by Louis XIV in 1661, social dancing (from the court and high society balls), hand and face pantomime and national dances (folk dancing), which added local colour, often well known to the audience, and enabled a distancing of the action from a French setting. Romantic ballet's choreographic richness emphasised the language of line, extension and verticality and a belief in the universality of the language of dance and mime. The radical new look of pointe work and adagio, of effortlessly graceful feminine bodies dressed in tutus disguised the increasingly strenuous technical virtuosity and extensive training for these performances. The silent solos of the practitioners, or the *pas de deux, pas de trois* or *pas de quatre* wove aesthetic and unified figures in space as their movements patterned their interconnectedness. The responsive corps de ballet's deployment over the entire stage around the individual performances revealed, allegorically, French notions of social hierarchy and power relations at home and abroad. It underscored as well the hierarchical divisions of the company and ballet's gendering (see Figs. 19 and 20).

Figure 20 Cut-out paper dolls, depicting Marie Taglioni and Fanny Elssler in contemporary fashionable frocks, 1830s.

Star appeal also played its part in romantic ballet's allure and accentuated the commodification of the female performer, as the directors of the Opéra sought to attract paying audiences by determining a ballerina's future with her Paris debut. Although many were foreigners, a good number of the *artistes* were products of the Académie's own school. Such dependable French dancers as the Dumilâtre and Noblet sisters, Pauline Leroux and Pauline Montessu established their reputation through hard work and often decried the unfair compensation which the foreign dancers like the Elssler sisters, and later Fanny Cerrito, reaped. By the century's second decade, pointe work, gendered as a feminine technique, appeared ubiquitous for the stars while masculine and feminine roles and styles no longer mirrored each other and became sharply gendered. The specific male and female roles undermined masculine dominance of the ballet stage. The ensuing introduction of the female travesty dancer in lead roles as well as in the corps de ballet produced a series of new role possibilities for the female dancers.[10] This trans-sexuality made ballet more and more feminine, an association which reached its apogee during the second half of the nineteenth century. Despite this feminisation of Western theatrical dance, the Opéra still employed a large number of men to dance and teach, to administer the institution and to hold the creative positions. The male stars, such as Mazilier, Barrez, Elie, Simon, Coralli, Petipa, who increasingly supported their partners during the *pas de deux*, tended to be known for their personal strengths – elevation and beaten footwork, character roles, bravoura, pantomime. They served long terms and could extend their careers as dancing masters – teaching and in some cases choreographing – options which were not readily accessible to women.[11]

By 1841, the Opéra, as state-sponsored or royal theatre or private enterprise, had accustomed its audiences to magnificent, stirring danced spectacles that served to sustain Paris's reputation as artistic capital of Europe. The fabulous shows evolved in dialogue with the current fashions and artistic trends as well as changes in knowledge bases about scientific enquiry and the new sciences, together with the codification of gender conventions which surrounded the emergence of the bourgeoisie's ideologies of gender and sexuality. As the dancers' bodies told stories against an ever more stunning representation of other historical moments and locations, the plots, which echoed their novelistic counterparts as well as the popular dramas of the time, outlined private affairs of the heart.

The ballets' titles, like their literary novelistic counterparts, often bore the (first) name of the female lead character, like la Sylphide, Giselle, la Péri, Paquita, while their subtitles, 'ballet-pantomime' or 'ballet-féerie', alluded to the hybrid nature of their mimed and danced form. Ballets frequently drew their inspiration from recognisable stories such as popular fairy tales (*Cinderella*, 1823; *Sleeping Beauty*, 1829); comic opera successes (*Nina ou la folle par amour*, 1823); or literary best-sellers (*Manon Lescaut*, 1830, adapted from Abbé Prévost's novel); *La Sylphide*, 1832 (based on Charles Nodier's short story *Trilby ou le lutin d'Argail*); *La Tempête ou l'île des génies*, 1834 (loosely inspired by Shakespeare's *Tempest*); *Le Diable amoureux*, 1840 (with key scenes from Cazotte's text). These blueprints travelled back and forth across the English Channel and circulated among the various theatrical genres, even though critics frequently denounced the librettists who borrowed effects and plot twists from the popular vaudevilles, *opéras-comiques* and *boulevard* theatre blockbusters as in the case of *Le Diable à quatre* (1845), and exerted pressure on the dancing masters to collaborate closely with their literary peers and composers.

The productions tended to fall into one of four, albeit overlapping, categories. The successful nuns' ballet in the opera *Robert le diable* determined the emergence of the *ballet blanc* as one constitutive aspect of romantic ballet. Those like *Giselle*, *La Sylphide*, *La Fille du Danube* generally incorporated an act which takes place in the world of the living and a second one which draws a male hero into a supernatural world – that of the *ballet blanc* – which he does not control. The second group of romantic ballets coheres due to the presence of a Mephistophelian or devilish character who allows the male hero to experiment with relationship choices, as in *Le Diable boiteux*, 1836, *Le Diable amoureux*, 1840, or *La Fille de marbre*, 1847. The third includes ballets like *La Péri* (1843) and *Ozaï* (1847) that expend their energy in 'exotic' settings (the Orient, an island, the Americas) and whose plots generally question French values by offering a political alternative, where, for example, women govern or determine their life choices, as in *La Révolte au sérail* (also known as *La Révolte des femmes*), 1833; *Brézilia ou la tribu des femmes*, 1835; *la Volière ou les oiseaux de Boccace*, 1838; *Nisida ou les Amazones des Açores*, 1848. The fourth grouping borrows most from melodramas with plots, which tend to portray a young woman – orphaned, exchanged and/or kidnapped, caught in another class or in a different culture's caste system – who is eventually restored to her birth rights: *La Gypsy*, 1839; *La Jolie Fille de Gand*, 1842; *Paquita*, 1846.

In allying itself with popular fiction, romantic ballet drew upon the fantastic, the exotic and the gothic. The ballets referenced the dislocation of the *Ancien Régime*'s principles and the new revolutionary institutions. They represented allegorically questions of nationalism and the erosion of the sacred as seen through the lens of marriage troubles.[12] The stories which the ballets conveyed used the fantastic to mirror human violence, betrayal, persecution, exclusion and marginalisation. In embracing a range of contradictions, the dancers embodied the romantic generation's afflictions. The ballets adopted the literary topos of forgiving the wayward male character who strays from the righteous path in order to take him back into the fold. At the same time they found a place for the female protagonist which did not infringe on male prerogatives and preserved her worth as an ideal. As sylph, wili, undine or péri – all archetypal forms – she pushed her plight to the limits of death or transformation. Whereas the *ballets d'action* used traditional, re-creational archetypes such as Pygmalion sculpting stone into living woman,[13] the romantic ballets offered a new individualism with a penchant for Narcissus's story. Framed by the proscenium arch, which served as a giant mirror, the spectators watched with fascination as the dancers performed for them a biography: their character's emotional turmoil and impassioned identity quest.

Not all romantic ballets ended with the tragic death of the ethereal "other" woman. In the modernising post-revolutionary French society, the female characters danced through a kind of cultural manipulation. They showed the fragility of their power in such a society, and exposed the male character's retrograde traditions.[14] Indeed the female characters neither championed a new order in gender relations nor in society, but rather seemed to indicate instead that the dancers, as they skimmed the ground in *glissades*, *pas de bourrée*, *jetés* and *assemblés* in a brilliant new technique, hinted at their renewed subordination in the Napoleonic civil code. Additionally, the public display of barely clothed female bodies created anxieties about women in the public and domestic or private spheres of society and complicated the social position of the female performers.

Figure 21 *The Dream of a Ballerina*. Léon F. Comerre, late nineteenth century.

As the house lights dimmed, spectators turned away from each other's appearance and looked to the stage where the performers figured as supernatural, exotic or domestic female icons in fantasy scenarios and settings, which evoked feminine private space. As an available yet unattainable character, repeatedly flitting just out of the male protagonist's reach, the dancer titillated the ogling males' desires. As the object of the gaze, whether portraying a fantastic, Spanish, Oriental, Amerindian being, or one of African descent, the female corporeal display created a voyeuristic sexualised and racialised image. The Opéra's directors used this impression and the dancers themselves to lure male spectators into subscribing to the theatre's season and paying for direct access to the *foyer de la danse*. This practice was particularly associated with Doctor Véron, who agreed to run the Opéra as a private enterprise for the first time in 1831. Thus the fashioning of the danced events contributed to the commodification of the ballerina and erased the fine line, which the artifice of the stage drew between desire and its actualisation. Increasingly, over the course of the second half of the nineteenth century, the spectacle of the dancers encoded femininity to signify eroticism and sexuality.

The commodification, to which the press reviews only added with their segmentation of the female dancing body into arrow-like legs, gracefully rounded arms, wasp-like waist and marble-white complexion, simultaneously translated her uncanny physical presence into a living incarnation of modernity's fleetingness. Whether otherworldly, supernatural, or down-to-earth, dressed as woman or young man, the female ballet dancer conferred upon romantic ballet an aura, which intrigued and yet masked and belied the financial and physical hardships most dancers endured as *rats de l'Opéra*[15] or members of the corps de ballet. In spite of the phallocentric foundation and patriarchal establishment of the Parisian Opéra, romantic ballet affected the history of bodies. Affirming roles for female dancers that carried the spotlight allowed women to envisage dancing as a career choice, and to perform in a repertoire of narrative ballets that address questions about sexual and gender identity, and socio-political configurations, as well as supporting France's national agenda to be Europe's cultural leader. The mirror, which such ballets as *Giselle* offered, reflected for some the narcissistic messages they wished for; for others, romantic ballet partnered illusion with realism to provoke the excitement of the subversive concept of a feminine art form (see Fig. 21).

11 Deadly sylphs and decent mermaids: the women in the Danish romantic world of August Bournonville

ANNE MIDDELBOE CHRISTENSEN

Is the Sylphide just a dream? Does she only exist as a supernatural being, split between dream and reality, in the thoughts of a romantic hero? Or is she a woman of flirtatious flesh and boiling blood?

There she is with her fragile wings, sitting right next to James in his armchair, shining in her pale whiteness and pointing a symbolic finger under her chin. She is so close that he could feel her fairy breath if he only woke up from his wedding nap in the armchair. When he actually does open his longing eyes, she immediately begins her unspoiled and natural dance of joy – only to vanish up the chimney without any warning the next minute...

As the spectator watches the Sylphide flying around in her beloved Scottish forest, she seems most of all to be an unreachable fairy-tale creature, collecting butterflies and looking at birds nests, just for the fun of it. As she loses her wings and her eyes go blind, with her hands creeping down her trembling arms in catastrophic fear, she is no longer a supernatural creature. At this moment, she is transformed into a mortal creature, conquered by gravity, dying in front of the man whom she loves above anything else in the world.

Silence. Tears. Curtain.

Nothing old-fashioned

Danish-French choreographer August Bournonville "borrowed" this dualistic story for his own *La Sylphide* from Filippo Taglioni's ballet at the Paris Opéra in 1832. Nevertheless, it is Bournonville's version that has stayed in the repertoire of romantic ballets – first danced in 1836 by the Royal Danish Ballet at the Royal Theatre in Copenhagen and danced ever since by the same company. Over the years, it has been staged by Bournonville-lovers such as Valborg Borchsenius together with Harald Lander in 1939, Hans Brenaa in 1967, Henning Kronstam in 1988, Dinna Bjørn in 1997, and lately Nikolaj Hübbe in 2003.

Figure 22 The Royal Danish Ballet, Season 2003/4. August Bournonville, *La Sylphide*. Gudrun Bojesen, Thomas Lund.

Even though August Bournonville created around fifty different ballets in his forty-seven years as ballet master between 1830 and 1877,[1] *La Sylphide* has survived as the ultimate favourite of both the audience and the dancers. It is one of his very few ballets with a true tragic ending – and it is the only one to deal so clearly with the bourgeois split of the new European citizen in the 1830s: the split between the compulsory marriage of convenience and the bohemian love of the heart (see Figs. 22 and 23).

The fascinating *La Sylphide* flew into the international ballet repertoire as well. In 1953, Harald Lander staged it for Grand Ballet du Marquis de Cuevas, in 1960 Elsa Marianne von Rosen reinterpretated it for the Scandinavian Ballet in Sweden – to be followed by Peter Schaufuss's dream version for London Festival Ballet in 1979, Flemming Flindt's interpretation for Dallas Ballet in 1984, and Frank Andersen's staging for Chinese National Ballet, Inoue Ballet and the Royal Swedish Ballet in 1999.

In Copenhagen, the characters of the Sylphide and James are like real-life figures, familiar to both the dancers and the spectators, very much in the same way as Hamlet and Ophelia are to actors and theatre-goers. They are considered a paradoxical and enticing mix: they become family members, they turn into reflections of human desire, or they hide symbolic meaning that performers and onlookers have to decipher.

"The Sylphide is innocent because she loves somebody", Royal Danish principal Rose Gad explained in 2002.[2] "I didn't know whether I was James

Figure 23 The Royal Danish Ballet, Season 2003/4. August Bournonville, *La Sylphide*, rehearsal.

or Alexander – whether I was standing on stage or was out somewhere flying", principal Alexander Kølpin recalled from his first, wild experience dancing James in 1987. As Nikolaj Hübbe, former principal with the Royal Danish Ballet, since 1992 with New York City Ballet, added: "Some people say: '*La Sylphide* is just something old.' But a young man, burning from affection and passion and love and lust, that is something archetypical. James is pumped by adrenaline and testosterone and dream and ideals – there is nothing old-fashioned about that."

The dualism of Bournonville seems as real as it can get. Dancers of the Royal Danish Ballet incessantly discuss the figures in rehearsal or in the canteen. However, if an outsider asks if James really dies from the powerful revenge of the witch Madge – or if he just falls to the ground in exhaustion – the answer has a condescending tone to it: "He dies of a broken heart, of course . . . " No question, falling in love with a sylph is deadly.

Danish romanticism

What we know of Bournonville's work fits perfectly into most of the existing definitions of romanticism. Let us use four central elements to analyse romanticism in ballet: *the supernaturalism, the diabolic, the exotic, and the fantasies of birth right*.[3] All these elements can be found in Bournonville's ballets.

Supernaturalism is most clearly embodied in Bournonville's flying female creature in white, *La Sylphide*. It is typical that the ballet carries the heroine's name, not that of James. This already points to a focus on the female, even though later interpretations tried to shift that focus more onto the figure of James (for instance in the version by Peter Schaufuss).

The appearance of a diabolic male figure who uses his power to take over an innocent woman also fascinated Bournonville. In *The Kermesse in Bruges* from 1851, the diabolic appears in the three gifts for three brothers, given by an old alchemist. Their magic makes the women lose their hearts and almost their bodies, in that piece at least in an innocent way. Carelis plays his magic fiddle so that Eleonore cannot stop her legs from dancing. She, of course, has no control over herself and does not understand what is happening to her body and why it reacts to his music in such a powerful way. However, this diabolic power is initially used as a joke; when it is used on his beloved Eleonore it seems a light-hearted jest – but later, that same power actually saves them from the death penalty.

The fancy for exotic settings and folkoristic dances dominate Bournonville's works. *Abdallah* from 1855, still in today's repertoire, takes place in Basra in Iraq; it shows off veils and harem dancing and sheikhs in violent conflicts. All of them are integrated into a story about Christian values of generosity, forgiveness and love.

Finally, there is the romantic fantasy about exchanged babies – the changelings who have been stolen and removed from their parents and their environment but who end up being granted their legitimate birth rights after all. This made-up dilemma is central to Bournonville's *A Folk Tale* from 1854 where the blond girl from the hills, Hilda, is discovered as the true heiress to the manor, replacing the red-haired Birthe, Hilda's troll changeling, who is forced to go back to the tough troll life.

Whereas the productions in Copenhagen have carried on the heritage from one generation of dancers to the next, the international stagings, which lack the more general cultural as well as specific dance traditions, had to invent the complete performance from scratch. If it were only for the steps, the *pas*, this would not have been very difficult since the choreographies do not contain advanced point work or complicated lifts. Nevertheless, foreign dancers often seem surprised by the hidden difficulties of the Bournonville steps that tend to look so easy.[4] A particular "Bournonville style " was recognised and internationally accepted after the first Bournonville Festival in 1979 and the scholarly discussions that took place at the same time. In the ballets, the style is most clearly demonstrated in *The Conservatory* from 1849. He allows no bravura, the arms are kept low, and the calves beat the air endlessly. At the same time the choreography never leaves a moment for the dancer to breathe in any corner or take any kind of rest. By dancing backwards upstage, the dancer has to continue conquering the space without breaking the soft flow of the movements – and without interrupting the tilted Bournonville "épaulement" where eyes focus downward, shoulders and head are directed towards the working foot – and has to question the earth-bound balance of the body as far as possible without disturbing the grace of the lines. Harmony is the ideal of every movement.

Subtle dualism

Bournonville's portrayal of dualism – the real and the unreal – at the peak of the romantic era in the 1830s and the 1840s should be considered very subtle. Admittedly, the definition of a truly romantic oeuvre might only apply to *La Sylphide* from 1836. Bournonville's later, so-called romantic ballets always seem to diverge from a strict romantic dualism. These ballets jump into a handy, happy ending instead of exploring the many deaths of the heroines. Nevertheless, their first acts often show the fascinations and temptations which distract a romantic, male hero from pursuing his proper, bourgeois plan of life. Bournonville simply never takes the romantic dualisms to their extremes. Sooner or later the hero realises what he is actually about to risk if he follows his improvidence and physical weakness – and his common sense wins.

Vilhelm in *Far from Denmark* from 1860 is such a challenged romantic male. Anchoring off the coast of South America, he has completely fallen for Rosita, his sensual South American hostess, who also charms all the other sailors on board his Danish frigate. The moment that he sees Rosita throwing his engagement ring into the water, he reacts with his Bournonville, bourgeois instincts: he throws himself into the water to rescue his golden ring – and to save his engagement to the faithful blonde, back home in Denmark (see Fig. 24).

Similarly, Edouard in *The King's Volunteers on Amager* from 1871 proves himself a reliable bourgeois male. At a Shrovetide party in a village outside Copenhagen, Edouard realises that the masked beauty he has been flirting with at the party is no one but his own wife. Embarrassed in front of every-body, he begs her for forgiveness. The male craving for women is depicted as something inevitable, just as the male apology is confirmed as a regularly emerging monologue within every marriage.

Naked secrets

Bournonville himself knew those promiscuous, masculine feelings quite well himself. As a young dancer at the Paris Opéra in the 1820s, he had

Figure 24 The Royal Danish Ballet, Season 2004/5. August Bournonville, *Far from Denmark*. Mads Blangstrup, Marie-Pierre Greve.

a love affair with a French dancer, Louise Simon. This led to one of his most well-kept secrets: in 1829, an illegitimate daughter, Louise Antoinette Simon, was born.

At this time, Bournonville was already engaged to the Swedish Helena Fredrika Håkonsson, whom he married the following year and to whom he remained married for the rest of his life. In his marriage, he had four daughters (born 1831, 1832, 1835 and 1840) and one son (born 1846) – besides an orphaned teenage girl whom he adopted in 1851. Obviously, he kept his child in Paris as a secret as its revelation would have created a serious threat both to his marriage and to his position at the Royal Theatre. What is less known, though, is that he continued to send money to the child and even visited her in Paris in the guise of her "Nordic uncle".[5]

Even though Bournonville did everything to support his reputation as a respectable family father and husband, he fancied several of his young female dancers. The most famous case is probably his affection for the young dancer Lucile Grahn whom he personally taught and coached – and allowed to mature – before her debut in 1834. His bad luck was that she did not return his feelings and, increasingly angry, rejected his advice. She was his first Sylphide but their relationship soured and became a problem impossible for the dancer to resolve. In 1839, she left for Paris and fame. In 1845, she danced herself in Jules Perrot's legendary *Pas de quatre* in London with, or more accurately, against Marie Taglioni, Carlotta Grisi and Fanny Cerrito – thus becoming the only Danish dancer who managed to leap to international fame before Toni Lander. As an example of a true, masculine seducer of his time, Bournonville had a paradoxical urge to improve the status of his female dancers. He truly wanted to lift the reputation of the Danish female corps de ballet from the French courtesan status to the position of respectable citizens. Accordingly, his hope was to make it desirable for members of the respectable middle class to send their young daughters to the ballet school at the Royal Theatre because they believed in artistic ambition, not because they were forced to do so out of poverty. He also fought for higher salaries and social security for the dancers, and in 1869 founded a special pension fund. According to Bournonville, the artists of the ballet should be granted the same rights as all other respectable citizens of Copenhagen.

However much he believed in social equality, he enjoyed being compared to his famous fellow artists of the time: the sculptor Bertel Thorvaldsen, the composer J. P. E. Hartmann, the writer Adam Oehlenschläger and the story-teller Hans Christian Andersen. All of them also shared his fascination with the exotic. In spite of his professed egalitarianism he relished royal marks of favour. In the four portraits that survive, he wears his medals with pride.[6] On the other hand he tended to take his relationship with the king for granted and in an age of monarchical absolutism that could be risky. During a perfor-mance of *Toreadoren* on 14 March 1841 a group of spectators began shouting whenever Bournonville danced and tried to hiss him off the stage. From the footlights, he had the impudence to turn to Christian VIII in his royal box and to ask for advice. His Majesty was not amused, ordered Bournonville off the stage and subsequently charged him with lese-majesty. He was punished first with house arrest and then with a six-month exile abroad without pay. The artistic result of this exile was the ballet *Napoli* of 1842.

In the so-called Danish Golden Age, women still had to face moral out-rage if they wished to abandon their roles as housewives and mothers. The urge to become a professional artist and not just to remain an educated amateur had a high price. Female writers and painters were often guarded by male professors who excluded them from respected artistic societies. Actresses were among the first to achieve public respect. They were seen as mediums, conveying poetry. Artists who used their own bodies, as ballet dancers did, seemed very far away from bourgeois decency and acceptance in Copenhagen, at least until Bournonville began his fight for "justice". He treated certain delicate matters with effective initiatives: for example, he insisted upon having the skirts of the ballerinas sewn together into wide pantalons, in order to prevent male spectators from getting more than what was considered just a glimpse of skin.

Nakedness, even the possibility of just a glimpse of flesh, posed a seri-ous threat to Christian Danish society. In the 1830s Danish Christianity worshipped the soul as superior and condescended to the body as inferior. The body on show and on stage was a constant, provocative reminder of its inherent sexual connotations. The arts were considered that sphere where the body constantly slipped through the closely guarded moral borders. In Copenhagen, the Academy of Fine Arts employed its first nude, female model in 1833; the fine arts were, contrary to ballet, after all, a very respectable art form.[7] The Danish Golden Age never really came to terms with the problem of the body, its nudity and its sexuality. There remained an underlying tension and fear. It needed the emergence of a radical modernism to allow open discussion of the place of women, marriage, freedom of thought, atheism, urban life, industrialisation and so on. In Denmark, modernism made its early mark around 1870; the literary critic Georg Brandes, one of the modernist protagonists, still attracts contemporary intellectuals with his appeal for cultural radicalism.[8]

Sweaty words

Bournonville attacked the bourgeois approach to the body with words instead – the safest way a cultivated soul in the Danish Golden Age could chose. He sensed that the ordinary bourgeois theatre-goer in little Copenhagen would probably never understand the fleshiness and physicality of muscular efforts and rehearsing in the ballet studios and the very un-aesthetic drops of sweat, which such training produced. Words were necessary and less offensive. Through his combative prose Bournonville made a name for himself within artistic and social circles. As a twenty-three-year-old in 1828 he made his debut as a writer with the booklet *Nytaarsgave for Dandseyndere* (A New Year's Gift for Dance Lovers). He soon gained an audience with his ability to express his choreographic ideals. Among his well-written books, the most popular have been his essayistic memoires *My Theatre Life* from 1848.[9] In his memoirs, Bournonville stated his "Choreographic credo"[10] which is still frequently quoted by his successors, both teachers and dancers. Several sayings are especially popular, such as: "*The beautiful* always retains the freshness of novelty, while *the astonishing* soon grows tiresome." The following is also: "The Art of Mime encompasses all the feelings of the soul. The Dance, on the other hand, is essentially an expression of joy, a desire to follow the rhythms of the music."

Furthermore, his credo has achieved a natural position of greatness and splendour in Bournonville discussions, mainly since the first Bournonville Festival in Copenhagen in 1979 when the Royal Danish Ballet celebrated the centenary of Bournonville's death. It was the first time that the specific Danish ballet tradition was seen by a wider circle of international ballet critics and historians. It was also around this time that his definition of "grace" from the "Credo" became the central explanation of the Bournonville secret:

> The Dance can, with the aid of music, rise to the heights of *poetry*. On the other hand, through an excess of gymnastics, it can also degenerate into *buffoonery*. So-called "difficult" feats can be executed by countless adepts, but the appearance of *ease* is achieved only by the chosen few. The height of the artistic skill is to know how to *conceal* the mechanical effort and strain beneath *harmonious calm*.

Diving dualism

The most joyful and harmonious ballet by Bournonville is probably *Napoli* from 1842. That sounds puzzling because in it romantic dualism between the real world and the dangers of the supernatural world turn into a question of life and death. The story is as follows: Gennaro, a fisherman, has been out on his boat together with his fiancée, Teresina, but a storm has made them fall overboard, and only Gennaro is saved. Teresina has disappeared. In his search for Teresina in a scene that takes place in the Blue Grotto somewhere in the sea outside Naples, Gennaro not only confronts the possible loss of his girlfriend but also the nature of his own sexuality, aroused by tempting mermaids. So does Teresina; she is saved by the king of the ocean, Golfo. In his Blue Grotto, he conveniently transforms her into a naiad, a mermaid, and strategically erases everything in her memory connected to her former life and her human lover Gennaro. Though mermaids are usually lesser divine pagan creatures, here a lesser mortal is granted the transformation in order to make her part of the sea god's submarine harem. The amnesia is supposed to induce feelings of physical attraction. Golfo almost succeeds in his seduction.

We can thus justify calling Bournonville a romantic because he extends the typical and subtle romantic dualism to the female character of *Napoli* and not just to the male. Gennaro delays his search for Teresina because he meets some irresistible naiads, glittering with seaweed in their long, wet hair. Teresina too confronts her sexuality as she flirts with the muscular king of the sea. At the last moment Gennaro disrupts the scene; he finally has found the way into the secret cave – only to discover that Teresina does not recognise him. Desperately, he points to the medallion of the Holy Madonna and the miracle works: Teresina recalls her past and because she can now remember her Christian faith she is restored to her old human form in her old dress.[11] Teresina is transformed back from a nautical creature into a human woman in love with a man, just as earthly as herself. To the heart-warming story are added the technical effects and stunts so typical of the romantic theatre (see Fig. 25).

The tale of Teresina and Gennaro has received many interpretations; fundamentally it is about a girl developing into a woman, rendered in the

Figure 25 The Royal Danish Ballet, Season 2004/5. August Bournonville, scene from *Napoli*, Act III.

way Marius Petipa and Pyotr Tchaikovsky pursued in their ballets some fifty years later. The story about the teenage Aurora in *The Sleeping Beauty*, who has to choose a man to marry, or the little girl Clara in *The Nutcracker*, revolve around that same exciting and terrifying moment when they realise that they are about to grow up. They dream about mice or cats, large, enchanted animalistic forces fighting not only their noble princes but above all enticing them into a sensuous world.

Teresina, the naughty mermaid and seductress, flirts more in her thoughts than with her legs. Bournonville manages to provide her with the necessary bourgeois strength: She does not give in to her instincts. Her bodily desires are controlled and then defeated by her religious faith: her body behaves itself and stays decent, thanks to the power of the Madonna. Her proper reputation is saved; Teresina is in the end a well-behaved mermaid.

This second act has challenged later choreographers. If they want to convert their inspirations into new versions of the ballet, they usually begin where Bournonville's second act left off: with the unanswered and unexplored dilemmas that occur when one dives into the subconscious. Bournonville could not have gone any further without seriously endangering his own and his society's sense of propriety, which demanded that a story always end with an intact couple. Psychologically focused artists such as Bournonville pioneers Elsa Marianne von Rosen and Allan Fridericia in the 1970s went further and challenged the notion of intactness. Dinna

Bjørn and Frank Andersen developed this idea even further in several of their stagings of *Napoli*, particularly in their latest version of the ballet for the Finnish National Ballet in 2005. More recently, modern dance forms of *Napoli* interpretations by Tim Rushton in his psychological, abstract style and by Thomas Lund and Johan Holten in their underwater video fusion[12] show the abiding fascination of the work.

The Danish Golden Age more or less seriously flirting with the ideas of romanticism is most interestingly portrayed in *A Folk Tale* from 1854. For once, Bournonville chose to bring a Danish folk tale into a ballet and focused on the superstition of peasants in the country. However, it is the young nobleman Ove who feels the longing for something more than a future in his manor house. He stays in the woods after a picnic with his angry fiancée Birthe and there experiences the powers of the subterranean creatures in the Danish summer night: A hill opens in front of his eyes and trolls are sitting there underground, hammering away at their forges. In their midst is Hilda, a beautiful, light creature, who carries a magic, golden cup, and who looks like a princess with a secret. In the end the power of the trolls is broken and Ove celebrates his wedding to Hilda by dancing their special Wedding Waltz around the maypole in the light midsummer night. That same waltz by Niels W. Gade is played at every Danish wedding even today.

A Folk Tale takes Bournonville's romanticism into a Danish reality where dreams come true. As such it is the complete opposite of the nightmare of the exotic supernaturalism of *La Sylphide*. Hilda proves that born virtue always defeats supernatural forces. And that true happiness only can be achieved in the real world. In a way, Hilda can be seen as a "happy end" transformation of the Sylphide, or as the tamed bourgeois version of the same dream of Bournonville.

Bournonville's ballets and their dualistic figures have been saved over time by the loyalty and enthusiasm of the dancers and the directors of the Royal Danish Ballet. Since the first Bournonville Festival in 1979, initiated by ballet director Henning Kronstam and assistant ballet director Kirsten Ralov, the Bournonville heritage has been treated as the international treasure it truly is. For the third Bournonville Festival at the Royal Theatre in 2005, just as for the second Bournonville Festival in 1992, the still-existing Bournonville repertoire reappeared, consisting of *La Sylphide* (1836), *Napoli* (1842), *The Conservatory* (1849), *Kermesse in Bruges* (1851), *A Folk Tale* (1854), *Abdallah* (1855),[13] *La Ventana* (1856), *Far from Denmark* (1860) and *The King's Volunteers on Amager* (1871) – and the *pas de deux* from *The Flower Festival in Genzano* (1858). Furthermore, the festival programme offered the two cheerful *pas de deuxs Polka Militaire* (1842) and *Jockey Dance* (from *From Siberia to Moscow* 1876).[14]

Lately, the company has had severe problems in maintaining its Bournonville tradition. On the one hand there is the influence of other dancing styles and on the other a massive intake of foreign dancers without the specific Bournonville style in their bodies. The fact that the company had five directors in eight years spanning 1994 to 2002, each with differing approaches to Bournonville, made it hard to perform the repertoire.[15] It seems that the third Bournonville Festival in 2005 has inspired the Royal Danish Ballet once again to take pride in the Bournonville tradition. It has also proved that the ongoing survival of this tradition depends upon the dancers' enthusiasm about one work above all: *La Sylphide*, the ballet with the love story that any dancer in the company would do almost anything to dance. The survival of Bournonville's ballet depends more on its peculiar erotic and social meanings: however adorable the troll queen Hilda might seem, it is the Sylphide who creates the ultimate attraction and who comes closest to Bournonville's concept of a truly romantic female, a dream creation of male imagination about feminine eroticism. As principal dancer and director Nikolaj Hübbe says about his dedication to *La Sylphide* in Ulrik Wivel's film *I Love You* (2005):[16] "I am part of that story." Apparently, the sylph is not just a dream.

12 The orchestra as translator: French nineteenth-century ballet

MARIAN E. SMITH

The Paris Opéra stood as perhaps the most influential house for ballet in nineteenth-century Europe until the ascendance of the Imperial Russian Theatres in the 1880s. Its stage attracted the talents of the great choreographers and dancers of Europe, and its audiences witnessed some of the most important phenomena in nineteenth-century ballet: the rivalry of Vestris and Duport in the first decade; the birth of the romantic style in the cloister scene of *Robert le diable* in 1831; the controversial failure (accompanied by the derisive whistles of the balletomaniac Jockey Club) of Richard Wagner's *Tannhäuser* in 1861. At the Opéra, audiences not only insisted that ballets be included within opera, but exalted independent ballets, sometimes praising them more highly than the operas with which they shared the stage.[1] The house's directors, with their generous budgets and top-notch teams of choreographers, composers, designers and librettists, oversaw the creation of new ballets at a steady pace – including such staples of today's repertoire as the other-worldly *Giselle* (1841), the heroic *Le Corsaire* (1856) and the comic *Coppélia* (1870) – and by popular demand exported many of them to other houses in Milan, Copenhagen, Moscow and Philadelphia, to name a few.

From century's beginning to century's end, custom at the Opéra dictated that for each new ballet a new musical score be produced. These scores did much more than provide background music; they helped constitute the ballet itself. Indeed, because they were tailor-made for each ballet, these scores stand as the best eyewitnesses to the century of stage action in question here. In this short chapter I shall offer an overview of this music, including its subdivision into two distinct types – dance music (including specialised music composed for "national" or "character" dance), and pantomime or dramatic music – followed by sketches of some of the most important composers of the century.

The ballet composer's explanatory mission

Perhaps the most striking feature of ballet music in the early decades of the century, at least to the latter-day observer, is its frequent use of borrowed music. Some ballets were taken over from comic operas – for instance, Mozart's *Le nozze di Figaro* – and these operas' original aria melodies were deployed in the corresponding scenes in the danced version. But even in operas with newly contrived plots and characters, composers typically made free use of pre-existing music, weaving it together with their own, not only to please the ear but to help the audience follow the action. The critic Castil-Blaze extolled both advantages as he bristled at the lack of borrowed music in *Alfred le grand* (1822) and complained, a bit prematurely, of the decline of musical borrowing by ballet composers:

> Un ballet étoit un concert plein d'intérêt, où tous les genres de musique se réunissoient pour plaire au moyen d'une séduisante variété ... D'ailleurs ... les airs d'opéra, même, après avoir perdu leurs paroles, conservent une expression mémorative bien précieuse pour expliquer les énigmes du langage mimique, tandis qu'une musique neuve et sans originalité ne frappe point assez l'imagination pour que son expression soit sentie.[2]

> (A ballet was an interesting concert, where all the genres of music came together to please the audience with seductive variety ... Moreover ... opera airs, even after losing their words, preserved an expressive memory of them, very precious for explaining the enigmas of the language of mimic. I would not [underestimate] the power of known melodies, and of the clarity they bring to the silent dialogues of pantomime.)

The relative novelty of wordless ballet in the early nineteenth century helps explain the need for musical interpretations of these "enigmas". In 1800, only twenty-odd years had passed since the advent of the Noverre-style *ballet d'action*, the narrative ballet. But at the Opéra, a tradition-bound house, such wordless narrative works, independent from the operas with which they had long been intertwined, still struck some stodgy observers as new-fangled as late as the 1830s and 1840s. Critics expressed in no uncertain terms the high expectations they held of ballet composers, revealing an assumption largely foreign to today's ballet aesthetic: that music must explain the story.

> La musique des ballets a son caractère particulier; elle sera plus accentuée, plus parlante, plus expressive que la musique d'opéra, car elle n'est pas destinée seulement à accompagner et à rehausser les paroles du poète, mais à être elle-même le poème tout entire.[3]

> (Ballet music has a particular character; it is more accented, more parlante [i.e. communicative], more expressive than opera music, because it is destined not only to accompany and enhance the librettists' words, but to be the entire libretto itself.)

En général, ce n'est pas de la musique qu'on demande à un compositeur de ballet-pantomime; c'est un orchestre qui soit la traduction, le commentaire du texte qu'on aurait pu ne pas saisir.[4]

(Generally, one does not ask for music from a ballet-pantomime composer, but for an orchestra that is the translation, the commentary of the text, which would not otherwise be understandable.)

si la musique n'exprime pas les sentimens des acteurs, qu'y a-t-il pour les exprimer? Les grands mouvements de bras sont une pauvre langue.[5]

(if music doesn't express the feelings of players, what else is there to express them? Arm movements are a poor language.)

[La] musique ... a mission d'expliquer ou de traduire [les scènes].[6]

(The music has a mission to explain or translate [the scenes].)

Le compositeur est presque chargé de raconter l'action.[7]

(The composer is virtually charged with telling the action.)

par leur caractère, par leur expression et par leur style, les mélodies peuvent and doivent compléter la signification du geste et du jeu de la physionomie.[8]

(By their character, their expression and their style, the melodies [in ballet music] can and must complete the meaning of the gestures and the play of the physiognomy.)

Most of the devices composers employed to fulfil this mission might strike us today as particularly explicit. One of these is the *air parlant*, used well into the 1840s, an excerpt of texted music from opera or popular song, sometimes only a phrase or less, which could make particular words pop into the spectator's mind.[9] (In Jean-Madeleine Schneitzhoeffer's *La Tempête*, for example, the orchestra plays "Je sens mon coeur qui bat, qui bat" from the moment in Grétry's *Richard Coeur de Lion* when Lea begins to fall in love.)[10]

Music often provided the sound of the human voice too. In some cases, a solo instrument played a recitative as performers on stage mimed. (A fine example may be heard today in the trombone "voice" of a street entertainer in August Bournonville's *Napoli*, first produced in Copenhagen in 1842.) In others, the rhythm of the music matched that of key phrases of text written in the libretto (for instance, "écoutez-moi" (listen to me) in a key scene in *La Somnambule*, 1827). In still others, composers used syncopation, dotted rhythms, a wide tessitura or a phrase-ending uptilt to imitate the sound of spoken French.[11] The instrumental voice became more subtle by the 1840s and 1850s but continued to be heard in ballet scores – for instance, the trilling violins and flutes that give us the sound of Paquita's rivals' derisive laughter in *Le Diable boiteux* (Gide, 1836); the syncopated clarinet and oboe melody that allow us to hear Berthe's admonition of the village girls to stop waltzing in *Giselle* (Adam, 1841); the high woodwind solo at the beginning of *Coppélia* (Delibes, 1870) for Swanilda's opening mime monologue. Thus, even when ballet music lost the blatantly vocal quality of the *parlante* music composed earlier in the century, it carried forward the tradition of acknowledging ballet characters' implicit vocality, and helped to deepen the performers' portrayals.

Recurring musical motifs evoking concepts, characters and emotional states also appeared in several Parisian ballet scores, including *Manon Lescaut* (Halévy, 1830), *Giselle* and *Coppélia*, taking their place among the constellation of other devices that helped the audience follow the action, and at the same time allowing the audience to hear for themselves the transformation of characters and emotions as the plot unfolded. Perhaps because Richard Wagner's anti-Terpsichorian stance is well known, little attention has been paid to the likely influence of Parisian ballet's recurring motifs upon the German master, who used the device in part to the same didactic end. Moreover, unlike the operatic and non-theatrical precursors of the Wagnerian leitmotif, recurring themes in French ballet were composed in an atmosphere in which audiences had made plain their desire for the intelligibility that could be furnished by the music.

Dramatic or pantomime music

It was largely in the dramatic or pantomime scenes, as opposed to the dance scenes, that the musical cues mentioned above are to be found. Though ballet composers were expected to write dance music too, and plenty of it, the dramatic segments constituted a vital component of the ballet and could take up a large portion of stage minutes – nearly half in some cases. They shrank in number and length as the century wore on and danced segments grew longer, yet remained a vital feature of ballet past 1900, for the simple reason that character and story remained crucial elements in ballet.

The music required for dramatic scenes served a wide variety of functions: it could express a character's feelings or reflect personality or ethnicity, set a mood, establish locale, and imitate ambient sounds such as a village band, a human voice or a thunderstorm. Composers deftly switched from type to type as the need arose. Consider, for example, the opening minutes of *Giselle*. At curtain-up, Adolphe Adam provides rustic music (with a drone in the lower instruments) to help situate the scene in a tiny Silesian village. The gamekeeper Hilarion soon appears, his furtive melody (played by lower strings) reflecting his mission to uncover information about his rival Albrecht. As he mimes his love for Giselle and points towards her cottage, the music becomes sweet and soft, but turns harsh for a moment as he points at Albrecht's dwelling. (These stage directions are indicated in the score.) Shortly thereafter Albrecht arrives, in the midst of a heated argument with his squire Wilfride, which is well brought out by tempestuous music. The ins and outs of their conversation are deftly followed by Adam, who provides warm, gentle music for Albrecht's declaration of love for Giselle and anxious, louder music for Wilfride's objections to his master's scheme to wear a disguise and woo the innocent peasant girl. Finally Wilfride accedes to his master's wishes and leaves him alone, and as the scene ends peacefully Adam matches Albrecht's words of relief: "Il est parti" (he has gone). Shortly thereafter Albrecht knocks on Giselle's door – pizzicato strings allow us to hear it – and Giselle makes her first appearance to the strains of a gay waltz, which helps express both her national character and her love of dance.

Dance music

Music for dancing was composed in a style more familiar to us today than that of the dramatic music, in part because of the enduring popularity of dance numbers often excerpted from such Parisian scores as Adam's *Giselle* (1841) and *Le Corsaire* (1856)[12] and Delibes's *Coppélia* (1870), and from later Russian scores carrying this style forward, including Ludwig Minkus's *Don Quixote* (1869) and *La Bayadère* (1877), Tchaikovsky's *Swan Lake* (1877) and Alexander Glazunov's *Raymonda* (1898). Indeed, when one thinks of nineteenth-century ballet music, one thinks of this style, and its familiar features make it instantly recognisable as such. These include regularity of phrasing and simplicity of melody, harmony and texture (two-voice textures are common, and often, for solo dances, composers wrote simply a solo for an obbligato melodic instrument and a pizzicato accompaniment), repetition by the full orchestra of a melody first stated by solo instrument, punctuation of sparsely textured passages with occasional tutti chords, extended tutti cadences increasing in volume and sometimes quickening in tempo towards the end, and a heavy reliance upon repetition, both of melodies and of catchy rhythmic patterns. Often, dances are preceded by an anticipatory-sounding introduction dwelling on the dominant, music often originally choreographed for a couple engaging in a "shall we dance?"/ "no – well, yes" dialogue.

The divertissement

Dance music found its most concentrated use in the divertissements that were featured in ballets and operas when the action was temporarily halted.

Such dancing was always carefully accounted for dramatically with such rationales as village festivals, masked balls, entertainments for royalty, celebrations of weddings and military victories. Moreover – this point is important for comprehending the popularity and accessibility of the ballet divertissement – a strong affinity existed between ballroom and stage. First, the overall musical structure of the ballroom dance set and the staged divertissement was roughly the same: a long series of short numbers in varying keys and metres, which could make for a pleasing variety of mood (a sweet and sentimental adagio, for example, was likely to be followed by a brisk and vigorous allegro). So too did the melody types, phrase structure and harmonic language of the dance music for the stage match those of ballroom music. It was also customary to end both *bals* and divertissements with a rousing galop, a fast dance in 2/4 with a strong back beat, the musical forerunner to the cancan.[13] Composers liked to end the grand *pas de deux* with a galop as well, a custom extended later in Russia in *Don Quixote* and *Swan Lake*.

Not only music but choreography easily glided back and forth between stage and ballroom. So receptive was the Paris Opéra to social dance fashion that dances new to the city's ballrooms in the 1830s and 1840s – for instance, the polka and galop – were virtually guaranteed to appear on the Opéra's stage.[14] By the same token, the Opéra's ballet stars sometimes ignited social dance crazes with their spectacular, crowd-pleasing performances of new social dances. And staged ball scenes at the Opéra looked so familiar and inviting that spectators occasionally tried to join in the dancing onstage, a reaction that confirms the close connection between social and theatrical dance. This familiarity was further fostered by the use of dance music from ballets and operas by orchestra leaders in ballrooms, and the prevalence of piano arrangements of such music for playing at home.

National or "character" dance

Among the favourite dances of stage and ballroom were so-called "national" dances, or "character dances" as they are more commonly called today. Though character dance had found a place on the Opéra's stage since well before the period under consideration here, Fanny Elssler's famous *cachucha* (danced in a scene from *Le Diable boiteux*, 1836) sparked an enthusiasm for the genre that carried through for decades, and choreographers commonly created both character dances appropriate to the setting of the work – like a jig in Scotland [*sic*] – and "foreign" dances as well, usually with the rationale that entertainers representing distant lands were dancing for the pleasure of onlookers. (This rationale was highly believable, for such entertainments did indeed take place as the revellers rested during real-life balls.) Composers, for their part, called upon a vocabulary of musical types, which like the steps and gestures used by choreographers, and the props, costumes and landscapes used by designers, were meant to convey an "authentic" sense of place. Germany was often signified by waltzes, France by minuets, Spain, by boleros, the Middle East by exotic-sounding minor-key oboe solos, Poland by mazurkas and *krakowiaks*, Sicily by tarantellas, Hungary by the *csárdás* and so forth. Occasionally, when generic "Others" from faraway lands were to be depicted, composers turned to the triangle, bass drum and cymbals that had signified Turks in the eighteenth-century West. Composers also made it a point to write music generally appropriate to the geographical setting and local character; Adolphe Adam, for example, was praised for demonstrating the "grace, the suavity and the vaporous poetry of the Germanic deities that inspired the composer";[15] Delibes's *Coppélia* featured rustic village music, mazurkas and a stirring *csárdás*, helping bring life to the Galician (Austro-Hungarian) setting; Messager's *Deux pigeons* imitated the gypsy violin, befitting the presence of gypsy characters. For "character-variety" divertissements, composers offered music to match each ethnic character as they appeared one by one. Even the wilis in *Giselle* – a few of them at least – had national identities, musically identifiable in their ball scene. National dance remained a popular feature of dance scenes, both in opera and ballet, and its continuing presence in the current repertoire (*Swan Lake* and *The Nutcracker*, for instance), serves as a reminder of its living quality for much of the nineteenth century, and of the crucial role that music played in bringing it to life.

Critical comments in the nineteenth century

By what standards did nineteenth-century critics assess ballet music? In the first few decades, as noted above, they often praised it for its sheer helpfulness in making the plot understood. Throughout the century they commended lively, graceful, varied, tasteful, inventive, danceable ("dansante") scores, expecting appropriateness to the setting and story. Melodies were to be accessible, plentiful, pretty and fresh, and orchestration interesting and colourful.

Occasionally, too, critics disclosed their assumptions about ballet music's place within the larger scheme of things. Most agreed it should be lighter in tone, more transparent, less complex, less ponderous than opera, and "in a more facile, more relaxed style", as one critic put it in 1863.[16] Any score too weighty or too rich in intrinsic interest was liable to be deemed operatic or symphonic.[17] In 1844 one critic of *Eucharis* wrote: "[Deldevez] would be more at ease with an opera libretto than a ballet ... his

talent is serious, elevated, instead of light and coquettish."[18] Another wrote
of *Le Diable amoureux* in 1840, "[Reber's] talent is better fitted to the
symphony" – perhaps because it was, in the assessment of a more favourable
observer, worth hearing even with one's back turned to the stage.[19] Lightness
could be taken too far, however: "one mustn't lose all sense of propriety, nor
forget that we are in the house where *Guillaume Tell* and *Les Huguenots* are
performed. It's a good idea to keep a distance between the Paris Opéra and
the neighbourhood tavern" – a distance one critic believed was breached by
Cesare Pugni in *Diavolina* (1863).[20]

In the 1880s, the debate raging in France over Wagnerianism seeped into
critics' assessments of ballet music's proper tone. A reviewer of Widor's *La
Korrigane* (1880), for example, found in ballet a synthesis of symphony and
drama – a quality ascribed by pro-Wagnerians to their hero:

> [ballet music is] a sort of free symphony in which [the young masters of the
> modern school] can let their imaginations roam freely. The melody follows
> the movement of the ballerina and the expression of the gesture; one
> thought is scarcely expressed before another one comes up to replace it.
> This art is both improvised and carefully planned (soigné) at the same
> time – a special art in which symphony merges with drama.[21]

This balance between the "improvised and soigné" struck one critic as lacking in Edouard Lalo's *Namouna* (1882). Though admired by the young
Debussy, among others, this score was thought to be too studied, and, moreover, its harmonic language too tangled – qualities found in Wagner's music
by his detractors. Lalo wrote good symphonies and operas, observed a critic,
but *Namouna* suffered from

> le raffinement excessif de l'idée musicale et d'inutiles, sinon regrettables,
> dissonances qui viennent troubler le cours et le mouvement d'une partition
> de ballet nullement appelée à prêcher les dogmes de la musique dite
> nouvelle. L'art de moduler à l'infini, avec plus ou moins de transition, a pris
> en ces derniers temps des proportions intolérables, – a ce point que l'on ne
> sait le plus souvent le ton dans lequel on se trouve. Par suite, des accords se
> précipitent, s'entre-choquent d'une façon peu harmonieuse; qu'on nous
> serve ce regal qui emport la bouche, puisque c'est la mode aujourd'hui,
> mais du moins, comme disait Rossini, qu'on y mette un peu de sucre.[22]

> (excessive refinement of musical ideas, and the useless – if not deplorable –
> dissonances which disturb the flow and sparkle of a ballet score. Ballet
> music is not at all appropriate for preaching the dogmas of the so-called
> new music. The art of modulating infinitely, with or without benefit of
> transition, has taken on intolerable proportions lately, to the point where
> you often don't even know what key you're in. As a result, chords dash into
> each other in a most inharmonious fashion. Serving up a feast so hot it takes

the roof off your mouth — that's the style these days. But at least, as Rossini said, you can add a little sugar.)

The very notion of defining ballet music as a separate genre with particular characteristics – serious, "soigné", improvisatory, light, "dansante", or otherwise – was discarded by the originators of "new ballet" in the early twentieth century. As Michel Fokine famously proclaimed in 1914:

> In contradistinction to the older ballet [the new ballet] does not demand "ballet music" of the composer as an accompaniment, to dancing; it accepts music of every kind, provided only that it is good and expressive . . . It does not impose any specific "ballet" conditions on the composer . . . but gives complete liberty to [the composer's] creative powers.[23]

Thus did the ballet world acquire the great commissioned scores of Stravinsky (including *Le Sacre du printemps*, 1913, composed with much liberty indeed), Ravel, Prokofiev, Copland, Khachaturian, and a host of others, as well as the habit of making choreographies to music never intended for dance.

Yet, while it is true that ballet benefited when traditional restrictions on composers were lifted, and an inexhaustible supply of non-dance music opened up to choreography – overdue developments as the young moderns of the early twentieth century saw it – some of the music composed for the nineteenth-century Parisian ballet remains as vital a part of the dance repertory today as ever. Aside from the continuing currency of such scores as *Giselle* and *Coppélia*, without which these ballets would likely not have survived into this century, others have been retrieved from the archives and used to great effect with new choreographies, including Donizetti's dance music for *Dom Sebastien* (Balanchine's *Donizetti Variations*), Verdi's for *Les Vêpres siciliennes* (MacMillan's *The Four Seasons*),[24] Delibes's for *La Source* (Balanchine's short ballet of the same name, and a *pas de deux* by John Cranko) and Ferdinand Hérold's full-length *La Fille mal gardée*, brought to Frederick Ashton's attention by the dance historian Ivor Guest, arranged by John Lanchbery and used in the Royal Ballet's highly successful production of that ballet.[25] Indeed, the great store of French ballet music remaining untouched in the archives could be profitably mined even more, for the necessary qualities of danceability and narrative vigour originally invested in the best of these scores remain as vibrant today as they were when the music was composed.

Composers

By way of concluding this study, I offer sketches of Adolphe Adam and Léo Delibes, the two most admired ballet composers in nineteenth-century France, followed by brief discussions of a few others of note.

Adolphe Adam

As a youth, Adam paid the Opéra-Comique's triangle player 40 sous for the privilege of taking his place for one performance. This enthusiasm for the theatre continued to manifest itself throughout his career, as he became one of most successful composers in Parisian history of comic opera and ballet, as well as founder of the Opéra-National in 1847 (forced by the political disturbances of 1848 to close its doors), Professor of Composition at the Conservatoire and writer of newspaper critiques as lively and open-hearted as his music. Most of his fourteen ballets scores (ten composed for Parisian premieres) were met with the unanimous approbation of critics, and when *La France musicale* declared in 1847 that the Opéra had "chosen the master of masters in this field to compose the music for the new ballet", there was no doubt about whom they meant.[26] Adam's ballets are notable for their danceability, apt characterisations, atmosphere and moment-to-moment adherence to the action. A particularly masterful example is the Act I finale of *Giselle* (structured like a grand opera finale), with its numerous characters, climactic confrontation, rapid mood changes, and the mad scene featuring Giselle's delusional recollections and death. Less known but equally effective is the opening of *La Jolie Fille de Gand*, Act II, in which the title character wakes up in a Venetian palace, takes a dancing lesson, meets her supercilious rival and quarrels with her, and then sets forth for the ball after hearing the sounds of carnival music. In both cases, Adam expertly interweaves strains of alluring dance music with *parlante* and descriptive music, focusing the audience's attention on the moods or actions of now this character's and now that one's, seamlessly sweeping the audience through changes in mode, tempo, metre, dynamics and instrumentation, making use of every gradation of volume from silence to full orchestra at *fortissimo*. Adam was also adept at keeping the audience's attention on the stage instead of the orchestra pit. For instance, he sometimes repeats a melody several times in mime scenes, as silent-film pianists did many decades later, but with small adjustments when needed, adapting to the particulars of the conversation and the moods of its interlocutors, as his annotations demonstrate. Like today's best film scores, Adam's ballets were never intended in their entirety for concert performance, but to serve as a vital partner in the drama.

A key to Adam's success was his sheer enjoyment of ballet composition; he fondly recalled his collaboration on *Giselle* with Carlotta Grisi and Jules Perrot "in my salon" and spiritedly rebutted critics' suggestions that he save his best ideas for opera: "Nothing pleases me more than the task for which the inspiration comes from observing the feet of dancers ... [Critics] scold me for using the springtime of my life in the production of [ballets] but so be it. This work is my muse and my life."[27]

Léo Delibes

Coppélia (1870), though Delibes's first ballet commission as sole composer (he shared compositional duties with Ludwig Minkus on *La Source*, 1866), shows his rare talent and sure-handedness in depicting stage action and character. Noël Goodwin has even averred that Delibes "could be called the first impressionist composer, for he shared similar principles with his contemporaries in pictorial art: he made colour and rhythm the most important elements in his compositions".[28] Indeed, Delibes's command over these two elements ensures the effectiveness of his characterisations; each major figure in this ballet (including the life-sized doll of the ballet's title) is strongly invested with musical character – Dr Coppelius's rhythm, for instance, is off-kilter and his sonorities thin and peculiar (foretelling Drosselmeyer in *Nutcracker*); Franz's music sounds eager and a bit impetuous. Of further note is the charming music of the character-variety scene (in which Swanilda, impersonating the inanimate Coppélia, comes to life, dances a bolero and a jig). The finale, a dedication of the new village clock, wittily and sweetly demonstrates Delibes's wide range in affect and style, with its lovely Waltz of the Hours and dances for each of the occasions for which the new clock will chime: dawn, prayers, work, village weddings, war (is this a light-hearted tribute to Beethoven's "Battle" Symphony and "Rage Over a Lost Penny"?) and peace.

Delibes demonstrates equal virtuosity in his only other full-length ballet, *Sylvia* (1876), though it is entirely different in spirit, since the scenario (based on the sixteenth-century pastoral drama *Aminta* of Torquato Tasso) aimed to be loftier and more sedate than the broadly comic *Coppélia*. The score, with its rich and full orchestration "reveals the hand of a master symphonist", wrote one critic, finding that "the picturesque choice of themes, the expressive variety of melodies, the attractive improvisation of harmonies, and the highly-coloured orchestration make this ballet, to my mind, an exquisite work, perhaps too refined and too delicate for the glare of the footlights".[29]

Others found the music too obscure (as did some of *Carmen's* first listeners), though today we would scarcely concur; its harmonic language is indeed more complicated than that of earlier ballet scores in Paris, and Diana's nymphs sound downright Walkurian. Yet, Delibes resisted the Germanic influence embraced by some of his contemporaries (for instance, César Franck) and made his loyalties to the French spirit explicit:

> Je professe pour Wagner une admiration sans borne. C'est un génie
> admirable ... Mais j'éstime qu'en musique, comme en tout autre art, chaque
> nation doit conserver son génie personnel, que les musicians français
> doivent conserver leur tempérament propre, en lieu de s'efforcer à des

imitations stériles. Pour ma part, je suis reconnaissant à Wagner des émotions très vives que sa musique m'a fait ressenti, des enthousiasmes qu'elle a soulevés en moi. Mais si, come auditeur, j'ai voué au maître allemand une profound admiration, je me refuse, comme producteur, à l'imiter.[30]

(My esteem for Wagner is boundless – he is a genius well worthy of admiration . . . But I reckon that in music, as in all the other arts, each nation must keep its own particular spirit; that French musicians must conserve their own temperament instead of trying to make sterile imitations. For my part, I am grateful to Wagner for the vivid emotions his music brought out in me, and for the rapturous feelings it raised. But if as a listener I admire the German master, I refuse, as a composer, to imitate him.)

Sylvia is widely considered the finest ballet score before *Swan Lake* (the first version of which appeared only a year later); Tchaikovsky himself declared *Sylvia* the better of the two. Upon his death, Delibes was deemed "incontestably without rival" as a ballet composer, and George Balanchine, in the next century, called him "one of the three great musicians of the dance", along with Tchaikovsky and Stravinsky.[31]

Other composers

Among the Opéra's many other notable musicians who produced ballet scores during the nineteenth century are the following (NB work lists in this section are not necessarily complete):

Pierre Gardel, the great ballet master whose career at the Opéra spanned the years of the turn of the century, including the tumultuous years of the Revolution. A fine violinist and dancer (who both danced the menuet and played the violin in *La Dansomanie*, 1800), Gardel owned copies of Haydn's music, and is likely to have arranged, or helped arrange, ballet scores for some of his choreographies. (*Le Jugement de Paris*, 1793, *Une demi-heure de Caprice*, 1804, *Le Retour des Lys*, 1814).

Ferdinand Hérold, whose early death left unfulfilled his ambition to compose grand opera. He composed and arranged witty and vibrant ballet scores in the late 1820s (including *La Fille mal gardée*, 1828), and composed comic operas so popular that his name, along with Mozart's and Rossini's, was inscribed in gold on the curtain at La Scala.[32] (*La Somnambule*, 1827, *La Belle au bois dormant*, 1829.)

Fromental Halévy, a major composer of French opera whose sole ballet *Manon Lescaut* (1830) is admired for its careful incorporation of eighteenth-century melodies (including Rameau) to evoke the period setting at the Opéra in the eighteenth century.

Jean-Madeleine Schneitzhoeffer, tympanist and composer of *La Sylphide*, 1832, striking for its evocations of Scotland in the divertissements, its dreaminess and its use of "airs parlants". This work remains a popular staple of the Opéra repertoire today. (August Bournonville, reportedly because of the high price of the Schneitzhoeffer score, commissioned music from Løvenskjold for his production of this ballet, first performed in Denmark in 1836 and still widely performed today.) (*Le Séducteur du village*, 1818, *Zémire et Azor*, l824, *Mars et Vénus*, l826, collab. *L'Orgie*, 1831, *La Tempête*, l834.)

Frederich Burgmüller, composer of over 100 piano pieces, as well as the music for the "peasant *pas de deux*" in *Giselle* (including his waltz "Souvenirs de Ratisbonne"), interpolated shortly before the premiere of that ballet. (*La Péri*,1843, collab. *Lady Henriette*,1844.)

Edouardo Deldevez, violinist and conductor, and composer of *Paquita*, 1846, of which he recalled that Mazilier waited to choreograph the ballet "until after he had heard the music and meditated for a long time upon it; until he had profited from the scenic intentions of the musician".[33] (collab. *Lady Henriette*, 1844, *Eucharis*, 1844, collab. *Vert-Vert*, 1851.)

André Messager, an ardent fan of Wagner, admired by Saint-Saëns and Fauré, and composer of comic operas and of *Les deux pigeons* (1886, rechoreographed by Frederick Ashton in 1961). (*Fleur d'oranger*, 1878, *Les Vins de France*, *Mignons et villains*, 1879, all for the Folies-Bergère.)

Ambroise Thomas, best known for his operas *Mignon* (1866) and *Hamlet* (1868) (collab. *Le Gipsy*, 1839, *Betty*, 1846), and composer of the ballet *La Tempête* (1889).

Charles Marie Widor, the great organist at St-Sulpice in Paris for sixty-four years, best known for his organ symphonies. His theatrical debut, the ballet *La Korrigane* (1880) (deemed a "master stroke" by *La Revue et gazette musicale*)[34] includes a syncopated mazurka clog dance, a gigue in the Breton style, and a number for humming chorus and typophone (a keyboard percussion instrument invented by Victor Mustel, and forerunner to the celesta made famous twelve years later by Tchaikovsky in *The Nutcracker*).[35]

13 Russian ballet in the age of Petipa

LYNN GARAFOLA

On 24 May 1847 Marius Petipa, a young French-born dancer and ballet master, landed in St Petersburg.[1] He was not the first dance artist to brave the long journey to Russia and the rigours of a Russian winter, nor even the only Petipa; only five months later, his own father signed a contract to teach the senior classes at the Imperial Ballet School.[2] Like so many other danseurs, Petipa *fils* was drawn to the "Venice of the North" because of decreasing opportunities for male dancers in the West and the unusually generous terms of an imperial contract, in his case, 10,000 francs a year and "half a benefit" for the position of premier danseur.[3] He accepted the offer with alacrity, little imagining that he would remain in Russia until his death in 1910, marry twice there (both times to Russian ballerinas), raise a family and rule the Imperial Ballet from 1869, when he became chief ballet master, to his retirement in 1903.

Petipa's long stewardship of the company had an incalculable effect on Russian ballet. He presided over the shift from romanticism to what is usually termed ballet "classicism", laid the foundation of the modern Russian school by marrying the new Italian bravura technique to its more lyrical French counterpart and helped transform an art dominated by foreigners and identified with the West into a Russian national expression. Petipa choreographed scores of ballets and innumerable dances, codifying their structure while expanding the lexicon of their movements, and created several generations of distinguished dancers. His works that survive, even in much altered form, *La Bayadère* (1877), *Giselle* (which he revived and significantly revised in 1884), *Swan Lake* (which he choreographed in 1895 with his assistant Lev Ivanov), *Raymonda* (1898), above all *The Sleeping Beauty* (1890), are the classics of an art with a performance tradition that goes back no further than the romantic period. Even if the designation of these works as "classics" came in the twentieth century and reflected a desire to establish a canon in the face of modernism, the fact remains that both in Russia and the West this canon was overwhelmingly identified with Petipa. Indeed, what we call "Russian ballet" in terms of repertory and style is virtually synonymous with Petipa, his colleagues and descendants.

The Imperial Ballet, renamed the Kirov Ballet during the Soviet period and the Maryinsky Ballet after the fall of the Soviet Union, is one of the world's oldest companies. It celebrated its 200th anniversary in 1983, but its origins date back to the 1730s and the court entertainments organised by Empress Anna Ivanovna. Although Russia was rich in folk performance traditions, ballet was an imported art nestled in the lap of the court. Ballet masters came from abroad (usually from France and Italy) and brought to Russia the dance fashions of the West. The first dance master of note was Jean-Baptiste Landé, who petitioned the empress for permission to establish a school to train dancers for court performances; the training was to take three years. In 1738 the first ballet school in Russia opened its doors, first in Landé's house, then in one of the wings of the imperial palace. The twenty-four pupils were children of palace servants.[4] The imperial court was generous to foreigners, especially artists, paying and treating them far better than the Russians who worked for them and whom they sometimes despised. In the decades following the establishment of Landé's school, numerous ballet masters made their way to St Petersburg. Sometimes they brought dancers with them, but by the 1760s, when the *ballet d'action* arrived in Russia with Franz Hilverding and Gaspero Angiolini, Petersburg-trained dancers could hold their own with foreign performers.

By then, the Imperial Theatres had come into existence. This state system, founded by decree of Catherine the Great in 1756, gave official status to the imperial opera, ballet and drama troupes, as well as the theatre school, and instituted pensions for artists.[5] The system was fully subsidised, with funding from the Ministry of the Court; it survived even the upheavals of the 1917 Russian Revolution. Suitably renamed, the former Imperial Theatres were nationalised and supported in full by the new Soviet state. When the socialist state collapsed in the 1990s, the post-Soviet government continued to pay for them. The state system had become so deeply entrenched that it outlasted any single form of government.

In 1783 the St Petersburg ballet moved into its first real home, the Bolshoi (not to be confused with the Moscow theatre of the same name) or Kamenny ("stone") Theatre, a huge, neoclassical building seating 2,000, opposite the site where the Maryinsky Theatre now stands. In 1885 the Imperial Ballet moved across the street to the Maryinsky, which remains the company's home today. Thus it was at the Bolshoi Theatre that most of the company's nineteenth-century history played out. Here, romantic sylphs took flight and designers from abroad created marvels of baroque perspective or shipwrecks on the high seas, as in Andreas Roller's famous design for *Le Corsaire* (1858).[6] There were scene-painting shops, costume shops and the finest stage machinery that money could buy. Dance personalities of the first rank found their way to St Petersburg, spending, in some cases, years with the company. Filippo Taglioni revived most of his ballets for the company, including *La Sylphide*,[7] which starred his daughter, Marie Taglioni, the most celebrated of romantic ballerinas. Balletomanes, a term coined in Russia for fanatical enthusiasts of ballet, crowded her performances and even, it is said, sipped champagne from her ballet slipper. "Taglioni is the synonym of Air!" enthused the novelist Nikolay Gogol. "Nothing more ethereal had existed heretofore on the stage."[8] Théophile Gautier, perhaps the foremost French dance critic of the time, visited St Petersburg in the 1850s. In *Voyage en Russie* (1858) he had nothing but praise for the Petersburg company: "The Russians are great connoisseurs . . . and the dancer who has withstood the marksmanship of their opera-glasses must be very confident of herself."[9] This was the Russia to which Petipa had come.

Marius Ivanovich Petipa, to give him his full Russian name, was born in Marseilles in 1818. Like so many nineteenth-century dancers, he came from a theatrical family. His father, Jean-Antoine Petipa, was a dancer and ballet master, his mother an actress who gave up the stage to raise a family.[10] His brother Lucien danced the role of Albrecht in the first *Giselle* (1841) and later became a ballet master at the Paris Opéra. Jean-Antoine was his son's first dance teacher. "At seven", Marius wrote in his memoirs many years later, "I started instruction in the art of dancing in the class of my father, who broke many bows on my hands in order to acquaint me with the mysteries of choreography."[11] He made his stage debut in Brussels at the age of nine in a ballet staged by his father and as a student danced in several of Jean-Antoine's original works. He got his first job in Nantes where he choreographed his first ballets, toured the United States with a small company organised by his father,[12] then settled in Paris to study with Auguste Vestris, one of the great teachers of the French school and a strict custodian of the academic tradition. Nevertheless, a place in the Paris sun eluded him. In 1847 he set out for St Petersburg and, except for vacations and the occasional sabbatical, never left.

During his first fifteen years in Russia, Petipa honed the craft that would distinguish his mature productions. Jules Perrot, the greatest of the romantic-era choreographers who spent more than a decade in St Petersburg, exerted a major influence over Petipa. Petipa danced in several of Perrot's ballets and also served as his assistant, at times even as his collaborator, rehearsing the "great *pas stratégique*" from *Catarina* and staging *Giselle* (1850) for Carlotta Grisi's Russian debut under the watchful eye of his mentor. A second influence on Petipa during these formative years as a choreographer was Arthur Saint-Léon, who followed Perrot to Russia in 1859 and held the post of ballet master for eleven successive seasons. A violinist of the Paganini school and sometime composer, Saint-Léon was an enormously musical choreographer; he had a facility for arranging dances, a fertile imagination and a gift for showing his dancers at their best.

In 1862 Petipa produced his first great success, *The Daughter of Pharaoh*. He had been working on it for nearly two years, commissioning a libretto

Figure 26 Gala performance at Peterhof, 11 July 1851, from Geirot's *Opisanie Petergofa*, 1868 (Carlotta Grisi and Jules Perrot in *The Naiade and the Fisherman*).

from Vernoy de Saint-Georges, who had written the "book" for *Giselle* and other ballets and a score from Cesare Pugni, a prolific ballet composer in the employ of the Imperial Theatres. A "grand ballet" in three acts and nine scenes, with prologue and epilogue, *The Daughter of Pharaoh* was set in Egypt. Gautier's short story "The Romance of the Mummy" (1857) inspired the plot, but the excitement generated by Egypt's fabulous monuments and the building of the Suez Canal gave the subject a topical interest.

The ballet was monumental in scale and a melodramatic tour de force. It was also a huge success, and Petipa was promoted to the rank of second ballet master. In 1869 came another success, *Don Quixote*, a ballet that has enjoyed continuous theatrical life. That year, promoted to chief ballet master, Petipa became sole master of Russia's choreographic revels. In his hands rested the fate of more than a half-dozen imperial enterprises: two theatres (the Bolshoi and the Maryinsky), a company, a school and several smaller court theatres (the Hermitage, Peterhof, Tsarskoe Selo, Krasnoe Selo and Kamennyi Ostrov) (see Fig. 26).[13]

Like the romantic ballets that fed his imagination, Petipa's works told stories. Many were romances touched with old-fashioned melodrama, with heroines who died of broken hearts or suffered in some way before wedding their rightful mates. Like their romantic predecessors, Petipa's ballets were always about women; more often than not, they took their titles from the heroine – hence, *The Daughter of Pharaoh* (1862), *La Bayadère* (1877), *The Sleeping Beauty* (1890), *Raymonda* (1898) and many others. Petipa revelled in his ballerinas, and in work after work, generation after generation, he displayed their growing prowess as technicians and their personalities as artists.

Although the romantic ballet had already identified the ballerina with the feminine mystique, emphasising her elusiveness and ethereality, Petipa added technical brilliance to the formula. In the post-romantic era, ballet technique developed rapidly, above all in Italy. By the 1860s the blocked shoe had come into use with its greater support; dancers began to run, jump, hop and perform multiple turns on pointe. Skirts rose, revealing greater expanses of leg and the prowess of "steel" toes. Not everyone welcomed the new virtuosity. To many the modern ballerina seemed akin to a machine, a miracle of industrial precision, nowhere more so than in the multiple *fouetté* turns introduced into Russia by visiting Italian ballerinas in the late 1880s and 1890s.

The emphasis on drill, as essential to the handling of Petipa's stage masses as to the manipulation of armies of "ballet girls" in the spectacular ballets popular in Western Europe and the United States, was another aspect of this mechanisation. Standing backstage at the Théâtre de la Gaîté in 1873, an American observer compared the production of an *opéra féerie*, with its spectacle effects and army of dancers, to "the manoeuvring of the great machine, which night after night worked so smoothly and so beautifully before the public".[14] Finally, unlike the sylphs and other romantic emblems of eternal girlhood, the ballerina of the closing decades of the nineteenth century was a full-bodied woman, wasp-waisted, corseted and glamorous, fully cognisant, when she stepped out on stage, of her star power. Utterly different from the chaste, "Christian" image of ballerinas like Marie Taglioni, she dominated the stage by her presence, not by the premonition of her absence. With flesh, sexuality and power as her weapons, she was all too real, anything but a metaphor for the spirit.

Petipa jettisoned other romantic conventions as well. Most romantic ballets (or "ballet-pantomimes", as they were usually called) consisted of two acts and were typically performed on a bill with opera. Petipa's ballets, by contrast, were usually three or four acts, full-evening entertainments. His ballets may have told stories like their romantic predecessors, but they embedded those stories in a vast array of dances and transformation scenes that enhanced the spectacular aspect of his work, while undermining its narrative power. Bigger meant better, so revising meant adding rather than trimming material. Instead of offering a simple contrast with the preceding realistic act, as in *La Sylphide* or *Giselle*, Petipa's *ballet blanc* was a jewel in an ever more elaborate setting.

In 1874 August Bournonville visited St Petersburg and saw several of Petipa's ballets, including *The Daughter of Pharaoh* and *Don Quixote*. Although he admired the "richly imaginative arrangement of the settings

and transformations", the corps of more than two hundred and the "superb
talent that displayed itself especially among the female members", the Danish
ballet master was also shocked by what he saw:

> I sought in vain to discover plot, dramatic interest, logical consistency, or
> anything which might remotely resemble sanity. And even if I were
> fortunate enough to come upon a trace of it in Petipa's *Don Quixote*, the
> impression was immediately effaced by an unending and monotonous host
> of feats of bravura, all of which were rewarded with salvos of applause and
> curtain calls.[15]

Bournonville also found appalling the "lascivious tendency" that pervaded
"the whole ballet movement", except for the Slavic national dances. He hated
the women's "excessively short skirts" and the "regulation *caleçons de bain*",
swimming trunks, that were "an established fact for the *danseurs*".[16]

However, at this very moment, Petipa was creating what a later generation
would regard as a defining moment in the genesis of Russian classicism –
the "Kingdom of the Shades" in *La Bayadère*. Produced in 1877 to a score
by Ludwig Minkus, the ballet marked Petipa's maturity as a choreographer,
with the "Shades scene" regarded as both a masterpiece of classical style and
one of his greatest dances. Here, in a story bathed in the romantic exoticism
of *The Daughter of Pharaoh*, was Petipa's vision of classical heaven – forty-
eight moonlit women in white descending one by one from the Himalayas
and winding slowly forward, all the while performing a simple arabesque
phrase with the hypnotic deliberateness of ritual.

Although the Imperial Ballet was largely insulated from outside events, the
1880s were a time of change. In 1881 Prince Ivan Vsevolozhsky became
the new director of the Imperial Theatres. In contrast to his predecessors, Vsevolozhsky was cultured, well-educated and polished, a European
in speech and manners.[17] Petipa adored him and the seventeen years that
followed his appointment were Petipa's happiest and most productive. As
conceived by Vsevolozhsky, the Maryinsky Theatre, where the Imperial
Ballet began to perform in 1885, was to be the temple of an art outside
time, unsullied by ugly nationalism, untouched by change except in "safe"
or ideologically neutral matters such as staging, technique and personnel.
Vsevolozhsky was above all a courtier and under his rule the Imperial Ballet
may have reached its apogee. But it did so at the price of cultural isolation; at no time did the company find itself so divorced from the society
around it or from the artistic trends – nationalism, realism, symbolism –
that transformed the Russian cultural landscape between the 1870s and early
1900s. Rather than a fully national art, ballet in nineteenth-century Russia
remained an appendage of the court.

In 1882 the monopoly of the Imperial Theatres was abolished, and for the first time ballet audiences in cities like St Petersburg and Moscow could see companies and entertainments from abroad. People flocked to the new establishments, although critics disagreed over the merits of the offerings, which included operettas, variety programmes and *ballets-féeries*. In marked contrast to the "grand ballet" as it had developed in Russia, the *ballet-féerie* depended on effects so spectacular as to overwhelm both the choreography and the story; at the same time it introduced the public to a new generation of virtuoso Italian ballerinas. However much Vsevolozhsky might disdain the new trends, he could hardly deny their appeal, and in several works of the mid- and late 1880s, he borrowed judiciously and selectively from the new genre.

Gradually, his vision of the Imperial Ballet took shape, which, as Roland John Wiley suggests, united "the dance-intensive grand ballet long favoured in Petersburg and the extraordinary *mise-en-scène* of the Franco-Italian *féerie* . . . Vsevolozhsky wanted to match the West European fashion for grandiose staging, then better it with elegant choreography and sophisticated music, which the West European model lacked."[18] He abolished the post of official ballet composer, thus partly abandoning the "specialist" tradition of nineteenth-century ballet music and sought "to develop new sources of ballet scores, principally from Russian composers".[19]

It was Vsevolozhsky who initiated the collaboration between Petipa and Tchaikovsky that became *The Sleeping Beauty*. "I have thought of writing a libretto based on Perrault's story 'La Belle au Bois Dormant'," he wrote to the composer in 1888. "I want to do the mise-en-scène in the style of Louis XIV. Here one can let one's musical fantasy play – and create melodies in the spirit of Lully, Bach, Rameau and so on. If the idea is to your liking, why couldn't you undertake the composition of the music?"[20] Tchaikovsky allowed himself to be tempted. "The subject is so poetic", he wrote to his patron Nadezhda von Meck, "so gratifying for music, that I was captivated by it."[21] Two years later the ballet was a reality. Petipa was fully aware of the importance of the collaboration. For the first time he was working with a major composer from outside the ballet "specialist" tradition, probably Russia's most distinguished musical artist. But Petipa did not significantly alter his usual working method. He wrote out a detailed plan for the ballet, breaking it down by section and for each section, describing the action, the quality of the music he wanted, the time signature, length (in terms of bars) and even suggestions for orchestration.[22] Tchaikovsky, for his part, responded with inventiveness to Petipa's call for expressive effects and almost always complied with his instructions regarding metre, tempo or scoring. The result was a score that followed the conventions of nineteenth-century ballet, even as it invested them with unusually high artistic quality.

The Sleeping Beauty premiered in 1890 and despite initial criticism of its weak libretto, *féerie*-style lavishness and Gallic source and setting, was soon hailed as a masterpiece.[23] The chief reason, wrote Alexandre Benois, was the music, which inspired Petipa to "a height of perfection hitherto unsurpassed by him. It is enough to recall the *variations* of the fairies in the prologue, the *grand pas de deux* in the third scene and, the greatest masterpiece of all, the dance of the Blue Bird and the enchanted Princess. But what innumerable other gems of choreographic art are scattered by Petipa throughout."[24]

A grand spectacle, four hours long, with a prologue, three acts and an apotheosis, *Beauty* was a summation of the conventions elaborated over the course of the century. Like all of Petipa's ballets, it drew on a multiplicity of movement idioms. There were long mime scenes, dances in national dance style, ballroom dances, as well as classical dancing in the vision scene, divertissements and a *grand pas d'action*.

It is impossible today even to imagine the human density on the imperial stage of the late nineteenth century. In 1903–4 the Imperial Ballet consisted of 122 female and 92 male dancers, plus ballet masters and régisseurs.[25] In addition, there were the children and advanced students of the ballet school, regularly used in productions. Dozens of them appeared in *The Sleeping Beauty*, as Cupids, pages, "young girls" with lutes, Tom Thumb and his brothers; in the Garland Waltz alone there were twenty-four children. Finally, there were the drama students and members of the imperial drama troupe, sometimes pressed into action as supers; in a pinch soldiers from one of the elite guards units stationed in St Petersburg could be called upon. The imperial stage teemed with life.

It also mirrored the hierarchy that governed all aspects of imperial life. Ranks determined the minimum or maximum number of dancers who could appear in a group. Coryphées could dance in groups of no more than eight; second soloists in groups of no more than four; first dancers in groups of no more than two. The ballerina danced alone. Thus hierarchy was built into the very substance of the choreography. It also went to the heart of the ballet's social "message". *Sleeping Beauty*, like *Swan Lake* (1895) and *Raymonda* (1898), invokes a monarchical ideal of the well-ordered polity ruled by its rightful king. Hence, the obsession in all three ballets with marriage as source of continuity in an absolutist state and the risk of choosing an inappropriate mate or (in the case of Aurora) no mate at all. The chaos produced by Carabosse in *Sleeping Beauty*, Odile in *Swan Lake* and Abderrakhman in *Raymonda* suggests that what is really at stake in these ballets is the idea of autocracy itself. To be sure none of these ballets (or any other ballets produced during Vsevolozhsky's directorship) takes place in Russia. But in their court settings and in the storyline that identifies them with outmoded forms of government, they celebrated a political vision that pointed directly to the Romanovs.

Sleeping Beauty and its successors, especially *Swan Lake* and *Raymonda*, offered a veritable encyclopedia of the codified forms constituting Petipa's "classicism". Among these was the *grand pas de deux*, a virtuoso dance for the ballerina and her partner that marked the climactic end of an act. Petipa did not invent the *pas de deux*, but he significantly transformed it, codifying it as a multi-part number that opened with a supported adagio, continued with one or two pairs of variations and ended in a triumphant coda. Just as Petipa had codified the *pas de deux*, so he did the same with the virtuoso variation. It was in three parts, with repeats, so that what was done first on one side was repeated on the other. Unlike the transitional ballets of the late 1880s, *Sleeping Beauty* did not simply display the new technical developments associated with the Italian school. Rather, for the first time, Petipa succeeded in fusing them with the elegance of the French school, the basis of traditional Russian training. This synthesis laid the foundation of the modern Russian school.

Petipa also brought a very high degree of perfection to what is sometimes called the *grand pas* or *grand pas d'action*. This was the climax of a ballet, a dance in classical style for a ballerina, premier danseur, soloists and corps de ballet that generalised the main idea of the ballet.[26] Although the number of characters might vary, a *grand pas* typically included the ballet's protagonists along with soloists, coryphées and corps members. The *grand pas* had a high degree of formal unity but little narrative function, the reason it could easily be extracted from the surrounding ballet and performed independently. The "Jardin Animé" in *Le Corsaire* is one such dance; another the *grand pas* of *Paquita*; still another the *grand pas classique* (also called the *grand pas Hongrois*) in Act III of *Raymonda*.

In the flush of excitement that followed the success of *The Sleeping Beauty*, Tchaikovsky agreed to do another ballet, *The Nutcracker*. Amazingly, given its longevity and protean identity, the ballet was ill-starred. Tchaikovsky disliked the libretto, based on a story by E. T. A. Hoffmann, and after the ballet went into rehearsal, Petipa fell ill and turned the choreography over to his assistant ballet master, Lev Ivanov. When the ballet finally opened in 1892, it met with sharp criticism. "*Nutcracker* can in no event be called a ballet," wrote one critic.[27]

Three years later, *Swan Lake*, the most iconic of nineteenth-century ballets, came to life at the Maryinsky. Petipa had choreographed Act I and most of Act III, the ball scene, including the "Black Swan" *pas de deux* for Odette's look-alike, Odile: the two roles were danced by the same ballerina. Here, writes Krasovskaya, Petipa "brilliantly [set] off Ivanov's Odette, with her elegiac arabesques, against Odile, the bird of prey, with her resilient and

Figure 27 *Swan Lake*, St Petersburg 1910, choreography by Lev Ivanov and Marius Petipa, music by Pyotr Ilyich Tchaikovsky.

commanding attitudes. His skill triumphed in the *fouetté*" – a sequence of thirty-two of those highly virtuosic turns – "which was no longer a technical stunt but the culmination in the depiction of cunning temptation: the swift repetition of the dancer's spins put the finishing touches to Odile's character."[28] Although Ivanov choreographed the lakeside dances of the last act, Petipa sketched out at least some of the action. He identified the dancers of various numbers and pondered the colour scheme of the costumes, deciding on black and white to underscore the theme of moral guilt and the presentiment of death.[29] The intonation of sorrow was intensified in the waltz, when the black swans cut through the lines of white swans and climaxed at the end of the act, when first Odette, then Siegfried died by their own hands, thereby breaking the spell. With the lovers united in death, Rothbart, the "evil genie", as he was called in the libretto, fell dead. In the apotheosis the lovers appeared in the clouds, seated on enormous swans,[30] giving the ballet a happy, if banal, ending (see Figs. 27 and 28).

Apart from *Giselle*, which Petipa revived and significantly revised in 1884, what survives of his work comes from the 1890s or turn-of-the-century recensions of earlier works such as *La Bayadère*, *Le Corsaire* and *Don Quixote* (although how much of Petipa remains in Aleksandr Gorsky's 1902 restaging is a matter of debate). Part of the reason these works have survived is because they were choreographed or revised towards the end of Petipa's career, thus representing his last word, so to speak, on an art that he had spent the previous fifty years perfecting. They also survive because they comprised the stock of works belonging to the "old ballet", as Petipa's work began to be called around 1910, that dancers of the 1910s and 1920s brought with them to the West and that the post-revolutionary generation in Russia made the cornerstone of the Soviet, "academic" repertory. Finally, the ballets of the 1890s have survived because of their high musical quality. This was especially true in the West, where Diaghilev's revolution in ballet music made composers like Pugni and Minkus sound hopelessly old-fashioned. It was not until the early 1960s, when the Kirov began to tour outside the Soviet bloc, that the "Kingdom of the Shades" was introduced to Western audiences. *Le Corsaire* and *Don Quixote* came later.

Although Russian ballet of the 1890s revealed an even greater Western focus than in previous decades, the number of foreigners in the Petersburg company was actually declining. Visiting ballerinas came and went, but with the departure of Pierina Legnani, the first Petersburg Odette–Odile, they pretty much left for good. Now, led by Mathilde Kshesinska, the company's *prima ballerina assoluta*, an extraordinary generation of Russian talent emerged from the Imperial Ballet School. The dancers themselves differed from their nineteenth-century predecessors in several important ways. Not only had the social class of the dancers risen, but so had salaries. Although these were not especially generous, they were far more than the pittance of the 1870s, when members of the corps earned between 174 and 240 roubles a year. (Yekaterina Vazem, the highest paid member of the company, received 1,143 roubles in salary plus 25 roubles per performance.)[31] Conditions at the school had also improved and memoirists like Tamara Karsavina describe the ample meals and generous allotment of clothing that the children received, regardless of means. A growing number of dancers, including Mikhail Fokine and Adolph Bolm, came from merchant families, a sure sign that the social status of the dancer was on the rise. Many dancers were now the children, siblings, or spouses of dancers, members of clans that formed an increasingly privileged caste within the Russian theatrical world. Some, like the Kshesinskys, were quite well off. Others, like the Karsavins, lived in "reduced circumstances" on the father's small pension and meagre salary as a part-time teacher.[32] Nevertheless, conditions at the end of the nineteenth century were far better than at mid-century, when poverty was well-nigh universal.[33]

Finally, the training had significantly changed during Petipa's years in Russia. Students who attended the Imperial Theatre School in the 1830s and 1840s studied acting, singing as well as dancing and were then placed according to their talents. By the 1890s ballet training had become highly specialised (although students continued to study music as well as academic subjects).[34] The result was a company with a very high degree of professionalism, which compared favourably with standards elsewhere in

Figure 28 Scene from *Swan Lake*, Bolshoi Ballet Moscow, 1959.

Europe, as became evident once the ban on private theatrical enterprise was lifted.

Despite the social changes, liaisons remained a fact of life. Some "protectors" eventually married the women who had been their lovers: this was the case of Agrippina Vaganova, the legendary Soviet-era pedagogue and her husband, Andrey Pomerantsev,[35] as well as Anna Pavlova and Victor Dandré. Kshesinska reserved her favours for Romanovs – first, the future Nicholas II, then his cousins, Grand Duke Sergey and Grand Duke André, whom she married years later in emigration. She collected houses as well as jewels and was not averse to throwing around her power. When Vsevolozhsky's successor (and nephew), Prince Serge Volkonsky, fined her for an unauthorised change of costume in the ballet *Camargo* (1872), she went straight to her former lover, Nicholas II, who requested that the fine be annulled. In Volkonsky's audience with Nicholas, he tried to explain "the impossible conditions . . . produced by interference with my dispositions, owing to the exceptional position in which one dancer was placed and her precedence before all the others".[36] Volkonsky ended by requesting permission to resign.

This incident, which took place in 1901, underscored the very close relationship between the Romanovs and the ballet. Members of the imperial family celebrated birthdays and name-days at the ballet; they attended school performances and distributed chocolates to the children; they made friends with the dancers, weighed in on performances, used their influence to promote their favourites and sometimes found mistresses. "How happy we felt at the thought of being allowed to dance in the presence of the Imperial Family!" exclaimed Kshesinska, recalling the school performance when Alexander III singled her out for praise.[37] Far more than any of the other arts, ballet in Russia was a reflection of what Richard Taruskin has called, "the last surviving eighteenth-century (hierarchical, aristocratic) society in Europe".[38]

Although Petipa remained very much a Frenchman, it was under his require that the Imperial Ballet began the slow transformation from an art of the court, understood in the broadest sense, to an art of the nation. By the 1890s nationalism was a recurring theme in ballet criticism, both with regard to genres like the *féerie* and foreign ballerinas who did not find favour with Russian audiences. Ironically, this identity was only fully realised after the triumph of Diaghilev's Ballets Russes in Paris beginning in 1909. Even though the Ballets Russes never performed in Russia and exemplified the "new ballet", it created for Russian ballet, old and new, a place in the European cultural imaginary and the international cultural marketplace.

By then the age of Petipa was long over and Russian ballet had ceased to be a purely Russian phenomenon. Now, through the diaspora of Russian dancers in the 1910s and 1920s, his last generation of dancers extended his influence far beyond the Imperial Theatres where Petipa had spent his most productive years. In an art where oblivion is the fate of all but the tiniest minority of works, his ballets, virtually unknown outside Russia during his lifetime, have become the "classics" of a common heritage, while his school, updated and transformed, continues to be its lingua franca.

14 Opening the door to a fairy-tale world: Tchaikovsky's ballet music

THÉRÈSE HURLEY

Ballet is the most innocent, the most moral of all the arts. If that is not so, then why do they always bring children to the ballet?[1]   (P. I. TCHAIKOVSKY)

Tchaikovsky's belief in the purity of ballet as well as its link to childhood lies at the core of his intent in and approach to composing ballet music. According to friend and music critic Herman Laroche, the composer welcomed writing for the ballet because, "in that magical world, it was pure fairy tale expressed by pantomime and dance".[2] Laroche added, "Tchaikovsky could not stand realism in ballet."[3] Tchaikovsky reserved ballet as the ideal genre for complete submersion into a child's fantasy world and so his *Swan Lake*, *The Sleeping Beauty* and *The Nutcracker* are all fantastic tales that draw the audience into a magical world of swan maidens, sorcerers, fairies, mouse kings, princes and princesses. In this chapter, I will show how Tchaikovsky's music for these ballets is the key that unlocks the door to a fairy-tale world. For pantomime and dance, the visual tools used to convey these stories cannot alone evoke the fantasy. It is Tchaikovsky's music, especially in his masterful choice of instruments and ways of deploying them, that transports his audience to a world of fantasy and magic.

Before delving into Tchaikovsky's ballet music, one first should recognise the role of a ballet composer in the nineteenth century, which was to highlight the actions on stage. The pantomimes required music that expressed the feelings of the characters, moment to moment, but the dance music often was simpler and somewhat repetitive in both melody and rhythm, allowing the audience's attention to be drawn to the dancers' steps rather than to complexities in the music. Composers were expected to meet the requests of the choreographers – usually known as "ballet masters" – and to compose music that helped express the action and accompany the dancing in suitable fashion.

Swan Lake

Swan Lake: A Ballet in Four Acts (composed August 1875–10 April 1876) was premiered in Moscow on 20 February 1877 to less than enthusiastic reviews, but the 1895 revival of the ballet by the choreographers Marius Petipa and Lev Ivanov, at the Maryinsky Theatre in St Petersburg, found much greater success. (Alas, Tchaikovsky did not live to see it.) For this later version – upon which today's productions are based – Tchaikovsky's brother Modest reworked the libretto and the Maryinsky conductor and composer Riccardo Drigo reorchestrated the score, adding to it three of Tchaikovsky's piano pieces from Op. 72, *L'Espiègle*, *Valse Bluette* and *Un poco di Chopin*, which he orchestrated as well.

Little evidence survives of the collaboration of *Swan Lake's* choreographer Julius Reisinger and the composer; we cannot know how Tchaikovsky might have responded to any specific requests Reisinger made. We do know that the composer took a keen interest in more than just the musical aspects of the ballet's first production. He was very specific about special effects, as machinist Karl Valts recalls:

> Peter Ilyich gave special attention to the final act. In the storm scene, when the lake overflows its banks and floods the entire stage, a real whirlwind was built at Tchaikovsky's insistence. Branches and twigs of trees were broken, fell into the water, and were carried away by the waves. After the storm, for the apotheosis, dawn came and the landscape was illuminated by the first rays of the rising sun at the curtain.[4]

His music brings out the drama of the storm scene, so much so that Laroche criticised the orchestration:

> For what do the trumpets, trombones and kettledrums roar when in the depth of an empty stage flies a band of swans? This moment demands soft peaceful sounds . . . I think . . . Tchaikovsky, as on many earlier occasions, was simply carried away by his peculiar weakness for loud sounds.[5]

Another critic remarked that "Tchaikovsky displayed an astonishing knowledge of instrumentation – a characteristic that is being admitted by friends and enemies alike. He gave new evidence of his ability to make masterful use of orchestral forces."[6]

Clearly, Tchaikovsky had a vision of the way in which his ballet was to come to life – not just the music, but also the visual and sound effects on stage combined. And he was more interested in conveying the tumult and despair felt in the final scene than the immediate picture of swans in flight. When he chose to depict the swans, he did so very effectively. Let us consider the case of the famous Swan Theme, which is heard for the first time at the end of Act I with the appearance of the swans at night. Tchaikovsky creates a sense of mystery and magic by simulating the rippling waves of the lake with B minor arpeggios on the harp over the shimmering tremolo of the strings. In the second bar, the oboe announces the theme, which bears a striking resemblance to Lohengrin's warning to Elsa in Wagner's opera.[7] (Fully acquainted with the score of *Lohengrin*, Tchaikovsky most likely chose to echo the tragedy that was to come in the musical warning to Siegfried.) When the Swan Theme recurs at the opening of Act II, the tempo is accelerated, adding a sense of urgency and making the oboe sound as a cry for help. Moreover, instead of modulating to major and adding a new theme (as he does in Act I), Tchaikovsky continues to develop the Swan Theme until the orchestra ends in *fff* (very loud) and finally fades with the B minor tremolo in the upper strings – the other-worldly tone is thus set for the rest for the act.

The famous love *pas de deux* of Act II provides not only another example of Tchaikovsky's deftness as an orchestrator, but also his ability to narrate the story (albeit subtly) through his music. The opening, virtuosic harp cadenza incorporates unresolved half-diminished seventh chords clearly meant to evoke the feeling of desire between Odette and Prince Siegfried. By giving this music to the harp, Tchaikovsky offers a sense of fantasy and paints a picture of what is (passion) and what is to be (magic and sorcery). The harp cadenza segues into a simple, chordal accompaniment for the solo violin's statement of the first theme in G major. The oboes and clarinets soon disrupt the heart-wrenching melody with a repetitive semiquaver rhythmic pattern (bars 34–42). This unusual rhythm causes a sense of anxiety as it chromatically ascends, modulating to E major, and arrives at the violin's playful second theme. When the first theme returns, the cello (representing Siegfried) plays the melody while the violin (Odette) sings a plaintive counterpoint.[8] After this moving and beautiful declaration of love, the two lovers and their fates are altered forever. The effect of this change is heard in the reprise of the Swan Waltz (Variation VI) when Tchaikovsky interpolates the repetitive, palpitating rhythm (this time as quavers) and confirms through his music that now everything (even the Swan Waltz) is different.

In Act III, Siegfried makes the fatal mistake of believing that the evil Odile is his beloved (though his friend Benno sees no resemblance at all between the two). How does Tchaikovsky fool Siegfried into this blunder? The answer is found in his instrumentation. For when Odile appears unexpectedly at the ball, she dances to an oboe solo accompanied by harp. Siegfried last heard this combination when he saw his Odette, so the return of this duo, he believes, must mean the return of the Swan Princess. In addition to creating the illusion that Odile is Odette, Tchaikovsky also leaves a musical clue that Odile is an impostor: we only have to look at the key signature to learn that the dance is not in one of Odette's keys, but rather in the sorcerer Rothbart's key of F minor – clearly Siegfried is doomed. His devastating mistake is revealed when he vows he will marry Odile.[9]

By the few musical examples above, we can glean that Tchaikovsky was very conscientious in his use of instruments to simulate nature (harp arpeggios as waves), affect the plot (instrumentation used to deceive Siegfried) and add a touch of magic (harp cadenza and accompaniment in the love pas de deux). Yet the composer himself was not satisfied with his instrumentation for Swan Lake and according to Drigo "had intended to take up the matter, but he never managed to do this".[10] We can only speculate what changes Tchaikovsky himself would have made had he lived long enough to collaborate on the Petipa/Ivanov production.

Sleeping Beauty

Eleven years after the premiere of Swan Lake, Tchaikovsky received a request from Ivan Alexandrovich Vsevolozhsky, the Director of the Imperial Theatres of St Petersburg, to compose a new ballet:

> I conceived the idea of writing a libretto on *La Belle au bois dormant* after Perrault's tale. I want to do the *mise-en-scène* in the style of Louis XIV. Here the musical imagination can be carried away, and melodies composed in the spirit of Lully, Bach, Rameau, etc., etc. In the last act indispensably necessary is a quadrille of all Perrault's tales.[11]

Tchaikovsky accepted enthusiastically:

> I very much want to tell you straight away that I'm charmed, delighted beyond all description. It suits me perfectly, and I would ask for nothing more than to set it to music. It would be impossible to make a better stage arrangement of the elements in this delicious subject.[12]

As he worked on the new ballet, the composer described his labour in a letter to his patroness, Nadezhda von Meck: "I worked on its instrumentation with special love and care and invented some completely new orchestral combinations which, I hope, will be very beautiful and interesting."[13] Indeed, *Sleeping Beauty*, upon its premiere on 2 January 1890 at the Maryinsky Theatre, was deemed by Herman Laroche "one of our theatre's pearls" and a musical triumph for Tchaikovsky as well.[14]

The choreographer Marius Petipa wrote out instructions for Tchaikovsky for *Sleeping Beauty,* and they make fascinating reading, for they show us how the composer responded musically to specific – and sometimes very narrow – requests. Petipa indicated expressive musical effects, metres, types and lengths of each dance in bars and, occasionally, he even requested instruments, as in "Variation d'Aurore" in Act I: "3/4 pizzicato for violins, cellos, and harp. (Excuse me for expressing myself so oddly.) And then lute [*sic*] and violin." For the evil Fairy Carabosse's appearance in the Prologue, for instance, Petipa requested "music of a fantastic character"; and Tchaikovsky responded with the menacing Carabosse Theme, in which horns and woodwinds strongly accent the offbeats as the clarinet sings out the chromatic melody, sometimes in duet with the bassoon. These darker woodwinds return to represent the mysterious and vengeful Carabosse throughout the ballet.

In contrast, for the Lilac Fairy's softening of the evil curse of Carabosse, Petipa suggested "tender and rather derisive music".[15] In response, Tchaikovsky presented the lullaby-like Lilac Fairy Theme, introduced by an ascending E major scale glissando on harp and performed by the oboe. Likewise, this theme reappears in the first and second acts. In fact, Tchaikovsky included both of these themes in his Introduction to the ballet, so the audience is made aware immediately of the contrasting forces in the story. The Carabosse Theme evokes danger and mystery and the Lilac Fairy Theme bodes tranquillity and magic; this sets up the opposing forces that provide the drama and suspense of the entire ballet.

Note further the close connection of the harp to the Lilac Fairy. From the beginning, the harp is used to represent magic and the mitigating of Carabosse's curse of certain death on the Princess Aurore to a mere hundred years of sleep. Throughout the Prologue and first two acts, the harp provides glissandos, arpeggios, lushly rolled chords and even harmonics (which make for a shimmering, celestial effect). However, the instrument is silent during the final act. What is the reasoning? First, let us recall that the final act is a set of dances at the wedding celebration of Princess Aurore and Prince Désiré. By this point, all fantastical activity has ceased. The Lilac Fairy is no longer needed and neither is her magic. Second, we encounter a new sound emerging from the orchestra pit: a piano. Just as the Lilac Fairy has given way to the Gold, Silver, Sapphire and Diamond Fairies, so has her supernatural instrument, the harp, been replaced by the earthly sound of the piano. The piano works especially well, for instance, for the Silver Fairy, for whom Petipa had specified that "the sound of coins must be heard". The clarity and percussive quality of the piano lends itself well to this music. Also, by engaging the flute to help project the melody over the *campanelli* (orchestra bells) and pizzicato string accompaniment, Tchaikovsky adds a sparkle to the piano's timbre.

In addition to expressive musical sound effects, Petipa also informed Tchaikovsky of the specific metre in which he was to compose. Although Tchaikovsky followed these suggestions, the dancers seemed to have difficulty with some of his metres and rhythms. Riccardo Drigo, conductor of the first production, mentioned that their "internal resistance . . . was great, as each variation went beyond the usual formulas to which the ear was accustomed".[16] It seems that the composer was continuing to push the boundaries of what was considered to be typical ballet music at the time. However, Petipa's prescribed metres were not always in simple duple or triple. For example, in the Dance of the Sapphire Fairy of Act III, Petipa wrote, "Sapphire – five points, music in quintuple time". Therefore, Tchaikovsky composed the dance in 5/4 – an unusual metre to be sure, but one that the choreographer had ordered.

Petipa also specified the types of dances such as the mazurka in Act II and the grand polonaise at the beginning of Act III. In addition to these requests, he described the character of the dances performed in Act II. For the Dance of the Duchesses, he merely wrote: "They are noble and proud." For the Dance of the Baronesses: "They are arrogant and conceited." To compose a minuet for the duchesses and a gavotte for the baronesses was entirely Tchaikovsky's decision. Since this act occurred a hundred years after the time of Louis XIV, it made perfect sense for Tchaikovsky to have composed the music in a Mozartian fashion. This classical style evokes the air of aristocracy while alluding to the change in time period.

As we have seen so far, Tchaikovsky did attempt to follow Petipa's requests for expressive effects, metre and dance. But the composer often exceeded the length requested by the choreographer. For the Act I waltz in *Sleeping Beauty* instead of the 16 bars of introduction and 150 bars of waltz Petipa had requested, Tchaikovsky supplied 36 and 261 bars respectively. He surpassed the length suggested for the introduction and polonaise at the beginning of Act III as well. One wonders how Petipa and Tchaikovsky handled discrepancies such as this. Fortunately, we have a hint from Alexander Shirayev (grandson of the composer Cesare Pugni and dancer with the Petersburg Imperial Ballet), who remarked that Tchaikovsky, like Glazunov, was willing to meet Petipa halfway regarding alterations to the score, but that the choreographer "was hesitant to make demands of them as he had of [minor composers] Pugni and Minkus, who at his wish reworked their compositions straightaway at rehearsal. Petipa had therefore to work quite hard on *Sleeping Beauty*. This he confessed to me."[17] From this recollection, we can surmise that Tchaikovsky was greatly respected by Petipa. The respect must have been mutual for when asked to collaborate again – this time for *The Nutcracker* – Tchaikovsky agreed.

The Nutcracker

Almost two years after finishing *The Sleeping Beauty*, Tchaikovsky wrote his final ballet, *The Nutcracker: Ballet in 2 Acts* (composed February 1891– 4 April 1892). Although somewhat sceptical of the subject matter, the composer set out to work on the ballet, which would become a worldwide Christmas favourite. Originally, the ballet was to have the same collaborators as *The Sleeping Beauty*, but Lev Ivanov replaced Petipa when the great ballet master fell ill. The ballet premiered at the Maryinsky Theatre on 6 December 1892 to mixed reviews, in part because the plot never seemed resolved and the heroine, Clara, never returned from *Confiturembourg*, the Palace of Sweets. Many critics complained that the story was pointless and were surprised to hear that Tchaikovsky would even consider working on such a ballet.[18] In any case, his efforts proved fruitful indeed, and his score surely accounts in great part for the continuing popularity of this work.

As with *The Sleeping Beauty*, Tchaikovsky received instructions from Petipa for *The Nutcracker* and responded with character-related instrumentation, musical sound effects and memorable melodies. He also borrowed music from other sources and worked them into the score. As in his earlier ballets, he adhered to an overall tonal plan and established a basic framework from which to compose music that draws the audience into a magical world.

For Councillor Drosselmayer's (later changed into Drosselmeier) first appearance, Petipa asked for "very serious, rather sinister and even droll music". At first, the Drosselmayer Theme is introduced by viola with trombone and tuba accompaniment, but then the clarinet and bassoon perform the mischievous melody with cello and bass accompaniment. We heard these lower woodwinds before: during Carabosse's Theme in *The Sleeping Beauty*. We can assume that Tchaikovsky wished to evoke the same mystery and darkness. This darkness returns at midnight when an eerie glow shrouds the Nutcracker. Although the melody is altered, the instruments of clarinet and bassoon remain the same and so does the sentiment of uneasiness and fear.

The battle scene between the Nutcracker and Mouse King (Act I, no. 7), which culminates in the transformation of the Nutcracker doll to an enchanting Prince, is the most action-filled part of the entire drama. Already a seasoned battle composer with the *1812 Overture* behind him, Tchaikovsky was certainly well equipped to simulate a "hail of grapeshot, volley of guns, piercing cries". The lower strings often play a galloping rhythmic motif with snare drums, woodwinds and brass sounding military calls. And at the point for which Petipa called for the Nutcracker to summon his men "To arms!" Tchaikovsky wrote a trumpet call to verbalise this order musically – there is no mistaking this as a military command in the midst of the belligerent action on stage. The choreographer was also specific in his requests for the post-ballet scene: "The mice are victorious and devour the gingerbread soldiers. 8 bars after the 48 b[ars] of battle, in order that the mice's teeth can be heard chewing on the gingerbread." Tchaikovsky responded with a repetitive descending scale in the strings to depict the ravenous rodents. For Clara's throwing of her slipper at the Mouse King, Petipa requested "2 bars for the piercing cry and 6 for the whistling of the mice, which disappear". Then follows the transformation of the Nutcracker into the Prince, for which Petipa instructed "One or two chords". The instructions seem rather minimal for the most triumphant scene of the entire production, but Tchaikovsky cleverly created a transition from the evil battle scene to the beauty and magic of *Confiturembourg* on the basis of these few suggestions. The oboe, clarinet and horns blare out a tritone for the King's cry in the suggested two bars. The clarinets and bassoons are called upon once more to add a feeling of dark magic as the mice scurry away in the suggested six bars. In the third bar of the scurrying mice, the cellos and basses pluck a pizzicato heartbeat. The trombones and tuba enter to sound the death knell of the Mouse King. Suddenly, we witness the transformation as the upper strings play a swelling ascending scale leaping to a high C and then quietly descending over the heartbeat motif. The Nutcracker is no longer a doll, for we hear his heartbeat and the scale sounds as the breath of life, bestowed upon the Prince. Although Petipa asked for a meagre two chords for this transformation, Tchaikovsky exceeded expectations again by creating a full-fledged musical metamorphosis.

With all signs and sounds of evil and mischief dispelled, the next scene opens with the rippling arpeggios of two harps. As in both earlier ballets, the composer continues to use the harp to signify magic. What was Clara's house at night has become a fir forest in winter. Gnomes with torches are paying homage to the Prince and Clara. All semblances of reality and evil disappear and the characters as well as the audience enter a childlike fairy-tale world. In this fantasy-land, the harp – aside from evoking the magic of the place – is used to create a whirlwind within the Waltz of the Snowflakes. (Petipa here noted that a "strong burst of wind breaks up the snowball and the dancers spin around".) By writing the harp glissandos for two parts in contrasting directions, Tchaikovsky achieves this blustery effect, demonstrating both his expertise in composing idiomatically for the instrument and his creativity in finding new ways to simulate non-musical sounds. Ever fascinated with new effects and the possibilities of the orchestra, Tchaikovsky made use of a newly invented instrument in *The Nutcracker*: the celesta. When he discovered it in Paris, he was so charmed by the instrument and its bell-like tones that he immediately asked his publisher to order one.[19] For the ballet, Petipa had requested that the Dance of the Sugar Plum Fairy should sound "as if drops of water shooting out of fountains are heard". Combining the delicacy of the harp with the percussive clarity of the piano, the celesta beautifully depicts staccato sprays of water; Tchaikovsky had found his fountain.

In addition to the celesta's famous solo, the instrument is heard often throughout the ballet, specifically in *Confiturembourg* and usually with the harps. In fact, Tchaikovsky (not content with just one new sound in this ballet) incorporated the quivering tones of a specific flute technique called flutter-tonguing (*frulato*) – something rarely used at the time. Together, these three instruments simulate the undulating currents of the river of rose oil, which flows through the kingdom of *Confiturembourg*. Therefore, just as the lower woodwinds evoked darkness and the brass and percussion led us into battle, the combination of celesta, harps and flutes create the sparkling sounds of the wintry fairy- tale land.

In addition to the usual suggestions of metre and dance style, Petipa asked Tchaikovsky to incorporate some previously composed music into the score, specifically the French song, "Bon voyage, Monsieur Dumolet", during the Christmas party in Act i, /no. 3 (bars 61–118). Tchaikovsky also included a German dance called the *Grossvater* for the party (Act i, no. 5, bars 187–219) – appropriate, since the Christmas party takes place in Germany.

In Act ii, Tchaikovsky used two popular French songs for the character dance of Mother Gigogne and her children as well as a Georgian lullaby for the Arabian Dance.[20] The inclusion of two merry French songs for Mother Gigogne seems a plausible choice. She is French and the songs, very playful and sprightly, fulfil Petipa's descriptions of dancing buffoons. But why did Tchaikovsky choose a Georgian lullaby for a sultry Arabian dance? Petipa's instructions call for an "Oriental Dance. From 24 to 32 bars of charming and voluptuous music" and he even specified the "kingdom of Yemen". Tchaikovsky's selection compels us to glance at the geographic location of Georgia as well as its history. Georgia (which shares borders with Turkey, Armenia and Azerbaijan) was part of Imperial Russia at this time, but had also endured many other invasions and occupations. The region had been part of the Persian and Ottoman empires in the sixteenth century and had been invaded by Arabs in the seventh century. With Georgia's longstanding relationship to the Middle East in mind, the melody choice begins to become clear. To Tchaikovsky, this melody must have been quite evocative of the Arabic musical genre and therefore an ideal choice. He accentuated the connection with his orchestration and his melodic ornamentation. We hear the violins softly playing the lullaby theme over a repetitive G and later a G–D drone in the lower strings. This string arrangement establishes a folk-like quality, but the woodwinds (specifically the oboe and cor anglais) decidedly add the timbre of Middle Eastern wind instruments. By this time in nineteenth-century ballet, an oboe solo in a minor key was considered a standard choice for a character (also called national) dance of Arabia. The subtle rattle of a tambourine punctuates the phrases and adds a finishing touch of exoticism to the music.

As noted above, Tchaikovsky tended to use simple melodies and frequent repetition for passages of virtuosic dance, so as to avoid diverting the audience's attention from the dancing to the music. In *The Nutcracker* he chose a simple repetitive melody to create the illusion of a growing Christmas tree in Act I, no. 6. Petipa instructed that "the Christmas tree becomes huge. 48 bars of fantastic music with a grandiose *crescendo*". At first, the horns provide the harmonic accompaniment beneath the melody of the first violins while the harp evokes images of the tree's growth. All this begins *pianissimo* and gradually increases in volume until the grand cymbals crash. Then the violas and cellos quietly introduce the melody in canon with the violins. This time, the woodwinds have joined the horns in harmonic accompaniment. The trombones and tubas soon play the melody with the cellos as the orchestra crescendoes once again. Another thunderous crash of the cymbals is heard followed by the violas and cellos playing the melody *piano* this time. The trumpets, flutes and clarinets take their turns at the short phrase while increasing to *ffff* and arriving at the triumphant metamorphosis of the tree. Although the audience can see the tree magically grow on stage during the performance, we can hear the fantastic change take place even without any visual aids. As Tchaikovsky's short ascending phrase gives the Christmas tree its height, the harp arpeggios add breadth as they cascade up and down the instrument. Simply by developing a short phrase, Tchaikovsky was able to create one of the most effective illusions in nineteenth-century theatrical music. In *The Nutcracker*, Tchaikovsky once more received instructions and fulfilled them with a keen ear for musically depicting the action on stage. He follows the choreographer's requests in most areas, but, as before, exceeds them in others – namely the number of bars. The Arabian Dance was meant to be 24–32 bars. Tchaikovsky wrote 102. The Final Waltz and Apotheosis of Act II was to be 128 and 16–24 bars and ended up at 239 and 55 respectively. Yet, it does not seem that his excessive productivity had any negative effect on the music or the ballet. On the contrary, it was surely his score that saved the ballet from being forgotten and elevated it to the status it enjoys today as a Christmas standard for so many ballet companies.

In *Swan Lake*, *The Sleeping Beauty* and *The Nutcracker*, Tchaikovsky, propelled by his belief in the innocence of ballet and perhaps his own happy recollection and longing for the early days of childhood, followed the requests of ballet masters (notably Petipa) and composed music for swan maidens, fairies and mice in all sorts of situations such as enchanted lakes, weddings and even battles. Like any ballet specialist composer, he wrote expressive music for the pantomimes and danceable music for the dances, but in his music we find something more than a mere fulfilment of choreographic demands. Tchaikovsky possessed a genius for melody (whether original or borrowed) – the Swan Theme, the Arabian Dance, the Dance of the Sugar Plum Fairy, to name only a few. But he also displayed an acute sensitivity to orchestral colour and the ability to evoke a magical sound world through his skilful approach to instrumentation and orchestration. Whether it is the swanlike cry of the oboe, the rushing waves of harp arpeggios or the fountain sprays of the celesta, it is through these means that the music springs forth with a vitality that sparks the imagination and opens the door to a fairy tale world.

15 The romantic ballet and its critics: dance goes public

LUCIA RUPRECHT

The extraordinarily successful phenomenon of the romantic ballet represents a period of renewal of theatre dance but also a symbiosis between the performed and the written, between dancer and critic. Romantic ballet is an aesthetic movement both embodied and discursive. Ballet in the 1830s and 1840s cannot be considered without taking into account its written testimonies, which described a new and sensational physical technique, suggestive stage technology and an elaborate dramatic style. A cult of the romantic ballerina grew up that soon reached the higher spheres of myth-making. While there had always been admiration for stellar dancers, the 'star system' came into its own in the nineteenth century. The new writing on dance followed an era of aesthetic redefinition and fits perfectly into Habermas's theory of the emergence of *Öffentlichkeit* or the "public sphere". The commercialisation of opera performance brought in its wake a demand for consumer information and led to a flood of journalistic and fictional writings that grounded ballet firmly in the rapidly developing field of publicity.[1] Audiences expanded and diversified. They extended to those who did not have to be present at a performance at all, to the "liseuses de feuilleton" and to those who enjoyed being able to observe the dancers through the eyes of a critic who might even allow glimpses into the secret spaces behind the stage, the green rooms of Europe's theatres to which only the lucky few were admitted.

If we think of criticism as a medium that makes art and aesthetic concepts public property, nineteenth-century ballet criticism distinguishes itself at first sight by its overtly voyeuristic attitude: it made the female performers public property, raising their attractiveness by an elaborate "hierarchy of proximity" as Marian Smith called it. It created an image of the opera house as a place where gaining access to dancers' bodies – whether visual or otherwise – was not just a privilege of the rich and influential. Through the voices of male critics, the ballerina gained a prominent place in the feuilleton, but as object not subject.

Since voyeurism among dance critics will hardly surprise readers, it may be more useful to look at a cross-section of a range of views of well-known and also lesser-known critics. Their writings display the specific characteristics of nineteenth-century dance journalism, situated between aesthetic theory, advertisement and purple prose.

The Paris Opéra ballet was at the heart of a movement that spread out via Milan, London, Copenhagen, Vienna and Berlin. French criticism set the tone by the sheer quantity, as well as the quality of the reviews. These reviews report on various aspects of the performances, and reveal the aesthetic taste or even political opinions of the individual critic. They discuss the economic strategies of the enterprise which the Paris Opéra had become in the 1830s. Louis Véron, its director from 1831 to 1835, certainly understood the importance of publicity. He elevated Marie Taglioni to the rank of principal dancer. He started a tradition that would lead over the course of the next two decades to an ever increasing level of concentration on the ballerina as celebrity.[2] Véron also raised the status of the critics. They were allowed to enter the inner circle at the Rue Lepeletier in exchange for their services as passionate promoters of the silent art. In spite of their privileged status, few had any real understanding or even appreciation of the choreography and the dancing. The nineteenth-century feuilleton indulged instead in lengthy descriptions of plots, costumes and scenery. Yet it did provide a continuous record, a verbal acknowledgement of an art form which at that time had almost no other way to leave traces of its existence. The professional critic wrote a new genre of reflection on dance. From the philosophical writings of classical antiquity and the Renaissance to eighteenth-century works by philosophers such as Jean-Baptiste Du Bos, Charles Batteux, Adam Smith, William Hogarth or Denis Diderot, dance had been included in aesthetic treatises, even if in rather marginal ways. More importantly, the choreographers and dancing masters themselves had articulated their critical positions in their manuals. Fabricio Caroso's *Nobiltà di dame* (1600–5), François de Lauze's *Apologie de la danse* (1623), John Weaver's *Anatomical and Mechanical Lectures upon Dancing* (1721), Jean-Georges Noverre's *Lettres sur la danse, et sur les ballets* (1760) and Gasparo Angiolini's writings on the eighteenth-century action ballet – to name only a few – all formulated aesthetic programmes, while at the same time dealing with theoretical or pedagogical aspects of dance. The ballet master Carlo Blasis continued this tradition well into the nineteenth century. Yet most of his publications (among them *An Elementary Treatise upon the Theory and Practice of the Art of Dancing*, 1820, and *The Code of Terpsichore*, 1830) were influential mainly because they codified the classical technique and constantly refined the essentially unchanged standards of ballet as we still know it today. However, for a critic 'it was unheard of ... to participate in a ballet class';[3] the aesthetic judgement of theatre dance fell therefore almost exclusively into the hands of spectators who may have been professional writers, but were amateurs in the art of dancing.

The early generation of critics like Castil-Blaze of the *Journal des débats*, from 1815 to 1832 considered the leading Parisian ballet critic of the time, knew their limits. For Castil-Blaze and his fellow reviewers, the onset of an aesthetic of pure dance that evoked abstract concepts rather than expressing a plot certainly posed a problem. His criticism still follows the lines of Noverre's dogmas, opposing the craft of meaningless mechanical virtuosity to the art of meaningful mimic expression. The extended mime scenes, which often dominated the action on stage more than the dancing, were criticised or ridiculed. Berlioz's comical desperation in his review of *La Chatte métamorphosée en femme* for the *Revue et gazette musicale de Paris* (22 October 1837) suggests that the writing of a scenario was an easy task compared to its analysis:

> Writing a programme for a ballet is not difficult in itself; it is much harder to write a critique of the plot, especially when one is unfortunate enough not to have understood anything of the pantomime and does not want to consult the libretto. I find myself in precisely that situation here. Innumerable experiences have shown me that the mimic art was a closed book for me.

Berlioz's account testifies to the fact that the reception of ballet was still in thrall to an aesthetic that had been formed in an age in which theatre dance was inseparable from opera, and had to match up to the latter's unique combination of music, words and mime. Thus the composer-critic cannot avoid expressing his frustration at what he perceives to be a deficiency of the performance, rather than of his expectations: "I have never been able to persuade myself that my mimic sense was so obtuse that I couldn't discover the ... fundamental idea, the basic idea, the I D E A, at the first performance of a work of this nature."[4]

The new generation of critics displayed such a degree of confidence or sophistication in taste, style and judgement that they in turn became stars of the ballet scene. Outstanding among these celebrities of criticism was the writer Théophile Gautier, the most widely known chronicler of the romantic ballet. He wrote his first proper review of a ballet as dramatic critic of *La Presse* in 1837, and continued to monitor dance in Paris until 1871. His career thus encompassed the heyday of the romantic ballet, as well as its decline and short-lived renaissance in the shape of Arthur Saint-Léon's *Coppélia*. Gautier's credentials as a dance writer were his enthusiasm – not least for the beauty of the ballerinas – his contacts in the profession, aesthetic insights into the art that grew with his experience and his talent for vivid prose. His virtuoso writing matched the virtuosity of the performances, and outlived the ephemeral glory of the feuilleton. The editors of the six volumes of the *Histoire de l'art dramatique en France depuis vingt-cinq ans*, a collection of Gautier's newspaper articles, elevated his criticism to a position of equality with the spectacle on stage; indeed they suggested that the review could enhance the experience of the performance for the retrospective reader.[5]

Although Gautier remained relatively ignorant of choreography, he also produced various ballet scenarios from 1838 onwards. No less than six libretti were actually staged. The most famous of them was *Giselle* (1841), based on Heinrich Heine's writings on the popular myth of female spirits of revenge known as the wilis. Gautier created it in collaboration with the librettist Vernoy de Saint-Georges and the choreographer Jean Coralli. He thus knew what he was talking about when in his review of *La Gipsy* in 1839 he complained: "It is not easy to write for the legs. There can be no proud bombastic tirades, no fine verse, no poetical clichés, no words for effect, no puns, no declamations against the nobles, nothing but one situation after another."[6] The writer laments the gap between his two preferred media, the word and the body. Reading this danced literature was equally difficult; the journalist who sought clear dramatic content and a decipherable message in a ballet could not find it. It was as hard to write *about* 'the legs' as it was to write *for* them – yet the possibilities of glamorous literary invention were almost limitless (see Fig. 29).

Jules Janin, the other most prominent critic similar to Gautier of the romantic ballet, abandoned the more content-oriented judgements of a Castil-Blaze. They expressed a new aesthetic of theatre dance. Janin succeeded Castil-Blaze at the *Journal des débats*. Some of his reviews, for instance that of *Nathalie* (9 November 1832), echo the mocking edge of Berlioz's account given above. Janin intersperses his text with italicised passages from the ballet's libretto, comparing them either to the incongruous activities on stage or ridiculing their general absurdity. Yet his critique of *La Révolte au sérail* (6 December 1833) shifted the emphasis from preoccupation with the tension between words and movement: "Some people claim that an idea was necessary in order to make a ballet; these people are wrong: for making a ballet, one only needs dancers, to be precise female dancers, since we have expelled the male dancers . . . The good Mr Taglioni is the living proof . . . Mr Taglioni has never any idea." The critic continues that the choreographer possessed something that surpasses ideas, for "he has his daughter", the incomparable Marie Taglioni, first among the gallery of female stars of the romantic ballet. His remark "Elle danse, tout est dit" (She danses, that says it all)[7] disarmingly proves the insignificance of such secondary aspects as "his dancing" or storylines. Over the course of Janin's critiques it turns into a genuine aesthetic appreciation of theatre dance as sufficiently expressive in and of itself.

Much has been written about the disregard for the male dancer during the romantic era, a disregard that is not necessarily reflected in the actual casting lists, but finds its strongest articulation in the views of male critics. Janin is the most outspoken among them, frequently spicing up his eulogies of the female stars with utterances like "Under no circumstances do I grant

M. Théophile Gauthier indiquant lui-même à Mme Ferraris les différens pas de son ballet qu'elle n'a fait qu'interpréter devant le public.

Figure 29 Caricature by Cham from *Le Charivari*, 1 August, 1858. "Monsieur Théophile Gautier himself demonstrating to Madame Ferraris various steps of his ballet which she has only to interpret for the public."

a man the right to dance in public".[8] Only the most impressive male dancers could challenge such an attitude. Was this suppression of the male dancer the result of a conceited sense of omnipotence and possessiveness on the part of the spectator? After all, Gautier declared that "the true husband of an actress ... is the public".[9]

The vogue for *danser en travestie* engaged the audience in the complex sexual subtext of the romantic ballet. Cleverly, through its playful understatement, travesty emphasised the femininity of the ballerinas. Even more than Gautier's, Janin's reviews are rich in invectives against those who occupied space on stage that could have been more pleasingly filled by the Taglionis, Elsslers or Grisis. Yet the writing of the two balletomanes has more to offer. Their articles reveal a clear sense of the renewal of dance that leaves the pre-romantic aesthetic behind. Echoing, at first sight, Castil-Blaze's tirade against mere mechanical virtuosity, Janin also directs his scorn against the poses and tricks, the vanities and the "Un, deux, trois!" of the traditional genre of the *danse noble*. Rather than opposing it to the powers of pantomime he celebrates "the revolution in dancing" (24 August 1832), which had been introduced by Marie Taglioni, "this young girl who has created modern dance" (22 July 1832). In a description of the choreography, which is rare in such detail, he praises the naturalness of her comportment, the suppleness of her arms and legs, her ability to simply walk on stage, and the absence of forced *pirouettes* and *entrechats*. He talks of an overall quality of her performance which he calls the absence of "dance" in her dancing (24 August 1832), a judgement which does not lack irony, since she was the first one to excel in the most explicitly artificial aspect of the classical technique, the dancing on the pointe. At the same time he documents Taglioni's extraordinary mastery of difficulties, which made the technical side of dancing disappear.

Janin and Gautier introduced an approach to ballet criticism which united formalist sensibility with the emphatic language of poetry and an outspoken appreciation of physical beauty. Apart from the mime scenes, movement was freed from its bondage to a plot. It became available for metaphorical readings that consolidated the much-praised abstract qualities of romantic ballet, epitomised in the *ballet blanc*: lightness, evasiveness, transparency and purity, titillatingly embodied by sensual dancers. Technique, dramatic framework and viewing situation were woven together into a maze of artful eroticism. The ballerina reflected, through her profession and through the specific characteristics of her dancing, the simultaneity of erotic availability and elusiveness which was at the heart of the roles she performed. The poetry of the dance begged to be matched by the poetry of the feuilleton. The following review of Carlotta Grisi dancing *Giselle*, written for *The Musical World* of 12 June 1847 by a critic called 'D.' who clearly adopts the French style, illustrates this to great effect:

> Nothing can be lovelier, nothing more ethereal, nothing more deeply imbued with poesy than her Giselle. She looks a thing of air that would melt away at your approach. It is impossible to imagine you could touch her, so transparent, so fragile is her appearance. She *floats* along the stage. Scarcely can you perceive the movements of her pretty feet. You might almost fancy her an animated lily of the valley, but that she is endowed with the power of locomotion. She shrinks instinctively at the approach of her mortal lover, feeling him near even when her face is turned away from him. Catch her he never can, though she makes not the least apparent effort to avoid him. It is as though she were a magnet with repulsive, instead of attractive power.

> And yet how entirely attractive and how entirely unrepulsive! How playful
> and seemingly full of life and spirits! How prettily she coquets with her
> lover, fleeing as he approaches and pursuing as he flies – but never coming
> into actual contact with him; like hope long deferred, always seeming to be
> realised but never really compassed. It is the very essence of imaginative art,
> and proves Carlotta what we have many times pronounced her, the true
> Poetess of the Dance.

Artists like Carlotta Grisi and Fanny Elssler complemented abstract and
sensual beauty with an expressiveness of mime that spoke directly to the
critics, as becomes evident in Janin's review of *Giselle* on 30 June 1841.
He writes after quoting a few of Giselle's "lines": "That's how she speaks,
and I can assure you that she speaks even better than that. Her gestures are
ideas, her dance is speech." When an anonymous critic of the *Revue et gazette
musicale de Paris* states that "the gaze of the viewer, seized by the deepest pain,
rests on the pale and devastated face" of Elssler performing the role in 1843,
he not only acknowledges the performer's talent for acting, but also indicates
a mode of spectatorship that engages the emotions and senses before the
intellect. Gautier draws a clear line between situations of intellectual and
sensual involvement by claiming that ballet was "directed only to the eyes".[10]
Thus Janin writes with regard to the rational inaccessibility of the ballet *La
Tentation*,

> the way in which you are able to judge all this is to surrender to the
> impression of the moment, to be nonchalant enough not to scrutinise your
> pleasure, to let yourself be guided, without resistance, by the painter, the
> musician, the *danseuse*, to whichever place they lead you, in short, to allow
> yourself to be happy: that's the secret of ballet' (27 June 1832).

This surrender simultaneously empowered the critic, since the non-
discursive allusiveness of the productions granted him the opportunity to
create his own spectacle on the blank page.

How to describe dance would become a major problem at the turn of
the twentieth century, but the critics of the romantic era were less troubled
by the problem of representation; they playfully evoke the ineffable, the
"grâce inexprimable",[11] and tease out the unsayable, the erotic charge of
the bodily display. While being important mediators of the new aesthetic
of dancing and seeing, they also took the liberty of producing their prose
on the occasion of, rather than *on* dance. They hid their amateurism under
a flamboyant style and anecdotal digressions. They mused; they described
physical features and revealed indiscretions. The explosion of journalism
in the first decades of the nineteenth century led to anxieties about a new
"self-interested instrumentality" of language as opposed to the truthfulness
of high literature.[12] Short-lived, consumer-oriented, amusing but superficial

and a potential battlefield of personal animosities, the feuilleton introduced a new written discourse whose characteristics echoed common prejudices about the entertainments which it depicted. Journalistic writing displayed a form of overstated showiness that was perceived in gendered terms as an unsettling feminisation of the masculine bourgeois domain of the word. Louis Gentil, author of the manuscript "Les Cancans de l'Opéra", failed journalist himself, holder of an administrative post at the Opéra and most sarcastic observer of the goings-on behind its wings, focused his scorn on Janin. Gentil's attack on the critic indeed recalls the latter's disdain of the effeminate male dancer: "He is provocative, mischievous, capricious, pretty, coquettish, sulky, playful, amorous without energy, quarrelsome without humour, irritable without anger, someone who speaks up without force, mumbles rather than murmurs, and chirps without singing . . . Fly-catchers of Paris, dilettantes of the big city, *voilà* Janin!"[13] In a less spicy manner, a Paris correspondent for the *Musical World* called 'S.S.' suggests that the writer got as carried away by the flow of his own prose as by the ballerinas whose praise he composed:

> All the world here is full of your *Pas de Quatre*, about which the London papers are so profusely eulogistic. The metaphrastic Jules Janin has ventured an article upon the subject, which is more remarkable for its verbosity than its truth. In apostrophising the four queens of the dance, he says Taglioni depended upon her laurels, Carlotta Grisi upon her beauty, Cerito [sic!] upon her freshness, and Lucile Grahn upon her talent, for maintaining their positions before a British public. Nothing can be more absurd. Janin dubs Cerito "The forbidden fruit" – "The unknown" – because, forsooth, she has never appeared before the Parisians. That admirable artist need not repine at this, since she has won her laurels from the severest public in Europe. (31 July 1845)

The press coverage of the *Pas de quatre* (1845), showcasing four of the most famous ballerinas of the day, not only documents the fact that criticism itself had developed its own star system, complete with glamorous hierarchies and resentments. It also represents a pinnacle in the cultivation of the female star. The popularity of the piece, still fuelled by the fame of outstandingly talented dancers, reveals the new dynamic of stardom that relied increasingly on media spectacle, rather than on artistic abilities. In *La Fanfarlo* (1847), Charles Baudelaire draws a highly entertaining and sarcastic picture of a self-appointed critic who embarks on the journalistic profession with the single goal of attracting the erotic interest of an infamously seductive celebrity of the Opéra. He wins her love by bombarding her with insulting reviews that only add to her fame:

From now on Fanfarlo was mauled every week at the tail-end of an important periodical. It was impossible to assert or suggest that she had an ugly leg or ankle or knee, as her skirts concealed them and every lorgnette would have denounced such blasphemy. But she was accused of being rough and common and tasteless, and doing her best to inflict German or Spanish mannerisms on the French theatre, with her castanets and spurs and high heels – apart from which, she drank like a trooper, was too fond of lapdogs and the caretaker's daughter, and suchlike dirty linen of domestic life which are the staple food and titbits of our dimmer newspapers.[14]

Baudelaire might well have had in mind the *danseuse terrible* Lola Montès, whose impulsiveness, extravagant life-style and illustrious affairs made up for her lack of dancing skills and gained her the attention of journalists over several years. Gautier, too much of an admirer of good dancing to yield entirely to Montès's aura, left ambivalent accounts of her performances. His colleague Pier-Angelo Fiorentino of *Le Corsaire-Satan* was among the many victims of the Irish-Creole conqueror and fervently defended her. On 8 March 1845, he reports on Montès's controversial appearance at Porte-Saint-Martin, where she had been engaged for a programme of popular national dances after having been expelled from the Opéra for allegedly throwing one of her shoes at the audience on the evening of her debut. Fiorentino writes: "From the moment in which the sound of the castanets indicated the first bars of the *cachucha*, an avalanche of bouquets landed on the stage and plastered the space in such a manner that the young dancer could hardly make a step." The cult of the dancer had literally taken over her performances. Whether we see the notoriety of Lola Montès as one of the indicators of the decline of the romantic ballet, which had become fixated on its stars, or as an entertaining exception, it shows to what extent acts of devotion and of discourse were involved in the aesthetic project. It seems a fitting end to these glimpses of the world of nineteenth-century criticism to evoke the image of a dance that is as much disfigured as it is enhanced by the flowers of the journalists' words. The vanities, the imagination and the discernment, the calculation and the enthusiasm of the reviews give evidence of a spectacle that developed alongside the main spectacles on stage; the writings bear witness to the fact that the romantic ballet was a multi-authored phenomenon.

16 The soul of the shoe

MARION KANT

Ask any young woman on her way to a performance of *Giselle* or *Sleeping Beauty* what most clearly symbolises ballet and she will probably answer – the skirt and the pointe shoe. She will not quote sentences from the story and may recall only a few names of the characters. But after the performance she will remember the ballet costume of the female dancer. If she ever had ballet lessons she will reminisce about her first pointe shoes; she might still have them in the attic. Why this cult of the costume? Has ballet no message? Is it merely a flighty art form of beautiful lines, of flowing skirts and satin shoes?

The history of these two items of dress tell us exactly the opposite. The skirt and the point shoe represented a complete change in the nature of the ballet as an art form. They have not always been there. When they were introduced in the 1830s, roughly 180 years ago, they initiated a revolution in artistic values and a fundamental shift in the attitude towards women in public life.

How and why the tutu and the slipper achieved this pride of place in ballet will be explained in what follows. Less clear is why much ballet today still uses a dress code frozen in time.

This new apparel, which ballet lovers know so well, was an inextricable part of the evolution of romanticism in the arts; during the nineteenth century romanticism gave dance its particular and enduring look. When Théophile Gautier described Marie Taglioni in 1834 he wrote about her delicate appearance: "She floats like a spirit in a transparent mist of white muslin with which she loves to surround herself, and she resembles a contented soul scarcely bending the petals of celestial flowers with the tips of her rosy feet." And then he continued with a description of Fanny Elssler, the other great ballerina of the day: "She recalls the muse Terpsichore with her tambourine and her tunic slit to reveal her thigh and caught up with clasps of gold."[1] Ten years later he defined romanticism in ballet through the figure of the seemingly weightless, fairy-like female performer:

> Mlle Taglioni dances the Sylphide: That says it all. This ballet opened the
> door for a whole new era in choreography, and through it romanticism
> entered the realm of Terpsichore. After La Sylphide, Les Filets de Vulcain
> and Flore et Zephyr were no longer possible. The Opéra was given over to

gnomes, ondines, salamanders, elfs, nixes, wilis, peris, all those strange,
mysterious creatures who lend themselves so wonderfully to the fantasies of
the ballet master. The twelve mansions of marble and gold of the Olympians
were relegated to the dust of the scenery store, and artists were
commissioned to produce only romantic forests and valleys lit by that pretty
German moon of Heinrich Heine's ballads. Pink tights remained pink, for
there can be no choreography without pink tights, and all that was changed
was the satin ballet slipper for the Greek cothurna. This new style brought
in its wake a great abuse of white gauze, tulle and tarlatan, and colours that
dissolved into mist by means of transparent skirts. White became almost the
only colour.[2]

Gautier's evocation of romanticism in dance focused on the female dancer
in a mist of white, with dainty, rosy feet that scarcely bent a petal. (In printed
illustrations of the early 1830s the dancers indeed were often barefooted.)

By the time Gautier wrote the second description in 1844 these distinct
elements had become the norm: the female dancer in white gauze, tulle and
tarlatan dissolving into transparency with pink tights and satin slippers.
All traces of classicism with its allegorical figures had given way to a stage
covered by mysterious romantic creatures.

The "transparent mist" of tulle conquered the stage as the standard
costume of nineteenth century ballet, sometimes white, sometimes more
colourful, the nuances in colour helping to define female characters. But
white, as Gautier remarked, became the prevalent colour and eventually lent
its name to a particular genre in ballet: the *ballet blanc*, or *white ballet*. In it
a group of female dancers (mostly in the second act) would all be dressed
in the same white skirts, they would look alike, they would move alike,
supernatural beings, neither alive nor dead. The world that they evoked lay
beyond life. White became the uniform colour and the colour of the ballet
uniform.

Romanticism marked a real break in the staging as well as the costuming
of ballet. Though many of the elements that made up ballet emerged
gradually, the whole came across as new and it challenged tradition. For
Jean-Georges Noverre[3] in the middle and late eighteenth century, the costume was but one part of the dance drama. It was one means among others –
story, design and steps – to express human emotion. Noverre thought a
reform of costume was necessary because he desired it to support rather
than hinder movement. The drama of the *ballet d'action* determined the
shape of the costumes. Nor could Carlo Blasis in his treatise on dance of 1820
imagine a dance costume detached from the ballet and its movement. His
descriptions and analyses focused on movement, technique, the acquisition
of muscular strength and flexibility. He assumed that costume followed
function. For Blasis, ballet was defined through the study of the legs, the

arms or the entire body, with shoes and dress an afterthought. The illustrations in his treatise show us today what his students in 1820 wore: white garments imitative of ancient Greek drapery, with a loose, sleeveless blouse and a free flowing skirt. This costume was complemented by soft-looking, snug shoes that allowed for easy and flexible stretches and extensions of the feet.[4]

Blasis's illustrations of his dancers reflect two aspects of the costume: practicality of dress for the dancer (male as well as female) and closeness to conventional fashion of the time. The craze for ancient Greek and Roman culture during the French Revolution had left its mark in a fashion that idealised tunic-frocks. From Napoleon's seizure of power in 1799 to the 1820s, high-waist "Empire" dresses became the rage, with the elegant Empress Josephine Bonaparte symbolising the age and many women competing for the highest waist. They too accented the body without imprisoning it. From the 1830s female fashion focused more on the tight corseted bodice and narrow waist with much fuller skirts. The relatively free and unrestricted movement increasingly became difficult. Ballet dancers also pressed their bodies into corsets (first reinforced with fishbone, later with steel wire) to acquire the "wasp" waist.

Romanticism embodied a paradox, in dance as well as in the other art forms. What today is regarded as the romantic movement's "other-worldly charms" and fairy-tale escape from reality depended on the real world's industrial progress and economic development. A few examples will illustrate the case: in 1832 Theobald Boehm, a Bavarian court musician, designed a new type of flute in his own factory, which used interlinked rod-axles to transmit the motion of fingers to remote tone holes. In other words, he devised a system of metallic levers and rings by which the opening or closing of the tone hole could be controlled. The new instrument, just like other new brass instruments invented around the same time, created a larger sound, corrected and maintained the pitch and, through its greater variety of instrumental volume and tone colour, made orchestras more expressive (and much louder). This improvement depended on the rapid advance of machine tools and metallurgy.[5] Stage lighting also shifted significantly. In the first half of the nineteenth century gas lighting was widely used. The limelight, an early type of a spotlight, relied on the chemical process of combining gases, oxygen and hydrogen with lime. Gas was particularly dangerous for dancers whose gauze dresses frequently caught fire, often burning the dancer, the entire stage or even the opera building. Fire prevention and protection became vital in theatres. With the invention of the first incandescent light bulb by Edison in 1879 the application of safer electric lighting and particular mood setting could begin; unheard-of effects – the gradual dimming of the chandeliers and the darkened auditorium – could be introduced and the audience would be enchanted and lured into a magical sphere.

The romantic ballet costume, too, was a product of industrialisation. The intensive use of muslin, tarlatan, gauze and tulle – all cotton products – coincided with the growth of cotton manufacturing in Europe, above all in England and France. Between the 1770s and the 1840s Britain increased its cotton production tenfold. The technological innovations that introduced industrialised processes into cotton production increased the availability of the material: mass production initiated mass use. It also forced female workers into the factory, turning them and their children into cheap labour. In fact, industrialisation in the textile industry depended on the allocation of female labour to factories. Cheap cotton made possible the special design of costumes for every new production instead of recycling from previous ballets, as had been the custom. It also introduced imitation and replication of costumes: the costume of the soloist could be replicated in the costumes of the corps. The great availability of material also facilitated the introduction of costume detail from ballets into wider fashion and vice versa. Fashion at rapid speed offered a new design of women's wear for every season.

The other two materials widely used in the making of clothing and household material – silk and wool – lost out to cotton. Wool was not yet as suited to fit into industrialised processing: spinning, bleaching, dying, weaving, cutting and so on. Lingerie could now be made of the cheaper cotton instead of silk, a relevant factor, above all, for the making of corsets, which were deemed an indispensable part of female fashion on stage and off in the nineteenth century.

The ballet costume up to 1830 had distinguished itself not by its complete difference from ordinary dress but by its aping and appropriation of society's fashions. During the previous centuries costume on stage was either randomly chosen (the dancer took what was available, however irrelevant the costume might have been in relation to the role performed, especially if she had to pay for it herself) or, more importantly, indicated the social class of the wearer and her position within an aristocratic hierarchy of order. The romantic costume shifted the focus from social or historic markers to gender indicators because the stories focused on gender battles. New costume and shift in storytelling happened at the same time and were closely linked and both indicate a reconceptualisation of dance.

The romantic ballet costume, that mass of white cotton products, was different from fashionable dress in the length of the skirts. The bare arms or the low-cut neckline exposing the bust were not unusual in female fashion – but exposing the ankles, the calves and or even the thighs definitely was. No decent woman would have allowed her legs to be seen, neither bare nor stockinged: yet the dancers on stage revealed what was not supposed to be visible in public. From the beginning, the romantic ballet costume emphasised gender as problematic and sexualised the female characters, and through them, the dancer herself. Let us look at one example, how the tension between being and appearance was created and manipulated: in 1831 in Paris Marie Taglioni exploded into attention in *Robert le diable*, a grand opera by Giacomo Meyerbeer. The dancer played a nun who had fallen for the devil and lost her faith.[6] Taglioni and the other dancers entered in costumes that copied nuns' habits; when they discarded their nuns' robes, white skirts became visible. Within a couple of years those infamous skirts would symbolise romanticism. Taglioni's abbess and her nuns were not the first to wear white on stage. But their costumes transformed the meaning of the scene through the connotations of white and thus made a deep impression on contemporary audiences. The shrewd use of this colour created a frightening uncertainty – satanic nuns whose white costume projected innocence. It called into question the romanticised ideal of woman. The colour defined the state of femaleness by confusing and reversing the moral categories of good or evil. These costumes broke another tradition; they had no equivalent in the world outside the theatre. The ballet costume was not "historic" but completely new: no social class, guild or profession wore such garb. Instead, the distance between the clothes worn on and off stage cleared the way for a new kind of appearance with a radically new symbolic content. It turned women on stage into an abstract category: *the* woman, *the* female per se, with a certain ethical value system attached. The plots of romantic ballets of the 1830s and 1840s involved murderous sylphs, rebellious female slaves and amazons fighting patriarchal society. They portrayed women as good or evil, caring or tempting, strong or weak but whatever their roles, they were primarily women, women opposite men.

The colour white had undergone an important philosophical and aesthetic transformation after Isaac Newton broke down sunlight into separate rays in 1672 and realised that colours were "Qualifications of Light ... but Original and connate properties". They could be simple or compound and they could be put on a wheel to show their physical relationships. But whatever was done, light was nothing but a physical phenomenon; it could be refracted, analysed and measured. With this recognition Newton destroyed the mystique behind light and colours. As he argued in his *Opticks: A Treatise of the Reflections, Refractions, Inflections & Colours of Light*, practical experiments could prove that white light was the additive result of the spectrum of colours and black nothing but their absence.

After the shock of Newton's reasoned analysis the German writer and poet Johann Wolfgang von Goethe in the last years of the eighteenth and the early years of the nineteenth century provided colour with a metaphysical dimension. For him, colours were expressions of energy and they could affect the psyche and the soul. His colour theory, less popular with physicists, enchanted and fascinated contemporary philosophers and artists like Arthur Schopenhauer, architects Otto Runge and Gottfried Semper and had a long-lasting impact on the humanities in the twentieth century. Colour had meaning again; colour was not simply an appearance of the physical world but a phenomenological problem that had to do with human perception and thus could stimulate, even harm, psychological moods, dispositions and sentiments. They could make people feel light, animated and happy or sad, agitated and sombre. One of Goethe's three fundamental emotional colour pairs was white–black, the ur-phenomenon representing the ur-polarity of light/darkness out of which all other colours evolved. In *Zur Farbenlehre* (*Colour Theory*) of 1810 Goethe wrote that colours were "deeds of light, actions and sufferings". Thus, during the early nineteenth century the meaning of the colour white changed once more; now it stood for innocence, virginity, chastity, clarity and purity.

By 1831 the evil nuns dressed in white created tension between the external, beautiful façade and the internal corruption of character. Hence they doubly deceived the audience: the dancer-nuns dressed in white signalled innocence and purity but acted its opposite. Finally, beneath the white nun's habit emerged the transparent white habit of the dancer. If the stage lanterns cast light from a particular angle her body appeared no longer covered at all but exposed as what it really was: a dangerous sexual challenge. Without the light shining through the fine cotton she could again act as the innocent, reliable lover. Within an instant the dancer shifted from one extreme to the other. Which part of the ambiguous costume/message was to be trusted?

The sylphs, wilis, the shadows in *La Bayadère*, the ghosts and spirits, the sylphs and immortal maidens, swans and butterflies of the nineteenth century ballet, were all dressed in white or very light translucent colours. They were fragile and tender creatures and at the same time destructive forces. Nowhere does this become more clear than in the second act of *Giselle*, which finally established the look and symbolism of the *ballet blanc*. The wilis, those "dead bacchantes",[7] arrive in uniform white costume – tight-fitting bodice and wide flowing skirt – instead of the faded colours of their former existence as Gautier had originally suggested.[8] They form battalions and execute their dance movements in military-style precision. The white gauze skirts and flowing hems soften the frighteningly martial image of the disciplined troop of wilis, led by Myrtha, their queen. They constitute a beautiful but threatening force out to destroy all men who cross their path. They are vengeful beasts that bring death; yet they wear the colour white, the colour of innocence and purity.

The costume of the ballerina was developed to help tell the hair-raising and horrific stories of women's lives and their transformation from alive to dead (or somewhere in between). The situations in which the heroines of ballet narratives found themselves differed slightly from one another. The geographical or time settings varied: some took place in a fantasy or fairy-tale world, others in a recognisable reality. But they were united by one common feature: the stories tested women in situations that questioned their very existence. These questions always revolved around the fundamental issues that had occupied citizens of European societies after the French Revolution: what if women are given equal rights? What might we to do with these emancipated women? What then happens to the familiar, traditional gender divisions? What happens with love relationships? The essential questions in these stories were so similar that the standard costume only needed small amendments.

Throughout the nineteenth century we can trace the woman in white as a romantic trope, in novels, paintings, operas, poems, but above all in ballets. At the end of the century Edgar Degas painted the dancers many times. He depicted them exhausted, happy, exhilarated, disengaged, training and practising or slumped over on the floor – they wear the light skirts that were introduced several decades before, now even shorter, cut just above the knee. They wear them with colourful sashes or ribbons, flowers, embroideries or other small ornaments and attributes – ballet added to the standard ballet costume whose absence by then would have been unthinkable. If the choreographies have not survived and the stories have been relegated with their music to the compartment of less important works of theatre history, the ballet costume invented in the same period still lives on. It is still the dream of many a young girl to fit into that pretty white tutu[9] and wear those beautiful satin slippers with their toughened caps that are so cruel to the feet.

The ballet shoe forms just as important and interesting a part of the costume as the skirt. The transformation that ballet underwent thanks to the employment of a special shoe is breathtaking. In fact, the development of the ballet shoe from a soft, satin slipper to a device made according to the latest technology with steel-hard cap is nothing short of a revolution in style, means and equipment. We cannot date the invention of the pointe shoe, but we can follow its changes that lead to the form and shape we know today. It began with the choreographer Charles Didelot, who used flying machines in several of his ballets at the turn of the eighteenth and early nineteenth centuries to sweep his ballerinas across the stages of Paris, London, Milan and St Petersburg. The performers were attached to wires to haul them from one corner to another while their feet flashed across the ground. From the early nineteenth century on, lithographs and etchings show female dancers

Figure 30 Fanny Elssler's pointe shoes.

hovering in the air. Their tiny feet, bare or clad, rest on petals or translucent insect wings. They barely touch the earth if at all. Dancers such as Amalia Brugnoli and Elisa Vaque-Moulin reaped applause for moving on the tips of their toes before Taglioni or Elssler became famous for feet sheathed in soft satin. This footwear was supple and where the toes touched the satin they were reinforced with stitches. The soles were made of flexible leather. Gautier noted:

> The sole, which is very hollowed out in the centre does not reach the top of the foot, but ends squarely, leaving about two finger-breadths of material projecting. The purpose of this is to enable the dancer to perform pointe work by giving a sort of jointed point of support, but as the whole weight of the body is borne on this part of the shoe, which would inevitably break, the dancer has to strengthen it by darning, almost as old-clothes menders do, the heels of stockings to make them last. The inside of the shoe is lined with strong canvas and at the very end, a strip of leather and cardboard, the thickness of which depends on the lightness of the wearer. The rest of the shoe is chevronned on the outside by a network of ribbons firmly sewn on, and there is also stitching on the quarter, which is adjusted by means of a little tag of ribbon in the Andalusian manner.[10] (Fig. 30)

Those brief moments on the tip of the toe appeared so breathtaking and amazing because technique beforehand had placed attention on other aspects of dance. The technique that would allow a dancer to rise smoothly onto point and linger – a moment that has come to define ballet as a genre – had not yet developed. In Taglioni's and Elssler's generation, the arms had to support the elevating body. (Cartoons of the time depict ballerinas flailing their arms around, adding a sense of instability and hysteria as inherent in women.) Gradually ballerinas learned to rise effortlessly or jump onto point and remain on their toes. The shoes in the 1830s and 1840s did not yet have any of the hard reinforcements, characteristic of shoes made later in the century. The development of the pointe technique in ballet thus depended on the interaction between the materiality of the shoe, its constant updating (in the same way the technology of the flute was continually bettered) and the revision of training methods. A. E. Théleur was probably the first teacher to develop a technique for the strengthening of the foot. In his *Letters on dancing* of 1832, the title an intentional reference to Noverre's book, Théleur came up with several exercises that resulted in a robust foot. He also described the way in which dancers should raise or lower their bodies by analysing what happened with the body weight in relation to ankles, heels and toes, though he was still concerned with training more than performance.

If we look at the printed illustrations of the time we see dancers with anomalous anatomies: long swan necks, small waists, extremely long, thin arms and miniature feet. It is remarkable that the entire dance style and technique depended on a body part that was more and more hidden away and distorted in images of ballerinas. The newly emerging technique depended on the strength and durability of the feet; the tip of the foot had to carry the entire body and make possible that technique. But the feet in popular printed illustrations cannot carry the dancer, they cannot sustain a jump, they cannot run the body across the stage. Under no circumstances can those tiny feet make the body spin in *pirouettes* and hold it, even briefly, on pointe to develop an arabesque. Why was the foot – the vital part of an entire aesthetic and technical approach to the body – so misrepresented? Because that new technique showed too much flesh? Was it to ease the shock and make the women on stage as inoffensive as possible? Or to pretend the provocation was not happening? Or because it was improper and tasteless to associate the feet of delicate dancers with those flat and clumsy organs of proletarian women who scuffled around in wooden clogs? Whatever the reason might have been, the result was astonishing. On the one hand, the printed illustrations demonstrate that the technique executed by women was considered an amazing accomplishment; they also suggest that it was an extreme problem. The visible aspect of ballet's technical revolution was made to disappear in illustrations of its performers, diminishing their feet to the point of non-existence.

Many critics of ballet from the 1830s on objected fervently to these new choreographic developments and proclaimed that the art form was in decline: the ballerinas were no doubt brilliant technicians, but their technique was nothing move than mindless acrobatics. (That seemed true even when the technique was engineered by male choreographers in the background though female choreographers were replacing their male colleagues and most famous ballerinas choreographed their own scenes.) Ballet had been hijacked by women who wanted to show off. Men no longer had significant roles to play, so it seemed, and had become superfluous. Other critics like Gautier or Jules Janin saw the new ballerinas as proof that men were neither beautiful nor useful. They argued that a feminised dance was the only tolerable one. But "hommes de lettres" like Gautier also believed in female emancipation, championing the beliefs of Count Saint-Simon, who fought for women's suffrage. The opponents replied with fury: women had no intelligent minds of their own. Philosophers could reason and science could prove that women were less intelligent than men. Female technique and its technology (costume and shoes) had to be treated with scorn. Through the influence of these hostile critics romantic ballet was declared to have had a short life span and after 1848 was not worth remembering. Then an odd reversal in historiography and criticism took place: in the late nineteenth century the Imperial Ballet in Russia was celebrated as a revival of ballet. That same romantic technique and costume, the tutu (now shorter)[11] and the ballet shoe (now more supportive), suddenly emerged like a phoenix from the ashes. For a man, the choreographer Marius Petipa, had clearly taken control again and there was nothing to fear. Since after mid-century the French romantic ballet, it was said, "perished", its Russian revival required a new name: general usage replaced *romantic* with *classical*, a confusion of terminology and concepts that has never been resolved.

From the 1860s on and certainly by the late 1870s the pointe shoe was no longer a slender leathery slipper but an instrument with which ballerina Pierina Legnani could turn thirty-two *fouettés pirouettes* in *Swan Lake*. It had a harder box to sustain the ballerina on point. The front of the shoe, the box, had been reinforced with layers of glued paper or burlap, allowing the dancer to stand on it for a much longer time. She had been trained in countless classes to jump onto pointe or rise gradually,[12] whatever the choreographer demanded. The shank, also inserted to support the dancer, was made of one or a split piece of leather or again glued paper (in the twentieth century of plastic). That is in principle what the shoe looks like today. Miniscule nails tacked the textile part of the shoe to the sole and the box (today, glue is preferred). Both were so hard, stiff and inflexible that the ballerina had to "break in" the shoe before she could dance in it. That literally meant damaging it: bending and making it more flexible by using a hammer or simply closing the door on the shoe. Of course this was a tricky moment as the shoe had to retain some stiffness; if it was rendered too soft it would be useless. Until recently, leading ballerinas would use up several pairs of pointe shoes during one performance. Improvements focused on making the shank and the box more durable, on increasing their flexibility and reliability. There was less need for a brutal "breaking in" process and the average shoe now supported the foot much better.

All of this technological progress had thus far never questioned the production process but merely enhanced features that were already there. This might change with the latest, truly innovative approach (only three years old and just patented): it treats the pointe shoe as a prosthetic tool. The approach to making a pointe shoe is slightly modified by looking at it as a "missing limb". It becomes more than an aid (that the traditional pointe shoe is) by providing something the foot cannot naturally do. It enhances technical possibilities by rethinking weight distribution, shifting weight away from the tip of the toe. The shoe is cast as a socket: the foot of the dancer is wrapped in plaster-impregnated gauze over which an elastic sock is pulled to hold the gauze tight to the foot. Over gauze and sock a plastic bag is placed to keep the layers clean. The entire foot-gauze-sock-plastic-bag-contraption is positioned in a pail, which is filled with sand, which provides a semi-weight-bearing environment while the splinting material is drying. The result: a negative impression of the foot in action made of flexible material. From the cast a flexible inner liner is custom-made, together with an outer shell, which can be standardised. The outer shell is also reinforced with a compact block and a tongue, which make point dancing possible by shifting the weight of the body away from the front of the foot and distributing it evenly upwards. In addition, the polyurethane and polypropylene materials diminish the impact of jumps – just like a lightning rod they direct the force away. Finally, inner liner and outer shell can be beautified with any colour satin. The new point shoe looks like its traditional cousin but is much healthier and lasts considerably longer (see Fig. 31). The drawback, of course, is the high costs of the individualised production process.[13]

By the twentieth century ballet costume and point shoes had been publicly accepted as symbols of the art as a whole. They carried all the representational implications for the female body. Around 1900, a new ideal of femininity led to an attack on ballet in the name of "nature" directed at its costume. The skirt and shoes became literally the critical points in the emergence of the so-called "modern" or free dance. Modern dancers around 1900 began articulating themselves and their revolt by discarding the costume. Out went corsets, pointe shoes and tutus, and in exchange came bare bodies and bare feet. Isadora Duncan declared that a free woman would have to free her body from traditional clothes. The body could be exposed in a "natural" way as long as the movements themselves embodied ideas. Nudity was more desirable than half-clothed bodies – indeed, it was more natural and less sexualised than transparent materials that suggestively veiled ballet dancers. Duncan's designs for her stage costumes harked back to the tunics of ancient Greece and Rome and the new loose garments were implicitly associated with Plato's, Aristotle's and Socrates' ancient ideals of freedom,

Figure 31 Pointe shoes 1950–2005 from the Soviet Union, Bulgaria, Germany, Great Britain and the United States.

republicanism and democracy. That, of course, had been exactly the same ideal with which the French Revolution had introduced its own tunics as a dress code. But neither Duncan nor any of her contemporaries recognised the irony that lay in the appropriation of exactly those notions that had once made ballet modern. For the modern rebels, ballet was outdated; it was no longer what it had been for Gautier (a critical analysis of an oppressive society) but instead misunderstood as a proponent of patriarchal dominance. The costume, the tutu and the pointe shoes, were tools to stifle women and, accordingly, any dancer who tolerated such dress made herself part of the repressive system. Even today advocates of modern or post-modern dance caricature ballet because of its costume and draw inspiration from the satire that the misapplication of toe shoes and frilly skirts offer. A modern dancer might not have been able to overturn the principles but at least she could change the exterior. By rejecting the look, she hoped to affect the reality. Whether the reformers of dance successfully introduced twentieth century modernity into ballet or whether ballet would have reformed itself on its own remains open to interpretation. But from the 1910s and 1920s onwards dancers in leotards or body stockings as gender-equalising, androgynous costumes increasingly populated half the stage, while traditional ballets and ballerinas occupied the other half. In the twenty-first century, the great ballets of the past still draw huge crowds to the opera houses of the world in spite of (or because of) their now stylised costumes and strict body movements.

Three questions arise at this point, none easy to answer:

1 How do we understand the romantic ballets today?
2 How do we see the costumes and the shoes?
3 Why have the *romantic* (turned *classical*) tutus and pointe shoes remained symbolic of the ballet as such?

The continuities in dress are remarkable. From the 1830s to the present, frocks with their tight bodices and wide fluffy skirts, the little sylph or butterfly wings, the satin shoes that hide the hardened pointe, the garlands of flowers, the parted hair, firmly combed back into a bun, have appeared over and over again. All those ingredients returned in every ballet and they were merged into the standard costume. There is a very clear, uninterrupted line between the *Sylphide* of 1832 and the sylphs in *Chopiniana* of 1908. Does that matter today? Does anybody bother to consider the meaning of these well-known costumes? Do mothers and grandmothers know what they are doing when they take their daughters to see a romantic ballet? Probably not. What once scandalised audiences in the Parisian opera has become quaint, unchanging and, above all, safe. Modern audiences marvel at the same movements of today's great ballerinas as the audiences of Gautier's time cheered Taglioni and Elssler. The magic of movement, plot and music, all well known and unthreatening, still draw comfortable crowds.

Do these audiences of a modern performance of *Giselle* know that they are about to confront an existential conflict about the place of women in society? Do they remember that romantic ballet used to ask many uncomfortable questions and challenge moral values?

Even if they wanted to do so, explanations and analyses which might take them behind the packaging are hard to find. It may well be that contemporary choreographers and audiences have made themselves accomplices of those forces, which undermined the emancipation of women in the 1830s and still do so today. Nevertheless, romantic ballet is not about fairy tales. It is about the very rough reality that women face. And the costumes once were able to tell that story of conflict.

What today's audience sees and demands to see is the ballerina in a costume that has been disconnected from its own history. Romantic ballet was once radical; the contrast between the weak and dependent female of the narratives and the strong female executing technique reflected the social status of women. The treatment of women able to create and perform their own technology echoes the discomfort and anxiety about women taking control and demanding equality, whether as suffragettes or factory workers in the cotton mills. Romantic ballet has been idealised and reduced to soppy stories that are seldom told in historical context. Romantic ballet is not merely about unhappy love affairs but about gender relations on the most profound level. What the audience gets with the tutu and the pointe shoe is a whole ideology, packed into the libretto and the music as much as the costume as an entity. That ideology did indeed evolve around the female performer and the ballerina became its carrier; she made it visible through the things she wore.

PART IV

The twentieth century: tradition becomes modern

17 The ballet avant-garde I: the Ballets Suédois and its modernist concept

ERIK NÄSLUND

Serge Diaghilev's Ballets Russes arrived in Paris in 1909 and immediately turned ballet into a high fashion in the Western hemisphere. But in 1920 a rival introduced itself to Paris: the Ballets Suédois. This company dared to perform in the Théâtre des Champs-Elysées, home ground of the Russians before the First World War. The newcomers quickly established themselves in the French capital and challenged Diaghilev's concept of avant-garde ballet. They took modernism to a new level and defined avant-garde not through the brilliance of ballet stars or spectacular extravaganza but through a concept that extended beyond all known theatrical conventions. Throughout its brief and hectic existence from 1920 to 1925, the Ballets Suédois were constantly criticised for being not Swedish enough as well as too Swedish, and above all for not presenting real ballet. In many ways the critics were right. The company was more international than Swedish in its character and instead of reinforcing the balletic tradition it searched for new paths in dance. The company's name pointed to its Swedish founders and its most prominent dancers. Its existence had come out of the art collection of the Swedish aristocrat Rolf de Maré, who had assembled significant modernist works by European, and particularly French, artists during the 1910s. He himself was the favourite grandchild of another great art collector in Sweden, the Countess Wilhelmina von Hallwyl. Around 1900 she was considered one of the wealthiest people in her country. Her grandson inherited her fascination for art and for collecting it. Both grandparents provided Rolf de Maré with the financial independence to pursue his exquisite but expensive interests. This financial independence also allowed him to feel secure enough to live his life as openly gay.

A turning point in his life was the encounter in 1912 with the Swedish painter Nils Dardel who was exactly the same age. He had settled in Paris in 1910 to study with Matisse and quickly made friends with leading painters, poets, composers and art dealers. Dardel was to cultivate his new friend's taste in art and he guided Maré towards modernism in general and cubism in particular.

Dardel began to buy works of art, paid for by his friend; the collection included established French masters such as Monet, Bonnard and Seurat.

Above all he turned to the artists who were experimenting with new shapes and forms and called themselves cubists, to Braque, Picasso and Léger. The high society to which Rolf de Maré belonged sneered and laughed at the acquisitions. He soon understood that there would be no place in his home country for his newest and boldest initiative – the founding of a dance company based on novel artistic concepts. It was the encounter in 1918 with the young dancer of the Royal Swedish Ballet Jean Börlin that spurred on this idea. Börlin had been inspired by and later studied with the famous Russian choreographer Michel Fokine, who fell out of Diaghilev's favour and choreographed his last work for the Ballets Russes in 1914. Fokine had visited Stockholm in 1913 and 1914 and had stirred up the dull, conventional repertory at the Swedish Royal Opera House. Now Börlin also began to choreograph; but because Stockholm was conservative he worked on a smaller, more careful scale, and invented pieces for himself or himself with a partner and organised tours to the Swedish provinces.

Fokine's tremendous success in Stockholm had inspired a project to establish a company with Swedish dancers and a repertory based on Swedish themes; he was to become artistic director, but the outbreak of the First World War in August 1914 made these initial plans obsolete. Fokine left Russia for good in the spring of 1918, after the effects of the Bolshevist Revolution were making themselves felt; he first came to Sweden and then settled in Denmark. After de Maré had met Fokine through Börlin the previous plan for a modern Swedish ballet company abroad must have been transplanted into his mind. By then the two men had no intention of involving the Russian master any more; instead the project mutated into providing support and opportunities for the budding Swedish choreographer.

At the same time, the development of the Ballets Suédois also was to be directly linked to Rolf de Maré's art collection. The inspiration for ballets would have to come from painters and paintings. Several of the artists represented in de Maré's collection – Pierre Bonnard, Nils Dardel, Fernand Léger – would also be engaged as stage designers. The paintings could be turned into a life form, into a new dance genre. "I wish to transfer something of the beauty found in these paintings into dance," as de Maré once explained it.[1] He soon confessed that it was his desire to see his El Greco paintings turned into dance motion because they had made him think of founding a ballet company.[2] The violent power of an El Greco painting or the sense of moving shapes in works by Léger such as his *L'Escalier* or *Le Soldat*, were to be transferred onto the living body and into movement. The repertory of the Ballets Suédois thus very concretely reflected de Maré's art collection. The El Greco paintings were developed into the piece *El Greco*, which was neither a ballet nor a dance drama but a visualised poetic vision of the works of the Toledo master; the expressionism of the Greek-Spanish painter was rediscovered during this period and mirrored in a dance theatre piece called *La Maison de fous* (The Madhouse). Rolf de Maré's large Léger collection found its natural continuation in the two Léger ballets *Skating Rink* and *La Création du monde*. Pierre Bonnard, one of several representatives of French impressionism in the de Maré collection, was commissioned to design *Jeux*. But Picasso, whose work de Maré also collected and who was a friend, could never be convinced to work for the Swedish company. Most likely he was bound by contracts he had received from Diaghilev.

In a metaphorical sense one can say that de Maré not only bought individual works of art or commissioned new ballets but made an entire modern art movement for himself. With the dance company he created his own living art gallery. His wealth made him independent from box-office success; he was his own patron and did not bother about any whims but his own.

In 1924 the painter Francis Picabia – one of de Maré's many collaborators – described the impresario's unique contribution to modern art by stating that he had been of much greater importance than even he himself thought. Maré, Picabia said, made it possible for an entire cosmopolitan generation in Paris to work with a purpose, to express itself freely and not have to give in to paralysing worries about the demands of a capricious audience.[3]

Yet the opening programme of the Ballets Suédois on 23 October 1920 was devised to please with a new version of Nijinsky's and Debussy's *Jeux*, the picturesque Spanish scenes *Iberia*, designed by the much-loved painter Steinlen, a light-hearted evocation of Swedish folklore entitled *La Nuit de Saint-Jean* and the exotic *Derviches*, designed in the style of an Indian miniature; this was indeed a safe way to programme and perform in the legendary footsteps of Fokine and the Ballets Russes. It was supposed to establish the company as a legitimate artistic enterprise. It did exactly that and in addition it made clear that the works of contemporary painters and composers would be closely related to a choreographed spectacle.

If we compare this fairly conventional opening with the very last new programme that the company presented in Paris on 4 December 1924 we realise that the Ballets Suédois underwent a remarkable aesthetic development: from a relatively conventional focus that defined choreography in the traditional way the company moved to the presentation of stage art that had disobeyed and dissolved all rules and accepted criteria.

When *Relâche* by Picabia and Satie was premiered on that last evening, together with the Léger works *Skating Rink* and *La Création du monde*, the Ballets Suédois had become much more than the name indicated: out of a ballet company had emerged the concept of multi art and total theatre.

The revolutionary development the Ballets Suédois gradually underwent was only possible with its international circle of collaborators, all of whom had been enticed to collaborate after the first autumn season in Paris. Again it was de Maré's close friend Nils Dardel who acted as an intermediary. It was to a great extent his close circle of friends, many of whom he introduced to the company, who came to inspire the Ballets Suédois and reflect publicly on the different art movements of the 1920s. It must be stressed that the ideas and concepts tried out by the Ballets Suédois did not exist in a vacuum. Similar impulses could be found among the Dadaists, the Russian constructivist avant-garde or the Bauhaus group. The many artists working within and around the Ballets Suédois functioned as agents and connectors. They were tempted by the stage as it offered an unique possibility to try out ideas on a larger scale, which they otherwise lacked. And the ballet gained innovative partners. Let us, for instance, take a painter like Fernand Léger, whose whole oeuvre strove towards a large, spatially minded art. Throughout his life he was a mural painter in soul and heart, although he rarely had access to that format. Considering this passion, one understands why he quickly became involved with the activities of the Ballets Suédois. Another friend of Dardel was Jean Cocteau who became an ardent propagandist for the Swedes and who generated new contacts. His attraction to the newly established company was different from Léger's. Cocteau's cooperation with Diaghilev in *Parade* in 1917 had disappointed the poet. Cocteau had imagined a fusion of dance and poetry; the Russian impresario had destroyed this vision by eliminating Cocteau's text. But the possibility of combining two artistic media was the reason why Cocteau had wanted to collaborate in the first place. Therefore he wanted to create his new piece, *Les Mariés de la Tour Eiffel*, with the Swedes instead of Diaghilev. Here was a young, un-established and unspoilt company, and one in which an authority like Diaghilev would not have the last word. Cocteau realised that he was himself the authority and that he could leave his mark on a production. *Les Mariés*, premiered in June 1921, was permeated with Cocteau's artistic taste and personality. The anti-naturalistic and ironical style, which Cocteau already had tried out in some previous works, pointed towards the theatre of the absurd; his multidisciplinary approach was reflected in a mixture of dance, spoken drama, music and visual arts, which created a new genre. Although Börlin was responsible for the choreography, Irène Lagut the décor, Jean Hugo the costumes and the masks and the young composing group labelled Les Six wrote the music, there is hardly a detail in the piece which does not carry Cocteau's "taste". This way of sharing the work became typical of the openness of the Ballets Suédois. Not only did the company venture further into the realm of experimental dance and theatrical spectacle, it also surrendered control of production aspects to the visual artists it employed. The involvement of Cocteau, Léger and Picabia in their respective productions extended far beyond ordinary stage designing and included and then merged concept with visual expression and invention of movement gestures. Börlin seems to have possessed an almost chameleon-like gift in adjusting to the different concepts and styles, to the different "isms", which the various collaborators represented.

At the time it had become fashionable to cross the borders between the arts as Cocteau did in *Les Mariés*. In music, composers moved briskly between different genres; popular musical forms were adopted and adapted by "serious" composers and in general artists were looking for popular art forms as circus, music-hall, *bal musettes* etc. It was a reaction to established bourgeois academic art and nineteenth-century romanticism. The use of quasi popular forms of expression was often intended as provocation, as was the case with Erik Satie and the group Les Six, all of whom collaborated with the Ballets Suédois. The mixture of high and low art and anti-romantic and anti-naturalistic attitudes was typical of Paris in the 1920s and also left its mark on the repertory of the Ballets Suédois. The company was often only too pleased to provoke and annoy its audience. The polemical approach reached its climax with the final production in December 1924 of Picabia's and Satie's *Relâche*, which in its anti-theatricality, its simultaneity and disintegration of all forms pointed to the happenings of the 1950s and 1960s.

This kind of simultaneity – where disparate as well as interrelated actions and expressions took place at the same time but independent of each other, with which futurists and Dadaists had experimented – was one of the immediate results of a concept that let various artistic forms work together or confront each other, with idiosyncratic effect. The search for a synthesis of movement, dramatic action, poetry, music and painting was even more evident as an artistic goal in the Ballets Suédois than it had been with its rival, the Ballets Russes. Jean Börlin often expressed his dream of creating a harmonious fusion of all these elements, forming a whole just like in a painting. This fusion was sometimes labelled "plastic theatre"; ballet in its traditional meaning it certainly was not. Hence the discussions around the Ballets Suédois were often very lively. The advocates of the classical ballet sharpened their pens, whereas those who were more sensitive to the company's ambitions tried to find new ways of appreciating the productions: "Ballet? No. Play? No. Tragedy? No. More of a secret wedding or ambiguous cross between the antique tragedy and the New Year's revue, between the ancient chorus and the numbers in a music hall," as Cocteau himself formulated the problem regarding *Les Mariés*.[4]

Plastic theatre, rhythmic pantomime, animated pictures, paintings with gestures, sculptures in space, plastic poems ... the attempts to find terms that would do justice to the Ballets Suédois's fusion between dance and pictorial art were many. "Ballet becomes more and more expressive," Börlin explained in an interview. "Some years ago it was only dance. Now it not only interprets the modern life, but also epochs in the past and the characteristics of different countries and peoples."[5]

It could be argued that it was with the Ballets Suédois that urban, modern life entered into the field of dance. Börlin and de Maré wanted something more than pure dance and technical skill, they wanted to give expression to a thought, an idea. Often outer action had to be disregarded in order to interpret the depth of the human soul. What they strove to do, de Maré explained in an interview, was to tell a story of real life by dancing and mimicry much as the actors in a play do with words and gestures. "Everything should convey a meaning, every movement, every phrasing in music, every scenic picture . . . all the ingredients should collaborate to create the same expressiveness as spoken theatre . . . It is a new and I think fascinating adventure into the realm of art," de Maré said. "If only we could find a new word for 'ballet' we would be better satisfied. The word 'ballet' is not comprehensive enough for the work which we are doing."[6]

The attempt to go beyond "ballet" made the Ballets Suédois create a genre that was often strongly symbolic and expressionistic. The full impact of expressionism came to its fore in works like *El Greco*, *La Maison de fous* and *Skating Rink*. *Maison de fous* (1920), set in a madhouse, where the dancers as its patients expressed grotesquely exaggerated emotions, represented an important step in the evolution of modern ballet. Dance was no longer limited to expressions of romantic longings or exotic beauty; it was also capable of finding means to express the horrific aspects of contemporary society. *Skating Rink* (1922) introduced an urban as well as modern aspect to ballet, presenting a cross-section of human society, including workers and fashionable types, engaged in a popular pastime. The circular arena stood for the panorama of life, which was in itself the material of art. Fernand Léger's decor with its geometric shapes and figurative elements provided a pictorial equivalent to the complex pattern of motions created by the dancers onstage. Léger's design resulted in the first completely abstract ballet design to be realised; he followed earlier experiments by Appia, Craig, Malevich, Depero and others. There was nothing decorative or virtuosic about the movement design either. Börlin had developed possibilities of plastic expression in the skating rink and had furnished them with angular gestures reflecting their frustrated inner selves and placed them in relationship to the geometrical patterns of the background (see Fig. 32).

No wonder, perhaps, that some critics reproached the Ballets Suédois for so poorly representing "pure" dance. Some critics complained that the dancers were too often squeezed into the straitjackets of futuristic and grotesque costumes. But de Maré and Börlin defined the word dance in a different way: against traditions and against the advocates of classical

Figure 32 *Skating Rink*, Les Ballets Suédois, 1931.

ballet who quickly turned against them. Börlin's teacher Michel Fokine found the entire concept wanting: "No dance!" he summarised laconically.[7] Others took offence at what they saw as a Scandinavian, or rather Germanic, bad habit: the urge to want to say "one million words" in every gesture, in every pose.[8] But there were critics who were fascinated by the new "Swedish" way to convey "dramatic feeling" to an audience. "Their productions are something between a ballet, a mimed play, and a series of tableaux vivants," explained an enthusiastic critic in *The Spectator* after the company's London debut in December 1920. An ordinary play, the reviewer said, conveyed itself by actions and words. Here the music had been substituted for the spoken words and rhythmic gesturing for the actions. It differed widely from the successful Russian style in that the characters often did not dance at all; it differed from mime play in that the music formed an essential yet invisible part. Indeed, the connection between movement and music – things seen and things heard – appeared perfect. The players – this critic could hardly call them dancers – all seemed to swim on the broad stream of the music.[9]

Dance was only one part of the total image that the Ballets Suédois strove to create and often it was not a matter of dance in the traditional meaning. "In classical dancing", Börlin once explained, "there is no correspondence between the movements of the legs and the movements of the upper part of the body... In searching for a remedy, it has been natural to try to transform dance into pantomime."[10] The Swedish choreographer sought an original and modern way of moving that stood in close relation to the contemporary pictorial art. In his new idiom, Börlin incorporated impulses from classical technique (especially Fokine), modern dance forms and pantomime. Such synthesis was guided by the experiments of visual arts. What he had in mind were moving images, set in motion by the many layers of a painting. In no better way could this aim have been demonstrated than in *La Creátion du monde* (1923), based on an African legend of how the world was created. Léger was once more able to use his ideas of an art work based on geometrical motifs in movement. Darius Milhaud's jazz-infused music surrounded the action like an atmospheric sound design. Music and movement existed independently of each other and yet together, in the same kind of universe and based on the same principles that Merce Cunningham and John Cage began to explore and adopt in the 1940s in the United States. The dancers were considered objects and became an integral part of the stage setting. They disappeared in and behind costume and design elements, which were set in constant movement. Thus the image of a painting was crafted, which constantly changed before the eyes of the audience. Léger's and Börlin's work pointed towards the form of total movement theatre later taken up by, among others, the American artist Alwin Nikolais: the dancer was and is only one part of a visual play with abstract forms, patterns, colours and sounds. *La Création du monde* presented itself as multi art, mixed media or movement in art work decades before these concepts had acquired the names that are now familiar to us. The dancers had been dehumanised and transformed into sculptures crawling or walking on stilts. This kind of "dance" had not been imagined before. As the company motto once went: we are the dancers who dare not dance!

La Création du monde was also the first jazz ballet, followed in the same programme by *Within the Quota*, for which Cole Porter composed his only "serious" score. Modernism was clearly linking popular musical forms and jazz, which became highly fashionable in Paris after the First World War, with "serious" music. Although there had been touches of an American sound beforehand in both *Parade* (1917) and *Le Boeuf sur le toit* (1920), *Within the Quota* was really the first ballet with an all-American theme. This satire on the American way of life reflected the contemporary interest in cinema and a cinematic quality, flashes of images, spread through the ballet (see Fig. 33). The modernity of the Ballets Suédois consisted in reflection upon contemporary life and art. In a more symbolic form a similar inner contemplation on existential themes was achieved in another work, *L'Homme et son désir* (1921), based on a poem by Paul Claudel and with a provocative musical score by Darius Milhaud. It was a plastic drama focused on "a man in his nakedness", who was born in the Brazilian forest, a setting that provided means to explore animalistic or atavistic instincts. The striking stage design

Figure 33 *Within the Quota*, Les Ballets Suédois, 1931.

by Audrey Parr consisted of four constructivist levels representing the different planes of symbolic action, which all took place simultaneously. Once more, this was neither ballet nor dance, but a gestured poem, in which the plastic expression of the poetic image correlated to Börlin's ideas of translating painted images and words into dynamic movements.

This urge to create a new idiom, a new way to express movement, can be compared to the development of modern dance in the US and in Europe during the 1960s and 1970s, when once more the boundaries of what constitutes dance were being investigated – this time by post-modernists. The Ballets Suédois can hence be regarded as one of the most important predecessors of experiments in modern dance later in the twentieth century. In terminology and perspective on dance traditions, techniques and content we are, for instance, not that far away from the 1965 manifesto of the radical American choreographer Yvonne Rainer, in which she said NO to most of the conventional notions of theatre and dance. She proclaimed her refusal in connection with her own performance of *Parts of some sextets* (1965).

It is therefore telling that the Ballets Suédois found perhaps its staunchest support in Central Europe where it presented its works during extensive tours. The idea of dance outside the ballet tradition that had gained strength after Isadora Duncan's appearances in European countries around the turn of the century had made possible a completely new genre: modern dance. This was no longer ballet but decidedly different in all of the most important aesthetic aspects. Modern dance per se made it its goal to work in opposition to and outside the theatrical tradition of ballet; this new dance genre pursued the search for new and unconventional forms to express movement. "These Swedes explore with their living material [the dancer], what earlier only painters on their canvases and modern musicians with their pianos and orchestras have done," exclaimed Hans Siemsen in *Die Weltbühne*. "They create expressionistic, cubistic yes even dadaistic ballets ... You can say that these Swedes have a different perception of the notion of dance than what you are used to and what tradition prescribes. They not only dance dances, they dance whole dramas."[11]

The earthliness, in other words the contemporaneity and sensitivity to social reality of the 1920s that often characterised Börlin's movements, began to appear in the choreographies of the German *Ausdruckstanz*. The dramatic impetus and the reinvented mimetic gestures of Rudolf von Laban's dance dramas for his Kammertanz Theater in Hamburg from 1923 onwards and the dramatic-pantomimic expressions of Kurt Jooss, who also tried to fuse classical and modern idioms, certainly can be compared to the achievements of the Ballets Suédois. The Börlin style is even more evident in the early works of Ninette de Valois. She not only recreated some of the Ballets Suédois repertory, but her theatrical style, the psychological or socially meaningful gesture, was very close to what Börlin tried to achieve. *Job*, for instance, created in 1931 and based on William Blake's famous visionary illustrations for the Book of Job, would not have been possible without Börlin's *El Greco*. In a characteristic Börlin manner de Valois described *Job* not as a ballet but as a serious dramatic production based on theatrical artistic conventions in general. The Hungarian Aurel von Milloss was another choreographer of the same generation as de Valois who openly conceded that he was influenced by Börlin. He too re-created a number of works from the Ballets Suédois repertory; above all it was the development of his dramatic dance-mime style that owed a lot to Börlin.

It is always difficult to assess exactly the influence of one movement on another, of the Ballets Suédois on later modern dance and ballet styles and concepts. But we can certainly compare the concepts of the Ballets Suédois to those of the emerging modern dance movements. And there we do see interesting cross-overs, continuations and developments that owe their core ideas to the earlier Ballets Suédois. It is in reality more difficult to distinguish and recognise exactly the stylistic impact and influence; can one speak of real influences or do we have to settle merely on similarities in aesthetics instead? Although many critics and their opinions split into decisive groups, they all unanimously praised the way in which the Ballets Suédois supported French art in general and music in particular. It appeared almost embarrassing that a Swedish company supported and spread French music around the world. By its example the Ballets Suédois also put pressure on Diaghilev and during the 1920s the legendary impresario felt obliged to turn away from his Russian heritage and employ French painters and composers instead. The fresh vision of the Ballets Suédois also challenged Diaghilev in another way: modernism had to be rethought and Diaghilev was forced to compete if he wanted to retain his avant-garde reputation.

Most of Jean Börlin's ballets represented a foray into the unknown, and thus demanded a new style. Unfortunately he never had the time to bring his ideas to maturity; he died in 1930, only thirty-seven years old. He was the company's principal dancer and producer as well as its only choreographer; he was also the manager and responsible for all the rehearsing and teaching. He created twenty-four new works in five years. It was an inhuman task and eventually he cracked under the strain. But the innovations of the Ballets Suédois were of considerable historical importance and many of the experimentations of later decades were foreshadowed or even forestalled by its modernist concepts.

18 The ballet avant-garde II: the 'new' Russian and Soviet dance in the twentieth century

TIM SCHOLL

In 1908, a collection of articles on contemporary Russian theatre appeared in St Petersburg. Modestly titled *Theatre. A Book on the New Theatre*, the volume featured contributions by the painter Alexandre Benois, theatre director Vsevolod Meyerhold, future Commissar of Enlightenment Anatoly Lunacharsky, the symbolist poets Andrey Bely and Valery Bryusov, and novelist Fyodor Sologub. The diversity of this group suggests the significance of Russian theatre in St Petersburg at the turn of the century and the breadth of the quest for new forms in the arts in Russia in the early years of the twentieth century. The writers mostly advocated the latest movement in Russian theatre, shaped as it was by a fascination with emerging symbolist tendencies that sought to correct, or at least to dethrone, the naturalism of Konstantin Stanislavsky's Moscow Art Theatre, though Stanislavsky's innovations were still relatively new.

One year after the theatre volume appeared, Sergey Diaghilev presented Russian dancers in five ballets in his *Saisons russes* in Paris. The fame and notoriety of this "new" dance from Russia would soon eclipse the discussion of new theatre – and outlast that earlier phenomenon. Nonetheless, Russia's new ballet owed much to the experimentation of new theatre. The new ballet emerged alongside it, and, like the new theatre, new dance was simpler to define by what it was not. However variously writers conceived of the 'new' ballet, one thing was clear: Marius Petipa and the large repertory he created for the Russian Imperial Ballet represented the old.

Petipa's 1898 production of *Raymonda* was the master choreographer's last "grand" ballet. He created a series of smaller-scaled works for the Hermitage (court) Theatre in 1900 and 1902; the production of his last ballet, *The Magic Mirror* met with unprecedented failure in 1903. Ironically, the reasons routinely cited for the fiasco could serve as the template for the innovations of the new ballet: the "symphonic" score, the sets by Aleksandr Golovin, a leading easel painter, and the curious provenance of the libretto, concocted from the unlikely pairing of the Brothers Grimm and Russia's great romantic poet, Aleksandr Pushkin. A mere six years after the failure of Petipa's *Magic Mirror*, Sergey Diaghilev's Ballets Russes stormed Paris with ballets set to "concert" music, with sets and costumes designed by fashionable painters, and libreti drawn from a variety of sources, including the poetry of Stéphane Mallarmé.

The ballets and choreographers eventually termed "new" were a loose collection of ballets and ballet innovators who worked mostly at the fringes of a ballet establishment centred in St Petersburg's Maryinsky Theatre, Petipa's laboratory since 1847. With ballet education and production the exclusive domain of the Imperial Theatre system, the new ballet had to emerge, with difficulty, from the old. And although foreign ballerinas, mostly from Italy, regularly received contracts to dance on the imperial stages, visiting ballet troupes (and choreography from beyond the Russian empire) only began to visit Russia once the Imperial Theatres' monopoly was relaxed in 1882. However Russian dance writers were none too impressed with the quality of the dancing or the choreography they saw when troupes such as Luigi Manzotti's staged their productions on the summer stages of suburban amusement parks.

The most stunning blow to the old ballet was delivered on the illustrious Maryinsky stage in St Petersburg, when Aleksandr Gorsky's production of *Don Quixote* (1900, Moscow), was brought in to replace Petipa's 1869 staging. Aleksandr Gorsky, a former dancer with the Petersburg troupe, established his reputation as a ballet master by staging Petipa works in Moscow (including *The Sleeping Beauty*, from dance notations, in 1899). Gorsky moved from these fundamentally faithful restagings of Petipa's ballets to full-scale revisions of his works in later years. As was typically the case in "new" ballets, Gorsky's attempts at revision were mostly attempts to make the old ballets more logical and dramatically viable. Gorsky was influenced by Konstantin Stanislavsky's work at the Moscow Art Theatre, which was then enjoying its artistic peak, staging premieres of Anton Chekhov's plays. From Stanislavsky, Gorsky learned the importance of the unity of the production as a whole, as well as the value of its details. In Gorsky's productions, dancers were encouraged to analyse their characters' motivations, decors were painted in a more realistic manner and costumes were increasingly designed for individuals rather than for groups. Most importantly, Gorsky focused his directorial attentions on establishing a clear line of action in his so-called choreo-dramas, revealing a clear debt to Stanislavsky.

When Gorsky's version of the Petipa classic *Don Quixote* arrived in St Petersburg, local critics were shocked at the asymmetry of Gorsky's choreography, his attempts to integrate the group dances into the dramatic fabric of the work and to rid the ballet of these conventionalised divertissements. The decors, painted by Konstantin Korovin and Aleksandr Golovin (who would design Petipa's *Magic Mirror* the following year) represented another departure from the work of Petipa's academically trained designers. Their works did not meet with general approval; they were deemed "decadent" for their lack of perspective and for the predominance of mottled colours.

Gorsky staged *Giselle* four times in Moscow (1901, 1907, 1918, and 1922). The evolution of this work in Gorsky's stagings offers a snapshot of the trajectory of his evolving approach to the classics, and to his evolution as a choreographer. His first staging remained faithful to Petipa's version and used old decors. Gorsky's 1907 staging of the work was for Vera Karalli, the dramatically gifted dancer who had graduated from the ballet school one year earlier. This staging of the ballet updated the action to the Directoire period and assigned individualised tasks to the crowd. Karalli clearly stepped outside the bounds of traditional interpretations of the classic role: she was criticised for laughing loudly in the mad scene. In the second act, the wilis, dressed in nightgowns, behaved more as seductresses than spirits from the underworld.

Gorsky's quite radical notions of ballet dramaturgy suited the new political and cultural climate that followed the decisive October 1917 Revolution – for a time. His attempts to democratise ballet institutions – as well as ballets – won him enemies at the Bolshoi, particularly among established virtuoso dancers who were replaced by a new generation of "dancing actors". Gorsky's favourite ballerinas were dramatically gifted but technically weak, and this preference for acting showed in the dances Gorsky created. Gorsky's 1918 version of the ballet was criticised as overly cinematic, as was the acting of the character dancers who played the lead. By 1922, Gorsky advised his ballerina not to dance on pointe, but to jump like a young goat, to really go mad, and die with her legs apart.[1] In Gorsky's hands, in successive stagings, *Giselle* became a mimed melodrama.

Gorsky played a central role in ballet reform in Russia in the early years of the twentieth century, but the radical nature of his later experiments made his innovations ultimately unworkable, and his productions were quickly replaced by more traditional treatments of the classic ballets Gorsky reconfigured. By the time of his death in 1924, little remained of the repertory Gorsky created for the Bolshoi Theatre.

Despite Gorsky's pioneering efforts in the creation of the new ballet, the body of work he created was little known beyond Moscow. Paradoxically, some of the most famous of Russia's new ballets were not seen in Russia until the wave of new ballet experimentation was over. Michel Fokine's *Schéhérazade*, *Firebird* and *Le Spectre de la rose*, essential to the early success of the Diaghilev ballet and exemplars of Russia's new ballet, did not become part of the Soviet repertory. Fokine's ballets, set mostly to concert music and therefore much shorter than the nineteenth-century's three- to five-act ballets, were deemed 'choreographic miniatures' in the Soviet Union, where works of epic length and scale were preferred.

Figure 34 Anna Pavlova, studio photograph.

Fokine began his choreographic career in 1905 with *Acis and Galatea*, a stylised Greek ballet for his students. His best-known and most-performed work, *The Swan*, was created for Anna Pavlova two years later (see Fig. 34). In these and subsequent works, the inspiration of Isadora Duncan is evident. Duncan began her first tour of Russia in 1904, and the self-taught, free-form dances she created furnished a ready model for Fokine and for others. Her dances were produced independently of state-supported academies and theatre bureaucracies. Duncan danced to concert music, without special sets, and with minimal costumes that revealed a freer body than tights and tutus allowed. Fokine responded to Duncan with a series of retrospective stylisations, yet *The Swan*, despite its conventional costuming and steps, was

Fokine's most significant contribution to the new ballet repertory. Its nearly naturalistic focus on the moment of death directed the new ballet's priorities towards expression, the watchword of so many modern dance innovators of Fokine's day.

Fokine drafted a manifesto of the new ballet that first appeared in *The Times* of London in July 1914, one month after the choreographers's last work for Diaghilev premiered. Fokine called for the ballet to abandon its usual conventions, including those of steps and costuming in favour of new forms better suited to the time and settings of individual ballets. Fokine believed that the ballet should also abandon the divertissement as a diversion from the action of the dance, and that dance and pantomime must be combined to express the idea of the ballet as a whole. Finally, the dance should unite with other art forms; the new ballet should function as a union of the arts, and dance should cease to be subordinate to music and the visual arts.

Fokine's *Chopiniana* (1907, the 1909 version for Diaghilev is known in the West as *Les Sylphides*), like his *Swan* from the same year, stylises the dance of the nineteenth century. These two works provide a fair representation of the principles of the new ballet that Fokine would later draft. They feature integrated dances, not divertissements, and relate events (relationships, death) that are readily understandable without recourse to pantomime. Although Gorsky had staged a similar work years earlier (*Valse fantaisie*, 1901), *Chopiniana* is generally regarded as the first plot-less ballet.

Fokine worked with the painter and set designer Alexandre Benois on the production of *Pavillon d'Armide* (1907). The first ballet shown by the Diaghilev ballet in Paris, *Pavillon* could serve as the template for the Ballets Russes and the works Diaghilev would produce. The ballet's opulent visuals were faithful to the rococo period. The dance was not; yet the harmonious blend of dance, drama, decor, and music captured the attention of the European public and established the choreographer's early fame. The ballets Fokine created for the Diaghilev ballet – *Schéhérazade* (1910), *Firebird* (1910) and *Le Spectre de la rose* (1911) – follow the choreographer's principles to varying degrees, though *Petrushka* (1911) is arguably the choreographer's most accomplished work. Fokine employed a variety of dance styles to create the world of the pre-Lenten urban Russian fairground. The divertissements for nurses, coachmen and others remain mostly in unison, as in the old ballet, but blend seamlessly into the fabric of the work. Fokine arrived at creative movement solutions to delineate his characters, utilising movements and gestures for his stars which were usually performed by character dancers. The Moor's splayed and Petrushka's turned-in positions built on grotesqueries from the Petipa ballet, although in *Petrushka*,

Figure 35 Vaclav Nijinsky in the title role of *Petrushka*, 1911, choreography by Mikhail Fokine.

these movements were given to soloists who were mostly deprived of virtuoso movement (see Fig. 35). Fokine responded in kind to the innovative character of Stravinsky's groundbreaking score, answering the simultaneous sounding of two melodies with two different dances performed at the same time, although Gorsky had already attracted attention with this device in his 1900 production of *Don Quixote*.

In a lifetime of making dances, Fokine never regained the success he achieved in his early works, or the fame he gained in his work for Diaghilev. A careful look at Fokine and his innovations reveals enormous debts to his predecessors: Petipa, Gorsky and Duncan. A clever packager of other choreographer's ideas, Fokine found an ideal outlet for their dissemination while he was part of the Diaghilev enterprise, an enormous travelling production company that put the best Russian and European designers, composers and dancers at the service of the choreographer. After breaking with Diaghilev, Fokine choreographed in Russia, Europe and North America, mostly restaging the hits of his early career. His early innovations, so central to the new ballet, soon became commonplaces of twentieth-century dance, while the Wagnerian hope for the total art work, the harmonious unification of dance with music and painting, required a constellation of collaborators and resources impossible to assemble outside Diaghilev's orbit. Nonetheless, many of the works Fokine created for the Ballets Russes have survived – a remarkable achievement (given the life expectancy of ballets from the early twentieth century) and a testament to Fokine's ability to translate important new cultural trends in Russia into ballets.

The decisive October Revolution of 1917 dramatically shifted the landscape of dance in Russia. For some time after the Revolution, the future of the Imperial (then State) Theatre system remained in doubt. Lenin's position on theatres and culture was ambivalent. The new Soviet leader believed vaguely in the need to preserve culture, but it was Anatoly Lunacharsky, the Commissar of Enlightenment (or education) who campaigned most vigorously on behalf of the theatres. Eventually, the State Theatres received a life-saving appellation: they were called "academic", to convey their status as educational tools. Government committees scrutinised their repertories, singling out supposed counter-revolutionary works and recommending revisions of others. The libretto of the ballet *Sleeping Beauty* was reworked as *The Sunny Commune*, for example, though the new version was never produced.

Meanwhile, lively debates on the future of dance in the new Soviet republic appeared in a variety of theatre and culture journals. These discussions focused on appropriate themes for contemporary dances and on the content of the new choreographic spectacles. The radical left recommended that the ballet vocabulary be jettisoned in favour of vernacular movement, acrobatics and folk dance. Others noted that many of the alternative movement idioms suggested (especially those from the West, such as Isadora Duncan and 'machine' dances) were as alien to Russia as the European court dances that flourished in Russia's theatres for two centuries. Until the crackdown on independent arts groups in the early 1930s, when the state gradually took control of all arts production in the Soviet Union, a number of experimental dance groups and choreographers flourished. Kasyan Goleizovsky and Fyodor Lopukhov are the best known of these vanguard choreographers, and well represent the range of the experimentation in Russian dance in the 1920s.

A dancer in the Bolshoi Theatre at the time of the Revolution, Goleizovsky had already opened his own school and was much in demand as a choreographer in Moscow's private theatres and cabarets. In the year following the Revolution, Goleizovsky took charge of the Bolshoi's theatre school, but left the company months later to choreograph full time. A harsh critic of the routine and the increasingly archaic repertories of the State Theatres, Goleizovsky nonetheless saw the professional ballet theatres as the sole repositories of skilled, well-trained dancers in Russia. Goleizovsky based his ever-expanding movement idiom on classical technique and required trained dancers, but nonetheless believed that all movement was legitimate and could be used to invigorate classical technique. Goleizovsky's dancers might perform somersaults, daring lifts, or lie on the stage, but the choreographer's diverse movement idiom relied on a foundation in ballet technique. A new attitude towards the visual elements of the ballet production marked Goleizovsky's new dance theatre and brought the ballet fully into the artistic vanguard of 1920s Russia. The costumes, however, lent the enterprise a hint of scandal. Goleizovsky believed in the nude body as both an aesthetic and a moral ideal, and although his dancers never appeared completely nude, they often appeared in minimal costumes. Like other dance reformers in the twentieth century, including George Balanchine, Goleizovsky preferred minimal costumes as a better way to reveal the body's movement. And like many theatre directors in Russia in the 1920s, Goleizovsky arranged these bodies on constructivist stage sets; dancers and dances were arranged on multiple planes.

Goleizovsky's best-known work, *The Legend of Joseph the Beautiful*, staged in 1925 for the Bolshoi's Experimental Theatre, made extensive use of stage platforms, stairs and constructions. Boris Erdman's costumes were asymmetrical and eccentric, updating the dress of Ancient Egypt for 1920s flappers. Goleizovsky's choreography avoided the archeological stylisations of Fokine and Gorsky, instead incorporating motifs from a variety of folk and historical dance traditions. Yet despite the fusion of dance styles Goleizovsky used in the ballet, contemporary commentators noted an unusual degree of coherence in the dances.

Work on *The Whirlwind* (1927) led to Goleizovsky's resignation from the Bolshoi Theatre, though he continued to contribute occasional works to the theatre until 1964. The choreographer's withdrawal from the Bolshoi anticipated the conservatism of the "academic" theatres in the 1930s and beyond, a time when Goleizovsky retreated to music halls and cabarets, and arranged dances for films.

If the work of Gorsky and Goleizovsky ultimately proved too radical and eccentric for the Bolshoi Theatre, St Petersburg's Maryinsky (called the State Academic Theatre of Opera and Ballet until it received the appellation "Kirov" in 1935) followed an even more conservative path to a Soviet approximation of modernity. The Revolution made for a very difficult situation within the former Maryinsky, not least because so many of the company's former stars (Nijinsky, Pavlova, Karsavina, to name a few) had established themselves in the West with the Diaghilev troupe and chose to remain there. Nikolay Sergeyev, the troupe's arch-conservative régisseur, left Russia in 1918 with the dance notations that recorded the bulk of the ballet repertory; Fokine left St Petersburg the same year. A series of male dancers staged ballets and worked as régisseurs for the company during the chaotic period following the Revolution until Fyodor Lopukhov was appointed director in 1922.

The first directive of Lopukhov's new administration amounted to a purge. A statement announced that Petipa's ballet would form the basis of the troupe's repertory and that special efforts would be made to cleanse them of the accretions of recent years (the work of other régisseurs from the time of Petipa's retirement in 1903 and death in 1910). Lopukhov began a process that continues to dominate discussions concerning the Maryinsky and its performance practices to the present day. His determination to return to a more pure or authentic version of Petipa's ballets inaugurated a quest as impossible as stepping twice into the same stream.

The complexity of Lopukhov's undertaking is demonstrated by a small, but telling moment in Russian ballet history in which Lopukhov played a leading role. In 1972, Lopukhov admitted that in 1914, he had choreographed the most commonly performed variation for the Lilac Fairy in Petipa's *Sleeping Beauty*. Lopukhov maintained that the variation was attributed to Petipa in order to escape the scrutiny of the régisseur, Nikolay Sergeyev. In his 1972 account of this history, Lopukhov nonetheless maintains that his variation functions as a kind of quintessence of the role, thus justifying his questionable maintenance of the Petipa legacy and congratulating himself for the deception. This pattern of "improving" Petipa continued throughout the Soviet era.

However questionable the authenticity of Lopukhov's revisions of Petipa, the decision to preserve the legacy proved more fruitful than the Moscow tendency to create increasingly eccentric versions of the nineteenth-century repertory. Throughout the Soviet period, the Petersburg/Leningrad ballet remained a repository (if an imperfect one) of the nineteenth-century repertory, whose productions were copied and reproduced for ballet companies around the Soviet empire and the world. And despite Lopukhov's reputation as a conservative, intent on preserving the classical legacy, the ballet master and choreographer was also interested in new forms.

His best-known work had only one performance; the dance-symphony *Magnificence of the Universe* was set to Beethoven's Fourth Symphony and featured dancers from George Balanchine's Young Ballet in its cast. Lopukhov's fascination with the symphony reflected a generalised anxiety over the ballet's place in some imagined hierarchy of the arts in the young Soviet republic. At a time when the score of *Sleeping Beauty* was singled out as the sole, musically acceptable score suitable for performance in the Soviet "academic" theatres, Lopukhov sensibly scrambled for the higher ground of an indisputable genre. Beethoven was admired in the Soviet Union in this period, both by conservatives and by radicals. The latter judged him close to the spirit of the French Revolution. The symphony quickly became an *idée fixe* for Soviet dance. Russian writers still use the term 'symphonic' to connote choreographic sophistication.

Lopukhov's choreography to the Beethoven score was perhaps less remarkable than the programme notes he wrote for the performance. With sections of the ballet titled *The Conception of Light*, and *Life in Death and Death in Life*, Lopukhov's vision for the new ballet wed pretension to naivety. The ballet proved an unpalatable concoction that, regrettably, suggested much of the future direction of Soviet dance. An uneasy step into the world of abstraction, Lopukhov's ballet retained narrative as an organising principle. At a time when flirtations with abstraction would be denounced as formalist experiments (the most damning denigration in Soviet arts criticism), Soviet choreographers intent on exploring the plot-less potential of dance were careful to disguise these "deviations" with an overlay of plot.

The theoretical foundations for Lopukhov's 1923 ballet may be found in a written work that appeared two years after the ballet, although he had begun it much earlier. In *Paths of a Ballet-Master*, Lopukhov outlined his notions of an ideal relationship between dance and music. Essentially, Lopukhov's tract calls for a unity between the two forms, though many of the specifics strike the modern reader as naive. Lopukhov's insistence on correspondence between the two forms included such particulars as the suggestion that minor keys be reflected in *en dedans* movement and major keys mirrored by movement *en dehors*.

Like Goleizovsky, Lopukhov worked only intermittently in the Soviet academic theatres after the 1920s. In both cases, the two men's notions of the future of dance proved too radical for an arts bureaucracy that came to favour slow evolution over new theories and "revolutionary" change. The future of Soviet dance lay with less progressive ballet masters who were willing to parrot formulaic approaches to art as handed down by party tribunals. It is not surprising, then, that the next important wave in Soviet ballet production had no identifiable author.

Much as Lopukhov, and others, sought to "symphonise" the ballet, choreographers in the 1930s and 1940s turned to another unshakeable genre from yet another art form as a basis for new ballets. The Stalin-era adoration of epic forms resulted in the Soviet ballet's new enthusiasm for adaptations of novels and the plays of literature's Beethoven: William Shakespeare. Rostislav Zakharov's *The Fountain of Bakhchisarai* (1934) and Leonid Lavrovsky's *Romeo and Juliet* (1940), both based on literary monuments, functioned as exemplars of the new wave in Soviet choreography, the *drambalet*. A contraction of "drama" and "ballet", the *drambalet* was meant to fuse the two seamlessly in a marriage of gesture and movement that avoided the nineteenth-century's division of pantomime and dancing. With time, it became clear that these dances privileged storytelling and pantomime over movement, and that dance as such took a second place to narrative conveyed in highly conventionalised gestures. The close-ups in the film version (1954) of Lavrovsky's *Romeo and Juliet* make it more accessible than the staged ballet and point out the genre's greatest deficiency: with so much of the story conveyed by silent-film gesturing, the live version of the ballet suffers by comparison.

The burst of creativity, experimentation and theorising that characterised Soviet arts in the 1920s was largely absent by the 1930s, when the state sought, and mostly achieved, control of avenues of creative expression. The ballet proved especially malleable, since dance activity was centred in the large theatres of large cities and the Western system of independent choreographers leading small troupes of dancers had not taken root in Russia. Despite a fervent period of activity in the dramatic theatre and the ballet theatre, the new Russian theatre and dance that captured the imagination of practitioners and writers in the first years of the twentieth century failed to blossom in Russia and the Soviet Union. The 1917 Revolution had drastically changed conditions in the Russian theatres; the emigrations of artists immediately thereafter left a creative vacuum impossible to fill in the lean and hungry years of civil war and cultural revolution that followed.

Russia's new dance, like new theatre, had a greater impact in the West, where experimentation and artistic collaboration were prized long after both became problematic in the Soviet Union. Abstraction and formalism, dangerous concepts for Soviet choreographers, became the rule in ballets created by Russian émigré dance-makers, especially George Balanchine. Balanchine's revolution in the ballet certainly drew upon his experience in 1920s Russia: his incorporation of a plentitude of dance idioms and styles echoed Goleizovsky's catholic approach to choreography; Balanchine's thorough investigation of the relationship of choreography to music revealed a debt to Lopukhov. In the hands of Russian émigrés, ballet became a prominent feature of the European and North American cultural landscape in the twentieth century. The dance that these émigrés created was no longer identified with Russian new ballet, yet it grew from the revolt against the old ballet begun by Gorsky, Fokine, and others in the first years of the twentieth century.

19 George Balanchine

MATILDE BUTKAS

It's like watching light pass through a prism. The music passes through him, and in the same natural yet marvellous way that a prism refracts light, he refracts music into dance."

(MARTHA GRAHAM)[1]

Balanchine has been likened to Mozart and Shakespeare for his universal appeal and prolific creative output and to Picasso and Matisse for his contributions to twentieth-century art. His friend and collaborator Igor Stravinsky, not famous for complimenting his peers, declared that "The world is full of pretty good concert pianists, but a choreographer such as Balanchine is, after all, the rarest of beings".[2] In the years since Balanchine's death in 1983 his ballets have remained a staple of New York City Ballet programmes each season and are widely performed by other companies as well, many of them led by former Balanchine dancers who work hard to recreate "Mr B's" ballets as faithfully as possible. It is rare for a choreographer to have this many works still in performance (to say nothing of the continuing influence of his school of technique – a streamlined version of classical ballet notable for its speed, energy, clarity, restylings of some of the original dance positions and emphasis on music as the heart of ballet).

What was so extraordinary about Balanchine as a working artist? First, he approached choreography as a craft akin to cooking or carpentry. He worked easily with what was available, adjusting his choreography to a dancer's strengths and was never fazed by the notion that a ballet might disappear forever after its performance. Moreover, Balanchine made ballets quickly and was, as a result, prolific, creating hundreds of ballets over the course of his life. He needed, most of all, to be in the studio working directly with his dancers and he found joy in the process of, as he liked to say, "assembling".

Second, Balanchine's working style inspired great loyalty in his dancers. He was, by many (albeit not all) accounts, easy to work with. In addition, he was a hands-on choreographer, intensely detail-oriented. His hand touched everything – from the sewing of costumes to the programme notes to the position of a ballerina's tiara – and he taught company class frequently until late in his life. These finer details, though perhaps unnoticed by the public, made the New York City Ballet distinct and the high quality of its dancers so consistent.

Third, his choreography was particularly responsive to music. This is widely acknowledged, but less often brought up in the literature than "Mr B's" personal life, his place in dance history, his technique, dancers, company and his choreographies. Balanchine's musical training and native abilities were unusual for a choreographer – he was a pianist who studied at the conservatory in St Petersburg, composed, made his own piano reductions of ballet scores, analysed these scores and even conducted. His deep interest in music led him to create choreographies that were, as Terry Teachout put it (describing his first experience of watching *Concerto Barocco*), "sound made visible, written in the air like fireworks glittering in the night sky".[3] Charles Joseph wrote, along the same lines, that Balanchine, "a musically astute choreographer, possessed the uncanny gift of clarifying what my ears heard through what my eyes saw".[4] However, as Edwin Denby pointed out, "the so-called imitations of music by the dancers, far from being literal, have a grace at once sophisticated and ingenious. The musical play and the play of dance figures, between them, create bit by bit a subtle strength"[5] Balanchine's choreography does not simply visualise or imitate the music, but rather, the musical structure determines the movement in more complex ways. A few scholars, led by the pioneering work of "choreo-musical" analyst Stephanie Jordan, have shed light on this much celebrated musical aspect of Balanchine's choreography.

That most Balanchine ballets are plotless provides further complexity; it also affected his choices and uses of music. Though his ballets are rich in drama, often that between a man and a woman, the story is left for the viewer to interpret (or not). Balanchine felt overt plots were unnecessary and that words were not needed to describe or discuss his ballets. "He always said that seeing [his ballets] was enough: words about them, how he came to make them, or about his life were of little use," wrote Francis Mason.[6] Since Balanchine so often did not rely on plot, he could focus purely on combining bodies in motion with sound, without undermining the importance of either. Important to his approach was to keep choreography from interfering with or obscuring the music.[7] He claimed to subdue his dances, submitting them to the music, taking a "less is more" attitude.[8] Indeed, the music itself provided drama and he underlined this with choreography. His approach to music and drama led to an amazing versatility in styles of both music and choreography, from Gershwin, Rodgers and Hart to Bach and Webern and from classic choreographies for prima ballerinas to dances for circus elephants.

The balance achieved in his work brings clarity to both the music and the dance in unprecedented ways. Stravinsky said that Balanchine's choreography "exposed relationships of which I had not been aware in the same way. Seeing it, therefore, was like touring a building for which I had drawn the plans but never completely explored the result."[9]

Origins: Russia and Europe

Georgi Melitonovich Balanchivadze was born in St Petersburg in 1904. His Georgian ancestry, the cosmopolitan and European influence of St Petersburg and a musical family all constitute important parts of Balanchine's heritage. His mother was his first piano teacher, his father a composer nicknamed "the Georgian Glinka". Though the details of accounts vary, Balanchinvadze ended up as a ballet student in the Imperial Theatre School of St Petersburg with his sister, instead of the Imperial Naval Academy of St Petersburg as his mother had wanted. At first he was miserable and lonely, more interested in music and religion classes.

One night, when he performed as a cupid in Petipa's *Sleeping Beauty* at the Maryinsky Theatre, he fell in love with ballet. Not long after this, in 1917, the Russian Revolution broke out, changing everything. The circumstances were dire as well as bizarre. Dances were performed in the freezing cold as interludes during political debates on the stage of the Maryinsky, which only a few years before had displayed the lush, extravagant performances for the tsar. During these deprived post-revolution years, Balanchivadze continued to pursue music and played the piano often at school. Yuri Slonimsky recalled him playing pieces by Chopin and Russian contemporaries Scriabin, Medtner and Rachmaninoff.[10] Balanchivadze graduated in 1921 and became a member of the ballet company but also enrolled in the conservatory of music, not sure yet in which direction he would travel: music or dance.

His first choreographies as a teenager were scandalous enough to raise eyebrows even though the early 1920s atmosphere was ripe for young artists' indulgence and experimentalism. At this time Balanchivadze was influenced by Fokine's "plotless" *Chopiniana* (*Les Sylphides*), Goleizovsky's barefoot and bare-skinned ballets, Lopukhov's avante-garde works such as *Dance Symphony*, and he even saw Isadora Duncan perform, though he was not favourably impressed. In 1923, Young Ballet, a new performing group Balanchine helped form, staged his choreography to Blok's poetry chanted by a chorus. The Maryinsky faculty prohibited the dancers from taking part in further Young Ballet programmes.

In 1924 Balanchivadze left Russia on a tour with a troupe of dancers including his wife, Tamara Geva, and Alexandra Danilova. Balanchine married three more times and made no attempt to disguise the fact that his inspiration was from women; he would later assert "ballet is woman". He would remain friendly with his former wives and worked professionally with them, creating ballets for them throughout his career. Years later, Danilova remembered taking one class with him at the School of American Ballet in which "there at the barre were all the wives and ex-wives: Geva, Zorina, Tallchief, Tanaquil LeClerq and myself".[11]

Surprised at having plentiful food for once, the Russian troupe ate their way across the Baltic Sea. They also decided not to return to Russia. They were eventually contacted by Diaghilev and auditioned for his famous Ballets Russes. Looking back we see this as a decisive moment; Diaghilev's Ballets Russes was at the cutting edge, providing an ideal atmosphere for Balanchine to continue developing choreographic skills and ideas. And so, Georgi Balanchivadze became George Balanchine at Diaghilev's request, the company's newest choreographer, and began creating works for the Ballets Russes and for the Opéra de Monte Carlo. Balanchine learned to appreciate painting and sculpture and also discovered his talent for cooking.

Early works

Apollo (Stravinsky, 1928),[12] a work that Balanchine considered a turning point in his creative life. Balanchine realised the value of economy in ideas and "that, like tones in music and shades in painting, gestures have certain family relations which, as groups, impose their own laws".[13] Diaghilev recognised Petipa-like qualities and Balanchine's ability to create classical ballets. But Balanchine became fascinated with jazz dance just as much as with classicism. In fact, jazz movements, though not necessarily new to Balanchine, entered his vocabulary during this time, probably through the influence of the Parisian star Josephine Baker, as Beth Genné has pointed out.[14] There is evidence that Balanchine not only choreographed for, danced with and admired Baker, but most importantly that the two traded material, with Baker learning to dance *en pointe* and Balanchine absorbing her jazz style. This yielded a hybrid, "a jazz infused classicism that integrates the angled arms akimbo, the crooked (cats paw) wrists with every finger displayed with the upright torso, precise placement and line lengthening point work of the *danse d'école*".[15] The meeting of these two young dancers during the 1920s and 1930s played a crucial part in Balanchine's future artistic development and his challenge of American race taboos. The jazz-influenced neoclassicism would characterise many of Balanchine's American works such as *The Four Temperaments* and *Agon*. Baker was probably the first "Balanchine ballerina"; she represented the American ideal with the much celebrated long legs, grace and athleticism, qualities that Balanchine would cherish in dancers such as Suzanne Farrell.[16]

Also during this period Balanchine began a lifelong friendship with Stravinsky; many of Balanchine's great neoclassic ballets were made to Stravinsky's music.[17] The choreographer and composer had much in common, from their shared love of pre-revolutionary St Petersburg to their artistic philosophy and aesthetic. Each of the two also felt a deep sympathy for the other's art. "If a dancer's heart beat within Stravinsky, that of a musician invigorated Balanchine," wrote Charles Joseph in his study of their relationship.[18]

Following Diaghilev's death, Balanchine battled with tuberculosis and after recovery, found work with Cochran's Revues, the Royal Danish Ballet, Sir Oswald's variety shows in England, the new Ballets Russes de Monte Carlo and then its competition, Les Ballets 1933. Many works from this period disappeared like the butterflies in Balanchine's famous metaphor: "[A ballet] is wonderful, it is now. It is like a butterfly. I always say butterflies of yesterday don't exist."[19] Balanchine was twenty-nine, dancing despite an injured knee, choreographing for whomever needed him and uncertain of his future. It was as this point of restlessness that Lincoln Kirstein saw a performance of his work in London and promptly proposed that he should become part of Kirstein's vision for a distinctly American ballet company, school, repertoire and audience. He arrived in New York in October 1933 (see Fig. 36).

America: Broadway and New Ballet

It took some time before Balanchine found resources and stability. But he loved his adopted country and its culture and found much to influence his art, including Broadway, hoe-downs, Hollywood, Fred Astaire and Ginger Rogers, Western movies (which he watched avidly), jazz, modern dance and composers such as Ives, Sousa and Gershwin. On 1 January, 1934, the School of American Ballet officially opened and in June of that year its students performed Balanchine's first American ballet: *Serenade. Serenade,* to Tchaikovsky's Serenade in C for string orchestra (1880)[20] begins with a ritual that not only evokes the elemental movements of ballet class, but records how Balanchine started from scratch, teaching his American students a basically unfamiliar art. Years later, tears would spring to Martha Graham's eyes when she saw the first section where the entire corps suddenly turns their feet out into first position, a striking and concise movement amidst a flowing and lyrical passage of dance and music.[21] Such precision would later be identified as a trademark of the Balanchine style.

Serenade illustrates an important aspect of Balanchine's choreographic process: working with what is available and whatever circumstances arise.

Figure 36 Pennsylvania Ballet Principal Dancer Riolama Lorenzo with Soloist Philip Colucci in *The Prodigal Son*, choreography by George Balanchine.

Each day of rehearsal, a different number of dancers were present and the day he put together the opening scene, the odd number of seventeen appeared, and so Balanchine used a bow-tie formation rather than standard parallel lines. One day a dancer rushed in late, another day a dancer fell; he would add these moments and mishaps to the choreography.

The structure of this ballet, like so many of Balanchine's works, derives not from a plot but from the music. Of *Serenade,* Balanchine tells us that, "making a ballet is the choreographer's way of showing how he understands a piece of music, not in words, not in narrative form (unless he has in mind a particular story), but in dancing."[22] Upon closer examination we see another example of Balanchine's classicism. Both Balanchine and Tchaikovsky use a limited set of themes, which are then explored and restated and brought back in variation. The dance reflects the music but not by merely imitating the musical events (high elevation equalling high pitch, fast movement equalling fast musical tempos, etc.). Balanchine and Mason wrote that in *Serenade,* "the only story is the music's story, a serenade, a dance, if you like, in the light of the moon".[23] Balanchine also alluded to fragments of a story, thought by many to be autobiographical: "It's like fate ... Each man going through the world with his destiny on his back. He meets a woman – he cares for her – but destiny has other plans."[24] Narrative drive in *Serenade* may be debated, but the music and choreography are dramatic, especially when one considers the myriad changes made in *Serenade's* "evolution" – changes which take place still with each new dancer, stager, conductor and orchestra. *Serenade,* whether it is about pure dance, music, fate, a woman, a process or inevitable loneliness, is enduringly popular, and still widely performed today.

Broadway and Hollywood

Balanchine soon found many venues for his talents. He felt just as comfortable choreographing for Broadway and Hollywood as he did for the ballet stage. He knew how to entertain and knew what was popular, sexy and funny. He worked easily with Rodgers and Hart and spoke fondly of Larry Hart teaching him English. Balanchine could sing Hart's "My Funny Valentine" in flawless English without a trace of Russian accent.[25] Balanchine brought the term "choreography" to the programmes of Broadway musicals, beginning with the hit *On Your Toes* in 1936. The time was just right. People were beginning to appreciate the dance in musicals and the choreography grew more sophisticated. That year he also choreographed for the *Ziegfeld Follies of 1936,* which included the stars Fanny Brice, Bob Hope and Josephine Baker, who hoped to make a triumphant return to her native country. The critics sharply disapproved of his casting Baker in a romantic lead role dancing with four white male suitors; the racist response was devastating.[26]

Also in 1937, he tried to get the American Ballet (the original Kirstein–Balanchine company) back on its feet with a Stravinsky Festival featuring *Apollo, Le Baiser de la fée* (The Fairy's Kiss) and the newly commissioned ballet about a poker game: *Jeu de cartes* (Card Game), "a ballet in three deals".

Ballet Society

Around 1940, "after all kinds of expenses", Balanchine said that he "still had five hundred dollars left. I thought, what should I do with the money? buy some extraordinary cigarette case or something? And then I decided, ah! I'll ask Hindemith to write something for me."[27] This is how *The Four Temperaments* for piano and strings came into existence, a work cherished today even by musicians unfamiliar with its choreography. It had its premiere in 1946 for a new, post-war Kirstein–Balanchine venture: Ballet Society, a subscription-only company (even for the press), with the purpose of performing newly commissioned or unfamiliar works. The American public was ready for such a company, for the mid-1940s was a time when, as a 1944 article title put it, "The Ballet Comes into its Own".[28] Balanchine was still working for Broadway and Hollywood and his contributions to *Song of Norway,* a musical on the life of Grieg, was seen as a "considerable part of the production's total assets".[29]

Two years later, the Ballet Society became the New York City Ballet at City Center. This would be Balanchine's (Mr B's) home company until his death.

The Four Temperaments became part of the new company's repertory. Subtitled "A Dance Ballet without Plot", it is a theme and four variations based on medieval cosmology: *I. Melancholic, II. Sanguinic, III. Phlegmatic and IV. Choleric.*[30] Dancing evolves out of the music, "it is the musical pulse, which provides rhythmic drive . . . , [the] pulse drive is celebrated too in movement style, most clearly with change of weight and in the work of legs and feet".[31] The "pulse drive", "change of weight" and "foot and leg work" form the basis of Balanchine's modernist vocabulary. In addition to the pairing of distinct musical themes with dance motifs and dancers, Balanchine subtly reformulated the strong correlations between the music and movement, between "family relations" and the economy of ideas, with which he had been concerned in earlier years. *The Four Temperaments* became known as one of the "black and white" ballets. In his incessant reshaping of choreography and costume, Balanchine soon after the premiere discarded the original costumes, which he thought were an impractical assortment of wraps, tubes and bandages. ("Balanchine was reportedly snipping away pieces of the costumes right up to curtain time."[32]) He made the dancers wear rehearsal clothes, simple black leotards and tights, and then set them against a solid-coloured backdrop. Thus, Balanchine shifted the focus from spectacle to the dance itself and especially to the unadorned body and its natural line, its flexibility, agility, strength and submission to the force of gravity. Gravity, the pull that ballet traditionally attempts to defy, is the force above all explored in *The Four Temperaments,* especially in the *Melancholic* variation where the male soloist succumbs to it, thwarted by the sinister marching of the corps women *en pointe* to the entrance of a prominent piano theme. Many of the lifts and supports clearly show the effort involved, and at times do not even accomplish a "heightening" of the dancer. The male soloist in

Melancholic exits with his torso arched backward as if being invisibly pulled. Next to the problem of gravity, Balanchine explored physical and spatial limitations. In addition to the restricted vocabulary of select "motifs", the dancers are often obstructing each other through entanglements of arms as in *Phlegmatic* or the holding of limbs of the female soloist in *Choleric*.[33] (These examples are now seen as Balanchine trademarks.) The dancers arch their backs forward and backward as if by pushed by an unseen force. Torsos are malleable and twisted, legs and hips are turned in at times, arms are angular and jagged and supporting legs are bent, even when on pointe. It often seems as though a dancer is trying to escape her body but is limited by unseen gravitational forces or the snares set up by other dancers. This ballet, though somewhat modified for the screen, was Balanchine's first choice for the PBS broadcast *Dance in America* in 1977. Balanchine had long been fascinated with the possibilities of filming dance and taking camera angles into account. One Hollywood anecdote tells of Balanchine, in 1937, constantly moving the exasperated director and others around the studio to demonstrate how differently the dance would look from different positions.[34]

In the years to come the company grew in strength; students who had been with the school from the start became its principal members. It was a slow battle for financial security with much hard work and sacrifice.Balanchine's *Firebird* (1949) to Stravinsky's newly arranged suite from the original score received overwhelming success and took the public by surprise. Maria Tallchief's demonically difficult solo caused gasps of awe. The *Firebird* and other successful pieces formed the repertoire for the extensive touring period in the 1950s.

In February 1954, Balanchine and the New York City Ballet presented *The Nutcracker*, a ballet that would reformulate the meaning of Christmas in America. From 1954 onwards, the New York City Ballet would not miss a single year of this holiday favourite and from year to year the Christmas tree grew. The ballet seemed to stand in odd juxtaposition to other, increasingly abstract choreographies and indulged in all those elements that seemed to be missing from many Balanchine choreographies, namely mime, costume, narrative.

1957 and Beyond

Disaster struck in 1956, as Tanaquil LeClerq, married to Balanchine and one of his leading dancers, fell ill with polio. Balanchine, devastated, set his work aside completely to care for her until November 1957. When he returned to the studio to choreograph, four ballets, completely different from anything he had ever done, spilled out in under three months: *Square Dance* (Vivaldi/Corelli), *Gounod Symphony, Stars and Stripes* (Sousa/arr. Kay) and *Agon* (Stravinsky). There was something for everyone is this season but it was *Agon* that received the most attention. Was it the nature of Balanchine's close collaboration with Stravinsky (he had proposed the idea of the ballet and Stravinsky took it up) or the daring and purposeful partnering of Diana Adams and African-American dancer Arthur Mitchell that astounded the audience once more? Duchamp compared *Agon* to *Le Sacre du printemps* and Arthur Mitchell wrote that it "set the standard for neoclassical dance today". The ballet represented "a perfect union between two great artists"[35] – composer and choreographer and female and male dancer.

Agon showed all the characteristics of previous ballets: the usual hard work, the craftsmanship, the eye for the strengths of particular dancers and the incorporation of personalities and banal events into the work. Arthur Mitchell echoed most dancers' sentiments, when he characterised Balanchine as "a master at knowing what looked good on a dancer's body and what movement could extend a dancer's body".[36] Mitchell recalled how, on a day when Balanchine's knee was bothering him, "he added a limp to the choreography. The 'toe, flat,' 'toe, flat' step that the boys do came out of that day".[37] Balanchine had exact timings in minutes and seconds in mind and even had stick figure drawings for the number of male and female dancers to be used for each part. *Agon*, Greek for "contest", best represents the ideal relationship between music and choreography as Balanchine and Stravinsky saw it: "a struggle between music and choreography to bring about harmony and synthesis . . . a strenuous working together of two independent forces".[38] Above all, rhythm as the constant from which movement derives is organised in such a way that "the most varied and complex inter-relationships between what we see and what we hear" occur.[39] Did Balanchine make the score visible? If so, then the visualising techniques used by Balanchine could be a step per note, mimicking musical highs and lows, or dancing the "look" of the score or its specific elements (such as the "tone row"). A major Balanchine trait is showing the underlying metre (including notes and rests or silences), such as in the opening of *Agon*, which serves to "[clarify] an ambiguous sense of musical pulse and metre".[40] Again, counterpoint (dance in opposition or tension with the musical score) is especially prominent. There are also places where the dancers anticipate or echo what is heard. Balanchine never strictly visualises what can be heard (sometimes called "mickey-mousing") rather, moments of visualisation pass quickly into the shifting flow, as in the short *Bransle Gay* female solo. Throughout, one hears the steady pattern on the castanets while the musical metre shifts. The dancer only lines up with the rhythm in an obvious way when the castanets are heard alone: at the opening, the ending and twice in the middle.

The focal point of the work is the *pas de deux*, which departs from an easily countable rhythmic pulse. The dancers must know the music extremely well and react while they "play along". Simply reading about these moments only serves to whet one's appetite for the actual performance, but it is this way of working with music that awed dancers and critics. One does not necessarily have to have music or dance training to appreciate or notice these things. In fact, Balanchine would say in his typical offhand way that, if people liked looking, that was fine, they would probably come again. If not, they could always close their eyes and listen to the wonderful music.

Balanchine was consistently creative throughout his life, pausing only infrequently, and the quality of his work rarely suffered. There were, of course, times of stress, political, cultural or personal. The emotionally intense tour of the Soviet Union in 1962 coincided with the Cuban missile crisis. During the challenging move to the Lincoln Center and New York State Theater in 1964, Balanchine discovered during the building process that the orchestra pit was half the size he expected. There was tension in the company and Balanchine faced problems in his relationships. But he was now accepted as the foremost American choreographer of ballet. He had finally found a home and stability. Soon he even received a salary – though he gave it all to his newly rehired secretary, Barbara Horgan (without her knowing). The Ballet started spending the summers in Saratoga Springs in upstate New York. There were many excellent dancers to work with. Balanchine began to make his ballets available to other companies and to produce them for film.

Of the many great ballets during this period only a few can be mentioned: *Episodes* (1959) – the famous collaboration with Martha Graham to Webern's complete orchestral works; *A Midsummer Night's Dream* (1962) – the first full-length original story-ballet to his own selections from Mendelssohn's music, complete with mime and a *pas de deux* between Titania and the perfectly choreographed Ass; *Movements for Piano and Orchestra* (1963) – the ballet that Stravinsky "heard with his eyes", which also marked the beginning of the "Suzanne Farrell years"; *Don Quixote* (1965) – commissioned from Nabokov, in which Balanchine, autobiographically, danced the role of Don with the young Farrell as Dulcinea. There were *Jewels* (1967) to music by Fauré, Stravinsky and Tchaikovsky (see Fig. 37), *Who Cares?* (1970) to music by Gershwin and *Mozartiana* (rev. 1981) to music by Tchaikovsky (hailed as his last great ballet). There were festivals for Stravinsky, Ravel and Tchaikovsky. Even on his deathbed he thought about choreography. Maria Tallchief remembers her last visit: "music was playing. Balanchine was tapping the fingers of both hands against each other." When she asked what he was doing, he replied, "You see, I'm making

Figure 37 Suzanne Farrell and Peter Martins in *Jewels – Diamonds*, choreography by George Balanchine.

steps."[41] He died on 30 April, 1983. That night Lincoln Kirstein announced to the audience, "I don't have to tell you that Mr. B. is with Mozart and Tchaikovsky and Stravinsky."[42]

Balanchine's legacy

In his will, Balanchine left his ballets to his friends and dancers. He thought that in fifty years no one would care; he was wrong. The efforts of the George

Balanchine Foundation and the George Balanchine Trust seek to ensure that the ballets are carefully preserved; many of his ballets have been filmed, and former students on video tapes demonstrate his technique. Many of his dancers have been interviewed, have written memoirs recounting his working practices and describing his technique. Balanchine has been turned into an ongoing new research project. If anything, Balanchine's legacy is not only secure but growing. Such policy goes against Balanchine's philosophy – that ballets are ephemeral, like butterflies and that they should be updated without concern for the "authenticity" of the first version. But his inspiration was too great, his ballets too beautiful and too compelling for his disciples, and the greater audience, to relinquish. Can his effect on the dance world be measured? Balanchine would say that "probably dance would stop if we didn't have Stravinsky"[43] but it is certain that without Balanchine, ballet would not be what it is today. It is not only his technique and his modernisation of classical ballet but his open-hearted and eclectic approach to the art that so altered it, and that continues to attract audiences to it. Moreover, his particular love for his adopted country, his commitment to create a truly American ballet company and to celebrate something American exerted an enormous influence on the ballet of the twentieth century.

20 Balanchine and the deconstruction of classicism

JULIET BELLOW

> I would say quite frankly that I detest the spirit of these parodies, and that the perpetual sniggering of the choreographer Mr Balanchine seems to me, at times, a sign of powerlessness. He uses and abuses classical dance by literally putting it to torture; with a type of sadistic satisfaction, he ... forces the leader of the Muses to play the clown.[1]

With this scathing critique André Levinson, the most prominent defender of the nineteenth-century balletic canon, assessed George Balanchine's *Le Bal* (*The Ball*, 1929). As anyone familiar with Balanchine's career knows, this is a surprisingly harsh treatment of the choreographer who has come to epitomise the resuscitation of classical ballet in the twentieth century. Scholars invariably place Balanchine within an "apostolic succession" of ballet masters "extending back in time through Petipa, and Didelot before him, to Noverre and Lully", the founding fathers of the genre.[2] Often, his irreverent attitude towards classicism in his early work is dismissed as lacking the mature, pure-dance approach of his later years. Balanchine himself set the tone of this interpretation by allowing more unorthodox works, including *Le Bal*, to fall out of repertory – and by altering the choreography of such early ballets as *Apollon musagète* (*Apollo, Leader of the Muses*, 1928) in order to stress their continuity with the classical tradition.

Yet Balanchine's early ballets, and the outraged responses of knowledgeable observers like Levinson, deserve to be taken seriously. Audiences of the 1920s saw in Balanchine's work an aggressive, even violent anti-classicism: an eagerness to "abuse" ballet by splicing it with modern and popular dance, vaudeville and gymnastic routines. This pastiche of different types of movement – which to late twentieth-century eyes seems a harmonious synthesis – struck its original viewers as a deliberately disjunctive, chaotic jumble of clashing styles. Placing the *danse d'école* in unfamiliar contexts, Balanchine's early choreography constituted a "composite, hybrid, inorganic spectacle" akin to the mismatching assemblage of architectural fragments featured in Giorgio de Chirico's set and costume designs for *Le Bal* (see Fig. 38).[3]

Balanchine's fusion of classical ballet with other dance forms did not just break the compositional rules codified by Marius Petipa in the nineteenth century. As several critics recognised, these works also deconstructed classicism's technique and structure, exposing its underlying conventions. Balanchine thus pitted himself directly against an emerging definition of classicism articulated most eloquently in Levinson's writings of the 1920s. Levinson conceived of classical ballet as a pure and autonomous art form

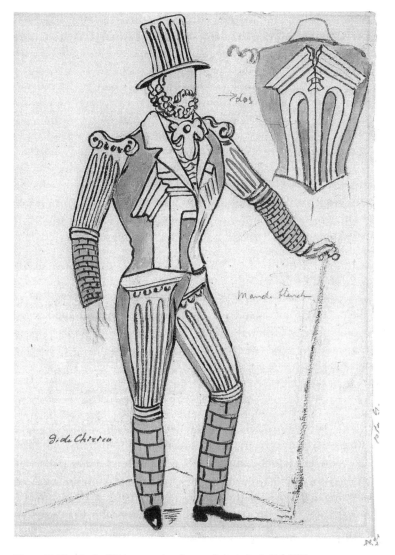

Figure 38 Giorgio de Chirico, costume for a male guest in *Le Bal*, 1929.

based on universal principles of corporeal symmetry and grace.[4] "The classical dance is not a label," he insisted, but "a determined and conscious servitude to spirit and body accepted with a view to a highly elevated aesthetic result. It is not a commodity, because it can only be realised through disinterested sacrifice."[5] At the beginning of his career, Balanchine refused classicism this status as a timeless, eternal order by treating it as simply one amongst a panoply of disparate styles of movement.

Balanchine came of age as a choreographer in the wake of Marius Petipa's death in 1910 and the October Revolution of 1917 – events that gave rise to a contentious debate about the relevance of classical ballet within the Russian dance community. While some choreographers and critics denounced classicism as bourgeois, decadent and obsolete, others viewed it as the foundation for a new Soviet style of dance. Under the auspices of Anatoly Lunacharsky's State Commissariat for Enlightenment, the Bolshoi and Petrograd (formerly Maryinsky) theatres continued to stage Petipa's most famous works, including *La Bayadère*, *The Nutcracker*, *Swan Lake* and *Sleeping Beauty*. Surprisingly, even such radical choreographers as Fyodor Lopukhov and Kasyan Goleizovsky worked from within the classical tradition by tweaking its basic positions, components and sequences. After Balanchine left the Soviet Union in 1924, he witnessed similar experiments by choreographers in Serge Diaghilev's Ballets Russes troupe. Critics noted despairingly the use of classical dance in Léonide Massine's *Pulcinella* (1920) "to create character, just as the czarda, the bolero and the jig [functioned in] ... *Coppélia*" and the "geometrical dessication of its vocabulary" in Bronislava Nijinska's *Les Noces* (*The Wedding*, 1923).[6] Several reviews claimed that rather than enriching classical ballet, these works impoverished the genre by making spectators feel as if they were attending a lowly circus or variety show.

Balanchine's work of the 1920s featured many of these choreographers' most infamous distortions of the *danse d'école*. His ballets broke with the classical ideal of bodily symmetry and balance, employing diagonal lines and uneven groupings, high leg extensions, extreme backbends, deep splits and overhead lifts. He invented unconventional forms of partnering and support in the *pas de deux*: in *La Pastorale* (1926), the ballerina executed *développés* over her partner's head, performed a promenade turn in which the male dancer pivoted her by supporting her calf, and assumed the "clip-on" pose, with her leg hitched to the danseur's torso. *Le Bal's pas de deux* likewise included a lift in which the ballerina, facing her partner, performed a plié on pointe, then jumped onto his chest, arching back.[7]

As this acrobatic sequence suggests, Balanchine juxtaposed classical or quasi-classical elements with movements perceived to be foreign to the *danse d'école*. He appropriated steps from folk and character dances, such as the jig, and from contemporary social dances including the foxtrot and cakewalk. Flexions of the torso in his works alluded to the modern dance vocabulary of Isadora Duncan. Intending to liberate the dancer's midsection, Duncan designed such movements in opposition to what she saw as the artificiality of classical ballet, symbolised by the constraints that the corseted tutu imposed upon the dancer's body. Balanchine also incorporated non-dance movements into his early choreography. Militaristic marches and music-hall gymnastics appeared in these ballets, as did sequences reminiscent of Vsevolod Meyerhold's biomechanical exercises: a system of theatrical training in which repeated motions allowed actors to transform their bodies into rationalised, controlled machines. In employing such an array of movement styles, Balanchine not only flouted the compositional rules that isolated classical steps from character dances and mime, but he also deliberately brought together movements that were aesthetically distinct and fundamentally incompatible in their underlying philosophy.

Moreover, abrupt transitions from one movement to the next exaggerated their inherent dissonance: the solo variation for *Le Bal*'s ballerina, for example, incorporated constant alternations of pointe and heel, as well as jumps from fifth position to second in the air to fifth again.[8] The middle of this leap, with legs spread wide, transformed the dance into an acrobatic routine that contrasted with its classical preparation and landing. Many viewers objected to such alterations of classical technique, accusing Balanchine of treating the dancers "like a docile and malleable material" and forcing them to "maneuver about jerkingly" with "angular movements [and] starchy gestures".[9] Crude and awkward, this choreography seemed an assault on ballet's fundamental principles – a "deformation … a drawing and quartering of the pure and graceful forms of the danse d'école", according to Levinson.[10]

While most critical commentary focused on his innovative (and purportedly torturous) choreography, Balanchine's dissection of classicism extended beyond the level of technique. His works of the 1920s also experimented with the traditional structure and subject matter of nineteenth-century ballets. He adapted standard plots involving love between human male and otherworldly female characters, which traditionally gave rise to a confrontation of the "real" world (dominated by national and character dances) with a dream or fantasy world (in which classical dance is privileged). *La Chatte* (*The Cat*, 1927), for example, was based on one of Aesop's fables in which a young man falls in love with a cat, and persuades the goddess Aphrodite to give her human form. When she chases a mouse, the woman turns back into a cat, and the young man dies of a broken heart.[11] *La Pastorale* translated this cross-species romance into modern-day characters: a movie starlet and a telegraph boy who meet on the set of a film.

That Balanchine used these flimsy scenarios to parody the standard balletic format is borne out in *The Triumph of Neptune* (1926), which multiplied the two acts of romantic-era productions into ten tableaux alternating between real and fictional worlds.[12] The ballet's narrative of a foreign correspondent who decides to travel to Fairyland for a story also allowed Balanchine to play with the conventional separation of character from classical dancing. Just after completing her solo variation for a classical *pas de deux* with Serge Lifar, Alexandra Danilova "ran quickly into the wings and put trousers on under [an] opera- or knee-length, tutu, ran back out onstage, and danced the hornpipe".[13] Cheekily combining the classical tutu with a more "realistic" costume typical of character dance, Balanchine referenced Petipa's strict rules of balletic composition in a "mélange of Taglionesque flight and fairground flashiness" that Levinson took to be a "deliberate parody of classical ballet".[14]

Nowhere is Balanchine's deconstruction of classicism more evident, however, than in his *pas de deux*, the "traditional classic ballet centerpiece", as he later termed it.[15] As noted earlier, Balanchine invented unusual forms of partnering, many of which exaggerated the gendered conventions of the *pas de deux*.[16] The female dancer was spun, twisted, held, lifted, dragged – in short, manipulated like an inanimate object. In *Le Fils prodigue* (*Prodigal Son*, 1929), still in repertory at the New York City Ballet, the character of the Prodigal Son holds the Siren by her armpits and lowers her down into a deep split, then lifts her to standing. At another point in the *pas de deux*, the Siren arches around the Prodigal Son's body, forming a belt around his torso; he holds her at the groin and waist and lowers her to the floor. A moment in *Le Bal* similarly featured the character of the Young Man straddling his partner, pinning her in place as she lay on the floor. Moving beyond the established vocabulary of partnering and support, such sequences emphasised the male dancer's control of the ballerina's movements.

Yet the female characters in Balanchine's early works also remained elusive sources of fear and desire: his heroes' fascination with their partners translated into a kind of passivity. In both *La Pastorale* and *Le Bal*, the male lead pursues the female dancer, allowing his movements to be dictated by hers – and dies when his quest fails. This lack of male agency was magnified by Balanchine's predilection for tall ballerinas. His male dancers often were the same height as, or shorter than, their female partners, thus reducing the association of masculinity with physical domination. Balanchine heightened this reversal by stressing the female dancer's weight, at times making her seem an almost unbearable burden (see Fig. 39). Supporting the ballerina from literally debased positions, his male dancers knelt, sat, and reclined, as when the Telegraph Boy in *Le Pastorale* turned the Star in arabesque from the ground, holding her by the knee.[17] Likewise, in the first encounter between the Prodigal Son and the Siren, the male dancer suddenly is thrust beneath his partner's legs; she straddles the nape of his neck and slides down his back. Drawing out the complexity of the classical *pas de deux*, Balanchine's dancers oscillated between activity and passivity, agency and objecthood.

Balanchine's *Apollon musagète* is described as the choreographer's first truly neoclassical work – a pure-dance *ballet blanc* that marked the end of his parodic experiments with the *danse d'école*.[18] However, the ballet also can be read as a profusion of distinct classicisms and neoclassicisms that

Figure 39 Alice Nikitina, Felia Doubrovska, Lubov Tchernicheva, Serge Lifar in *Apollon musagète (Apollo, Leader of the Muses)*, 1928, choreography by George Balanchine, music by Igor Stravinsky. First performance 12 June 1928, Théâtre Sarah-Bernhardt, Paris. Ballets Russes de Serge Diaghilev.

refuse to cohere. Juxtaposing the gods of antiquity, the seventeenth-century *ballet d'action*, and the nineteenth-century Petipa tradition – all forms that have been described as "classical" – *Apollon musagète* exposed the tensions underlying the concept of classicism. The ballet subtly demonstrates that the meaning of this slippery term has changed over time, and carries different connotations when applied to visual art, music and dance. A close reading of *Apollon musagète* reveals the ways in which Balanchine and his collaborators strategically heightened the confrontation of these various "classicisms".

Apollon musagète's characters and story come from classical Greek mythology: the god Apollo in his role as master of the Muses, represented by Calliope (muse of poetry), Polyhymnia (muse of mime) and Terpsichore (muse of dance). As the souvenir programme for the Ballets Russes'

1928–9 Paris season noted, *Apollon musagète* began with a short prologue "representing Apollo's birth" that Balanchine later removed from the ballet.[19] Leto, Apollo's mother, kneels to the ground and gives birth to the god; two goddesses arrive, swaddling him in white clothes and a golden belt, present him with nectar and ambrosia, and carry him off to Olympus. The second tableau centres around a "Judgment of Paris" scenario, with each muse demonstrating her art for Apollo in a solo variation. Apollo chooses Terpsichore as his favorite muse and they dance a *pas de deux*, followed by a coda with all four dancers. "These allegorical scenes end", according to the programme notes, "with an apotheosis in which Apollo leads the muses, Terpsichore at the front, to Parnassus, which will henceforth be their residence".

In addition to its explicit invocation of the gods and demi-gods of classical antiquity, the ballet implicitly alluded to the seventeenth-century neoclassical court ballets of Louis XIV and their subsequent development into the eighteenth-century *ballets d'action*. The Sun King often used the figure of Apollo as his symbol and alter ego, playing the role in several ballets, including *Le Ballet de la nuit* and *Les Noces de Pelée et Thétis*, which also featured his Muses. Balanchine's inclusion of sun imagery, with the Muses' extended legs creating a burst of rays behind Apollo, further cemented *Apollon musagète*'s references to seventeenth- and eighteenth-century neoclassicism. So did André Bauchant's set, with its incarnation of Mount Parnassus and Apollo's chariot onstage. One critic noted that "nothing is lacking in [the ballet's] wilful positioning in bygone days, not even the flying mechanism hitched to cardboard horses, as in an opera-ballet by [Jean-Philippe] Rameau".[20]

This reference to one of the French Royal Academy's most famous eighteenth-century composers was just: with its emphasis on order, clarity and simplicity, Stravinsky's score for *Apollon musagète* deliberately recalled that era's musical classicism. Moving away from the constant shifts in tempo, rhythm and tonality that characterised Stravinsky's earlier works for the Ballets Russes, *Apollon musagète* established a structure of theme and variations that remained stable throughout. The critic for the *Nouvelle revue française* termed this score a "notary's contract", arguing that "in abandoning Bach and Handel", Stravinsky "appeared to want to revive the tradition of eighteenth-century French ballet, and even recalled Lully", Louis XIV's chief composer.[21] *Apollon musagète* thus conveyed to its first listeners a self-conscious flatness or "intentional frost", as critic Louis Laloy put it, produced by Stravinsky's pastiche of eighteenth-century classicism.[22]

Balanchine, of course, added Petipa's classicism to the mix, complete with the knee-length tutus worn by the three Muses. As Levinson noted in his review, *Apollon musagète* "submits itself to the form, always common in the classical ballet, of theme and variations", with traditional solo and ensemble dances and a *pas de deux*.[23] Yet, as in his other works of the period, Balanchine added "angular attitudes", "cut and dried movements", and "vague acrobatic impulses" abutting the graceful steps of the *danse d'école*.[24] For example, Terpsichore begins her solo variation with a series of classical steps: *coupés*, *grands jetés*, and *soutenu* turns. This traditional variation quickly morphs into unfamiliar territory as the dancer twice repeats a sequence consisting of two consecutive *relevés* in *arabesque à la seconde* with her arms overhead in fifth position. She then lowers herself down from her pointe and ambles around in a flat-footed circle; arranging her arms in a diagonal line, with hands flexed at the wrist, she breaks with classical rules of alignment in her upper body. This sequence is accompanied by a syncopated musical phrase that emphasises the disjunctiveness of the two different forms of movement. Later in the same variation, Terpsichore assumes a position straight out of *La Sylphide*, with her front knee in *plié*, her back leg angled back gracefully. She then pivots to face her back leg, which she raises onto pointe and bends deeply, her knee extending beyond her planted foot to form a hard angle.

The *pas de deux* between Apollo and Terpsichore also juxtaposed classical and unclassical movements. The dance begins with Apollo seated on the floor. Terpsichore takes his hand and performs a *développé*, then strides over his shoulder and turns in arabesque, allowing her extended leg to pass over his head, and takes a seat on his raised knees. An equally unusual sequence occurs later when Terpsichore stands in *relevé* in arabesque, supported by Apollo, who holds her waist in the traditional manner. He then grabs her inner thigh and lifts Terpsichore overhead; with her torso draped over his back, her legs remain in a split, as if performing a leap upside down. Apollo lowers her down and both dancers lean forward, lunging deeply. Together, they repeat the sequence in Terpsichore's variation in which she moves from *grand battement* to flat-footed circle, this time with Apollo's support. Later, in the famous end to this *pas de deux*, Apollo kneels on the ground as Terpsichore performs a *grand battement développé* behind him. He lifts her onto the back of his neck and she balances there. Both partners sweep their arms forward and back, as if swimming. Apollo places Terpsichore back down on the ground as he rises up, one foot forward and slanting his body diagonally; she rests her body on his as they arch their backs in unison.

While admitting in his review of *Apollo musagète* that "some [of Balanchine's] groups are ingeniously constructed", Levinson seconded Louis Laloy's assertion that the ballet conveyed an air of "intentional frost". Balanchine's aim, he declared, was "that of 'refrigerating' classical ballet" in a manner that "borders on parody".[25] Balanchine preserved the *danse d'école*, Levinson seems to say, but not the hierarchy within which it occupied the premier rank. To put it in Levinson's terms, Balanchine's choreography of the 1920s treated classicism as a "label" or "commodity" – as an artefact or set of arbitrary conventions rather than a universal principle of movement transcending time and place.

In a 1971 essay entitled "The Greatest Master of them All", Balanchine claimed that "the movements that Petipa used are essentially the same movements we know today". While on occasion "I myself turned those steps upside down", he wrote, "the language of classic dance is unchanging, universal and eternal".[26] When did Balanchine come around to Levinson's point of view? What precipitated this change of heart? Was it simply a maturation that moved him away from the rebelliousness of his youth, as most scholars maintain? Did it emerge from his relationship with Lincoln Kirstein, or reflect the turn towards formalism in the United States after the Second World War? Or was Balanchine responding to the tastes of an audience for ballet that he had helped to create? Answers to these questions are speculative, stymied in large measure by Balanchine's constant rewriting of his own history – rendering himself, in retrospect, into an apostle of the classical tradition.

21 *The Nutcracker*: a cultural icon

JENNIFER FISHER

In 1892, when *The Nutcracker* premiered at the Maryinsky Theatre in St Petersburg, it received mixed reviews. Like other Imperial Russian ballets, it featured flashes of brilliance from a talented cast, but it had a rather ordinary plot about a girl who receives a magical Christmas gift. Even the Tchaikovsky score failed to win unequivocal approval because it was more symphonic than the music that usually accompanied a ballet at the time. No one suspected *The Nutcracker* would eventually become the most popular and most often performed ballet in the world. This transformation from the least respected of the three Tchaikovsky ballets (the other two are *Swan Lake* and *The Sleeping Beauty*) into the most visible and lucrative of all classical ballets, is a story of virtual immigration. There are no borders at which ballets must clear customs and *The Nutcracker* never actually left its homeland, as other immigrants do; nonetheless, like all successful transplants, it thrived in a new location by adapting in creative and unexpected ways. Through all the changes, the ballet has retained much of its "genetic material" – the Tchaikovsky score, a version of the original libretto, some ideas and steps from the original Lev Ivanov choreography and the aura of its distinguished ballet heritage.

The Russian pedigree of *The Nutcracker* was a strong factor in recommending the ballet to North Americans. St Petersburg and Moscow, like Paris and Copenhagen before them, were ballet capitals long before reputable schools and companies were established in the United States and Canada. Imperial Theatre director Ivan Vsevolozhsky first had the idea to make a ballet based on E.T.A. Hoffmann's 1816 short story, "The Nutcracker and the Mouse King". Simplifying the plot considerably, he wrote the libretto, with contributions from master choreographer Marius Petipa. Although the ballet has undergone countless changes since it first appeared, elements of the following story tend to reappear: at a Christmas party, the mysterious Herr Drosselmeier gives a nutcracker doll to Clara, also called Marie in some productions, following Hoffmann's story. Dressed as a soldier, this doll represents the tradition of nutcracker carving developed by miners in the Erzgebirge Mountains of Germany as a way of lampooning figures of authority. After the guests leave, Clara falls asleep near her nutcracker and, when a battle between mice and tin soldiers breaks out in her living room, discovers the doll has come to life. She helps her Nutcracker Prince conquer the wicked Mouse King, then accompanies her hero to a land of snow, where the first significant classical dancing takes place in the form of waltzing snowflakes. In the second act, Clara and her Nutcracker Prince arrive in the Land of the Sweets, where plot development halts, while a series of dances are performed in their honour. These include fancifully imagined ballet versions of national dances, and those performed by swirling bits of candy, a few storybook characters, and waltzing flowers. The reigning monarch, the Sugar Plum Fairy, partnered by her cavalier, appears for her *pas de deux* near the end of the ballet. Then, Clara says goodbye to her fantasy land.

Tchaikovsky had been commissioned to write the score, but he had doubts about whether the story would provide as much scope as that of *The Sleeping Beauty*. Still, he went to work, following the meticulous written instructions from Petipa as to what kind of music each scene required. In letters, Tchaikovsky worried about the quality of his music, but it would be hard to separate his disparaging remarks from the emotional turmoil of his life at the time. In the spring before the ballet premiered, he received ovations after conducting some selections from *The Nutcracker* as a concert suite. Petipa may also have had doubts about the ballet's potential, and before rehearsals began, he pleaded illness and turned the project over to his assistant, Lev Ivanov. There was no dearth of talent to help Ivanov with *Nutcracker* chores. His dancers vied with visiting Italian ballerinas to amaze audiences with their athleticism and charm and together with the resources of copious Maryinsky designers, seamstresses and set builders, a certain amount of excellence was practically guaranteed.

On opening night in January 1892 *The Nutcracker* evidently had a few problems. The critics praised only parts of the score and a few group dances and individual performances. They condemned other aspects of the ballet in such definitive terms that those comments are perhaps best remembered: "For the artistic fate of our ballet it is yet one more step downwards", one critic lamented.[1] The plot was deemed unlikely and imbalanced, the battle scene called chaotic, and the use of children in major roles considered a mistake. Nor did it help that Antonietta Dell'Era, the first Sugar Plum Fairy, appeared very late in the evening, near midnight, because Tchaikovsky's opera *Iolanthe* premiered on the same programme, before the ballet.

It took a few decades for Tchaikovsky's ballet scores to gain acceptance as eminently "danceable" masterworks, but the composer died in 1893, never knowing the lasting impact his ballets would have. *The Nutcracker* was slower than most to gain popularity and then, not in its homeland. Although the Russians did not abandon *The Nutcracker*, neither did they embrace it very firmly. It remained in the repertory of the Maryinsky (known as the Kirov later) and other Russian and Soviet ballet companies, occasionally enjoying a revival or appearing in a new version, but its reputation languished. Often, only the second act appeared on a mixed programme, or it was relegated to school performances and dismissed as a children's ballet, not serious enough to match the emotionally sophisticated score.

In the second half of the twentieth century, *The Nutcracker* came into its own. It all began when Russian artists started to travel across Europe in the decades just before and after the First World War, taking various versions of their classical repertoire with them. Bits of *Nutcracker* music showed up out of context in works performed by Diaghilev's Ballets Russes in Europe, and Anna Pavlova's company toured the world with a version of the snow scene choreographed by Ivan Clustine. This one-act ballet, called "Snowflakes", featured the former Maryinsky ballerina in a *pas de deux* and may have started today's tradition of having a "Snow Queen" in that scene (there was none in Ivanov's original).[2] The Russian Revolution and two world wars made returning to Russia difficult for many dancers and choreographers, so they ended up touring and settling abroad. Memories of *The Nutcracker* travelled with them, and in London the full ballet was staged in 1934 by the Vic-Wells Ballet, with the help of Russian émigré Nikolay Sergeyev.[3]

It was not until *The Nutcracker* reached the United States in the 1940s that it took root in a more significant way. The culturally young country welcomed a ballet with a dual personality, on one hand featuring serious music and classical vocabulary, and on the other, an atmosphere of child-like fun and fantasy. In 1940, Alexandra Federova made a condensed version that criss-crossed the continent for a few decades with the Ballet Russe de Monte Carlo, one of the companies formed in the wake of Diaghilev's death in 1929.

Another introduction to *The Nutcracker* came in the unlikely form of the 1940 Walt Disney film *Fantasia*, which began with a segment featuring animated figures "dancing" to selections from the ballet's second act. It may well have introduced many people who would never go to a ballet performance to the graceful, rhythmic aesthetics of ballet. Disney animators used dancers as models, and made a group of ordinary thistles perform a respectable Russian character dance. The rest of the figures often move like a corps de ballet: fairies skating on frozen ponds, flowers spinning down a stream or fish swirling their fanned tails and fins. If the "high" arts that came from Europe and Russia seemed remote and elitist to many Americans, cartoons did not; *Fantasia*, in many ways, brought ballet "down to earth" for them.

The first full-length American *Nutcracker* came about in San Francisco in 1944, through a series of coincidences. Willem Christensen, artistic director of the San Francisco Ballet, had begun to do a ballet at Christmas the year before, because the city's War Memorial Auditorium happened to be free.

The next year, local Russian immigrants convinced him to try a *Nutcracker*. He had never seen the full ballet and therefore asked for advice from George Balanchine and Alexandra Danilova, ex-Maryinsky dancers by then based in New York. Danilova dutifully tried to recall the original choreography, but Balanchine advised Christensen to make his own version.[4] It was a course Balanchine himself took in 1954, when his New York City Ballet needed a classical challenge, as well as an evening-length crowd pleaser. The choreographer was well suited to both tasks, he had been schooled in Russian imperial style, which he energised by incorporating modernistic streamlining and jazzy elements from African-American cultural forms.[5] He seemed to have a special affection for *The Nutcracker*, had danced in it at the Maryinsky while still a student. In interviews, he remembered old-fashioned Christmases (though he thought of Russian Easter as a much more festive time), and he added touches to his *Nutcracker* that made it particularly appealing in his new homeland.[6] Even with a relatively small budget at the time, he insisted on having a tree that expanded impressively to Tchaikovsky's soaring crescendos, snow that fell so quickly that dancers traced paths in it across the stage, and flying reindeer to whisk Clara away.

Balanchine's commitment to training young dancers dovetailed nicely with the audience's interest in seeing their children onstage. In his party scene, young dancers break out of the formal, starchy mode seen in other versions, playing leapfrog, bursting with emotion, and urging the comically scary Drosselmeier to perform magic. Balanchine created a picture-postcard Christmas, with Marie's mother coming to check on her daughter after she has fallen asleep in the living room. To a sweetly serene violin solo, she crosses the stage holding a candle, then covers her sleeping daughter solicitously with a shawl and closes a window against draught.[7]

With all the nostalgic touches and special effects, there is still enough complex, technical dancing to keep aficionados happy, so that Balanchine seems to have succeeded where other choreographers failed: he trusted the music, his choreography and the holiday season to provide enough resonance for both a good ballet and a new holiday tradition. The "immigrant Nutcracker" was indeed fortunate to be adopted and adapted by a "countryman" who was already established in the United States. Because of New York City's centrality in the world of American ballet and Balanchine's influential artistic leadership, his production had a major impact on the "annual Nutcracker" trend. Not only did other choreographers start thinking about the financial benefits from return ticket buyers, but dancers who left the company staged a *Nutcracker* wherever they settled. City Ballet sometimes took its production on tour (even in the summer at first) and used local children, further planting *Nutcracker* seeds in various communities. In 1957 and

1958, an even larger audience saw the ballet during Christmas day television broadcasts, with Balanchine himself as Drosselmeier the second year.

Starting in the 1960s, scores of North American ballet companies mounted their own *Nutcrackers*, with newly created choreographies or with influences from elsewhere, until it seemed there was a production anywhere that had a ballet school and a Tchaikovsky recording. An influential 1985 video of a Royal Ballet production, with choreography credited to Ivanov and Peter Wright, was perhaps as widely imitated as Balanchine at first. Perceived to have strong connections to the first St Petersburg production, it benefited from the incomplete Sergeyev notation, as well as research contributed by musicologist Roland John Wiley, who has studied the original *Nutcracker* extensively. But it was not long before choreographers started to go their own way. Although most of them created a picturesque version of Christmas traditions inherited from Germany and Victorian England, some choreographers opted to shift its location to represent their own communities more directly. In cities with a significant immigrant population of Germans or Scots, Clara's home was located in the German section of an American town, or became the scene of Scottish country dancing in kilts. A Mexican piñata and cowboys found their way into productions in the American south-west; hula was added in Hawaii and hockey in Canada. More than one urban *Nutcracker* has reflected inner-city realities, and satiric versions have featured political commentary that outshines the dancing. By the 1990s, there even was a Barbie film version, starring the popular doll as the most plastic of Sugar Plum Fairies. In 2001 English National Ballet struck a deal with toymaker Mattel who sponsored the six-week run of *The Nutcracker* around Christmas at London's Coliseum with $85,000, in order to cover the deficit the ballet had incurred.[8]

Perhaps because of its ubiquitous nature, choreographers have felt compelled to put a unique stamp on *The Nutcracker*. Both John Cranko and John Neumeier, American choreographers who made careers in Germany, turned the ballet's Christmas gathering into a birthday party for Clara in their versions, in 1966 and 1971 respectively. Graeme Murphy's 1992 adaptation for the Australian Ballet makes Clara a Russian ballerina who emigrates to Australia. In England, Matthew Bourne set his first act in an orphanage straight out of Dickens's *Oliver Twist*. Two of the more notable departures in the 1990s were Mark Morris's *The Hard Nut*, and Donald Byrd's *Harlem Nutcracker*. Morris set the ballet in the 1960s, adding an op-art set, cross-dressing and much irreverence, as well as his own brand of modern dance musicality. Byrd changed the location to current-day Harlem, where Clara is a grandmother who has a flashback to her youthful days during the Harlem Renaissance. Her "Land of the Sweets" becomes "Club Sweets" and swings to the rhythms of Duke Ellington's arrangement of the score.[9] Byrd's

Figure 40 The American department store chain Lord & Taylor announces its presentation of *The Nutcracker* in the 1974 catalogue.

Nutcracker, like other versions with African-American influences, changed Euro-American customs and names to reflect another cultural reality; it featured a gospel choir in the first act, and a jazzy "Sugar Rum Cherry" in the second. In 2000 Maurice Béjart used his own life to create a *Nutcracker* for the Théâtre Musical de Paris-Châtelet. He replaced the mother and Clara characters with his own mother and himself as a young boy growing up in Marseilles, also adding the character of Petipa to represent Russian ballet tradition.

In many American locations, the impulse to "customise" the ballet has reached epic proportions: There have been tap dancing *Nutcrackers*, *Nutcrackers* on ice, dance-along versions (bring your own tutu and tiara), and even a short-lived production in Southern California that tried to tell the story with bharata natyam. Every ballet company that makes an adaptation of *The Nutcracker* seeks an ingenious way to keep audiences interested. Some convince local celebrities or politicians to appear in walk-on roles. Or they surround the performance with related events – a "*Nutcracker* Fair", a "Tea Party with Clara", or a *Nutty Nutcracker*, a performance in which dancers switch roles or send up their characters in some way. They also entertain audiences with ever-expanding lobby boutiques that sell nutcracker dolls of all sizes, as well as *Nutcracker* themed T-shirts, socks, scarves, foodstuffs, placemats, finger puppets, soap and stationery (see Fig. 40).

Along with the wide popularity of *The Nutcracker* has come a certain amount of scepticism about its artistic merit. Can a ballet featuring such childlike glee and spin-off products be taken all that seriously? Aficionados and critics have tended to look down on it as too accessible, too lopsided in plot (all story in the first act, all dancing in the second) and too full of children. But these elements, echoing critical condemnation back in Russia, only seemed to recommend the ballet in North America. Accessibility was a good thing for newcomers to ballet, helping to educate and build audiences; and the story's quick switch from the everyday world to fantasy did not seem so unbelievable; it resembled the great American rags-to-riches dream. Another discourse that grew up around many *Nutcrackers*, especially those by regional and amateur ballet companies, was that of "community togetherness". Many productions rely on volunteers to mount the ballet, often involving whole families, onstage and backstage. For them, and even for audiences who identify strongly with their local professional company, the yearly *Nutcracker* has evolved into a secular holiday ritual that you celebrate with family, real or imagined.

Edwin Denby was one of the first American dance writers to provide a meaningful subtext for the ballet. In the 1940s and 1950s he used a psychological framework and a light tone in deciding why the simple structure of the ballet works. At the seemingly ordinary Christmas party, he said, with its grounded dancing and fractious squabbling, we can imagine the social pressures that make Clara's childhood fraught. Then, the quick transition into fantasy provides a release for her, and for the audience, because friendly characters provide stability and warmth with their graceful, clear dancing. It is really a dream about Christmas, Denby proposed, "since it succeeds in turning envy and pain into a lovely invention and social harmony".[10] For Denby, and perhaps for many people in the *Nutcracker*'s new home, classical dancing spoke a language of hope and reassurance, and the ballet's focus on children enabled audiences to recall youthful dreams and excitement. Denby's emphasis on underlying themes and the way the dancing itself conveys moods make perceived plot deficiencies less problematic. Look beyond the narrative, he advised. The ballet is not confusing or meaningless to a viewer who can link the real and fantasy worlds well enough in his or her mind. Nor is the second act flawed for stalling the story to offer a suite of dances, he said. It allows the viewer to savour each dance individually, then proceed, satisfied, to the next.[11]

When lauding *The Nutcracker* as a perceived site of Christmas ideals, it is also necessary to note the potential pitfalls of the ballet's so-called "national dances". Appearing in the second act, they are called "Hot Chocolate", "Tea", "Coffee", and "Trepak", but are more commonly known as "Spanish", "Chinese", "Arabian", and "Russian". These dances are meant to represent Clara's encounter with an innocently exotic treat, but they have in the past also reflected negative stereotypes of the "Other", inherited from nineteenth-century ballet. Not surprisingly, the least contentious of them is usually "Russian", which often is staged as an athletic character dance, and other times is a dance of candy canes (Balanchine followed Ivanov in the latter choice). The "Spanish" dance also poses few problems, because it tends to resemble some form of dancing actually done in Spain, except that it is more "balleticised". But "Chinese" and "Arabian" rarely resemble any dance done in Asia or the Middle East; instead, some versions can feature distorted, insulting stereotypes.

Though it is hard to generalise, and impossible to consider every specific production, there are certain trends when it comes to staging these dances.[12] They can be divided into two basic categories: those that are more or less respectful and naively combine elements of Asian or Middle Eastern dance with ballet; and those that are oblivious to potential ethnic slurs, reproducing iniquitous images of lounging villains, obsequious servants and loose women. The two key discourses for understanding the difference between these "insensitive and insulting" and "naive but respectful" versions are "Orientalism" and "artistic hybridisation". Orientalism, as first defined by Edward Said, refers to the ways in which Western colonialists (specifically the British, French and Americans) stereotyped the Middle East as "a place of romance, exotic beings, haunting memories and landscapes, remarkable experiences".[13] Whether or not ballet audiences who see *The Nutcracker* are familiar with this definition, they may be absorbing its negative reverberations when "Arabian dance" soloists portray one-dimensional sensualists, or Chinese dancers bob and scurry in clown-like fashion.

On the other hand, some versions may simply combine classical lines with fanciful angles and costumes without suggesting anything more negative than an incomplete ethnographic understanding. This brings to mind historian John M. MacKenzie's proposal that a kind of benign artistic borrowing has always gone on in the world of the arts, and that choreographers may have a genuine admiration for the cultures in question.[14] In other words, a balleticised "Arabian" or "Chinese" dance can be an artistic hybrid,

Figure 41 Pennsylvania Ballet Company Member Heidi Cruz in *The Nutcracker*, 2005, choreography by George Balanchine.

not made "to reinforce colonial power or superiority, but to enable artistic innovation".

Some companies have experimented with practitioners from the countries in question; others have eliminated the dances or changed their character to something less specific. Whatever the version, there has been little productive discussion in the ballet world about how the "Chinese" and "Arabian" dances might have evolved historically and how they might be staged today. With *The Nutcracker*'s long history of adjusting to new people and places, it may be the right classical ballet to continue experimentation with new strategies in eliminating potentially injurious stereotypes in old story ballets. Often fitting into the parameters of any classical ballet, it has also become a nexus point for attitudes, opinions, allegiances and renovations to the classical ballet world itself. Because *The Nutcracker* appears so often and is critiqued in so many situations, it can stimulate questioning of the usually conservative ballet world. How much of ballet's ethnocentric past will survive? How much of it do we want? How can the glorious nineteenth-century ballets evolve and yet retain core values that are worthy? (See Fig. 41.)

Although revenues have sometimes dropped off in economic hard times, the annual *Nutcracker* tradition still grows. Far from being a children's ballet that got out of hand in a country that did not know any better (a common notion among *Nutcracker* detractors), it has become an annual phenomenon that gathers resonance in many ways in many locations. Increasingly, ballet companies outside North America also make December *Nutcracker* season. For many, it is still a Russian ballet, and critics may lament the distance between current incarnations and the original. But for today's *Nutcracker*, the discourse of "authenticity" regarding St Petersburg origins seems less relevant than the ways in which the ballet has become meaningful in many new places. In that case, the idea of repeating *The Nutcracker* each year does not seem a bore or an accident; it seems like a powerful tradition.

22 From *Swan Lake* to *Red Girl's Regiment*: ballet's sinicisation

ZHENG YANGWEN

Chinese dance is a riot of identities – court, folk, ethnic and dynastic. It has a glorious history and is a topic on its own.[1] It draws inspiration from martial arts and "the art of sex" as the quintessential man of letters and leisure Li Yu wrote: "When people teach girls to sing and dance, they do not really teach them how to sing and dance but how to be sensual. If you want her body to be so, then you must have her dance."[2] Several legendary sensual dancers rose to be Senior Consorts and Empresses during the Han (206 BC– AD 220) and Tang (618–960) dynasties. Yang Yuhuan, the most beautiful woman in Chinese history, was a sensual dancer. She captivated the Tang emperor Xianzong (685–762), became his favourite consort and came to shape Chinese history.[3] The splendid history of court dance, like Chinese dance itself, waits to be researched. Chinese dance absorbed its properties and values from many cultures, especially Central Asia, during the Han and Tang dynasties. This pattern of assimilation continued as the Mongols conquered China in 1279 and the Manchus in 1644. It developed rapidly after the Opium War (1839–42) when China began to have direct intercourse with the world beyond greater Asia. This exposure not only dramatically changed China's history but also the very fibre of Chinese culture. Dance in the form of ballet is a great example of such cultural change.

I cannot discuss the introduction and naturalisation of ballet without situating it in the landscape of late Qing, Republican and communist China. Art in general and ballet in particular had to develop within the larger political and socio-cultural framework. Many believe that the West viewed the East as exotic and stereotyped its culture; hence the impact of Western art and thinking has been labelled cultural imperialism. The study of China itself falls into four intellectual frameworks: impact-response, tradition-modernity, imperialism and China-centred. Chinese ballet would fall under any but the fourth paradigm. The story itself is, however, more complicated than that. Ballet, like opium and communism, was foreign to China. Important in its introduction and naturalisation, similar to the stories of opium and communism, were agents and mechanisms of transmission.

Mainland historians credit the introduction of ballet to Yu Ronglin, daughter of late Qing diplomat Yu Geng and sister of author Yu Deling.[4]

Born in 1882, Ronglin followed her father to Japan where he served as China's ambassador in 1893. She was exposed to and began to learn ballet. The family moved to Paris in the late 1890s and Ronglin took classes from the famous Isadora Duncan. They returned to Beijing in 1903; she and her sister became the Empress Dowager Cixi's ladies-in-waiting. Ronglin performed ballet for Cixi and the court at large. She also began to use ballet techniques to choreograph Chinese dance; this can be considered to be the beginning of the naturalisation of ballet in China. One of her enduring works was *Dance of the Lotus Fairy Maiden*, inspired by the Zhongyuan Festival where lotus-shaped lanterns were set floating on water on the fifteenth day of the seventh month of the Chinese lunar calendar. The old Buddha, as Dowager Cixi was reverently addressed, took a liking to Ronglin's dance and to the two sisters.[5] Imperial exposure and endorsement helped promote ballet among the late Qing elite and upper classes; it had set the tone for the twentieth century.

Late Qing (1842–1911) was a stirring time as imperial China disintegrated and something new was in the making. The Nationalist Revolution in 1911 ushered in the May-Fourth or New Culture movement where Chinese intellectuals criticised, if not abandoned, China's heritage in their effort to modernise the ancient culture. *Yangwu* or "foreign dance", as early newspapers and pictorials labelled it, did not mean ballet exclusively but included it.[6] Along with other non-Chinese art forms, it was making its way into treaty port cities like Shanghai where early performances took place. Russian ballerina Anna Pavlova brought *The Dying Swan* to Shanghai in 1922, while a whole array of foreign dance companies and dancers, Denishawn and Irma Duncan for example, gave classic and modern dance performances between 1925 and 1928. They attracted the serious attention of native artists, both traditional and modern. Denishawn fascinated the master of Peking opera, Mei Lanfang, whereas Duncan attracted left-wing writers like Tian Han.[7] This was significant as indigenous artists and progressive men of letters welcomed and began to explore Western art and dance. China's cultural elite appreciated, if not completely accepted, ballet in the 1920s. Soon, first-generation Chinese ballet dancers and choreographers emerged.

Most important among them was Wu Xiaobang, the founding father of Chinese ballet. Wu attended an American school in Shanghai in the 1910s and loved modern dance *and* ballet.[8] He went to study in Japan in 1929, came back to found a dance school in Shanghai and gave China's first public modern dance-ballet performance in 1935. Wu choreographed and performed before and during the Japanese war; his works have become classic repertoire for ballet students in China. Another ballerina who was instrumental in the spread of ballet was Trinidad-born and London-trained

Dai Ailian or "Mother of Chinese dance". She studied at the Mary Wigman and Jooss-Leeder schools and with masters like Rudolf Laban.[9] Like many patriotic overseas Chinese, Dai returned to her ancestral land in 1940 or during the height of the Japanese war where Madam Sun Yat-sen welcomed her. Dai, Wu and Sheng Jie were the dynamic trio in the wartime capital Chongqing. They choreographed patriotic dances and helped mobilise the war against Japan in an extremely difficult time. Patriotism was injected into a performing art; this had set the precedent for the communist era. The trio threw their lot in with the communists at the end of the war. Dai and Wu became the Chair and Vice-chair of the National Dancers Association in 1949. The Beijing Academy of Dance was founded in 1954; Dai became its first Master and Dean. Between 1957 and 1960, the Academy mounted *La Fille mal gardée*, *Swan Lake*, *Le Corsaire* and *Giselle* with the help of such Russian artists as O. A. Yealina.

The 1950s gave birth to a new generation of outstanding ballerinas. Dance theatre in general, ballet in particular, flourished into the mid-1960s when the country was in a mood of revolutionary optimism and originality. Chinese ballet classics, *Hongse Nianzijun* or *Red Girl's Regiment* for example, emerged. It was choreographed and first performed by the Ballet Troupe of the Central Song and Dance Ensemble in Beijing in 1964. It tells an old story, set in the 1920s Hainan Island, Guangdong province. Slave girl Wu Qionghua was captured every time she ran away from Landlord Nan Batian. She was caught again, beaten badly and left to die in the coconut forest. Hong Changqing, Party Secretary of the Red Girl's Regiment who pretended to be a rich overseas merchant, was on assignment in close proximity. He saved Wu and led her to the revolutionary base where she joined the Red Girl's Regiment. After much struggle, Wu killed Landlord Nan and rose to become the Regiment's Party Secretary when Hong died.

Another, similar classic hit was *White Haired Girl*. It was choreographed and performed by the Shanghai Academy of Dance in 1965. It is also a tale of oppression and class struggle. It seemed ironic that Chinese drama and class struggle were told in a quintessentially imperialistic and bourgeois artistic form. It certainly enlightens us about the making of the communist performing arts and, more importantly, ballet's naturalisation in China.

Red Girl's Regiment serves as an excellent example of ballet's "sinicisation". It used the language of ballet, a Western European vocabulary foreign to the Chinese dance dictionary, to tell a Chinese story in its indigenous customs and setting. It introduced ballet techniques into Chinese dance and enriched its dance theatre. First of all, the use of the unique ballet shoes and poses signalled a new style of dance even though the costumes and stage settings were still Chinese. Poses specific to ballet were used to portray Chinese characters whose circumstances were familiar to the Chinese audi-

Figure 42 Escape Scene from the ballet *Red Girl's Regiment*.

ence. Some ballet poses proved better suited to portray narrative moments than others. A great example is Slave Girl Wu's escape from Landlord Nan's estate. The forty-five degree mid-air pose with her two fists tightened in the air highlighted her hatred for the Landlord and her determination to escape (see Fig. 42). This was not a dance vocabulary which the choreographer could find in the dictionary of Chinese dance because oppression and class struggle had not been the focus of traditional dance theatre. The choreographer used ballet techniques to emphasise class struggle, dramatise the escape and build a strong character; this laid the foundation for the climax.

The following act, when Wu changed into the Red Army uniform and joined the Communist Party, was electrifying (see Fig. 43). To the classic ballet pose, the choreographer simply added a gesture every communist understood and millions wished to act out – holding the right fist high above the head to swear one's allegiance to the Party. It is a brilliant combination of

Figure 43 Shooting Scene from the ballet *Red Girl's Regiment.*

ballet and communist politics. Even more electrifying was the drilling scene. The all-female regiment with rifles in their hands and short hair in Mao caps and puttees conveyed the essence of "Red Girls". This was breathtaking because it was something the audience could easily comprehend even in its foreign pose and gear. Traditional Chinese drama had featured female fighters but none with rifles and short hair in Mao caps, the emblem of liberation and revolution. Many such scenes in *Red Girl's Regiment* and *White Haired Girl* signalled the arrival of a different era with its own artistic language.

If innovation was key in ballet's sinicisation, even more important was the integration of traditional Chinese dance techniques that choreographers skilfully incorporated: the performance would have to be indigenous because the story took place in the ethnic *Li* minority village, hence the village scene, where young men and women gathered to dance, provided that native flavour. In essence, it is similar to the Chinese dance in *Swan Lake, Nutcracker* and other ethnic dances in Western ballets and operas. Chinese martial art techniques and drama poses were embedded in the battle scenes when the "Red Girls" fought their enemies. Such integrating approaches made it easier for the ordinary Chinese to understand and accept ballet. The communist regime was injecting revolutionary ideas into the construction of a new China; their platform was to advance and uphold the interests of the proletariat. The regime and this unprecedented era therefore demanded new performing art styles. The introduction of new techniques was welcome and opportune; it brought new life to the Chinese dance theatre. It inspired and facilitated creativity in the process of character-building and storytelling. It enriched the vocabulary of Chinese dance and enhanced its *narrative* power. The process also transformed, if not modernised, Chinese dance.

Two years after *Red Girl's Regiment*, the Culture Revolution (1966–76) threw the country into chaos. Politically, it was a power struggle between

Mao Zedong, the ideologue, and his colleagues who were more pragmatic in their approach to the construction of a new China. The "cultural" aspect of the revolution involved Mao, his extreme supporters, his wife Jiang Qing among them, in a campaign to destroy old elements of Chinese culture and society in order to build a communist utopia in his lifetime. Mao believed strongly in the superstructure theory of Karl Marx whereas Jiang Qing led the "gang of four" to define and dictate what communist art and culture should be. Performing art classics like *Red Girl's Regiment* were turned into what was called "revolutionary model plays". Jiang, originally an actress, had a personal interest in pushing forward the revolution in culture and refashioning the arts for the proletariat. She intervened in the making of "model plays", that is the remaking of classics like *Red Girl's Regiment*. She will remain infamous for her destruction of Chinese art and culture. However, the Culture Revolution itself had undoubtedly contributed to the spread and indigenisation of ballet in China.

Dance was the best device because it could be reduced to a body language that was so basic that even a child would understand it. The "revolutionary model play" was directed towards the proletariat; it had to be simplified so that every worker and peasant could understand it. In the frenzy to popularise the "model plays", hundreds of *Red Girl's Regiments* were produced around the country as the whole nation was thrown into a fervour of making revolutionary art. The "model play" politicised ballet and it spread the idea of the proletarian consciousness and its class struggle through ballet language. Many peasants knew about ballet; some could even name the "eight big revolutionary model plays". The Culture Revolution on the one hand disfigured the original art and its sinicised form; on the other hand it helped to spread ballet among the masses. *Red Girl's Regiment* served more than just its artistic purposes. Like other artistic forms in the communist era, it helped popularise Marxist ideology and promote its key platform – class struggle – advance feminism and strengthen communist rule. It also bred a generation of outstanding dancers, some of whom have won the recognition of the international ballet community as we can see from Li Cunxin, one of the ballerinas handpicked by Jiang Qing's followers. The star, whose fame depended on the Cultural Revolution, defected while performing with the Houston Ballet in 1979 and continued her career on the global stage.[10]

The sinicisation of ballet had much to do with patriotism and politics. In the late Qing, it was limited to the court and elite. In the Republican era, it was embedded in the New Culture movement and in the war against Japan. Under the communist regime, it was used to popularise an ideology and deepen authoritarian rule. This government-sponsored political cultural extravaganza was most effective when it came to the indigenisation of ballet. It became a household name overnight during the Culture

Revolution. It is now part of a common Chinese vocabulary and artistic heritage. The sinicisation of Buddhism and opium consumption took a few hundred years, but the naturalisation of ballet, alongside communism, took only a few decades. The involvement of a political regime is key to the quick indigenisation of a foreign art and ideology. China was ready for a new political thought with which the communists could build a new state; it was ready for a new performing art genre with which the regime could educate and re-educate its new/old citizens. China provided the best soil for both ballet and communism to grow; it gave birth to the most brilliant dancers and choreographers. It enriched the language of dance and vocabulary of ballet. The post-Mao era has seen a revival of Chinese arts and culture. Chinese dance theatre in general and ballet in particular will undoubtedly continue to draw inspiration from other cultures in this age of globalisation.

23 *Giselle* in a Cuban accent

LESTER TOME

In New York, on 2nd November, 1943 Alicia Alonso, a Cuban ballerina, danced the title role of *Giselle* replacing a sick Alicia Markova in a performance of Ballet Theatre.

In 1943, a Cuban ballet dancer was a rarity, even more if she starred in a work considered the epitome of the European Romantic tradition. Though Cuba was immensely popular in the United States in the 1940s, it was by no means associated with ballet. Since the early 1920s, Hollywood and Broadway had made Americans familiar with images of Cuba as an exotic destination offering exuberant women, hot rhythms, beaches, casinos and endless nights of romance and alcohol. *I'll See You in Cuba* (1920), *The Cuban Love Song* (1931), *Girl from Havana* (1940) and *Week-End in Havana* (1941) were among the era's numerous films and musicals with Cuba as their subject or background. Cuban songs topped American charts while rumbas, congas, cha-cha-chas and mambos took centre stage in dance halls from New York to Los Angeles.

Rising to fame as a ballet dancer and becoming one of the most celebrated Giselles of the twentieth century, Alonso undermined Americans' stereotypical images of Cuba and Cubans. She also challenged the assumption that ballet belonged to Europeans. Asked about the reactions that her nationality elicited at the beginning of her career, she said: "A lot of people were astonished. I danced the more classical works, like *Giselle* and *Swan Lake*. In my first visits to England and France, the audience could not believe that a Latina represented classicism. In England, a critic even asked me how I had the courage to dance *Giselle*. Regardless of their disbelief, I achieved success".[1]

Alonso's nationality, always brought to attention by critics, was a problematic factor in the early years of her career. Impresarios suggested that she drop her Spanish name and adopt a Russian or British one for the sake of commercial success. She refused. "I firmly believed that achieving success under my name would help to debunk false and discriminatory concepts about Latinos' possibilities in ballet".[2] Alonso's national identity was beyond her name. It emerged through her dancing: "When I performed, something different was always noticed in my dance. We Latinos have specific features," she said in an interview.[3] In 1945, the *New York Herald Tribune*'s critic Edwin Denby emphasised her ethnic origin: "Alonso is a delightfully young and a

Figure 44 Alicia Alonso in Act ɪ of *Giselle*.

very Latin Giselle, quick, clear, direct in her relation to her lover. She is passionate rather than sensuous. She is brilliant in allegro, not so convincing in sustained grace . . . She has little patience for those slow-motion, vaporous effects that we Northerners find so touching".[4]

Denby, who focused on Alonso's Latin foreignness in contrast to an audience of "Northerners", classified her according to prevalent clichés of the time. Brilliance of movement, quickness and passion were seen as characteristics that represented the common superficial American views on Cuban dance stirred by the rumba and conga crazes. Grace, slow motion and vaporous effects, on the other hand, were contrary to the stereotype. Hence Denby had to see them as "Northern" features inaccessible to the dancer from the South.

A decade later, Alonso had achieved artistic maturity; she was receiving widespread critical acclaim. By 1955, she had been dancing *Giselle* for twelve years and had perfected her interpretation of the title role. In the *New York Herald Tribune*, Walter Terry described her as "one of the great Giselles of the time" with an "impeccable classicism". Yet her national or ethnic identity remained a significant factor in how critics judged her work. In the context of Alonso's undisputable stardom, her geographical origin was now perceived as enhancing her rendering of Giselle. Terry pointed out "a Latin warmth which (. . .) suffuses the entire ballet with a rich range of dramatic colors".[5]

Departing from the opposition between Latin and Northern sensibilities that Denby had seen, Terry connected Alonso to both Cuba and Europe,

Figure 45 Alicia Alonso in Act ii of *Giselle*.

pointing out "Latin warmth" and "impeccable classicism". Most critics seemed surprised at Alonso's mastery of classicism, which, after all, was essentially European with its French, Danish, Russian and British roots.

Here lies the paradox: Alonso's dancing was a perfect embodiment of European classicism and yet it was infused with Cuban accents. From her own point of view, this was not necessarily a contradiction. Cubans perceive their national identity not in opposition to but in dialogue with the European culture brought by colonisers and settlers who mixed with the native and African population of the country. The island takes pride on its links to Europe. But this does not make the paradox of Alonso's dancing less striking. How could something be Cuban and European at the same time? How could Alonso's classicism be faithful to its European origins if her dance had a Cuban tone? How could her Cubanness be authentic if it was tackled through a European canon?

The key to Alonso's excellence as a classicist was her discipline, her determination, and her understanding of the history of the works that she danced. After first seeing *Giselle* in a performance by Markova and Anton Dolin, she fell in love with the ballet and decided that she too would dance it someday. Even before the opportunity appeared, she began to prepare for it:

> I read all the books. I tracked the ballerinas that had performed the part: how were they, what had been said about them, how were their costumes, makeup, hairdos and headdresses . . . In 1943, Markova was going to dance *Giselle* during the season of Ballet Theatre but she became sick. Nobody wanted to replace her. When impresario Sol Hurok asked me if I would dare to do it, I said yes. By then, I had learned not only the part for the title character but also the choreography for the rest of the soloists and the corps de ballet. I knew the ballet by heart. I felt completely identified with Giselle, to the point of having planned even the movements for the fingers and eyelashes. [After the debut,] I continued my study of the piece, deepening into its style, defining the profile of each character, questioning the transitions between scenes . . . I loved studying the lithographs of the romantic ballerinas from the nineteenth century. I looked at every detail, paying attention to their way of using every part of the body to resemble a volatile creature. Looking at their poses and the position of their torsos, arms and heads, I tried to imagine how these women danced. It was like putting a puzzle together.[6]

It was this dedicated study of the background of Giselle together with her very own interpretation that represented the curious mixture of cultures. Some of the most influential critics of the twentieth century, such as Walter Terry or Arnold Haskell, praised her as the most outstanding Giselle of her generation. In a review that captured the tone of many critics' opinion on Alonso, Olivier Merlin wrote for *Le Monde* in 1966: "In the past, Olga Spessivtseva, Alicia Markova, Galina Ulanova; today, Margot Fonteyn and Ivette Chauviré: these are the only great, moving Giselles. Nevertheless, Alonso, for some mystery, keeps her rank as the leader in this constellation."[7] In a personal letter from the same year, Anton Dolin, the famous Albrecht who had danced with most of the great Giselles of the era, wrote to Alonso: "[Before] the intelligence of your interpretation of the ballet *Giselle*, I lay myself again at your feet."[8] The paradox now manifested itself through the tension between "intelligence" and "passion". Dolin's acknowledgement of Alonso's intelligence evidences how she challenged the stereotypical view that identified Latinos with uncontrolled passion and a lack of rationality. Alonso's performances of Giselle were both impassioned and intelligent.

Again and again during Alonso's career as a ballerina her detailed knowledge of the romantic style was highlighted, together with the blurring between her person and the character she danced, her psychological insight into the role, her intense emotional expressiveness, the simplicity and lack of affectation of her acting, her refined musicality in phrasing, her virtuosic technique and the subordination of herself to the stylistic and dramatic demands of the ballet.

Her own choreographic production of the ballet, premiered in Cuba in 1948 by the Alicia Alonso Ballet and perfected over the years, achieved the same level of recognition. In 1972, the Paris Opéra, where *Giselle* had been born in 1841, discarded its ossified version of the piece and adopted Alonso's. Her production, applauded for bringing the romantic style of the original back to life, was also incorporated into the repertoire of the Vienna State Opera, the San Carlo Theatre in Naples, and the Colón Theatre in Buenos Aires.

But there remained the difficulty for dancer as well as critic of pinpointing the bodily manifestations of her national identity. There was the inadequacy of words to describe dance in the first place. The greater problem consisted in identifying what was essentially Cuban in her dancing. Asked for a definition, Alonso replied: "Cubanness exists. Who doubts it? But, at the same time, who is able to define it? Cubanness is not a single thing but many; it is something alive and difficult to capture."[9] Critics Arnold Haskell and Pedro Simón, who believed that a Cuban School in ballet exists, faced the same problem. Haskell acknowledged that he was not able to describe what was particular about it: "I can recognize it, but it is almost impossible to explain the movement in words".[10] In a similar way, Simón explained that "a School is not a phenomenon as defined as a recipe that one can put on paper".[11]

Vagueness predominated even when particular Cuban or Latin inflections were pointed out in Alonso's dancing. For instance, Terry indicated the "Latin warmth" that brought a rich range of dramatic colours to Alonso's style. But he offered no further explanations on its specific Latin- or Cubanness. In an interview, Alonso suggested that femininity was another Cuban feature in her dancing. However, it was not clear how she was more feminine than other ballerinas or how her femininity differed from theirs. She also observed that "phrasing, the mode of joining the steps, is among the characteristics of Cuban dancers. It is mentioned that we follow the melody instead of the rhythm."[12] But are melody and rhythm separate in the choreography of Giselle, and is it possible for a dancer to follow one instead of the other?

In spite of the vagueness and ambiguity of the Cuban elements in her style, Alonso was conscious that her national identity made her dancing unique. She nurtured those characteristics and tried to turn them into a national style: "In those early days I wasn't exactly clear about the style we would later develop . . . But I did know that I wanted things to look a certain way . . . When the Latin, Cuban qualities appeared, they just seemed to come out, as if the richness of the earth were coming into my art. This was not calculated. Home and the richness of its heritage were always there. I took it, just instinctively, and used it".[13]

The paradox of Alonso's simultaneous embodiment of Cuban sensibility and a European aesthetics turned into an attitude that attempted to be truthful to the factors in a relationship that had hitherto been seen as irreconcilable. Alonso achieved complete identification with the European romantic style and, at the same time, channelled her national identity through her dance; she was truthful to both a European and a Cuban legacy. Both became equal instead of Cuban culture subordinate to European tradition.

The artist's double identity created a curious dynamic between Eurocentrism and nationalism that affected how she saw herself and how she was perceived by the international dance community. Alonso, who initially was subject to cliché views on Latinos and expelled from the European canon, became interested herself in developing a national style. In this endeavour, triumphing in the European repertory was indispensable to attaining recognition for herself as a Latin ballet dancer as well as for her Cuban-inflected classical dancing. Her repertory included pieces by Cuban choreographers and twentieth-century Western creators such as Fokine, Balanchine, Robbins and Tudor. Yet, nineteenth-century European works such as *Giselle* remained her letter of presentation and she took steps to secure her status as a legendary performer of the piece. She made sure that popular and academic publications alike commemorated her in her career as Giselle and assured her a definite place in history. In a self-celebratory note, the introduction to a book issued by the company in 1988 for her forty-fifth anniversary in the role states: "The eternity of the role of Giselle and the work itself . . . owes a fundamental breath to Alicia Alonso, a resurrection that points towards the future with the certainty of permanence . . . For future generations, the pictures of Alicia Alonso in *Giselle* will be equivalent . . . to the drawings of Marie Taglioni in *La Sylphide*, Fanny Elssler in *The Gipsy*, and Carlotta Grisi in *La Peri*."[14] Further reinforcing her status as mythical Giselle, the National Ballet of Cuba frequently performed gala evenings dedicated to the romantic ballet that emphasised Alonso's authority as a performer of that repertory and her success in passing down its style to successive generations of Cuban dancers. One of those Romantic Galas "in tribute to Giselle-Alonso" was offered in Havana on 2 November 1993, as part the celebrations for the ballerina's fiftieth anniversary in the role. It included landmark romantic works such as Jules Perrot's *Grand pas de quatre* (restaged by Alonso) and fragments from August Bournonville's *Le Sylphide*, *Napoli* and *Flower Festival in Genzano*, as well as Arthur Saint-Léon's *La Vivandiére*.[15]

Alonso followed her nationalist agenda persistently; she pursued it at the same time as she positioned herself as the keeper of a European legacy. In 1948, she founded the Ballet Alicia Alonso in Havana and, two years later, she opened the National School of Ballet Alicia Alonso. Her goal was not only to solidify ballet in Cuba but also to develop a Cuban hallmark in classical dance. Nationalism had been a strong force in the development of Cuban culture during the 1930s, 1940s and 1950s, permeating the realms of philosophy, history, music, literature, drama, musical theatre and the visual arts. Zarzuela, the Spanish equivalent to opera and operetta, experienced a boom and acquired a defined national profile in the works of Ernesto Lecuona and Gonzalo Roig during the 1920s and the 1930s. Simultaneously, the trend known as *afrocubanismo* drove the attention of classical composers such as Amadeo Roldán and Alejandro García Caturla to the African Cuban cultural legacy. In 1928, Jorge Mañach published his *Indagación del choteo*, an essay on Cuban national identity. In these years, Fernando Ortiz introduced anthropological research as a tool for studying Cuban culture. His essay "Los factores humanos de la cubanidad" appeared in 1939, a year after Medardo Vitier published the first history of ideas in Cuba (*Las ideas en Cuba*). In 1940, the University of Havana organised the first retrospective exhibition of Cuban art, covering three centuries of painting. In that same year, another crucial book by Ortiz examined the formation of Cuban identity, *Contrapunteo cubano del tabaco y el azúcar*, while Martha de Castro published her *Contribución al estudio de la arquitectura cubana*, an analysis of Cuban architecture. During the 1940s, Cuban-ness became a conscious element in the work of national painters such as Wilfredo Lam, Amelia Peláez, René Portocarrero and Mariano Rodríguez. In 1944, a group of writers led by Vitier, José Lezama Lima and Virgilio Piñera founded the literary magazine *Orígenes*, concerned with expressing a national sensibility in poetry. Two years later, Carpentier presented his pioneer study *La música en Cuba*. Also, over the 1940s and 1950s, five histories of Cuban literature were published, authored by Salvador Bueno, Max Henríquez Ureña and three other scholars.

This national context informed Alonso's attitudes and evolution as an artist as well as the development of her company. In the early 1950s, the group was already staging experimental works by Cuban choreographer Alberto Alonso, "using Cuban music and our folklore, utilising Cuban elements, enriching our ballet technique, artistry and way of dancing", according to the ballerina.[16] Sociedad Pro-Arte Musical,[17] umbrella organisation for the company and the school at the time, preferred Alonso and her company to perform the nineteenth-century European classics that satisfied the taste of Havana's bourgeois audiences. Pro-Arte did not regard the innovative works by Cuban choreographers with sympathy. The organisation censored and prohibited some of these pieces, but Alonso pushed them forward and negotiated a deal with Pro-Arte: she would dance in these new productions as a guarantee of their quality. In those early years of Cuban ballet, the credentials and money that Alonso needed to nurture a national style could be obtained only if she continued to dance the European classical repertory both inside and outside Cuba. Her nationalist agenda depended on the Eurocentrism associated to audience's preferences and box-office decisions.

After Fidel Castro took political and economic control of the country in 1959, the company became the National Ballet of Cuba. The dancer, at the height of her career, chose to remain on the socialist island. The communist government never prevented Alonso from travelling abroad. But Cuba's isolation and the tense diplomatic relationship with the United States had a negative impact on Alonso's international career. For this loyalty towards Cuba she received state support for her truly Cuban ballet. Her company was recognised as a national institution, officially affiliated to the Ministry of Culture; ballet schools across the country were opened. Alonso and her collaborators distilled a Cuban methodology for the teaching of ballet to ensure that the students in these schools learned to dance within the consistent style that she was developing. Another goal of the policy of enforcing a Cuban methodology was to safeguard the national elements of the style by preventing members of her company from copying foreign dancers. According to Alonso, "dancers from other Schools move in their own way and it's beautiful that they do so. But let *them* dance in a way that fits *their* character and *their* culture. We should dance in our own differentiated style. Only the most qualified, knowledgeable and mature ballet teachers, those who truly know the Cuban School and are able to discuss and arrive at the right conclusions on these matters should decide, which foreign elements can be assimilated. Otherwise, we start to copy things that are not related to us and our School becomes blurred".[18]

The evolution of Cuban ballet was determined, in part, by the political reality of Cuba. Alonso was aware of the impact that communism had on the island and paid special attention to align her nationalist goals with the philosophy of Castro's Revolution. In 1978, she pointed out: "We are living fabulous events in our homeland, where new elements, life styles and ways of expression are constantly emerging. But we cannot lose our identity or national roots. That's why the enrichment of the [Cuban] School should be done in an orderly and careful way." Alonso's objectives fitted within communist cultural policies that encouraged a nationalist type of art. In 1993 Fidel Castro wrote a letter to mark the forty-fifth anniversary of the National Ballet of Cuba. He addressed Alonso: "Your great achievement has been to know how to take advantage of the potential that the Revolution has offered the people to develop all the art forms and dance in particular, an art that is part of the essence of Cubans. The Revolution and the Cuban people are proud of the National Ballet of Cuba."[19]

Alonso and her company became cultural ambassadors for the Revolution, spreading the gospel of communist ideology through the arts during tours abroad and at home. The pride that the government took in Cuban ballet was not exempt from Eurocentrism. Dance might be "part of the essence of Cubans", as Castro stated, but ballet was a form that Cubans had adopted from Europe and North America. Such pride contained implicit satisfaction that the state-supported company triumphed within an art that had belonged to Europe and, most recently, North America. Communist Cuba's achievements in the arts and in education compared well to the developed world and formed an important part of the official rhetoric that made Europe once more a point of reference.

The interaction between nationalist and Eurocentric interests also shaped the repertory of the National Ballet of Cuba. *Fiesta negra*, *Floras*, *El solar*, *El río y el bosque*, *Sóngoro cosongo* are some of the numerous pieces by Cuban choreographers that explore national legends, dances and traditions. During international tours though, the ensemble usually presents European battle horses such as *Giselle*, *Swan Lake*, *Coppélia* and *Don Quixote*, polished performances of the classics that situate the dancers on the same level as the finest ballet companies of Europe and North America.[20]

In conclusion, the career of Alicia Alonso and the emergence of Cuban ballet have been shaped by a dialectic interaction between a strong interest in nurturing Cuban-ness in classical dance on the one hand, and Eurocentric perspectives inherent to the art form on the other. Although the creation of a Cuban school of ballet demanded the reaffirmation of a national identity on Alonso's part, it did not presuppose that the ballerina and her company distanced themselves from the European balletic tradition. Quite the contrary; Alonso conceived Cuban-ness in ballet as a continuation of a European dance legacy. In the artist's view, the Cuban tone in her dance and her embodiment of a European aesthetics were equally valid. That interplay between national and European components has become complex, with the emphasis shifting from one area to the other, depending on the opinions of the critics, the demands of the presenters, the preferences of the audiences, the stereotypes and expectations in diverse political scenarios and the tactics that Alonso displayed to secure recognition for herself and her troupe.

24 European ballet in the age of ideologies

MARION KANT

Between 1789 and 1989 Europe and then the world chased the rapidly receding hope that human society could be remade. The struggle to renew the social order reached its zenith in the years before 1945 in modernism, socialism, Freudianism, expressionism, Bolshevism, Fascism, Nazism, the New Deal, the Mexican Revolution, Peronism and Gandhian nationalism. After 1945, the world froze into two blocks in which both the West and the East feared and suppressed experimentation, hunted and imprisoned radicals and stamped out the danger represented by the "youth movements", the last and least powerful of the great attempts to transform human nature. The collapse of the Soviet Union and its satellite states ended the French revolutionary age and its attendant "isms". Since 1991 Western capitalism has become the universal form of economic enterprise but with unexpected consequences. The two most populous states of the world, India and China, have turned out to be very good at capitalism and now threaten the economic futures of the United States and the European Union. Globalisation has also called forth the genie of resistance from the ancient Arab bottle – Wahabi Islam has emerged to reject every aspect of the great European experiment, especially the emancipation of women, in the name of an ancient theocratic puritanism.

Ballet has been at the centre of these developments both as protagonist and as victim, because – that is the central argument that emerges from the preceding chapters – ballet like all art reflects the social, economic, political, legal, institutional and intellectual environment in which its creators work. Yet the history of ballet raises a new issue, a possibility, which I shall consider at the end of the chapter: the effect of new technology on the theatre and on the public sphere. The year that the Soviet Union disappeared was the year that Dr Tim Berners-Lee inaugurated the World Wide Web: a revolution so profound that we all reel from its impact. In the decade and a half since that "giant step for mankind" the instant transmission, storage, reproduction and consumption of culture has been so fundamentally transformed that nobody, not the great movie moguls, the newspaper barons, the record companies, the publishers, the museums and universities, theatres and opera houses, know whether they can survive. When millions of people contribute to their own "Wiki" encyclopedia, what happens to the Britannica? When I-Pods owned by millions store more music than any library in the world before 1991, why go to concerts? Where will ballet be in this new environment if theatrical culture crumbles under the explosion of new forms of technology, or, as Walter Benjamin famously put it, what happens to "art in an age of technical reproduction"?

Ballet was thus inevitably affected by the huge changes in culture and society after 1900. They disrupted the continuous dialogue in which ballet had found itself: the heated, aggressive, emotional, often insulting, debates that involved the artists who produced it and the public that received it shifted between 1890 and 1914. Ballet had now also to deal with the emergence of a rival, a self-proclaimed "modern dance" evolving around a new sense of self. Dance and ballet were forced to take sides.

The ideologies of the body and the mind

Ballet, once it had become an art performed by professionals, depended on the opera house and the theatre. As court ballet it had been a theatrical performance for several centuries but, with the growth of the public sphere in the eighteenth century, it needed professional performers and audiences, critics, costume and stage designers, composers, orchestras with conductors, stage hands, cleaners, ushers, choreographers, directors, managers, financial and press officers and so on. It was now performed in special buildings that were designed to bring together people who bought tickets and then entered that architectural space. Future dancers went to special ballet schools to follow a career: after an admissions process that tested talent and physical suitability, young students, often from the age of six years old, would be trained for years and years so that they could carry out the ballet technique and embody the characters of the narratives. Writers invented stories, composers wrote music, choreographers devised movements that would convey the stories. Ballet as part of theatre was a concerted effort of a large staff of people, all gathered to create the performance event evening after evening (or matinee after matinee performance). The theatre was (and is) a hierarchical institution that very much reflected the social order into which it was born, out of which it grew and within which it remained. The hierarchy shifted but was always characterised by allocating people to certain places, making them work towards the performance. That produced a particular division of labour, with certain dependencies and the need for equilibrium among the competing departments: power structures, financial viabilities, economic incentives, aesthetic ideas played their part to keep the theatre going, to stabilise the balance or tip it towards the dangerous and existential edge. Ballet cannot be taken out of the theatrical landscape and European civilisation is unthinkable without its theatrical culture.

But at the end of the nineteenth century something fundamental happened: a diffuse rebellion against bourgeois society bubbled out of the new mass urbanised society. Irrational and anti-rational ideas – the cult of violence, crowd psychology, anti-semitism as a mass movement, nudism, vegetarianism – spread across the traditional cultural landscape. Drama, opera, ballet – that entire theatrical culture – was questioned and its mere survival could no longer be taken for granted. The questions came from within by those who knew how theatre worked and who suggested reform and adaptation to the changing world. Such changes, in a sense, had always been an important part of the constant evolution of theatre itself and were reflected in new aesthetic movements and new technologies (for instance photography and film in the early twentieth century). More importantly though, attacks came from outside the theatrical sphere and its proponents demanded radical transformations, even abolition of the entire institution of "theatre" or "opera house" or "ballet".

One of the first to articulate these concerns in the dance sphere was Isadora Duncan, an American who came to Europe to find the meaning of life. Her concept of dance was completely different from ballet. Dance had to be made an expression of modern life. For her, ballet as an old-fashioned, antiquated and outmoded art could not fulfil the demands of the new era, it could not express modernity. "Modern" and "expression" became the catchwords of the time and programmatic for the future. Duncan's theory of dance sought to interpret the German philosopher Friedrich Nietzsche's writings. Through him she hoped to enter into the mysteries of artistic creation and human existence. After she had been introduced to his work in 1903 in Germany, she proclaimed his book *The Birth of Tragedy out of the Spirit of Music* of 1871 her "bible". With it she found a guide that would enable her to express her female humanness in movement. It would equip her to go back to the original sources of artistic inspiration with which she could restore the art of movement to its former glory and place. Dance had once been magnificent, in antiquity, and it now needed Nietzsche's conception of tragedy to resuscitate it by incorporating the primal principles of the Apollonian and Dionysian in humanity. Those powerful forces of creation supplied Duncan with the means to translate idea, inspiration and feeling into movement and make it visible. Dance without the backbone of an idea, a philosophy, was dead, worthless. Yet thought could only stand at the beginning of the creative process because motion was driven then by emotion and thinking had to be fused into feeling. Her physical preparation could not have been more different from that of a ballet dancer:

> For hours I would stand quite still, my two hands folded between my
> breasts, covering the solar plexus . . . I was seeking, and finally discovered the

central spring of all movement, the creator of motor power, the unity from
which all diversities of movements are born. I ... sought the source of the
spiritual expression to flow into the channels of the body filling it with
vibrating light ... [1]

She danced as though she were in trance, without technical drill. Ballet
was decadent because it followed mindless repetition and had particularly
disastrous effects on the female frame. Ballet training harmed limbs and
tore muscles, it bloodied the feet with the cruel and unnecessary pointe
shoes, the corset imprisoned the nature of femininity; it took away the natural beauty born out of music and the ebb and tide of water or the gentle
swaying of branches in the wind or sand blown over the shores, in short,
the flow of nature. Her dance, infused with Nietzschean philosophy, would
also resurrect the female body by liberating it from all previous social constraints. Out of her dance would materialise the beautifully contemporary
and essentially natural embodiment of womanhood. Her fervent feminism
took up the "woman question" of the Victorian age but gave it a different
perspective and outlook. Duncan did not need the theatre but she cleverly
used it if available. For her, any space was good enough for dance, which
meant that Duncan performed anywhere – in parks, tea rooms, salons, on
the stage of theatres or opera houses.

Isadora Duncan soon turned into the icon of modernity and exerted the
greatest influence on dance and on its perception in the twentieth century.
From choreographer Mikhail Fokine to dancers Anna Pavlova and Vaclav
Nijinsky – hardly any artist remained untouched by her passionate appeal
to renew the arts, particularly dance, and many changed their aesthetics and
performance styles, inspired by Duncan.

Following Isadora Duncan's forceful impact, Rudolf von Laban became
the defining authority within the movement that labelled itself modern
and avant-garde. In looking for new principles and a new understanding
of dance, Laban, a Hungarian officer who moved to Germany after the
First World War, formulated, devised and organised a theory and dance
practice which concentrated on expression of the inner soul of the human
being. Hence this movement called itself and was recognised as *Ausdruckstanz* or expressive dance. Very much like Isadora Duncan, Laban searched
for the source that had made an *Ur-Tanz*, an original, untainted dance
before civilisation and history had left its nasty traces and contaminated it.
And like Duncan, Laban and his followers were convinced that they had to
look outside European high culture and far beyond ballet. Laban, as many
other modernists, mistrusted Western civilisation. Ballet clearly epitomised
Western culture and therefore needed to be eliminated together with its
entire history. He admired Duncan for her intuition and originality but

particularly for what he deemed a non-rationalistic approach to dance, for the courage to find the "soul" through dance. As he wrote:

> At a time when science, and especially psychology, endeavoured to abolish radically any notion of a "soul", this dancer had the courage to demonstrate successfully that there exists in the flow of man's movement some ordering principle which cannot be explained in the usual rationalistic manner.[2]

The essential principles of his modern dance can be found in a new theory of space, followed by a new theory of the performer. His space redefined performers and audiences; Laban made a dance space outside the theatrical realm and restructured dance as performance. In fact he rejected the notion of "performing" and replaced it with "experiencing". Thus he reformulated the performer's attitude to originality and self-expression and addressed the preparation and training for dance events so that they no longer had to rely on talent or technique but on belief. Modern dancers followed their convictions; anyone could dance who shared a deep faith in movement as source of humanity. Laban also "wrote dance" by devising a notation as a language of movement and, finally, he reorganised the dance networks.

Germany together with the United States provided the environments for modernist experiments. In both countries the battle between ballet and modern dance was decided in favour of modernism though the fight was less violent and antagonistic in America. In both countries national identities were being altered not through ballet but modern dance. Only after Balanchine's arrival in America did attitudes towards ballet alter, gradually but substantially.

One primary concern of the theatre and performing arts avant-garde had been to change the nature of the performer–audience relationship by examining the theatrical space. Reforms in spatial arrangements of theatre/performance space developed in parallel: Laban rethought dance at the same time as Bertolt Brecht developed the principles of epic theatre, Vsevolod Meyerhold advanced a new movement theory called biomechanics and Walter Gropius and Erwin Piscator discussed their project of "total theatre". Theatre turned into a weapon to to realise social changes and bring about the utopian future; art and artists were supposed to accept social responsibilities and make their art an active social presence.

Laban, also troubled by the state of urban civilisation at that time, attempted to create a new religious order that followed a cosmological idea of wholeness and oneness of mind, soul and body. He founded dance communities in which his dancers underwent conversion experiences before connecting to the cosmic universe. Dance, a community affair, functioned as a ritual, which created the community, held it together and brought harmony back into individual human lives and thus to the community. Dance was healing, soothing, a way of life and no longer merely a paid profession. He intended to go beyond the mechanical, meticulous movement structure of ballet and instead make and celebrate the whole and unified person. Laban's movement system and his system of spatial and movement analysis attempted to unify life with art in a way which had not been envisaged by anyone in the dance world. Though he built on knowledge created by ballet masters such as Pierre Beauchamps and Raoul Feuillet so as to invent a new system to write dance according to his new rules, he surpassed every convention on which ballet rested. He had to deny ballet its past in order to prevent its future and instead secure that of his modern dance. Coexistence was not an option. He could not accept that the balletic system had developed through the centuries according to claims and necessities of the society to which it belonged: from representation of worldly power in the aristocratic courts, particularly of northern Italy, in the fifteenth century to the bourgeois theatre dance of the romantic era, first in France then throughout Europe, presenting social conflicts and telling stories of a contemporary world to a paying audience. To acknowledge that the stage, the theatrical space, had changed considerably over the centuries would mean to admit the possibility of further change and adaptation of ballet to the modern world.

The ballet of the nineteenth and twentieth centuries belonged to exactly that society that many modernists intended to overthrow. Laban's relationship to the theatre therefore had to be contradictory: he felt drawn to it for the possibility of creating another imaginary world; yet he disliked, even loathed, the "lies" and the "falseness", the pretentiousness and artificiality, of the theatre. He imagined a performance space "true" to values, which had been destroyed by modernisation, urbanisation and technology. Ideally, dance would not be a performance in the common sense, there would be no paying audience because no commodity would be bought. Instead, he needed a space for devotion and transfiguration, which also severed itself from social connotations; it had to be accountable to the community not the society. Laban's image of space broke totally with traditional dance and theatrical spaces; in fact it was a break with the inheritance of Western culture. It disconnected dance from its history and replaced it with an imagined archaic tradition. At the end of the twentieth century his complete, self-reliant system once more became attractive to choreographers of post-modern dance as well as ballet who also had lost confidence in civilisation and Western culture.

The modern or avant-garde movements in dance represent an interesting paradox: they planned an ideal world in opposition to the existing modern world yet needed the modern world they detested to make their ideals. In the years before the First World War ballet was blamed together with other cultural phenomena for a world falling apart: ballet had run its course, very soon it would be replaced by one of the modernist movements. Most modernists could not or would not apprehend that ballet had more survival strength than anticipated and that it had not outlived its time but lived with it – though in a different way from the modernist projects. Renewal within ballet might have been painful for those involved in it, but it took place. The Ballets Russes or the Ballets Suédois were examples of the successful reform of the art form, not despite of the century-old ballet tradition or because of its weakness but because of its vigour.[3] But not even at the end of the twentieth century was this view commonly shared in the dance world. It is still a contentious issue.

The new ideologies

The modernist concepts of the body and the mind grew out of the discontent with civilisation. They were an expression of the desire to solve the conflicts brought about by a world in rapid transition. Economic crises, unemployment, women's liberations, secularisation, urbanisation turned the world upside down – where was this society going? What was going to happen next? The loss of securities, the loss of the certainty that there was a future, the collapse of value systems, the disappearance of social frameworks, the fading of economic stability led to new political movements with new ideologies. They counteracted fear and ambiguity with enticing projections of a future world. For most of these radical movements the French Revolution of 1789 still provided a model for social change: that of a revolution combined with the intention to generate a new man who would inhabit the revolutionised world.[4] Dance, just as the other arts, played an important role in those projects. It became part of the activist ideologies, it was a propaganda device, a medium to convey the message and forge an alliance between the believers of the new movements and their prospective members. Above all, it was the practice field to discover and test suitable embodiments of the new ideal. On this level too, the struggle between ballet and modern dance continued, as modern dancers argued that their movement concepts were more suited than ballet to produce future man, that they were better able to rule the masses out of which the new man was to emerge. Once more, ballet's history and tradition were considered proof of its elitism and backwardness. On the other hand, ballet's history and tradition lent legitimacy to the new movements. Hence confused messages surfaced. The odd mixture of preserving and destroying traditional movement concepts become clear in Italian futurism. It was one of the first organised assaults on traditional aesthetic concepts in the twentieth century. Filippo Tommaso Marinetti established futurism by issuing a founding manifesto in 1909. There was hardly an art form, artistic phenomenon or aesthetic idea that was not examined, denounced and reinvented with a better, futuristic outlook, from painting, to film, to theatre, to noise in general, to collage, to sensuality and sexuality. In another passionate manifesto Marinetti celebrated war as the grand hygienic cleansing of the decaying old world. Dance, of course, could not be left out. In July 1917 Marinetti surprised his followers with a manifesto of futurist dance in which he did not propound a modern dance movement above ballet. Instead he managed to fuse all sorts of national or folkloric dances with ballet:

> Once the glorious Italian ballet had died and been buried, there began in Europe a stylisation of savage dances, an eleganticisation of exotic dances and a modernisation of ancient ones. Parisian red pepper + helmet + shield + lance + ecstasy before idols that no longer mean a thing + undulations of the thighs of Montmartre = a passé anachronistic eroticism for foreigners ...
>
> From an artistic point of view the *ballet russe* [sic] organised by Diaghilev is extremely interesting. It modernises Russian popular dancing in a marvellous fusion of music and dance, the one penetrated by the other, and thus gives to the spectator an original and perfect expression of the essential force of the race. With Nijinsky there appeared for the first time pure geometry in dance liberated from mimicry and without sexual excitement. We have here the apotheosis of musculature.[5]

Isadora Duncan as an over-emotional, childish woman did not appeal to Marinetti, she was of little interest to manly futurism. He ended his manifesto with several ballet libretti which rejoiced in shrapnel, aeroplanes and machine guns: to visualise Vaclav Nijinsky not as Faun or Spectre of the Rose but as bullet shooting across stage. Futurism set its hopes on Benito Mussolini, the leader of the Fascist movement, anticipating that the Duce would march towards the "futuristic future". In a similar way German Modern Dance, forged by Rudolf von Laban, aligned itself with racist concepts of the body and collaborated with Nazism. Adolf Hitler would create the folk community and exalt Laban's religious dancing cult. Thus many dancers could shift their movement theories, whether modern or ballet, towards the right, but they could also move towards the left. After the Russian Bolshevik Revolution in 1917 a surge in radically politicised ideas took hold of the dance world. Isadora Duncan had a short-lived dalliance with Bolshevism for which she was never forgiven in her native United States but remembered as the "red hussy". Her notion of dance as education made a deep impression on Russians even though, in the long run, ballet became the representative dance culture of the communist state. Why did ballet win over modern dance in the Soviet Union, why preservation instead of continuous exploration?

Because after the revolutionary mastermind Vladimir Ilyich Lenin's death in 1924 the conservative, regressive and oppressive flank of the Bolshevik party won. After ambiguous statements by state bureaucrats, ballet advanced to state art, the art representing Soviet Russia. Here, its strong traditional past and glamour, its imperial grandeur reinforced the link to an intact Russian past that the rulers of the regime needed and that in turn would make itself felt on the European scene. Ballet legitimised the regime that paid and sustained it on a historical and political level. If ballet from the mid nineteenth century on had failed in Western Europe, which dance scholars seemed to agree on, then the Russian Imperial ballet after 1917 was one example of how Russian artists could revitalise European ballet, and Europe on the whole. Ballet might just be part of that proletarian world revolution and thus not by its nature anti-revolutionary but worth incorporating into the revolution. It would now set out to tell the well-established fairy tales together with the revolutionary stories of the people of Soviet Russia, the heroes of the kolkhoz – the peasants, the heroes of the factories – the proletariat, the heroes of the Red Army who protected the united workers and peasants. The immediate nineteenth century past also bestowed its narrative and dramaturgical structure on many ballets of the Soviet era. Realistic storytelling won over dream-like abstract, symphonic ballets. It took several decades after the Second World War before any experiments in abstraction occurred again. The ideological and aesthetic ideal was called "socialist realism". It grew out of political demands that the Stalinist state placed on artists and relied on the belief that they, the artists, had an obligation to fulfil towards the masses, the people. In 1934, at the First All-Union Congress of Soviet Writers, "socialist realism" was declared standard for all arts: they had to glorify the political and social achievements of communism.

Soviet bureaucracies left the institutional structure of opera and ballet intact. In fact, even tsarist obligations to artists were taken seriously and payments of pensions to former ballerinas who had performed at the court in St Petersburg were still made into the 1940s and later. Ballet schooling continued in the traditional way, the hierarchical order was upheld with great shining stars, slightly less great and twinkling stars and the corps de ballet. Like their predecessors, the Taglionis, Elsslers, Grisis or Grahns, the ballerinas of the Soviet age became national idols: Galina Ulanova, Maya Plisetskaya, Marina Semenova, Natalya Dudinskaya, Olga Lepeshinskaya ... The technical standard and rigidity were also maintained; Agrippina Vaganova who, after her dance career, began teaching at the Leningrad State Choreographic School (formerly the Imperial Ballet School) in 1921 modernised and at the same time canonised the training system and methods.[6] Both, school as well as training principles, bear her name today (see Figs. 46 and 47).

Figure 46 Galina Ulanova in Act II of *Giselle*, Bolshoi Ballet Moscow, 1954.

The Russian Revolution spread ballet back to the West. In the years after the Revolution of 1917 dozens and dozens of choreographers, ballerinas and their entourages left for the West. In Berlin and Paris, the largest Russian émigré communities in Europe came together and ballet schools and studios teaching classical Russian style with Russian teachers multiplied though they did not carry the proletarian dogmas with them. European ballet culture experienced a tremendously vitalising force. In Germany, with a relatively weak ballet tradition but strong theatrical network, Russian ballet seriously threatened the modernist claim to power. In France and Great Britain it

Figure 47 Maya Plisetskaya as Odette in *Swan Lake*, Bolshoi Ballet Moscow, 1966.

rejuvenated and infused with new life a respected cultural heritage. Two companies, above all others, broadcast ballet across the globe: the Ballets Russes de Monte Carlo in its twofold manifestations.[7] Both ensembles were born with the intention to exploit the fame of Diaghilev's Ballets Russes. Both lived off the eminence of Russian ballet and Russian ballerinas. The waves of refugees fed the ranks of the two companies from the 1930s onwards; adoration and notoriety accompanied them but also helped business and reinforced name recognition. Scandal, though, was founded on real originality and imagination: Léonide Massine explored abstract formal structures in his ballet symphonies and George Balanchine began his experiments with ballet's form and structure. Russian ballet as "classical" ballet entered the minds of the audiences from London and Paris to New York and Buenos Aires as a fusion of the old – French and the new – Russian.

European and American ballet, invigorated, carried on, more or less pragmatically in the municipal or court theatres, in the smaller opera houses and in the many provincial companies, neither making itself part of the political right nor the left. It found a powerful defence against any ideological claim and the attack of any political movement: *l'art pour l'art*, art for art's sake. This slogan constituted the most successful creed or ideology claimed by artists to protect themselves as well as their art from the onslaught of political programmes and demands. It was (and is) ideology masquerading as anti-ideology. Théophile Gautier, the man who had invented *Giselle* and had written many other ballet libretti, had picked up the motto and used it to rescue art (and ballet) from the claws of utilitarian politicians in 1834. *L'art pour l'art* declared then, as it does now, that art is only an aesthetic means unto itself, that it serves no ulterior purpose. "Only those things that are altogether useless can be truly beautiful; anything that is useful is ugly, for it is the expression of some need, and the needs of man are base and disgusting, as his nature is weak and poor."[8] Hence the most useful thing for Gautier, and the least artful, was the toilet bowl. (Marcel Duchamp in his Dada phase answered in kind by exhibiting a urinal – *Fountain* – in 1917 as ultimate art object.) With the idea of *l'art pour l'art*, artists could declare their independence and resist attempts at political take-over. It also implied that the artist was somehow removed from society, alienated to such a degree that art need not enter into a direct and immediate relationship or dialogue with social forces. In the age of ideologies, art for art's sake proved itself as the most powerful shield for ballet; any philosophies that did not support the aesthetic integrity of the work of art were – and are – considered unacceptable. The separation of technique from narrative had been undertaken in the nineteenth century and conveniently continued. A *plié*, an *attitude*, an arabesque, a *développé*, a *battement* or any other element of the ballet method was beautiful in itself; it meant nothing and hence could not be appropriated by ideologies. If there existed any ideological trace it was embedded in a story or narrative. Those, though, were exchangeable and negligible. The contradiction between abstract movement principles and concrete narrative could not be revoked, but it could be neutralised. Ballet had been classified as mindless physical activity by the advocates of modern dance; ballet dancers – by repeating the same steps in every story and by using a universalised technique – paradoxically confirmed the case. Ballet's presumed intellectual emptiness was tied to *l'art pour l'art*'s intention of keeping the movement component as pure as possible and making it valuable in itself; the lines and shapes that the body achieves within a balletic movement sequence constituted then – and now – ultimate beauty. The arch of the foot preparing to rise on pointe had to be more important than the arch of the foot rising on pointe as a means to convey a story, be it in *Sleeping Beauty, Romeo and Juliet* or *The Red Poppy*. Thus it has always been possible to disconnect the technical aspect of ballet from the content of the story, which the technique is supposed to help tell. An example of the peculiar dynamics of ballet, *l'art pour l'art*, self-supporting technique and the endeavour to instil ballet with a new spirituality can be found in Oskar Schlemmer's *Triadic Ballet* of 1922. When Schlemmer conceived the idea, he was working at the Bauhaus, the college that tried to unite and unify the arts, to explore new ways of manufacturing and crafting in the age of mechanisation. With Schlemmer (as with Laban's student Kurt Joos who in 1932 choreographed *The Green Table* and founded the Ballets Jooss), a careful cross-fertilisation between ballet and modern dance began. Schlemmer studied dance history and deliberately called his stage work "ballet" though the ballet world either ignored or laughed at his strange experiments. He imagined a ballet that found a new meaningful subject through technique as abstraction and condensation of human movement. Ballet was taken to the extreme limit of coherence by replacing the human body with costumes representing elementary geometrical shapes, which led to intensely focused applications of movement principles: circles, lines, ellipses, diagonals, colours all emanated from primary human gestures. Non-ideology, *l'art pour l'art*, made a new and acceptable belief-system. The reduction of movement to essential factors and the constant repetition of the Holy Trinity as symbol of a new spirituality, Schlemmer predicted, would lead to a fresh awareness of religiosity. But Europe was moving towards the next disastrous war. Dancers made good soldiers, for any army, German or Russian, Italian or French or English. Dancers entertained soldiers of every army, whether the Wehrmacht, the Red Army or the Allied Forces. Dancers joined the resistance in France or danced for the Nazi occupiers, they went underground in Italy, they fought in the eastern forests with the partisans or on the eastern front with the SS, they entered ammunition factories in Germany or supported the war effort in Britain. They were thrown into prison and taken to concentration camps if they were Jews, or communists, or socialists or gay. And they danced in the camps and in the prisons, secretly using dance to survive and subvert the systems. They entered the ever growing army of refugees, which took them to every part of the world. Wherever they went, they carried with them their dance, modern or traditional, opened up schools, taught and performed.

The ideology and politics of the state

In 1945, at the end of the Second World War Europe was destroyed and though its theatres and opera houses were largely bombed, burnt and razed, its performance culture was among the first utterances to come alive again. If dance had provided hope during the war then dance was the art form that sparked new energy and belief in the future in peace time. Germany, now a smoking ruin, had to endure the dance culture of the allied forces – ballet. Modern dance, tainted by its association with Nazism, had to retreat for a time. Ballet now was imported from the victorious United States and Soviet Union. The United States brought their own very young ballet and theatrical dance culture, to which they had been introduced through European soloists and their accompanying groups in the nineteenth century and through artists who emigrated in the twentieth century.

With the beginning of the Cold War, that battle between the capitalist West, led by the Americans and the communist East, led by the Soviets, Europe entered the next period. The American Marshall Plan, designed to restore European industry and provide dollars for imports of new US machinery and technology, in the long run also paid for and fed theatres. Growing economic wealth was measured not only in higher production or increasing wages but in the number and quality of orchestras, operas and ballets. Liberalism could be distinguished by its manifold artistic approaches and styles. Ballet companies were proud to engage foreigners because ballet was international, a shield against the destructive nationalist forces: Stuttgart from 1961 had John Cranko from South Africa, Hamburg since 1973 has John Neumeier, born in Milwaukee, Frankfurt since 1984 has William Forsythe, born in New York City in 1949, who had danced under Cranko in Stuttgart. Glen Tetley, born in Cleveland was invited to the Nederlands Dans Theatre in 1962; Jiří Kylián, born in Czechoslovakia in 1947, trained at London's Royal Ballet School and encouraged by John Cranko to choreograph, became artistic director of the Nederlands Dans Theatre in 1975. In Western Europe, internationalism and international exchange, openness to experiments and personal styles, were advanced, and in the face of socialist realism, abstraction and aesthetic independence, *l'art pour l'art* was ever more promoted. But internationalisation meant Americanisation.

In the East, internationalism meant Sovietisation. The Russian school, above all the Vaganova method, prevailed and Russian dancers came to teach in the new state ballet schools in Berlin, Prague, Warsaw, Sofia, Budapest. The Soviet system superimposed socialist realism, "the truthful, historically concrete representation of reality in its revolutionary development . . . linked [to] the task of ideological transformation and education of workers in the spirit of socialism", onto all the states in the Eastern bloc with ballets like *The Flames of Paris*, *The Fountain of Bakhchisarai*, *Spartacus*, *Romeo and Juliet*.

In the West as well as the East, ballet offered itself as a cultural export article. Imperialism (here understood in the context of the Western and Eastern empires) once more spread ballet and made it a global asset with an ideological dimension, just as in the nineteenth century. The West believed in liberalism and democracy, the East in socialism and dictatorship of the proletariat, and both sides promoted the ballets that best represented these ideologies. After decades of isolation Russian ballet companies made startling appearance, on the stages of the Western world in the early 1950s, with a huge impact, from Paris to New York. Long queues formed and the audiences wept with Julia – Ulanova and rejoiced with Kitry – Plisetskaya. The Russians and the West utterly misunderstood each other in this process of exchange. For the East their triumphant dancers promoted socialism with a human face. These tours took place at the height of the Cold War, a war fought with every means except nuclear weapons. The Soviet leaders assumed that the triumphs of Russian ballet would establish a dialogue but at the same time convince Western audiences of the superiority of their system. An unfortunate side effect of the international tours lay in the defection of dancers like Natalia Makarova, Rudolf Nureyev or Mikhail Baryshnikov. To the East, these were traitors who abandoned their ideals, to the West they were heroes who had jumped into freedom. Their physical rejection of socialism was always turned into a political coup: when ballet dancers left, they more clearly than anyone else seemed to prove the physical disintegration of the Soviet system; to provide proof also of the correctness of Western propaganda that the East was intolerable. The east counter-argued that the West corrupted the minds and the souls of the weak and therefore borders needed to be fortified. For the West, *l'art pour l'art*, the dominant and apolitical ideology of post-war modernism, ensured that the Russian political message could not remotely attract Western audiences. The great Russian ballerinas were symbols of pure art not of the workers' and peasants' state.

Though the focus on ballet was very much determined by political factors, and interest concentrated on those dancers, choreographers and companies who would best satisfy political ambition, ballet flourished in the West as representation of *l'art pour l'art*. In France and Great Britain the steady and enduring ballet cultures were never endangered species. Both countries have always produced choreographers who challenged and broadened the system from within. The visionary Maurice Béjart came to attention with his philosophical ballet *Symphonie pour un homme seul* in 1955. No aspect of life has since been too trivial for him to investigate, no culture not interesting enough to compare or work into Western ballet, no political event not worth using as reference (see Fig. 48). Ever since his first success he fused ideas and styles; used Nô Theatre or Indian drama, existential philosophy or Zen Buddhism to enhance ballet. In 1960 he founded the Ballet de XXe siècle with a school attached. Béjart's biography reminds us of an important aspect of ballet: its interconnectedness throughout the world. Béjart had danced with Roland Petit (who cultivated dramatic, realistic ballet and

Figure 48 Maina Gielgud in *Forme et ligne* (*Squeaky Door*) by Maurice Béjart. Australian Ballet, 1974.

explored twentieth-century literary sources) and Birgit Cullberg (the force behind Swedish modern dance and ballet and author of a specific danced drama) before making himself independent. The centres of schooling and performance in Paris, London, Milan, Moscow and so on functioned as central network points from which talents emerged and spread – in the nineteenth just as much as in the twentieth centuries.

In Great Britain, the confrontation between ballet and modern dance can also be traced though it seemed to have taken less acrimonious forms. The oldest modern dance company was founded by Marie Rambert in 1926, whereas Dame Ninette de Valois had trained and danced with Enrico Cecchetti and Serge Diaghilev and from 1928 built Sadlers Well's Ballet, later the Royal Ballet. With these two companies the foundations were laid for artists like Frederic Ashton, Anthony Tudor, Kenneth MacMillan and ballerinas

Figure 49 Felia Doubrovska as Bride in *Les Noces*, choreography by Bronislava Nijinska.

like Alicia Markova or Margot Fonteyn to employ their skills and nurture the narrative tradition and dramaturgical structure of nineteenth century ballet. Famed for its wit and amusing quality, British ballet for a long time struck a balance between the old and the new (though it remains to be seen what happens next at The Royal Ballet).[9]

Ballet in Europe always had to cope with its past and learn to modernise. It managed to preserve and at the same time depart from its own tradition, the shadow of the past looming over it, as burden or inspiration (see Fig. 49). Its survival rested on maintaining the balance between invigorating explorations and reverence for the well-worn repertoire. That is just as true today: ballet has to transform itself constantly, otherwise it will lose its vitality and turn into a stale, museum-like artefact, smelling of moth balls.

Figure 50 *Three Atmospheric Studies* by William Forsythe, the Forsythe Company 2005.

This is an ongoing challenge. Contemporary interpretations of nineteenth century favourites often split audiences and professionals alike: Mats Ek's vision of *Giselle*, Mark Morris's *Hard Nut* or Maurice Béjart's autobiographical *Nutcracker* do what art is supposed to do, question the canon and push the boundaries. They keep the art form alive as much as those who go far beyond the known repertoire: choreographers like William Forsythe, who deconstruct human movement through the categories and methods that Laban had once invented, to infuse his ideal community with core values. Forsythe seeks that same kinetic energy and essence that Laban studied and contemplated. Movement as defining category of humanity therefore provides the structures with which to experiment and which to manipulate (see Fig. 50).

Ballet's further survival does not rest on the debates around how much invigoration it needs or receives from adventurous dance artists nor on its relationship to modern dance, a movement genre in its own right. Neither is it threatened by internationalisation; just as great violinists or cellists come from China, Japan or Korea, so the traditional ballets schools from Buenos Aires to Shanghai continue its structures, institutions and cultural legacies. It depends on the effect that globalised capitalism will have on the place and the fabric of the art form.

Ballet is not a universal art form, but a Western cultural articulation. It spread with European trade, commerce and cultural exchange. It depends still on the public sphere and human interaction but both of which may now be disintegrating in the twenty-first century. Ballet has up to the present day retained certain characteristics that guarantee constancy: the stage, the schools, the company structures and hierarchies, the international competitions. Ballet technique – its technology – has not yet substantially changed in this globalised era. It is still a training method supposed to shape dancers' bodies for the performance. Training at the barre, with a ballet mistress or master remains a purely technical preparation for dance events that follow the most diverse performance principles and incorporate movement vocabulary that is no longer limited to ballet technique. The school, the training, the traditions emerged and survived because the institution "theatre" survived. The great ballet companies depend on the state and its subsidies everywhere except America, where they rest on private philanthropy. Whatever the source of funding, the ballet system requires its institutional casing and framework. In the age of globalised communication, the cell phone, the I-Pod, the Blackberry, all of which isolate and individualise human interaction with culture understood in its widest sense, can a collective enterprise, born in the first period of the commodification of art in the public sphere of the early nineteenth century, survive when other institutions of that period – the daily newspaper, for example – seem to be in terminal decline? Is there a public sphere out there any more? When great media moguls worry about the fragmentation of the public into ever smaller coagulations of special interests, when hundreds of specialised TV channels confuse the viewer, when the traditional weekly and monthly journals born in the eighteenth-century market for ideas and coffee houses for *a single* public give way to blogs and pods and other electronic avenues to private consumption of culture, what will happen to ballet?

With the loss of the common public sphere to which ballet was and is linked, the transition is open to an art form that is no longer ballet. This transition could be the end of the art form in that it makes superfluous and eventually abolishes the institution. If ballet technique, taken out of its context, is nothing more than an article that is used by anyone who can buy it for whatever reasons, then the art form begins to give way to the relentless onslaught of consumerism. Will it now, finally, succumb to the ultimate commodification of culture and the arts, unimagined and unimaginable to the modernists of the previous centuries? And will ballet then leave the public sphere – the theatre, which is consistently being undermined and destroyed – and appear occasionally as reflection of its former self and of what it can never be again, once it has been turned into a corporate ornament?

Notes

1 The early dance manuals and the structure of ballet: a basis for Italian, French and English ballet

1 Guglielmo Ebreo da Pesaro, *Guilielmi Hebraei pisauriensis de pratica seu arte tripudii vulgare opusculum incipit*, 1463, Paris, Bibliothèque Nationale, MS fonds it. 973, fo. 19r. (The translation is the author's.)

2 For a detailed discussion of improvisation and ornamentation in the *balli* and *bassadanze*, see Jennifer Nevile, "Disorder in Order: Improvisation in Italian Choreographed Dances of the Fifteenth and Sixteenth Centuries", in Timothy J. McGee (ed.), *Improvisation in the Arts of the Middle Ages and Renaissance* (Kalamazoo, Mich.: Medieval Institute Publications, 2003), pp. 145–69.

3 See Anne Daye, "Skill and Invention in the Renaissance Ballroom", *Historical Dance* 2/6 (1988–91), pp. 12–15, for further details on these virtuosic steps.

4 For a detailed discussion of improvisation and ornamentation in sixteenth-century Italian dances, see G. Yvonne Kendall, "Ornamentation and Improvisation in Sixteenth-Century Dance", in McGee, *Improvisation in the Arts of the Middle Ages and Renaissance*, pp. 170–90.

5 Timothy J. McGee, "Dancing Masters and the Medici Court in the Fifteenth Century", *Studi musicali* 17/2 (1988), p. 205.

6 Francis Ames-Lewis, *The Intellectual Life of the Early Renaissance Artist* (New Haven: Yale University Press, 2000), p. 74.

7 Keith Polk, *German Instrumental Music of the Late Middle Ages: Players, Patrons and Performance Practice* (Cambridge: Cambridge University Press, 1992), p. 11.

8 The anonymous fifteenth-century French *basse danse* treatises were far closer to a collection of choreographies, with very little additional information being included. Dance records from England in this period are scarce. For information on English sources see David Fallows, "The Gresley Dance Collection, *c*. 1500", *RMA Research Chronicle* 29 (1996), pp. 1–20; and Jennifer Nevile, "Dance in Early Tudor England: An Italian Connection?", *Early Music* 26/2 (1998), pp. 230–44. The sixteenth-century French and Italian dance manuals follow the fifteenth-century Italian model.

9 See chapter 4 in Jennifer Nevile, *The Eloquent Body: Dance and Humanist Culture in Fifteenth-Century Italy* (Bloomington: Indiana University Press, 2004), for a detailed discussion of the four *misure* and how the dance masters married the practical concerns of the dancer to the intellectual ideas about the nature of the cosmos.

10 None of the terms is defined precisely by Domenico, Guglielmo or Cornazano, but it is clear all refer to subtle movements of the dancer's body performed as part of the execution of each step. The meaning of *campeggiare* is not entirely clear, although the word seems to refer to a horizontal shading movement of the body above the foot which makes the step. This horizontal movement is contrasted with *ondeggiare*, a vertical movement like the waves of the sea, with a slow rising of the dancer's body followed by a quicker lowering of the body. (For further discussion of *campeggiare* see Mark Franko, *The Dancing Body in Renaissance Choreography (c. 1416–1589)* (Birmingham, Ala.: Summa Publications, 1986), pp. 59–61.) In his treatise Domenico likens *maniera* to the movement of a gondola that in its passage across the sea rises slowly and falls quickly (Domenico da Piacenza, *De arte saltandj & choreas ducendj De la arte di ballare et danzare*, Paris, Bibliothèque Nationale, MS fonds it. 972, fo. 1v). Cornazano also defines *maniera* as a rising and falling movement of the body, encompassing both *ondeggiare* and *campeggiare* (Antonio Cornazano, *Libro dell'arte del danzare*, Rome, Biblioteca Apostolica Vaticana, Codex Capponiano, 203, fo. 3v). Guglielmo describes *aiere* as "an act of airy presence and elevated movement, with one's own person showing with agility a sweet and gentle rising movement in the dance" (fo. 10r).

11 The term *fantasmata* referred to the way a step should be phrased. Domenico (fo. 2r) describes how at the end of every step the dancer should freeze briefly for a fraction of a second before commencing the next step, and this should all be done with so little effort that the dancer appears to be like a falcon taking wing. For further discussion of *fantasmata* see Mark Franko, "The Notion of 'Fantasmata' in Fifteenth-Century Italian Dance Treatises", *Dance Research Annual* 16 (1987), pp. 68–86.

12 Nicholas Clulee, *John Dee's Natural Philosophy Between Science and Religion* (London: Routledge, 1988), p. 77.

13 Marsilio Ficino, *Three Books on Life*, critical edn and trans. with intro. and notes by Carol V. Kaske and John R. Clark (Binghamton, N.Y.: Medieval and Renaissance Texts and Studies, 1989), pp. 331–3 and 363.

14 See Françoise Carter, "Celestial Dance: A Search for Perfection", *Dance Research* 5/2 (1987), pp. 3–17, for further discussion on divine dance from Plato to the seventeenth century.

15 The translation is Margaret M. McGowan's from her book, *Ideal Forms in the Age of Ronsard*, (Berkeley: University of California Press, 1985), p. 224, from Ronsard's sonnet "Le soir qu'Amour vous fist en las salle descendre".

16 See Thomas M. Greene, "Labyrinth Dances in the French and English Renaissance", *Renaissance Quarterly* 54/4.2 (2001), pp. 1403–66. Similarly, the English court masques, on one level, can be viewed as "one vast moving talisman with emblematic figures in diverse colours moving amongst incantatory scenes designed to draw down influences on the British court" (Vaughan Hart, *Art and Magic in the Courts of the Stuarts* (London: Routledge, 1994), p. 187).

17 Stockholm, Kungliga Biblioteket, Cod. Holm S 253.

18 For further information on this manuscript and on other surviving notated dance figures, see Jennifer Nevile, "Dance Patterns of the Early Seventeenth Century: The Stockholm Manuscript and *Le Ballet de Monseigneur de Vendosme*", *Dance Research* 18/2 (2000), pp. 186–203; and Mark Franko, "Writing Dancing, 1573", in Ann Dils and Ann Cooper Albright (eds.), *Moving History / Dancing Cultures. A Dance History Reader* (Middleton, Conn.: Wesleyan University Press, 2001), pp. 191–201.

19 Charles Nicholl, *The Chemical Theatre* (London: Routledge & Kegan Paul, 1980), p. 97.

20 Lyndy Abraham, *Marvel and Alchemy* (Aldershot: Scolar Press, 1990), p. 26.

21 Very similar sentiments were expressed at the end of the sixteenth century by Caroso, who repeats this belief that movements of the body represent inward emotional states (Fabritio Caroso, *Nobiltà di dame* (Venice, 1600; facs. edn, Bologna: Forni, 1980), p. 1).

22 Guglielmo, *De pratica seu arte*, fos. 19r–19v (the translation is the author's).

23 Prudence represented the knowledge of things men and women ought to desire and of things they ought to avoid.

24 Thomas Elyot, *The Boke Named the Governour* (London, 1531), repr. ed. S. E. Lehmberg (London: Dent, 1962), pp. 79–80.

2 *Ballet de cour*

1 Mark Franko, *Dance as Text: Ideology of the Baroque Body* (Cambridge: Cambridge University Press, 1993), p. 1.

2 Paul Lacroix, *Ballets et mascarades de cour sous Henri IV et Louis XIII (de 1581 à 1652)* (Geneva: J. Gay et fils, 1868–70; repr. Geneva: Slatkine, 1968).

3 In addition to Lacroix cited above, for a review of ballets and masquerades with indications of the sources which document them see appendix in Margaret M. McGowan, *L'Art du ballet de cour en France 1581–1643* (Paris: Centre National de la Recherche Scientifique, 1965, repr. 1978), pp. 251–309; for the later phase see Philippe Hourcade, *Mascarades et ballets du Grand Siècle, 1643–1715* (Paris: Desjonquières et Centre National de la Danse 2002), pp. 253–336.

4 The success of some ballets led to a series of repeats as was the case with the *Ballet de la douairière de Billebahaut*, staged first in 1626 at the Louvre and a few days later by popular demand at the Hôtel de Ville.

5 See, for example, the *Ballet de la prosperité des armes de la France* (1641), ordered by Richelieu to celebrate recent French military successes for which he considered himself to be responsible.

6 McGowan established a periodisation for the *ballet de cour* that focuses on the themes presented: allegorical and political from 1581 to 1610, melodramatic from 1610 to 1620 and burlesque until 1636. Cf. McGowan, *L'Art du ballet de cour*.

7 Susan Foster, *Reading Dancing: Bodies and Subjects in Contemporary American Dance* (Berkeley: University of California Press), p. 101.

8 François De Lauze, *Apologie de la danse et parfaite méthode de l'enseigner tant aux Cavaliers qu'aux dames* (n.p., 1623), pp. 35–6. McGowan (*L'Art du ballet de cour*, p. 33) concludes on that basis that "the ballet had already evolved into a genre in which all amateurs would be excluded".

9 Michel de Pure, *Idée des spectacles anciens et nouveaux* (Paris 1668; facs. edn Geneva: Minkoff, 1972), p. 215.

10 Jerôme de la Gorce, "Un aspetto del mestiere teatrale di Torelli: la riutilizzazione delle scenografie dell' 'Andromède' per il 'Ballet de la nuit' ", in Francesco Milesi (ed.), *Giacomo Torelli. L'invenzione scenica nell'Europa barocca* (Fano: Fondazione Cassa di Risparmio di Fano, 2000), pp. 235–41.

11 Marie Françoise Christout, *Le Ballet de cour au XVII° siècle* (Geneva: Minkoff, 1987), p. 76. This volume presents a rich iconografic documentation. By the same author, *Le Ballet de cour de Louis XIV. 1643–1672* (Paris: A. et J. Picard, 1967; new edition Paris: Centre national de la danse and Picard, 2005).

12 Christout, *Le Ballet de cour au XVII° siécle*, p. 148.

13 Henry Prunières in his *Le Ballet de cour en France avant Benserade et Lully* (Paris: Henri Laurens, 1914; New York and London: Johnson Reprint, 1970) argue for the Italian origins, with James R. Anthony, *French Baroque Music from Beaujoyeulx to Rameau* (New York and London: Norton, 1974; rev. edn 1981); and Barbara Sparti, "Dance and Historiography. Le Balet Comique de la Royne: an Italian Perspective", in Ann Buckley and Cynthis Cyrus (eds.), *Festschrift for Ingrid Brainard*, forthcoming (I thank Barbara Sparti for putting at my disposal two diverse versions of the unedited manuscript of her essay).

14 The masquerade consists of a parade or a stage action, for the most part improvised, and executed by characters who are dressed up or wearing masks. The dramatic content was limited and rather basic, resting on allegory and myth. Some parts could have been recited and others accompanied by instruments or voices. The main purpose was to create a spectacular impression by using lavish costumes and accessories. *Intermedii* that were placed between the courses of a banquet or the acts of a comedy were normally composed of recited texts and instrumental or vocal music and various types of bodily moves such as dance, pantomime, acrobatics or fighting scenes. The theoreticians of the sixteenth century saw in its theatrical form the functions of the ancient Greek chorus: temporal and technical transitions between acts, a pause for the actors, time to change the scenery, time for the spectators to relax from the dramatic tension of the main work.

15 McGowan, *L'Art du ballet de cour*, p. 7.

16 De Pure, *Idée des spectacles*; Claude-François Ménestrier, *Des représentations en musique anciennes et modernes* (Paris: René Guignard, 1681; repr. Geneva: Minkoff, 1992); Claude-François Ménestrier, *Des ballets anciens et modernes selon les règles du théâtre* (Paris: René Guignard, 1682; repr. Geneva: Minkoff, 1972); M. de Saint-Hubert, *La Manière de composer et de faire réussir les ballets* (Paris: Targa, 1641; repr. Geneva: Minkoff, 1993).

17 De Pure, *Idée des spectacles*, p. 214.

18 From the libretto for the ballet cited in McGowan, *L'Art du ballet de cour*, p. 152.

19 Marie-Thérèse Bouquet-Boyer (ed.), *Les Noces de Pélée et de Thétis. Venise, 1639–Paris, 1654*, Actes du colloque international de Chambéry et de Turin, 3–7 novembre 1999 (Bern, New York, Oxford and Vienna: Peter Lang, 2001).

20 Franko, *Dance as Text*, p. 21.

21 Ibid.

22 De Pure, *Idée des spectacles*, p. 249.

23 Menestrier, *Des ballets anciens et modernes*, p. 154.

24 See Bibliography for more information.

25 For analysis of the Italian antecedents, see Sparti, "Dance and Historiography". It is worth remembering that in a sort of obsession with research on origins, Italian historiography has for a long time identified Begonzio Botta as the inventor of the ballet on the basis of an equivocal story due to a distorted reading of a fifteenth-century chronicle which refers to the wedding of Galeazzo Sforza and Isabella of Aragon in 1489. In reality, Botta, who was a wealthy landowner, financed and occupied himself with the organisation of that event, which took place in his residence in Tortona. There is no evidence that he was author of the stage actions of a mythological kind, which included dance or mimed parts specially prepared for the occasion. See Eugenia Casini Ropa, "Il banchetto di Bergonzio Botta per le nozze di Isabella d'Aragona e Gian Galeazzo Sforza nel 1489: quando la storiografia si sostituisce alla storia", in Myriam Chiabò and Federico Doglio (eds.), *Spettacoli conviviali dall'antichità alle corti italiane del '400* (Viterbo: Tipolitografia Agnescotti, 1983), pp. 291–306. The origin of the historiographical error is probably to be found in Ménestrier, *Des représentations*, p. 157.

26 He has passed into history as the first choreographer of the first ballet. It could be the case that he never composed a single dance. Balthasar de Beaujoyeulx, born Baltazarini o Baldassarre (born before 1535 and died about 1587) was of Italian origin but not precisely identified. He went to France in the entourage of the Marechal de Brissac, governor of Piedmont, at the request of Catherine de' Medici. He was an excellent violinist and integrated himself rapidly at court, frenchifying his name. He rose rapidly from simple *valet de chambre* to become an *officier*. Some scholars think that the real author of the *Balet comique de la Royne* was the court poet Agrippa d'Aubigny. Carol and Lander MacClintock (eds.), *Le Balet comique de la Royne 1581* (New York: American Institute of Musicology, Musicological Studies and Documents 25, 1971), p. 12.

27 Cf. Diane L. Woodruff, "The 'Balet Comique' in the Petit Bourbon: A practical View", *Proceedings of the Society of Dance History Scholars* (Riverside: University of California, 1986), p. 123.
28 Translation in Selma Jeanne Cohen, "Balthasar de Beaujoyeulx, Ballet Comique de la Reine Paris, 1582", in *Dance as a Theatre Art: Source Readings in Dance History from 1581 to the Present* (New York: Harper & Row, 1974), p. 19.
29 See Sparti, "Dance and Historiography".
30 Franko, *Dance as Text*, p. 2.
31 Ibid., p. 1.

3 English masques
1 Inga-Stina Ewbank, "'These Pretty Devices': A Study of Masques in Plays", in *A Book of Masques*, ed. T. J. B. Spencer and S. Wells (Cambridge: Cambridge University Press, 1967), pp. 405–48.
2 William Shakespeare, *The Tempest*, ed. David Lindley (Cambridge: Cambridge University Press, 2002), iv. i. 138 and stage direction.
3 *Henry Purcell's Operas: The Complete Texts*, ed. Michael Burden (Oxford: Oxford University Press, 2000), pp. 6, 9–10.
4 Edward Hall, *The Union of the Two Noble and Illustre Famelies of Lancaster [and] Yorke* (London: R. Grafton, 1550), third year of Henry's reign, sig. ciiii^r. See also Enid Welsford, *The Court Masque: A Study in the Relationship between Poetry and the Revels* (Cambridge: Cambridge University Press, 1927), pp. 130–5.
5 John Stevens, *Music and Poetry in the Early Tudor Court* (Cambridge: Cambridge University Press, corr. repr., 1979), pp. 244–5.
6 André Hurault, Sieur de Maisse, *A Journal . . . Anno Domini 1597*, ed. G. B. Harrison and R. A. Jones (London: Nonsuch, 1931), p. 95.
7 B. Ravelhofer, "Dancing at the Court of Queen Elizabeth", in Christa Jansohn (ed.), *Queen Elizabeth I: Past and Present* (Münster: LIT, 2004), pp. 101–15; p. 104. Robert Mullally, "*Measure* as a Choreographic Term in the Stuart Masque", *Dance Research* 16/1 (1998), pp. 67–73.
8 *A Letter . . . of the Entertainment . . . at Killingwoorth Castl* (London: s.n., 1575), p. 24. Traditionally ascribed to Robert Laneham but apparently produced by the scholar William Patten. See Benjamin Griffin, "The Breaking of the Giants: Historical Drama in Coventry and London", *ELR* 29/1 (1999), pp. 3–21.
9 Cited from Judy Smith and Ian Gatiss, "What Did Prince Henry Do with His Feet on Sunday 19 August 1604?", *Early Music* 14/2 (1986), pp. 198–207; p. 199; my translation.
10 Gatiss and Smith point out that early British Library catalogues mention Italian dance books.

It remains speculation whether (a) these dance books were already available in the early Stuart period, and (b) whether readers really used them as dance manuals rather than bibliophile objects. Late seventeenth-century book lists in the Royal Collection are, for example, MSS Royal App. 73 and 86. Barbara Ravelhofer, *The Early Stuart Masque: Dance, Costume, and Music* (Oxford: Oxford University Press, 2006), ch. 2.
11 Roy Strong, *Henry Prince of Wales: The Lost Renaissance* (London: Thames & Hudson, 1986), pp. 92, 95.
12 They have attracted a massive amount of criticism, for instance: Stephen Orgel's *The Jonsonian Masque* (1967, repr. New York: Columbia University Press, 1981, with new introduction) and *The Illusion of Power* (Berkeley: University of California Press, 1975); D. Bevington and P. Holbrook (eds.), *The Politics of the Stuart Court Masque* (Cambridge: Cambridge University Press, 1998); Kevin Sharpe, *Criticism and Compliment: The Politics of Literature in the England of Charles I* (Cambridge: Cambridge University Press, 1987); numerous articles by Martin Butler.
13 Thomas Middleton, *A Courtly Masque: The Device Called The World Tost at Tennis* (London: G. Purslowe, 1620), sig. B^r.
14 For instance, in *Oberon*.
15 Huntington Library, MS HA 10543. Letter to the Earl of Huntingdon, date estimated 1627 by cataloguer and 1633 by John Yoklavich in "The Seven-Thousand-Pound Pastoral", *Huntington Library Quarterly* 28 (1964), pp. 83–7. I am indebted to Eva Griffith for a transcription of this document.
16 Edwin Nungezer, *A Dictionary of Actors* (1929; repr. New York: Greenwood, 1968), p. 270.
17 Walter Salmen, *Der Tanzmeister: Geschichte und Profile eines Berufes vom 14. bis zum 19. Jahrhundert* (Hildesheim: Olms, 1997), pp. 49–52.
18 Ben Jonson, *The Masque of Queens*, in *Court Masques: Jacobean and Cardline Entertainments, 1605–1640*, ed. David Lindley (Oxford: Oxford University Press, 1995), pp. 43–4, ll. 318–24. A topic explored in Anne Daye's work.
19 Francis Beaumont, *The Masque of the Inner Temple and Gray's Inn*, in *A Book of Masques*, ed. Spencer and Wells, p. 139, ll. 241–8.
20 An exception is *Luminalia* (1638), where aristocrats and professionals performed together in an entry. Interestingly, this masque was commissioned by Henrietta Maria. On Anglo-French relations see also Peter Walls, *Music in the English Courtley Masque, 1604–1604* (Oxford: Clarendon Press, 1996), ch. 6; and

Marie-Claude Canova-Green, *La Politique-spectacle au grand siècle: les rapports franco-anglais* (Paris: Papers on French Seventeenth Century Literature, 1993).

21 Martin Butler, "'We Are One Mans All': Jonson's *The Gipsies Metamorphosed*", *Yearbook of English Studies* 21 (1991), pp. 253–73. For masques away from Whitehall see also James Knowles, "The 'Running Masque' Recovered: A Masque for the Marquess of Buckingham (c. 1619–20)", *English Manuscript Studies* 8 (2000), pp. 79–135; Timothy Raylor, *The Essex House Masque of 1621* (Pittsburgh: Duquesne University Press, 2000).

22 Margaret M. McGowan, "Ballets for the Bourgeois", *Dance Research* 19/2 (2001), pp. 106–26.

23 William Whiteway's diary, February 1634, in C. E. McGee, "'Strangest Consequence from Remotest Cause': The Second Performance of *The Triumph of Peace*", *MRDE* 5 (1991), pp. 309–42; p. 320.

24 Orgel and Strong, *Inigo Jones*, p. 95, ll. 264, 272–3.

25 Jennifer Nevile's "Dance and the Garden: Moving and Static Choreography in Renaissance Europe", *Renaissance Quarterly* 52/3 (1999), pp. 805–36; p. 819.

26 John Milton, *Complete Shorter Poems*, ed. John Carey (London: Longman, 2nd edn, 1997), p. 185, stage direction, p. 189, l. 171, p. 229, l. 959.

27 See Anne Daye, "'Youthful Revels, Masks, and Courtly Sights': An Introductory Study of the Revels Within the Stuart Masque", *Historical Dance* 3/4 (1996), pp. 5–22.

28 Jean E. Knowlton, "Some Dances of the Stuart Masque Identified and Analyzed", 2 vols., Ph.D. diss., Indiana University, 1966, vol. I, ch. 2.

29 John Ward, "Newly Devis'd Measures for Jacobean Masques", *Acta Musicologica* 60/2 (1988), pp. 111–42, and "Apropos 'The olde Measures'", *Records of Early English Drama* 18/2 (1993), pp. 2–21.

30 Dudley Carleton on *The Vision of the Twelve Goddesses* (1604). *Dudley Carleton to John Chamberlain*, ed. Maurice Lee (New Brunswick, N.J.: Rutgers University Press, 1972), p. 56.

31 Marshall McLuhan, "Roles, Masks, and Performances", *New Literary History* 2/3 (1971), pp. 517–31; p. 518.

32 François de Lauze, *Apologie de la danse* (n.p., 1623; facs. edn Geneva: Minkoff, 1977), and J. Wildeblood's edition of the same (London: Muller, 1952). Barthélemy de Montagut, *Louange de la danse*, a manuscript treatise

plagiarised from an early version of *Apologie*, ed. B. Ravelhofer (Cambridge: RTM, 2000).

33 BL MS Harl. 1026, fo. 7^r, *c*.1633–1635 (date according to HMC/NRA database, February 2003).

34 For instance, BL MSS Add. 41996, Lansd. 1115; Oxford Bodl. MSS Douce 280, Rawl. D 864, Rawl. poet. 108; London Royal College of Music, MS 1119. Also BL MS Sloane 3858 – "Chorea".

35 Oxford, Bodl. MS Rawl. C 799. All citations from the excellent *The Travel Diary of Robert Bargrave*, ed. Michael Brennan (London: Haykluyt Society, 1999), pp. 88–99; p. 96.

36 Bargrave, *Diary*, p. 97. Bargrave's idiosyncratic vocabulary includes more theatrical terminology than Playford's first edition. In this it is reminiscent of another mid- to late seventeenth-century country dance source, the "Lovelace" or "Pattricke Manuscript". On the latter, see Carol Marsh, "The Lovelace Manuscript: A Preliminary Study", in Uwe Schlottermüller and Maria Richter (eds.) *Morgenröte des Barock: Tanz im 17. Jahrhundert* (Freiburg: fa-gisis, 2004), pp. 81–90, and a full transcription by Carol Marsh and John Ward, *Harvard Library Bulletin* (forthcoming).

37 *A Book of Masques*, ed. Spencer and Wells, p. 382, l. 43.

38 For cast lists and bills see Eleanore Boswell, *The Restoration Court Stage* (1929; London: Allen & Unwin, 1969). Andrew R. Walkling, "Masque and Politics at the Restoration Court: John Crowne's *Calisto*", *Early Music* 24/1 (1996), pp. 27–62.

39 Peter Holman, *Four and Twenty Fiddlers: The Violin at the English Court, 1540–1690* (Oxford: Clarendon Press, 1993), p. 367.

40 Michel de Pure, *Idée des spectacles anciens et nouveaux* (Paris 1668; facs. edn Geneva: Minkoff, 1972), pp. 248–9, my translation.

41 John Crown, *Calisto* (London: Th. Newcomb, 1675), "To the Reader", sig. a^r.

42 Walkling, "Masque and Politics at the Restoration Court", p. 51.

43 Thomas Carew, *Coelum Britannicum*, in *Court Masques*, p. 192, ll. 1023–5.

44 *Calisto*, Act V, p. 79. – I would like to thank Lisa Vargo for her comments on this chapter.

4 The baroque body

1 See Susan Leigh Foster, *Dance and Narrative: Ballet's Staging of Story and Desire* (Bloomington: Indiana University Press, 1996).

2 Alfred Heuss, "Eine Vorführung altfranzösischer Tänze", *Gesellschaft* (1910), year 2, part 12, pp. 386–9.

3 See Patrizia Veroli, "The Mirror and the Hieroglyph: Alexander Sacharoff and Dance Modernism", in Frank-Manuel Peter and Rainer Stamm (eds.), *Die Sacharoffs. Two Dancers within the Blaue Reiter Circle* (Cologne: Wienand Verlag, 2002), pp. 169–217.

4 Georges Detaille and Gérard Mulys, *Les Ballets de Monte-Carlo, 1911–1944* (Paris: Arc-en-ciel, 1954), pp. 104–7. Tim Scholl argues for "a reasonably authentic homage to the court of Louis XIV" in Petipa's *Sleeping Beauty* (1890). The retrospectivism of the Russian ballet spilled over into Diaghilev's repertoire. See Tim Scholl, *From Petipa to Balanchine: Classical Revival and the Modernization of Ballet* (London and New York: Routledge, 1994).

5 See Charles M. Joseph, "The Making of *Agon*", in Lynn Garafola with Eric Foner (eds.), *Dance for a City: Fifty Years of the New York City Ballet* (New York: Columbia University Press, 1999), pp. 99–118.

6 See Raoul Auger Feuillet, *Chorégraphie ou l'art de décrire la dance* (Paris: Feuillet & Bruncl, 1700); and Pierre Rameau, *Le Maître à danser* (Paris: Jean Villette, 1725). For an interesting discussions of Feuillet notation, see Jean Noel Laurenti, "Feuillet's Thinking", Laurence Louppe (ed.), in *Traces of Dance: Drawing and Notations of Choreographers* (Paris: Editions Dis Voir, n.d.). For a discussion of alternative seventeenth-century notational systems, see Rebecca Harris-Warrick and Carol G. Marsh, *Musical Theatre at the Court of Louis XIV: Le Mariage de la Grosse Cathos* (Cambridge: Cambridge University Press, 1994).

7 See Wendy Hilton, *Dance of Court and Theater: The French Noble Style, 1690–1725* (Princeton: Princeton Book Company Publishers, 1981). Also important for the interpretation and production of baroque dance were Melusine Wood, Belinda Quirey and Shirley Wynne.

8 Despite her involvement with and significance to performance, Francine Lancelot was primarily involved in a research project, the capstone of which was the publication of *La Belle Danse: catalogue raisonné fait en l'an 1995* (Paris: Van Dieren, 1996).

9 See Linda Tomko, "Reconstruction", in *International Encyclopedia of Dance* (New York: Oxford University Press, 1998).

10 Dene Barnett, "The Performance Practice of Acting: The Eighteenth Century", in *Theatre Research International* (1977). Three articles appeared in this series; one devoted to

the hands, one the arms and the last to the ensemble.

11 See "Repeatability, Reconstruction and Beyond", in *Theatre Journal* 41/1 (March 1989), pp. 56–74. ("Reproduction, reconstruction et par-delà", *Degrés* 63 (Fall 1990), pp. 1–18). For the musical context of this debate, see Richard Taruskin, *Text and Act: Essays on Music and Performance* (New York: Oxford University Press, 1995).

12 Marie Françoise Christout, *Le Ballet de cour de Louis XIV, 1643–1762: Mises en scène* (Paris: A. et J. Picard, 1967); Margaret M. McGowan, *L'Art du ballet de cour en France 1581–1643* (Paris: CNRS, 1978); Rudolf zur Lippe, *Naturbeherrschung am Menschen* (Frankfurt/M: Syndikat Reprise, 1979); Mark Franko, *Dance as Text: Ideologies of the Baroque Body* (Cambridge: Cambridge University Press, 1993), also translated into French as *La Danse comme texte: ideologies du corps baroque* (Paris: Editions Kargo, 2005).

13 Giovanni Careri, *Gestes d'amour et de guerre. La Jérusalem délivrée, images et affects (XVIe–XVIIIe siècle)* (Paris: Editions EHESS, 2005).

14 William Forsythe discussed baroque dance with German dance scholar Rudolf zur Lippe before creating *Artifact* (personal communication, October 2000).

15 Gilles Deleuze, *The Fold: Leibniz and the Baroque*, English trans. and foreword Tom Conley (Minneapolis: University of Minnesota Press, 1992).

16 Guy Debord, *Society of the Spectacle*, English trans. Donald Nicholson-Smith (New York: Zone Books, 1994).

17 Louis Marin, *Portrait of the King*, trans. Martha M. Houle (Minneapolis: University of Minnesota Press, 1988); Stephen Orgel, *The Illusion of Power: Political Theater in the English Renaissance* (Berkeley and Los Angeles: University of California Press, 1975); Jean-Marie Apostolidès, *Le Roi-machine. Spectacle et politique au temps de Louis XIV* (Paris: Editions de minuit, 1981).

18 For an overview of these affinities, see Omar Calabrese, *Neo-Baroque: A Sign of the Times*, trans. Charles Lambert (Princeton: Princeton University Press, 1992).

19 Mark Franko, "Majestic Drag: Monarchical Performativity and the King's Body Theatrical", in *Drama Review* 47/2 (T178) (Summer 2003), pp. 71–87. See also, Mark Franko, "Figural Inversions of Louis XIV's Dancing Body", in Mark Franko and Annette Richards (eds.), *Acting on the Past: Historical Performance Across the Disciplines* (Hanover, N.H.: Wesleyan

University Press University Press of New England, 2000), pp. 35–51.

20 See Louise Fradenburg and Carla Freccero (eds.) *Premodern Sexualities* (New York and London: Routledge, 1996).

21 Morris spoke of the relation of his ballet to the AIDS crisis of the 1980s at a talk he gave at Barnard College, New York City, on 11 October 2004.

22 Oskar Schlemmer, *The Letters and Diaries of Oskar Schlemmer* (Middletown, Conn.: Wesleyan University Press, 1972), p. 196.

23 Paul Lacroix, *Ballets et mascarades de cour sous Henri IV et Louis XIII (de 1581 à 1652)* (1868–70; repr. Geneva: Slatkine, 1968); and Victor Fournel, *Les Contemporains de Molière, receuil de comédies rares ou peu connues, jouées de 1650 à 1680* (Paris: 1866).

24 Collection housed in the Bibliothèque Nationale de France in Paris.

25 See Harry Haskell, *The Early Music Revival: A History* (London: Thames & Hudson, 1988).

26 For a corrective to the neglect of this repertory, see Kate Van Orden, *Music, Discipline, and Arms in Early Modern France* (Chicago: University of Chicago Press, 2005).

27 See Margaret M. McGowan, *The Court Ballet of Louis XIII: A Collection of Working Designs for Costumes 1615–33* (London: Victoria and Albert Museum, n.d.).

5 Choreography and narrative: the *ballet d'action* of the eighteenth century

1 Louis de Cahusac, *La Danse ancienne et moderne ou Traité historique de la Danse* (Paris: Jean Neaulme, 1754), vol. III, p. 118.

2 Jean-Georges Noverre, *Lettres sur la danse, et sur les ballets* (Lyons: Delaroche, 1760).

3 John Weaver, *Essay towards a History of Dancing* (London: J.Tonson 1712).

4 Ibid., p. 159.

5 Ibid., p. 137.

6 Ibid., p. 167.

7 Ibid., p. 159.

8 Ibid., p. 160.

9 John Weaver, *The Love of Mars and Venus* (London: W. Mears, J. Browne, 1717), p. 1.

10 Mark Franko, *Dance as Text. Ideologies of the Baroque Body* (Cambridge: Cambridge University Press 1993), p. 33.

11 Feuillet, *Chorégraphie ou L'art de décrire la danse* (Paris: Feuillet & Brunel 1700).

12 Cahusac, *Danse*, vol. III, p. 125.

13 Ibid., p. 139.

14 Noverre, *Lettres*, p. 84.

15 Ibid., p. 262.

16 Ibid., p. 262.

17 Malpied, *Traité sur l'art de la danse* (Paris: Bouïn, 1770), p. 84.

18 Cf. Gennaro Magri, *Theoretical and Practical Treatise on Dancing*, trans Mary Skeaping (London: Dance Books, 1988), chs. 13–58; originally *Trattato teorico-prattico di ballo* (Naples: Vicenzo Orsino, 1779).

19 Cf. George Touchard-Lafosse, *Chroniques secrètes et galantes de l'Opéra*, 4 vols., (Paris: Schneider, 1846); Emile Campardon, *L'Académie Royale de Musique au XVIII siècle* (Paris: Berger-Levrault & cie, 1884); François Henri Joseph Castil-Blaze, *L'Academie Impériale de Musique. Histoire littéraire, musicale, chorégraphique, pittoresque, morale, critique et galante de ce théâtre de 1645 à 1855*, 2 vols. (Paris: Castil-Blaze, 1855).

20 Noverre, *Lettres*, p. 53.

6 The rise of ballet technique and training: the professionalisation of an art form

1 Debra Craine and Judith Mackrell, *Oxford Dictionary of Dance* (Oxford: Oxford University Press, 2000), p. 40.

2 Rose A. Pruiksma, "Generational Conflict and the Foundation of the Académie Royale de Danse: A Reexamination", *Dance Chronicle* 26/2 (2003), p. 169.

3 Ibid., p. 182. Pruiksma postulates that the original membership of the academy may have included a woman, as the list includes a Moliere La Jeune, who might well be Marie Blanche Molier, daughter of a court musician and dancer, Louis Mollier.

4 Régine Astier, "Académie Royale de Danse", in Selma Jeanne Cohen et al. (eds.), *International Encyclopedia of Dance* (New York and Oxford: Oxford University Press, 1998), vol. I, p. 3.

5 Astier, "Académie Royale de Danse". See also, Régine Astier, "In Search of L'Académie Royale de Danse", *York Dance Review* 7 (1978), pp. 2–14.

6 Régine Astier, "Pierre Beauchamps", in *International Encyclopedia of Dance*, vol. I, p. 397.

7 Astier, "Académie Royale de Danse", p. 3.

8 See Pierre Rameau, *Le Maître à danser* (Paris: Jean Villette, 1725), p. 9. A contemporary English translation was published by John Essex as *The Dancing-Master* (London: J. Essex and J. Brotherton, 1728) and will be cited hereafter in translated material from Rameau.

9 Raoul Auger Feuillet, *Chorégraphie ou l'art de décrire la danse* (Paris: Feuillet & Brunel, 1700).

10 They included fifteen theatrical dances composed by Feuillet and nine ballroom dances composed by Guillaume-Louis Pécour, a leading ballet master of the time.

11 Ivor Guest, *Le Ballet de l'Opéra de Paris* (Paris: Théâtre National de l'Opéra/Flammarion, 1976), p. 19.

12 Quoted in Ivor Guest, *The Ballet of the Enlightenment* (London: Dance Books 1996), p. 23.

13 Johann Pasch, *Beschreibung wahrer Tantz-Kunst* (Frankfurt: Wolffgang Michahelles and Johann Adolph 1707), p. 369. I am grateful to Edmund Fairfax for this citation.

14 Cited in Régine Astier, "Marie Sallé", in *International Encyclopedia of Dance*, vol. v, p. 503.

15 Régine Astier, "La Vie quotidienne des danseurs sous l'Ancién Régime", *Les Gôuts reunis*, 3rd series/1 (1982), p. 35.

16 Rameau/Essex, *The Dancing Master*, p. 125.

17 Ibid., p. 2.

18 Joan Wildeblood, *The Polite World* (London: Davis-Poynter, 1973), p. 94.

19 Jean-Georges Noverre, *Lettres sur la danse, sur les ballets et les arts* (St Petersburg 1803), transl. Cyril W. Beaumont as *Letters on Dancing and on Ballets* (New York: Dance Horizons 1968), p. 117.

20 Giambattista Dufort, *Trattato del ballo nobile* (Naples: Felice Mosca 1728), pp. 4–5.

21 C. Sol, *Méthode très facile et fort nécessaire, pour montrer à la jeunesse de l'un et l'autre sexe la manière de bien dancer* (La Haye: l'Auteur 1725), p. 52.

22 Rameau/Essex, *The Dancing Master*, p. 11.

23 Sol, *Méthode*, p. 18.

24 Gennaro Magri, *Trattato teorico-prattico di ballo* (Naples: Vicenzo Orsino 1779), vol. ii, pp. 10–11. Hereafter, translated material from Magri will be from the English translation by Mary Skeaping, *Theoretical and Practical Treatise on Dancing* (London: Dance Books, 1988).

25 Noverre/Beaumont, *Letters on Dancing*, p. 119.

26 Magri/Skeaping, *Theoretical and Practical Treatise*, p. 75.

27 Ibid., p. 74.

28 Carlo Blasis, *The Code of Terpsichore*, trans. R. Barton (London: printed for James Bullock 1828), p. 102.

29 Noverre/Beaumont, *Letters on Dancing*, p. 19.

30 Ibid., p. 91.

31 Giovanni-Andrea Gallini, *A Treatise on the Art of Dancing* (London: The author, 1762), p. 236.

32 G. Léopold Adice, *Théorie de la gymnastique de la danse théâtrale* (Paris: Chais 1859), p. 80. A portion of his book dealing with the ballet class is translated by Leonore Loft in Selma Jeanne Cohen, *Dance as a Theatre Art* (New York: Harper & Row, 1974), p. 76.

33 Magri/Skeaping, *Theoretical and Practical Treatise*, pp. 48–9, 143.

34 Noverre/Beaumont, *Letters on Dancing*, p. 18.

35 Magri/Skeaping, *Theoretical and Practical Treatise*, p. 61.

36 Cited in Edmund Fairfax, *The Styles of Eighteenth-Century Ballet* (Lanham, Md.: Scarecrow Press, 2003), p. 19.

37 Magri/Skeaping, *Theoretical and Practical Treatise*, p. 128.

38 Cited in Guest, *The Ballet of the Enlightenment*, pp. 205-6.

39 Quoted in Régine Astier, "Marie Camargo", in *International Encyclopedia of Dance*, vol. ii, p. 27.

40 Ibid., p. 28.

41 Ivor Guest, *Ballet under Napoleon* (Alton: Dance Books, 2002), p. 9.

42 Fairfax, *Styles of Eighteenth-Century Ballet*, p. 276.

43 John Chapman, "Auguste Vestris", in *International Dictionary of Ballet*, ed. Martha Bremser (London: St James Press, 1993), vol. ii, p. 1485.

44 Guest, *The Ballet of the Enlightenment*, p. 24.

45 John V. Chapman, "The Paris Opera Ballet School, 1798–1827", *Dance Chronicle* 12/2 (1989), pp. 196–220.

46 Carlo Blasis, *Notes Upon Dancing, Historical and Practical*, transl. R. Barton (London: M. Delaporte, 1847), pp. 56–61.

47 Carlo Blasis, *Traité élémentaire, théorique et pratique de l'art de la danse* (Milan: Joseph Beati et Antoine Tenenti, 1820), trans. Mary Stewart Evans as *An Elementary Treatise upon the Theory and Practice of the Art of Dancing* (New York: Dover 1968), p. 5.

48 Blasis, *Notes*, p. 62.

7 The making of history: John Weaver and the Enlightenment

1 Quoted in Richard Ralph, *The Life and Works of John Weaver. An Account of his Life, Writings and Theatrical Productions, with an Annotated Reprint of his Complete Publications* (London: Dance Books 1985), p. 50.

2 Richard Ralph, *The Life and Works of John Weaver*, Ibid., p. 108.

3 John Weaver, *An Essay Towards an History of Dancing* (London: Printed for Jack Tonson, 1712), reproduced in Ralph, *The Life and Works of John Weaver*, p. 395.

4 Ralph, *The Life and Works of John Weaver* p. 405.

5 Ibid.

6 Ibid. p. 469.

7 Carol Lee, *Ballet in Western Culture: A History of its Origins and Evolution* (New York and London: Routledge, 2002), p. 368.

8 *Poems by Soame Jenyns, containing Art of dancing, To Lord Lovelace, Essay on virtue, Written in Locke, Epitaph on Doctor Johnson; to which is prefixed a sketch of the author's life* (Manchester 1797). Canto 2, p. 8

9 John Essex, *The dancing-master: or, The art of dancing explained. Wherein the manner of performing all steps in ball dancing is made easy by a new and familiar method. In two parts . . . The whole containing sixty figures drawn from the life, and curiously engraved on copper plates. Done from the French of Monsieur Rameau* (London: Printed and sold by him, and J. Brotherton, 1728), p. x.

10 Quoted in Ralph, *The Life and Works of John Weaver*, p. 107; Charles Burney, *Choregraphy, The Cyclopaedia*, ed. Abraham Rees (1819), vol. VII.

11 Ralph, *The Life and Works of John Weaver*, p. 142.

12 Cf. ibid., p. 49.

13 Considered one of the greatest British playwrights of comedy.

14 Quoted in Hugh Arthur Scott, "London's earliest public concerts", *Musical Quarterly* 22 (1936), p. 454.

15 Roger North, *Memoirs of Musick being some Historio-criticall Collections of that Subject* (1728), ed. Edward F. Rimbault (London, 1846), p. 111.

16 George Savile Marquis of Halifax, *Advice to a Daughter, Chiefly with Regard to Religion* (Aberdeen: printed for and by Francis Douglass and William Murray, 1688; 7th edn 1701), p. 141.

17 Petition to the Vice-Chamberlain.

18 Weaver, *Essay Towards the History of Dancing*, p. 658.

19 Ibid., p. 612.

20 Ibid., p. 614.

21 Ibid., p. 666.

22 Ibid., p. 436.

23 Ibid.

24 Ibid.

25 Ibid.

26 Ibid.

27 Charles Rosen, *The Classical Style: Haydn, Mozart, Beethoven* (New York: W.W. Norton, 1972; 1997), p. 172 n. 1.

28 Anthony Ashley Cooper, Third Earl of Shaftesbury, *Soliloquy: Or, Advice to an author* (London: Printed for John Morphew, 1710), p. 65.

29 Ibid., p. 135.

30 Ibid.

31 Weaver, *Essay Towards the History of Dancing*, p. 403.

32 Weaver, *A Small Treatise of time and Cadence in Dancing*, reproduced in Ralph, *The Life and Works of John Weaver*, p. 365.

33 William Wycherly, *The Gentleman Dancing Master*, www3.shropshire-cc.gov.uk/etexts/E000294.htm.

34 Ibid., Act II, scene ii.

35 Joshua Reynolds, *Seven Discourses on Art* (delivered between 1769 and 1776), www.authorama.com/book/seven-discourses-on-art.html.

8 Jean-Georges Noverre: dance and reform

1 Samuel Johnson, *A Dictionary of the English Language* (London, 1755).

2 Cf. Horst Koegler, "The Northern Heirs of Noverre", *Dance and Dancers* (London, 1987), p. 24.

3 Deryck Lynham, *The Chevalier Noverre: Father of Modern Ballet*. (London: Dance Books, 1972), p. 117.

4 Lillian Moore, "Noverre, First of the Moderns", *Dance Magazine* 9(1952), p. 44.

5 Artur Michel, "Le Ballet d'action avant Noverre", *Archives Internationale de Dance*, pt. 2 (Octobre 1935), p. 116.

6 Cf. Denis Diderot, *Oeuvres complètes de Diderot*, 20 vols., ed. J. Asśezat and M. Tourneux (Paris: Garnier frères, 1875–7), vol. VII, p. 157.

7 Cf. Jean-Jacques Rousseau, *Julie ou la Nouvelle Héloïse, Oeuvres complètes* (Geneva: Editions Gallimard, Bibliothéque de la Pléiade, 1964), vol. II, pp. 287–9.

8 *International Encyclopaedia of Dance* (New York: Oxford University Press, 1998), p. 174.

9 Voltaire (François-Marie Arouet), *Correspondance, Oeuvres complétes*, 50 vols., ed. L. Moland (Paris: Garnier, 1877–85), vol. LIII, p. 76.

10 Voltaire, *Correspondance*, vol. LIV, pp. 18–85.

11 Noverre, *Lettres sur La danse* (Paris: Editions Lieutier, 1952), 92. This edition is based on that of St Petersburg, 1807). Subsequent references in the text are to the English translation, *Letters on Dancing and on Ballets*, trans. Cyril Beaumont (New York: Dance Horizons, 1968).

9 The French Revolution and its spectacles

1 See Ivor Guest, *Ballet under Napoleon* (Alton: Dance Books, 2002), p. 20: "Aristocratic appropriation of the court ballet's sensuous techniques likely reinforced the overall image of royal authority, but it also established a fascination with bodily display and attraction that would catalyze the art forms associated with 'aristocracy' in the following decades."

2 Cf. Sarah Cohen, *Art, Dance and the Body in French Culture of the Ancien Régime.* (Cambridge: Cambridge University Press, 2000).

3 Cf. Inge Baxmann, *Die Feste der Französischen Revolution. Inszenierung von Gesellschaft als Natur* (Weinheim/Basel: Beltz, 1989).

4 Boullée, cited in Fritz Wagner, *Isaac Newton im Zwielicht zwischen Mythos und Forschung.* (Freiburg/München: Verlag Karl Alber, 1976), p. 127.

5 Abbé Emmanuel Joseph Sieyès, *Qu'est-ce que le tiers état?* (Paris: Flammarion, 1989), pp. 173–4. *What is the Third Estate?* Trans. M. Blondel, ed. S. E. Finer (London and Dunmow: Pall Mall Press, 1963), p. 162.

6 Jacques Grenier, *Opinion sur la question de savoir si l'on doit supprimer de la formule du serment civique les mots de haine à l'anarchie.* Paris, an VII, cited in Mona Ozouf, *La Fête Révolutionnaire* (Paris: Gallimard 1976), p. 339.

7 See Guest, *Ballet under Napoleon*, pp. 17–18.

8 S. Thomas, *Nancy avant et après 1830*, cited in Ozouf, *La Fête Révolutionnaire*, p. 135.

9 *Plan de la Fête de l'Etre Suprême*, qui sera célébrée à Tours, le 20 Prairial en exécution du Décret du 18 Floréal, l'an second de la République, une et indivisible. Bibliolegue Nationale Paris, p. 8/9.

10 Ibid., p. 6.

11 *Receuil de chants philosophiques, civiques et moraux, à l'usage des Fêtes Nationales et Décadaires.* Paris An VII, p. 58.

10 Romantic ballet in France: 1830–1850

1 Gas lighting to illuminate the stage was introduced in 1822 while the dimming of house lights occurred in 1831.

2 Susan Leigh Foster, "The Ballerina's Phallic Pointe", in Susan Leigh Foster (ed.), *Corporealities: Dancing Knowledge, Culture and Power* (London: Routledge, 1996), p. 5. For the tie to sexuality, see Felicia McCarren, *Dance Pathologies: Performance, Poetics, Medicine* (Stanford, Calif.: Stanford University Press, 1998).

3 Later in the late 1840s and 1850s, Arthur Saint-Léon returned to Filippo Taglioni's practice and devised the plot, the choreography and often partnered the leading dancer, sometimes even playing the telling tune on his violin on stage.

4 See Sally Banes's section "The Marriage plot" in her introduction and the chapter "The Romantic Ballet: *La Sylphide, Giselle, Coppélia*", in *Dancing Women: Female Bodies on Stage* (London and New York: Routledge, 1998), pp. 5–7 and 12–42, where she argues against reading the ballets as simple depictions

supporting bourgeois and patriarchal marriage practices.

5 René Girard's concept of mimetic desire, or triangular desire, captures aptly the romantic love element of the ballets' plots. He argues that the desire, which a subject, a man, has for an object (a woman, for example) has more to do with the prestige associated with the person who possesses or is about to desire the same object than with the object's intrinsic worth. Simultaneously the person is not passive. He too is invested in the object's worth and thus seeks to awaken desire in the subject. As they copy one another, the triangulation of the mimetic desire turns them into rivals. See in particular his *Deceit, Desire, and the Novel: Self and Other in Literary Structure*, trans. Yvonne Freccero (Baltimore: Johns Hopkins Press, 1965).

6 For the circulation of répétiteurs, see Marian Smith, "The Earliest *Giselle*? A Preliminary Report on a St Petersburg Manuscript", *Dance Chronicle: Studies in Dance and the Related Arts* 23/1 (2000), pp. 29–48.

7 More exact dates would be 1831 to 1847, marked by the premiere of the opera *Robert le diable* with its "*Ballet des nonnes*" and finishing with *Ozaï* (26 April) and *La Fille de marbre* (20 October).

8 The various transformations *Giselle* has undergone in its history has pulled it towards more class- or race-conscious readings. Others have looked at Giselle's madness in terms of drug addiction.

9 I am indebted to Marion Kant's essay "Giselle – la jolie morte", which traces and contextualises through a reading of *Giselle* the transformations the wili has undergone, and Christianity's manipulation of dancing, in *Musik und Gesellschaft*, ed. Verband der Komponisten und Musikwissenschaftler der DDR (Berlin: Henschelverlag), no. 3 (1988).

10 For travesty dancing, see Lynn Garafola, "The Travesty Dancer in Nineteenth Century Ballet", *Dance Research Journal* 17/2 (Fall–Spring 1985–6), pp. 35–40. Examples of ballets with dancers *en travesti* include: *Le Diable boiteux, Le Diable amoureux*, and *Paquita* with its squadron of hussars.

11 Few women worked as teachers or choreographers at the Paris Opéra until the 1860s. Thérèse Elssler stands out for her choreographic work on her sister Fanny Elssler. Her ballet, *La Volière ou les oiseaux de Boccace* (1838), set in the Caribbean on a plantation, from which all men have been banished, configured gender differently and asserted women's emotional growth. Fanny Elssler (or her sister) choreographed a ballet entitled *La*

Salamandrine, which was first produced at Covent Garden on 22 May 1847 (see the Bibliothèque de l'Opéra's libretto (Liv m. 149)), some 113 years after Marie Sallé's staging and performance of *Pygmalion.* Marie Taglioni would return later to teach and she choreographed and produced the ballet *Le Papillon* at the Paris Opéra in 1860. Other female teachers, such as Madame Dominique, developed a loyal following of students during the latter part of the century.

12 For romanticism's use of the fantastic and the question of marriage see Scott M. Sprenger, "Figures du fantastique: la logique du mariage raté chez Gautier et chez Zola", *Bulletin de la Société Théophile Gautier* 21 (1999), pp. 191–207; esp. p. 192.

13 Susan Leigh Foster elaborates the recurrence of this story in *Choreography and Narrative: Ballet's Staging of Story and Desire* (Bloomington and Indianapolis: Indiana University Press, 1996).

14 For a similar argument regarding the novelistic characters, see Jann Matlock, "Novels of Testimony and the 'Invention' of the Modern French Novel", *Cambridge Companion to the French Novel from 1800 to the Present* (Cambridge: Cambridge University Press, 1997), pp. 10-35; p. 33.

15 The origin of this appellation is disputed, but Théophile Gautier used it consistently to refer to the dancers of the Paris Opéra who performed walk-on roles or as part of the corps de ballet ("Le Rat", *Les Français peints par eux-mêmes: encyclopédie morale du dix-neuvième siècle* (Paris: L. Curmer, 1841–2), vol. iii, pp. 249–56). Honoré de Balzac also uses the term.

11 Deadly sylphs and decent mermaids: the women in the Danish romantic world of August Bournonville

1 Bournonville was ballet master at the Royal Danish Ballet 1830–77, except for his time as ballet master in Vienna, Austria 1855–6 and as director in Stockholm, Sweden 1861–4.

2 *Hvor danser Den Kgl. Ballet hen?* pp. 52 and 55. www.schoenbergske.dk.

3 Cf. Chapter 10 by Sarah Davis Cordova "Romantic ballet in France: 1830–1850".

4 Examples of the Bournonville style and its basic exercises can be seen on the video *Bournonville Ballet Technique: Fifty Enchaînements annotated by Hans Beck* (London: Dance Books 1993), featuring Rose Gad and Johan Kobborg, directed by Vivi Flindt and published along with the book *Bournonville Ballet Technique: Fifty Enchaînements* by Vivi Flindt and Knud Arne Jürgensen (London:

Dance Books, 1992). Besides that, the Royal Danish Ballet has published *The Bournonville Schools* – the DVD, coached by Frank Andersen, Anne Marie Vessel Schlüter, Eva Kloborg, Flemming Ryberg and Dinna Bjørn. Director: Ulrik Wivel, 2005.

5 According to the Danish ballet critic Erik Aschengreen, Bournonville's illegitimate child had always been known about within a small circle of people, but only in 1997 did it become public knowledge when Danish ballet historian Knud Arne Jürgensen included the daughter in his article on "The Ballet Tradition" (1997), also in his Bournonville biography for the catalogue for the exhibition *Europæeren Bournonville* (Bournonville the European), vol. i, p. 20 at the Royal Library, Copenhagen, 2000.

6 The most famous painting is that by the Danish painter Carl Bloch from 1876 where the seventy-one-year-old Bournonville is portrayed with five different medals. He received the royal honour of being knighted Ridder af Dannebrogordenen 1848. Cf. *Dansk Biografisk Leksikon* (Copenhagen: J. H. Schultz, 1979).

7 *Den nøgne Guldalder* (The Nude Golden Age), exhibition catalogue by Annette Johansen, Emma Salling, Marianne Saabye (Copenhagen: The Hirschsprung Collection 1994), p. 164 (with English summary and translation).

8 Women were not seriously invited to share these intellectual discussions in the circles around Brandes and they were not accepted as students at the University of Copenhagen until 1875.

9 *Mit Theaterliv* was published in five volumes: vol. i in 1847 (and 1848), vol. ii in 1865 and the others in 1877–8 (Copenhagen: C. A. Reitzel). Niels Birger Wamberg created a new edition, linguistically revised, for the centenary celebration of Bournonville's death: *Mit Teaterliv* (Copenhagen: Thaning & Appel, 1979). On the same occasion, Patricia McAndrew translated this gigantic work into English, with a foreword by ballet dancer Erik Bruhn and an introduction by ballet critic Svend Kragh-Jacobsen: *My Theatre Life* (London: A. & C. Black, 1979).

10 "Choreografisk Troesbekjendelse" (Choreographic Credo) was published in his *My Theatre Life,* vol. ii, ch. 1. It was reprinted in Erik Aschengreen's *Ballettens Digter. 3 Bournonville essays* (Copenhagen: Rhodos, 1977) (Danish only). Translations taken from Patricia McAndrew, see n. 9.

11 In *Napoli,* the change of dress for Teresina takes place so quickly that the surprised sigh of the audience has become part of the transformation. The secret consists of two

dresses on top of each other – and a decisive, masculine hand from underneath.

12 Elsa Marianne von Rosen and Allan Fridericia: *Napoli*, Gothenburg Ballet, 1971. The same production was later staged for the Kirov Ballet in St Petersburg and the Royal Swedish Ballet in Stockholm. Tim Rushton, *Napoli – den nye by* (Napoli – The New Town), New Danish Dance Theatre, Copenhagen, 2003. www.nddt.dk. Thomas Lund and Johan Holten, *En anden akt* (Another Act), Copenhagen International Ballet, Bellevue Teatret, Copenhagen, 2004. www.sommerballet.dk. Dinna Bjørn and Frank Andersen, *Napoli*, stagings for the Royal Danish Ballet in 1992, 1998, 2005 and for the Finnish National Ballet in 2005.

13 In Bournonville's time, *Abdallah* was performed between 1855 and 1858. Then it was practically forgotten until ballet director Bruce Marks and his wife, Toni Lander, bought Bournonville's handwritten libretto at an auction in New York in 1970. In 1985, they reconstructed the ballet, together with Danish Bournonville teacher Flemming Ryberg. At that time, Toni Lander had accepted the position as ballet director of the Royal Danish Ballet and she had planned to bring *Abdallah* to Copenhagen with her. Tragically, Toni Lander died of a sudden illness. In spite of this, Bruce Marks and Flemming Ryberg together with Bournonville coach Sorella Englundand managed to stage the ballet for the Royal Danish Ballet in 1986: *Abdallah* had come back home.

14 At the gala for the third Bournonville Festival in 2005, the *Jockey Dance* was danced as a unisex duet by two principal ballerinas *en travestie*, Gudrun Bojesen and Gitte Lindstrøm.

15 Artistic directors of the Royal Danish Ballet since the first Bournonville Festival: Henning Kronstam 1978–85, Frank Andersen 1985–94, Peter Schaufuss 1994–5, Johnny Eliasen (temporary appointment) 1995–7, Maina Gielgud 1997–9, Aage Thordal-Christensen 1999–2002, Frank Andersen 2002–8. Frank Andersen (born 1953), was a Danish principal dancer and Bournonville instructor. He was artistic director at the Royal Danish Ballet 1985–94. He then was ballet director for the Royal Swedish Ballet 1995–9 and artistic adviser for the Chinese National Ballet, and judge at international dancer competitions, before he returned to his position as artistic director of the Royal Danish Ballet in 2002. Abroad, he has staged *Napoli* and *La Sylphide*. For the Royal Danish Ballet, he has staged *A Folk Tale* in 1991 (together with Anne Marie Vessel Schlüter and

with decor by her majesty, Queen Margrethe II) and *Napoli* several times since 1992 (with Henning Kronstam, Dinna Bjørn and Anne Marie Vessel Schlüter).

16 *Jeg Dig Elsker* (I love you). An interpretation of *La Sylphide* with ballet director Nikolaj Hübbe, directed by Ulrik Wivel. Dancers: Mads Blangstrup, Gudrun Bojesen, Lis Jeppesen. DVD, 25 minutes. The Royal Theatre and the Danish Film Institute 2005.

12 The orchestra as translator: French nineteenth-century ballet

1 Operas of four acts or longer nearly always included a ballet; shorter operas (or shortened versions of longer operas) were performed on the same evening as independent ballets.

2 *Le Journal des débats*, 28 September 1822. The score for *Alfred le grand*, first performed 18 September 1822, was by Gallenberg and Dugazon.

3 Auguste Baron, *Lettres et entretiens sur la danse* (Paris: Dondey-Dupré, 1824), p. 296.

4 *Le Moniteur universel*, 21 September 1827.

5 *La Siècle*, 23 September 1836.

6 *La Sylphide*, 26 September 1840.

7 *Le Constitutionnel*, 11 August 1845.

8 Gustave Chouquet, *Histoire de la musique dramatique en France* (Paris: Librairie Firmin Didot Frères, 1873), p. 170.

9 See Stephanie Jordan, "The Role of the Ballet Composer at the Paris Opéra: 1820–1850", *Dance Chronicle*, 4/4 (1982), pp. 374-88; and Ivor Guest, *The Romantic Ballet in Paris* (London: Dance Books, 1980), p. 10.

10 Over a half-century later, Tchaikovsky wove the royalist tune "Vive Henri Quatre" into the final scene of *Sleeping Beauty* (1890) to help conclude that ballet "with great pomp and ostentation", and a royalist flair, recalling the Parisian tradition of using it to suggest just those qualities.

11 Such "vocal" passages were frequently indicated in rehearsal scores, and the text "spoken" by the characters written below the staff.

12 To *Le Corsaire*, 1856, a new divertissement was added by Delibes in 1857. The ballet was restaged by Petipa at the St Petersburg Maryinsky Theatre, with additional music by Drigo, Minkus and Pugni. The music for the famous *pas de deux* so often performed without the rest of the ballet is by Drigo.

13 Galops may be found, to name only a few examples from the stage of the Paris Opéra, in the ballets *La Jolie Fille de Gand*, *Le Diable à*

quatre, *La Fille de marbre*, *Diavolina*, *La Korrigane*, and the operas *Dom Sébastien*, *Gustave III* and *Le Prophète*.

14 The polka, which was according to Guest (*The Romantic Ballet in Paris*, p. 229) "all the rage in the ballrooms and public balls" in the early 1840s, is said to have made its first appearance on the stage of the Opéra in the ballet *Lady Henriette* (first performed 21 February 1844).

15 *La France musicale*, 17 August 1845.

16 *Le Nord*, 13 July 1863.

17 Such levity proved a valuable counterbalance to the serious and even violent tone of many operas with which ballet shared the stage. See Smith, *Ballet and Opera*, pp. 59–96.

18 *La France musicale*, 11 August 1844.

19 *La Revue et gazette musicale*, 27 September 1840.

20 *Le Nord*, 13 July 1863.

21 *La Revue et gazette musicale*, 5 December 1880.

22 *Le Menéstrel*, 12 March 1882. This music fared well in the next century, in Serge Lifar's *Suite en blanc* (1943), revived as *Noir et blanc*, and as a concert suite.

23 Letter to *The Times* of London of 6 July 1914, reprinted in Roger Copeland and Marshall Cohen (eds.), *What is Dance? Readings in Theory and Criticism* (Oxford: Oxford University Press, 1983), p. 260.

24 This choreography also uses ballet music from Verdi's *Jérusalem* and *Don Carlos*.

25 Music of Delibes's *La Source* and *Naila* was used for Balanchine's *La Source* (1968); parts of the *Sylvia* score have also been choreographed by, among others, Balanchine and Ashton. The many other choreographies to Delibes's ballet music include Léo Staats's *Soir de fête* (1921), using *Le Corsaire* and *La Source*, which has been performed over 250 times.

26 1 August 1847. His ballets include *La Chatte blanche* (Paris, 1830), *Faust* (London, 1833), *La Fille du Danube* (Paris, 1836), *Les Mohicans* (Paris, 1837), *L'Ecumeur de mer* (St Petersburg, 1840), *Die Hamadryaden* (Berlin, 1840), *Giselle* (Paris, 1841), *La Jolie Fille de Gand* (Paris, 1842), *Le Diable à quatre* (1845), *The Marble Maiden* (London, 1845), *Griseldis ou les cinq senses* (Paris,1848), *La Filleule des fées* (Paris, 1849), *Orfa* (Paris, 1852), and *Le Corsaire* (Paris, 1856).

27 Remarks made by Adam while working on *La Filleule des fées*, quoted in Benoît Jouvin, *Hérold, sa vie et ses oeuvres* (Paris: Heugel, 1868), p. 148.

28 "Léo Delibes", in Selma Jeanne Cohen and Elizabeth Aldrich (eds.), *International*

Encyclopedia of Dance (New York and Oxford: Oxford University Press, 1998), vol. ii, p. 368.

29 *L'Opinion*, trans. Cyril Beaumont, in *Complete Book of Ballets* (London: Putnam, 1937; repr. 1956), p. 495.

30 *Le Telegraphe*, 3 June 1885.

31 "Le XIX Siècle" (in Delibes dossier d'artiste, Bibliothèque de l'Opéra); George Balanchine and Francis Mason, *Balanchine's Complete Stories of the Great Ballets* (Garden City, N.Y.: Doubleday, 1977), p. 608.

32 Jouvin, *Hérold*, p. 194.

33 Edouard Deldevez, *Mes Mémoires* (Paris: Marchessou fils, 1890), p. 34.

34 5 December 1880.

35 See Ivor Guest, *Le Ballet de l'Opéra de Paris* (Paris: Flammarion, 2001), pp. 297–314, for a list of the Opéra's ballets and their composers, 1776–2000.

13 Russian ballet in the age of Petipa

1 *Russian Ballet Master: The Memoirs of Marius Petipa*, ed. Lillian Moore, trans. Helen Whittaker (London: A. & C. Black, 1958), p. 23.

2 Vera M. Krasovskaya, "Petipa, Marius", *International Encyclopedia of Dance*, ed. Selma Jean Cohen and Dance Perspectives Foundation (Oxford: Oxford University Press, 1998, 2005) (hereafter *IED*), p. 150. Jean-Antoine Petipa died in St Petersburg in 1855, at which point Marius took over his position, which he continued to occupy until 1863, when at Petipa's request, the director of the Imperial Theatres appointed Christian Johansson to succeed him.

3 Petipa, *Memoirs*, p. 22. A "benefit" refers to a performance of which all or part of the proceeds were earmarked for a particular artist or group (such as the corps de ballet).

4 Natalia Roslavleva, *Era of the Russian Ballet*, foreword Ninette de Valois (London: Gollancz, 1966), p. 22.

5 Ibid., p. 32.

6 This is the date of the Russian as opposed to the French premiere, which took place at the Paris Opéra in 1856. The 1858 St Petersburg production was by Jules Perrot. Petipa restaged the ballet five years later, with significant revisions in 1868 (when he choreographed the "Jardin Animé"), 1885 and 1899. See "Works by Marius Petipa in Russia", in *The Diaries of Marius Petipa*, ed., trans. and intro. Lynn Garafola, *Studies in Dance History*, 3/1 (Spring 1992), pp. 81–2.

7 *La Sylphide* premiered at the Paris Opéra in 1832. Three years later, Antoine Titus staged the ballet after Taglioni at the Bolshoi Theatre,

St Petersburg. The ballet was restaged by Taglioni in 1837. Petipa restaged the work, again after Taglioni but with additional music by Riccardo Drigo, in 1892. "Sil'fida", *Balet Entsiklopediia* (hereafter *Soviet Ballet Encyclopedia*) (Moscow: Sovetskaia Entsiklopediia, 1981); Cyril W. Beaumont, *Complete Book of Ballets* (London: Putnam, 1937), p. 103.

8 Quoted in Roslavleva, *Era of the Russian Ballet*, p. 59.

9 Quoted ibid., pp. 66–7.

10 Krasovskaya, "Petipa", p. 149.

11 Petipa, *Memoirs*, p. 2. The "bow" is a reference to the small violin or "pochette" that ballet teachers played as accompaniment in class.

12 For an account of this unsuccessful tour, see Lillian Moore, "The Petipa Family in Europe and America", *Dance Index*, 1/5 (May 1942), pp. 76–8.

13 Yury Slonimsky, "Marius Petipa", trans. Anatole Chujoy, *Dance Index*, 6/5–6 (May–June 1947), p. 106.

14 "A Glance Behind the Scenes", *Appleton's Journal of Literature, Science and Art*, 1 April 1876, p. 433. According to the author, some fifty dancers appeared in the divertissement.

15 August Bournonville, *My Theatre Life*, trans. Patricia N. McAndrew, intro. Svend Kragh-Jacobsen (Middletown, Conn.: Wesleyan University Press, 1979), p. 581.

16 Ibid., pp. 581–2.

17 Slonimsky, "Marius Petipa", p. 115.

18 Roland John Wiley, *The Life and Ballets of Lev Ivanov* (Oxford: Clarendon Press, 1997), p. 106.

19 Ibid., p. 93. For abolishing the post of official ballet composer, see *A Century of Russian Ballet: Documents and Accounts, 1810–1910*, ed. and trans. Roland John Wiley (Oxford: Clarendon Press, 1990), p. 350.

20 Quoted in Vera Krasovskaya, "Marius Petipa and 'The Sleeping Beauty'", trans. Cynthia Read, *Dance Perspectives* 49 (Spring 1972), p. 21.

21 Ibid.

22 Wiley reproduces Petipa's instructions to Tchaikovsky and his "plan" for the ballet in *Tchaikovsky's Ballets: Swan Lake, Sleeping Beauty, Nutcracker* (Oxford: Clarendon Press, 1985), Appendix D, pp. 354–70.

23 For criticism of the ballet, see Tim Scholl, *Sleeping Beauty: A Legend in Progress* (New Haven: Yale University Press, 2004), ch. 1 ("Genre Trouble").

24 Alexandre Benois, *Reminiscences of the Russian Ballet*, trans. Mary Britnieva (London: Putnam, 1941), Reminiscences, p. 128.

25 The *Yearbooks of the Imperial Theatres* (*Yezhegodniki Imperatorskikh Teatrov* (St Petersburg/Petrograd, 1890–1915) listed all the dancers and artistic personnel in the employ of the St Petersburg and Moscow companies.

26 Krasovskaya, "Petipa", pp. 153–4.

27 Quoted in Wiley, *Tchaikovsky's Ballets*, p. 221.

28 Vera M. Krasovskaya, "Ivanov, Lev", *IED*, pp. 565-6.

29 Wiley, *Ivanov*, p. 174.

30 Ibid., p. 176.

31 Sergei Khudekov, "The Petersburg Ballet During the Production of *The Little Humpbacked Horse* (Recollections)", in Wiley, *A Century of Russian Ballet*, pp. 266–7.

32 Tamara Karsavina, "Platon Karsavin", *Dancing Times* (October 1964), p. 12.

33 "Before graduation . . . many students never imagined the poverty in which their parents lived", wrote the dancer Anna Natarova in her recollections of theatre life in the 1840s. "However badly they fed us at school, it was worse at home" ("From the 'Recollections of the Artiste A. P. Natarova", in Wiley, *A Century of Russian Ballet*, p. 160).

34 For a description of training in the 1830s and 1840s, see "Recollections of T. A. Stukolkin", ibid., pp. 108-9. For training in the late nineteenth and early twentieth centuries, see Tamara Karsavina, *Theatre Street: The Reminiscences of Tamara Karsavina*, foreword J. M. Barrie (London: Heinemann, 1930), ch. 7 ("The Pupil"); Princess Romanovsky-Krassinsky [Kshesinska], *Dancing in Petersburg: The Memoirs of Kschessinska*, trans. Arnold Haskell (London: Gollancz, 1960), ch. 3 ("The Imperial Ballet School"); Michel Fokine, *Memoirs of a Ballet Master*, trans. Vitale Fokine, ed. Anatole Chujoy (Boston: Little, Brown, 1961), ch. 2 ("Life in School"); and Bronislava Nijinska, *Early Memoirs*, ed. and trans. Irina Nijinska and Jean Rawlinson (New York: Holt, Rinehart & Winston, 1981), chs. 11–17.

35 Vera Krasovskaya, *Vaganova: A Dance Journey from Petersburg to Leningrad*, trans. Vera M. Siegel, intro. Lynn Garafola (Gainesville: University Press of Florida, 2005), p. 51.

36 Prince Serge Wolkonsky, *My Reminiscences*, trans. A. E. Chamot (London: Hutchinson, n.d.), p. 107. For Kshesinska's account of the incident, see Kschessinska [Kshesinska], *Dancing in Petersburg*, pp. 81–2.

37 Ksehessinska, *Dancing in Petersburg*, p. 27.

38 Richard Taruskin, *The Oxford History of Western Music*, vol. IV (New York: Oxford University Press, 2005), p. 142.

14 Opening the door to a fairy-tale world: Tchaikovsky's ballet music

1 Solomon Volkov, *Balanchine's Tchaikovsky: Interviews with George Balanchine*, trans. Antonina Bouis (New York: Simon & Schuster, 1985), p. 144. From letter to Taneyev (Taneev).

2 Volkov, *Balanchine*, p. 153. Herman Laroche recalls Tchaikovsky's turn from opera to ballet.

3 Volkov, *Balanchine*, p. 153.

4 Karl Fedorovich Valts, *Shest'desyat pyat' let v teatre* (Sixty-five Years in the Theatre) (Leningrad 1928), p. 108. Translation in Roland John Wiley, *Tchaikovsky's Ballets: Swan Lake, Sleeping Beauty, Nutcracker* (Oxford: Oxford University Press, 1985), p. 56.

5 German Avgustovich Larosh (Laroche), *Izbrannye stat'i* (Collected Articles), 5 vols. (Leningrad, 1974), vol. I, pp. ii, 99. Translated in: Wiley, *Tchaikovsky's Ballets*, pp. 52–3.

6 "Sovremennye izvestiya" (25 February 1877), p. 3. Translated in Wiley, *Tchaikovsky's Ballets*, p. 52.

7 As Wiley points out, St Petersburg newspapers commented on this similarity: *Novosti i birzhevaya gazeta*, 17 January 1895, p. 3; *Novoe vremya* 17 January 1895, p. 3. Tchaikovsky earlier used the Swan Theme for a children's play at his sister Alexandra Davydov's estate in 1870. Cf. Wiley, *Tchaikovsky's Ballets*, p. 37.

8 Wiley, *Tchaikovsky's Ballets*, p. 85. Tchaikovsky originally composed this duet for Undine and her mortal lover, who must die for having betrayed her, in his opera *Undine* (1869). In *Swan Lake*, the soprano and baritone parts are played by violin and cello respectively.

9 Wiley, *Tchaikovsky's Ballets*, pp. 80–8. Wiley provides a detailed analysis of the use of keys throughout the ballet and how they relate to the characters.

10 Ibid., p. 244.

11 Ibid., p. 104. Ivan Alexandrovich Vsevolozhsky was Director of Imperial Theatres 1881–99. He had eliminated the post of a resident ballet composer, making it easier to give commissions to composers such as Tchaikovsky.

12 Tchaikovsky's response was written in Moscow on 22 August 1888 – more than three months after Vsevolozhsky's initial enquiry (my trans.). Wiley speculates that the director's original letter may have been lost (Wiley, *Tchaikovsky's Ballets*, p. 104).

13 Wiley, *Tchaikovsky's Ballets*, p. 125.

14 Laroche. *Izbranniye stat'i* vol. II (Leningrad, 1975), pp. 140–3, trans. David Brown, *Tchaikovsky Remembered*. (London: Faber & Faber, 1993), p. 190. In addition to praising Tchaikovsky's achievement with *Sleeping Beauty*, Laroche's review for the *Moscow Gazette* defends

the use of a children's tale for the ballet, remarks on the composer's skill at writing music of both a serious, melancholic nature as well as happy, lively material, and touches on the Russianness of his music.

15 Wiley, *Tchaikovsky's Ballets*, p. 361: "Musique douce et un peu ricaneuse". This request seems rather confusing. How can the Lilac Fairy be sweet and derisive at the same time? Perhaps Tchaikovsky thought similarly, since the end result is a theme that is *très douce* and not *ricaneuse* at all.

16 Wiley, *Tchaikovsky's Ballets*, p. 161.

17 Ibid., p. 161.

18 Brown, *Tchaikovsky*, p. 339.

19 Wiley, *Tchaikovsky's Ballets*, p. 228. Auguste Mustel was the inventor of the celesta.

20 Wiley, *Tchaikovsky's Ballets*, p. 234. Composer Mikhail Ippolitov-Ivanov had notated the Georgian lullaby and sent it to Tchaikovsky.

15 The romantic ballet and its critics: dance goes public

1 See also Jeremy Noble's article on Opera criticism in *Grove Music Online*. Among the fictional accounts of life at the Opéra are Albéric Second, *Les Petits Mystères de l'Opéra* (Paris: G. Kugelman/Bernard Latte 1844); and Albert Smith, *The Natural History of the Ballet Girl* (London: D. Bogue 1847).

2 See Ivor Guest, *The Romantic Ballet in Paris* (London: Dance Books, 1980), p. 109.

3 Ivor Guest, "Introduction", in Théophile Gautier, *Gautier on Dance*, ed. Ivor Guest (London: Dance Books 1986), pp. xix–xxvi; p. xxii.

4 Quoted in Marian Smith, "About the House", in Roger Parker and Mary Ann Smart (eds.), *Reading Critics Reading: Opera and Ballet Criticism in France from the Revolution to 1848* (Oxford: Oxford University Press, 2001), p. 225.

5 Théophile Gautier, *Histoire de l'art dramatique en France depuis vingt-cinq ans*, 6 vols. (Leipzig: Edition Hetzel, 1858–9) (Geneva: Slatkine Reprints 1968), vol. I, p. i.

6 Gautier, *Gautier on Dance*, p. 58.

7 Jules Janin, *Journal des débats*, 6 December 1833.

8 Janin, *Journal des débats*, 27 June 1832.

9 Gautier, *Histoire de l'art dramatique*, vol. I, p. 127.

10 Gautier, *Gautier on Dance*, p. 6.

11 Anonymous critic of the *Revue et gazette musicale de Paris*, 18 August 1839, on Fanny Elssler dancing the *cachucha*.

12 Susan Bernstein, *Virtuosity of the Nineteenth Century: Performing Music and Language in Heine, Liszt, and Baudelaire* (Stanford, Calif.: Stanford University Press, 1998), p. 11.

13 Louis Gentil, in Jean-Louis Tamvaco (ed.), *Les Cancans de l'Opéra*, 2 vols. (Paris : CNRS, 2000), vol. i, p. 338.

14 Charles Baudelaire, *La Fanfarlo*, in *The Poems in Prose*, vol. ii, ed. and trans. Francis Scarfe (London: Anvil Press, 1989), pp. 214–63; pp. 245–7.

16 The soul of the shoe

1 Théophile Gautier, in: *Gautier on Dance*, selected, trans. and annotated Ivor Guest (London: Dance Books, 1986), p. 15.

2 Ibid., p. 140.

3 Cf. Judith Chazin-Bennahum on Jean-Georges Noverre in Chapter 2.

4 Carlo Blasis, *Traité élémentaire, théorique, et pratique de l'art de la danse* was published in 1820. See Fig. 14.

5 Cf. *New Grove Dictionary of Music and Musicians*, ed. Stanley Sadie and John Tyrrell, 2nd edn (London: Macmillan, 2001). Entry Theobald Boehm.

6 The scene was later immortalised in Edgar Degas's painting *The Ballet Scene from Meyerbeer's Opera, "Robert le Diable"*, 1876.

7 Heinrich Heine, *Elementargeister* (Berlin, Paris: Säkularausgabe Akademieverlag and Edn. du CNRS 1979), vol. ix, p. 95. Trans. Marion Kant.

8 First draft of libretto for *Giselle*. Cf. Théophile Gautier, "Théatres, Mystère, Comédies et Ballets", in *OEuvres complètes* (Geneva: Slatkine Reprints, 1978), vol. viii, p. 267.

9 Tutu, "childish alteration of *cucu*, dim. of *cul* – rump or buttock", term used since around 1910. *Oxford English Dictionary* (Oxford: Clarendon Press, New York: Oxford University Press, 1991), entry "tutu". Cf. the comprehensive overview of the evolution of the tutu in Martine Kahane et al., *Le tutu* (Paris: Flammarion, Les petits guides de l'Opéra, 2000).

10 Théophile Gautier, *Peau de Tigre*. (Paris, 1866), pp. 335–6, quoted in Judith Chazin-Bennahum, *The Lure of Perfection*, (London and New York: Routledge, 2005), p. 194.

11 When the tutu was shortened even further and nothing remained but the tulle sticking out at the hip, the tutu required a metal hoop to keep it in shape.

12 This is one of the distinctions between the Russian and the American school. George Balanchine preferred a gentle rise, whereas the Vaganova style emphasised forcefulness and strength.

13 Dr Janice Bruckner, anthropologist, formerly Director of Research for the department of physical therapy at Philadelphia's Jefferson University, now at Widener University Pennsylvania, is the inventor of this pointe shoe. She developed it together with Prosthetic Orthotic Solutions International. Cf. Marion Kant, "The New Ballet Shoe", in *Ballettanz* (Berlin: Friedrich Verlag, 2004), p. 74.

17 Ballet avant-garde I: the Ballets Suédois and its modernist concept

1 *Berlingske Tidende* (Copenhagen), 12 September 1922.

2 *Pall Mall Gazette*, 21 October 1922.

3 Francis Picabia, "Rolf de Maré", *La Danse* (November–December 1924), unpaginated.

4 Jean Cocteau, *La Danse* (June 1921), unpaginated.

5 *The Minneapolis Tribune*, 22 May 1930.

6 *New York Telegraph*, 17 November 1923.

7 *Dagens Nyheter* (Stockholm), 26 May 1925.

8 Reynaldo Hahn in *Excelsior*, 10 November 1920.

9 *The Spectator*, 25 December 1920.

10 *Midi* (Brussels), 3 June 1921.

11 *Die Weltbühne*, 27 April 1922.

18 Ballet avant-garde II: The 'New' Ballet – Russian and Soviet dance in the twentieth century

1 Elizabeth Souritz, *Soviet Choreographers in the 1920s*, trans. Lynn Visson, ed. Sally Banes (Durham, N.C.: Duke University Press, 1990), p. 140.

19 George Balanchine

1 Michael Walsh, "The Joy of Pure Movement", *Time Magazine*, 9 May, 1983.

2 Quoted in Bernard Taper, *Balanchine: A Biography* (New York: Times Books, 1984), p. 51.

3 Terry Teachout, *All in the Dances: A Brief Life of George Balanchine*. (Orlando, Fla: Harcourt, 2004), p. 3.

4 Charles Joseph, *Stravinsky and Balanchine: A Journey of Invention* (New Haven: Yale University Press, 2002), p. xi.

5 Edwin Denby, *Dancers, Buildings and People in the Streets* (New York: Horizon Press, 1965), p. 84.

6 Francis Mason, *I Remember Balanchine* (New York: Doubleday, 1991), p. vii.

7 See Stephanie Jordan, *Moving Music: Dialogues with Music in Twentieth-Century Ballet* (London: Dance Books, 2000), pp. 123 and 87.

8 Balanchine picked music for its *dansante* quality; he held steadfast opinions about what kind of music was danceable.

9 Quoted in Joseph, *Stravinsky and Balanchine*, p. 295. Originally from Igor Stravinsky's *Themes and Conclusions* (repr. Berkeley: University of California Press, 1982). On the dispute over the authenticity of this well-known quotation, see Joseph, Stravinsky and Balanchine, p. 411, n. 35. Stravinsky is referring to *Movements for Piano and Orchestra*.

10 For a detailed account from this time period, see Yuri Slonimsky's memoir in Mason, *I Remember Balanchine*, pp. 19–78.

11 Mason, *I Remember Balanchine*, p. 7. Danilova and Balanchine were never legally married but were seen as such within their circle during the time they were together.

12 *Apollo* was originally entitled *Apollon musagète*. For its various titles, see Harvey Simmonds (ed.), *Choreography by George Balanchine: A Catalogue of Works* (New York: Eakins Press Foundation, 1983), p. 86. Adolph Bolm was the first to choreograph to this score; his version made its debut 27 April 1928, and Balanchine's followed June 12 of the same year.

13 Taper, *Balanchine*, p. 100.

14 See Beth Genné, "'Glorifying the American Woman': Josephine Baker and George Balanchine", *Discourses in Dance*, 3/1 (2006), pp. 29–65.

15 Ibid., p. 35.

16 See ibid.

17 *Apollo* was not composed for Balanchine; Balanchine only commissioned four scores from the composer.

18 Joseph, *Stravinsky and Balanchine*, p. 14.

19 Robert Gottlieb, *George Balanchine: The Ballet Maker* (New York: Harper Collins, 2004), p. 206. (From a reprint of an interview published in *Life* magazine, 11 June, 1965.)

20 See Simmonds, *Choreography by Balanchine*, p. 117. Listed as "Serenade in C for string orchestra, Op. 48, 1880, first three movements; arranged and reorchestrated by George Antheil". The fourth movement (*Tema Russo*) was added in 1940 and inserted before the *Elegy*.

21 See Costas (ed.), *Balanchine: Celebrating a Life in Dance* (Windsor, Conn.: Tide-mark Press, 2003), p. 149.

22 Balanchine, *Balanchine's New Complete Stories of the Great Ballets*, (ed.) Francis Mason (New York: Doubleday, 1968), p. 363.

23 Balanchine, *Balanchine's New Complete Stories*, p. 365.

24 Taper, *Balanchine*, p. 160.

25 Gottlieb, *George Balanchine*, pp. 167–8. A memory of Barbara Horgan.

26 See Genné, "Glorifying the American Woman".

27 Solomon Volkov, *Balanchine's Tchaikovsky: Interviews with George Balanchine* (New York: Sunon & Schuster, 1985), pp. 147–8.

28 Anon., "Ballet Comes into its Own", *Musical America*, 64 (April 1944), p. 16. The author cites successful American-themed ballets such as *Rodeo, Billy the Kid, Filling Station* and *Fancy Free* (by Jerome Robbins – soon Balanchine's associate artistic director of NYCB).

29 Ronald Eyer, "'Song of Norway' Scores Hit" (Review), *Musical Times* 64 (September 1944), p. 15.

30 Balanchine, *New Complete Stories*, p. 171.

31 Jordan, *Moving Music*, pp. 112–13.

32 Teachout, *All in the Dances*, p. 87.

33 See Tim Scholl, *From Petipa to Balanchine* (London: Routledge, 1994).

34 See Taper, *Balanchine*, pp. 187–8. Balanchine's choreography was to Gershwin's *American in Paris,* which was dropped by director Samuel Goldwyn due to his "too experimental camera techniques" (Robert Gottlieb, *George Balanchine*, p. 92).

35 Costas, *Balanchine: Celebrating a Life in Dance*, pp. 23–5.

36 Ibid.

37 Ibid.

38 Jordan, *Moving Music*, pp. 122–3.

39 Jordan, *Music Dances* (video recording).

40 Jordan, *Moving Music*, p. 114.

41 Quoted in Gottlieb, *George Balanchine*, p. 181.

42 Ibid., p. 182.

43 Richard Buckle in collaboration with John Taras, *George Balanchine: Ballet Master* (New York: Random House, 1988) p. 269.

20 Balanchine and the deconstruction of classicism

1 André Levinson, "Le Deuxième Spectacle des Ballets Russes: *Le Bal*", *Comoedia* (30 May 1929), clipping in the collection of the Bibliothèque Nationale, Archives Rondel (hereafter abbreviated AR). All translations are mine unless otherwise indicated.

2 Bernard Taper, *Balanchine: A Biography* (Berkeley: University of California Press, 1996), p. 292.

3 André Levinson, "Grandeur et décadence des 'ballets russes'", in *La Danse d'aujourd'hui* (Paris: Editions Duchartre et Van Buggenhoudt, 1929), pp. 9–10.

4 André Levinson, "Some Commonplaces on the Dance" (1922), in Joan Acocella and Lynn Garafola, (eds.), *André Levinson on Dance: Writings from Paris in the Twenties* (Hanover,

N. H.: University Press of New England/Wesleyan University Press, 1991), p. 30.

5 "Grandeur", pp. 20–1.

6 Ibid., p. 17; D. Sordet, Review of the Ballets Russes (27 June 1928), AR.

7 Alexandra Danilova, *Choura: The Memoirs of Alexandra Danilova* (New York: Alfred A. Knopf, 1986), pp. 102–3. See also M. Hunt, "*The Prodigal Son*'s Russian Roots: Avant-Garde and Icons", *Dance Chronicle* 5/1 (1982), p. 33.

8 Danilova, *Choura*, pp. 102–3.

9 Levinson, "Le Deuxième Spectacle"; L. Laloy, "Théâtre Sarah-Bernhardt (Ballets Diaghilev): *Le Bal*", *L'Ere nouvelle* (30 May 1929), AR; W. George, "L'art à la scène: En marge des Ballets Russes", *Scène* (5 June 1929), AR.

10 André Levinson, *Les Visages de la danse* (Paris: Bernard Grasset, 1933); in Acocella and Garafola, *Levinson on Danse*, caption accompanying plate 11.

11 André Levinson, "La Chorégraphie et l'interprétation", *Comoedia* (29 May 1927), AR.

12 Ibid.

13 Danilova Choura, p. 87.

14 Levinson, "La Chorégraphie".

15 George Balanchine, *Balanchine's New Complete Stories of the Great Ballets*, ed. Francis Mason (Garden City, N.Y.: Doubleday, 1954), p. 10.

16 On Balanchine and gender, see the analysis of *Agon* (1957) in Sally Banes, *Dancing Women: Female Bodies on Stage* (London: Routledge, 1998) as well as Ann Daly, "The Balanchine Woman: Of Hummingbirds and Channel Swimmers", *Drama Review* 31/1 (Spring 1987), pp. 9–21.

17 Richard Buckle, *Diaghilev* (New York: Atheneum, 1979), p. 470.

18 See, for example, Tim Scholl, *From Petipa to Balanchine: Classical Revival and the Modernization of Ballet* (London: Routledge, 1994), p. 97.

19 Souvenir programme from the December 1928–January 1929 season at the Théâtre de l'Opéra, Paris, AR.

20 P.-B. Gheusi, "Les Ballets Russes", *Figaro* (19 June 1928), AR. These links are discussed in D. Harris, "Balanchine: Working with Stravinsky", *Ballet Review* 10/2 (Summer 1982), p. 20.

21 B. de Schoelzer, "Chronique Musicale: Les Ballets Russes de 1928", *Nouvelle revue française* (1 July 1928), AR.

22 Louis Laloy, "'Apollon musagète,' ballet de Stravinsky", *Ere nouvelle* (17 June 1928), AR.

23 André Levinson, "Apollon-Musagète", *Candide* (21 June 1928), AR.

24 André Levinson, "Une escale des 'Ballets Russes'", *Candide* (3 January 1929), AR.

25 André Levinson, "Apollon-Musagète".

26 George Balanchine, "Vyshe vsyekh masterov" ("The Greatest Master of them All"), in *Marius Petipa: materialy, vospominaniia, stat'i* (*Marius Petipa: Documents, Reminiscences, Essays*), ed. A. Nekhendzi (Leningrad: Leningrad State Theatre Museum, 1971), pp. 277–82. Trans. Irina Klyagin.

21 *The Nutcracker*: a cultural icon

1 Quoted in Roland John Wiley, *The Life and Ballets of Lev Ivanov: Choreographer of The Nutcracker and "Swan Lake"* (Oxford: Clarendon Press, 1997), p. 140. Wiley offers many details of the 1892 *Nutcracker* premiere.

2 Jack Anderson, *The Nutcracker Ballet* (New York: Gallery Books, 1979), p. 82. Anderson was the first to chronicle the many versions of the ballet and suggest it had become an American tradition.

3 Ibid., pp. 92–6. Anderson spells the Russian's name "Sergueeff".

4 Cobbett Steinberg, *San Francisco Ballet: The First Fifty Years* (San Francisco: The San Francisco Ballet Association, 1983), pp. 63–4.

5 Discussion of the ways in which Balanchine incorporated Africanist influences in his version of neoclassical ballet can be found in Brenda Dixon Gottschild's *Digging the Africanist Presence in American Performance: Dance and Other Contexts*. (Westport, Conn.: Greenwood Press, 1996).

6 Solomon Volkov, *Balanchine's Tchaikovsky: Interviews with George Balanchine*. (New York: Simon & Schuster, 1985), pp. 192–3.

7 This violin solo, which does not appear in the original *Nutcracker* score, was cut from the composer's *Sleeping Beauty* score (it is sometimes restored in current versions). Tchaikovsky had used its melody again in *The Nutcracker*, so Balanchine's bringing the two together with this interpolation made musical sense (Volkov, *Balanchine's Tchaikovsky*, p. 188).

8 Cf. Tania Branigan. "Barbie sponsors Nutcracker ballet", *Guardian*, Monday, 10 September 2001.

9 Billy Strayhorn collaborated with Ellington on the original adaptation, which only used excerpts of the ballet. For the Bird *Nutcracker*, composer and musical director David Berger added to the score.

10 Edwin Denby, *Dance Writings*, ed. Robert Cornfield and William MacKay (New York: Knopf, 1986), pp. 272–5.

11 Ibid., pp. 272–3.

12 These dances are discussed at more length in Jennifer Fisher, "Arabian Coffee in the Land of the Sweets", *Dance Research Journal* 35/2 and

36/1 (Winter 2003 and Summer 2004), pp. 146–63.

13 Edward Said, *Orientalism* (London: Routledge & Kegan Paul, 1978), p. 1.

14 John M. MacKenzie, *Orientalism: History, Theory and the Arts* (Manchester and New York: Manchester University Press, 1995), p. 211.

22 From *Swan Lake* to *Red Girl's Regiment*: ballet's sinicisation

1 Marcel Granet, *Danses et legends de la Chine ancienne*, 2 vols. (Paris: Presses Universitaires de France, 1959). See also E. Yuan, *Zhongguo Wudao Yixianglun* (Beijing: Wenhua Yishu, 1995).

2 Li Yu, *Xianqing Ouji*, 16 vols. (Shanghai: Shanghai Guji, 1995), vol. VII, pp. 593–4.

3 Their love story and history has been the subject of many writers, poets and historians.

4 Wang Kefen and Long Yingpei, *Zhongguo Jinxiandai Dangdai Wudao Fazhangshi* (Beijing: Renmin Yingyu Chubanshe, 1999), pp. 40–3; Wang Ningning, Jiang Dong and Du Xiaoqing, *Zhongguo Wudaoshi* (Beijing: Wenhua Yishu, 1998), pp. 69–71. See also Ou Jian-ping, "From 'Beasts' to 'Flowers': Modern Dance in China", in Ruth and John Solomon (eds.), *East Meets West in Dance: Voices in the Cross-Cultural Dialogue* (Chur, Switzerland: Harwood Academic Publishers, 1995), pp. 29–35.

5 Ronglin continued to promote ballet during the nationalist and communist eras. She died in Beijing in 1973. She left a memoir *Qinggong Suiji* or "The Miscellaneous of the Qing Court".

6 The illustrious *Dianshizhai Huabao* is one of them.

7 Mei Lanfang was the most famous Peking opera singer from the late Qing through the communist era. He was the founder of a new style of singing. He held numerous positions during the communist era. Tian Han was a famous writer and poet. He wrote more than one hundred plays, many songs/poems, and the lyric for the National Anthem.

8 Wang Kefen and Long Yingpei, *Zhongguo Jinxiandai Dangdai Wudao Fazhangshi* (Beijing: Renmin Yingyu Chubanshe, 1999), pp. 64–72; Wang Ningning, Jiang Dong and Du Xiaoqing, *Zhongguo Wudaoshi* (Beijing: Wenhua Yishu, 1998), pp. 83–7. Ou Jian-ping, "From 'Beasts' to 'Flowers': Modern Dance in China", pp. 29–35.

9 Wang Kefen and Long Yingpei, *Zhongguo Jinxiandai Dangdai Wudao Fazhangshi* (Beijing: Renmin Yingyu Chubanshe, 1999), pp.72–80; Wang Ningning, Jiang Dong and Du Xiaoqing, *Zhongguo Wudaoshi* (Beijing: Wenhua Yishu, 1998), pp. 88–92. Ou Jian-ping, "From 'Beasts' to 'Flowers': Modern Dance in China", pp. 29–35.

10 Lin Cunxin, *Mao's Last Dancer: A Memoir* (New York: G. P. Putnam's Sons, 2003).

23 *Giselle* in a Cuban accent

1 See A. Alonso, "Bailar ha sido mi vida", interview by Lester Tome, in *El Mercurio*, 19 November, 2000 (Santiago, Chile), p. E24.

2 See A. Alonso, "Primeros recuerdos, primeros pasos en la danza", originally issued in T. Gutiérrez, *Alicia Alonso prima ballerina assoluta, imagen de una plenitud (testimonios y recuerdos de la artista)* (Barcelona: Edición Salvat, 1981), repr. in A. Alonso, *Diálogos con la danza*, ed. P. Simón (La Habana: Letras Cubanas, 1986), p. 13.

3 See Alonso, "Bailar ha sido mi vida", p. E24.

4 See E. Denby, "Youth and Old Giselle", in *New York Herald Tribune*, 24 October, 1945, repr. In E. Denby, *Looking at the Dance* (New York: Horizon Press, 1968), p. 167.

5 See W. Terry, "The Ballet Theatre", in *New York Herald Tribune*, 15 April, 1955, repr. in W. Terry, *I Was There: Selected Dance Reviews and Articles, 1936–1976* (New York: Dekker, 1978), p. 295.

6 See A. Alonso, "Bailar ha sido mi vida", p. E24.

7 Olivier Merlin's review (*Le Monde*, 1966) is quoted in the booklet *XLV Aniversario de Alicia Alonso en el personaje de Giselle* (Havana: Gran Teatro de la Habana, 1988), no pages.

8 A facsimile of Anton Dolin's letter, written in Montreal on 24 and 26 June 1967, is reproduced in *XLV Aniversario de Alicia Alonso en el personaje de Giselle*, no pages.

9 See A. Alonso, "El arte no tiene patria, pero el artista sí", transcript of an interview by Raúl Rivero, in Alonso, *Diálogos con la danza*, p. 177.

10 Arnold Haskell is quoted by Pedro Simón in A. Alonso and P. Simón, "Fuentes y antecedentes de la escuela cubana de ballet" (Sources and antecedents of the Cuban School of ballet), transcript of a lecture offered by Simón and Alonso at the offices of the Union of Cuban Journalist on 10 November 1978, in Alonso, *Diálogos con la danza*, pp. 44–5.

11 See Alonso and Simón, "Fuentes y antecedentes de la escuela cubana de ballet", p. 25.

12 See Alonso, "Bailar ha sido mi vida", p. E24.

13 Alonso is quoted by Walter Terry in W. Terry, *Alicia and her Ballet Nacional de Cuba* (Garden City, N.Y.: Anchor Books, 1981), pp. 34–5.

14 See the prologue to *XLV Aniversario de Alicia Alonso en el personaje de Giselle*, no pages. The author of the prologue is unknown. Its content was probably sanctioned by Alonso as director of the National Ballet of Cuba and the Havana Grand Theatre, which issued the publication.

15 The programme is reproduced in F. Rey Alfonso and P. Simón, *Alicia Alonso: Órbita de una Leyenda* (Madrid: SGAE, 1996), pp. 190–1.

16 See Alonso and Simón, "Fuentes y antecedentes de la escuela cubana de ballet", p. 35.

17 Sociedad Pro-Arte Musical, founded in 1919 in Havana. Alonso received her first ballet classes in Pro-Arte's studios. Later in her career, the Ballet Alicia Alonso appeared at the Auditorium Theatre as part of Pro-Arte's series.

18 See Alonso and Simón, "Fuentes y antecedentes de la escuela cubana de ballet", p. 55. Italics added.

19 See Alfonso and Simón, *Alicia Alonso: Órbita de una Leyenda*, pp. 135–4.

20 In 1978 and 1979, the company danced *Giselle, Coppélia, Grand pas de quatre* and *Les Sylphides*. The programme for these two initial tours also included pieces by Cuban choreographers, but their choreography did not receive positive criticism. For later visits the group therefore focused on its European repertory. Recent tours have featured the company in a production of *Cinderella* by Cuban-French choreographer Pedro Consuegra (1998), *Giselle* (1999), excerpts from *Don Quixote, Nutcracker, Sleeping Beauty, Giselle, Coppélia* and *Swan Lake* (2001), *Don Quixote* (2003) and *Swan Lake*, Azari Plissetski's *Canto Vital* and Antonio Gades's *Blood Wedding* (2004).

24 European ballet in the age of ideologies

1 Isadora Duncan, *My Life* (New York: H. Liveright, 1928), p. 32.

2 Rudolf von Laban, *Modern Educational Dance* (London: Macdonald & Evans 1948), p. 5

3 Cf. Chapter 18 by Tim Scholl, "The 'New' ballet: Russian and Soviet dance in the twentieth century" and chapter 17 by Erik Näslund, "The Ballets Suédois and its modernist concept" in this volume.

4 Cf. Chapter 9 by Inge Baxmann "The French Revolution and its spectacles" in this volume.

5 F. T. Marinetti, *Teoria e invenzione futurista*, ed. Luciano De Maria (Milan: Arnaldo Mondadori Editore, 1983), pp. 144–52. trans. Jonathan Steinberg.

6 Cf. Agrippina Vaganova, *Basic Principles of Classical Ballet*, trans. Anatak Chujoy (1953; New York: Dover Publications 1969); the book is still in print and widely used.

7 The Ballets Russes de Monte Carlo were founded in 1932, as a fusion of the Ballets de l'Opéra de Monte Carlo and the Ballet de l'Opéra Russe à Paris, with Colonel de Basil as director and René Blum as artistic director. The Ballets de Monte Carlo, founded by René Blum at Monte Carlo in 1936 were the result of a row between him and Colonel de Basil. Léonide Massine took over as artistic director in 1938 and the company's name was changed to Ballet Russe de Monte Carlo. In 1985 Les Ballets de Monte Carlo saw a brief revival. The Ballet Russe de Monte Carlo, a descendant of René Blum's Ballets de Monte Carlo opened in 1938 and lasted into the 1950s.

8 Théophile Gautier, *Mademoiselle Maupin* (Paris: 1834), p. 22.

9 According to ballet critic Clement Crisp, the future is bleak: "We have stopped being a nation of ballet choreographers, we have stopped being a nation of interesting ballet-dancers, and we have stopped being a nation who go to ballet to enjoy ourselves." Interview with Ismene Brown, *Dance Magazine* (December 2001). http://www.dance.co.uk/magazines/yr_01/dec01/ismene_b_int_clement_c.htm

Bibliography and further reading

Part I
Dance treatises
Arbeau, Thoinot, *Orchésographie*. Langres, 1588. Facsimile edition, Geneva: Minkoff, 1972, English trans. Mary Steward Evans, 1948. Reprinted with introduction and notes by Julia Sutton, New York: Dover Publications, 1967.

Arena, Antonius, *Ad suos compagniones studiantes*. *c*.1529. English trans. in John Guthrie and Marino Zorzi, "Rules of Dancing: Antonius Arena", *Dance Research* 4/2 (1986).

Brussels, Bibliothèque Royale 9085. *Le Manuscrit dit des Basses Danses de la Bibliothèque de Bourgogne*. Facsimile edition Graz: Akademische Druck-u. Verlagsanstalt, 1988. Transcript and edition in David Wilson and Véronique Daniels, "The Basse Dance Handbook", forthcoming.

Caroso, Fabritio, *Il Ballarino*. Venice, 1581. Facs. edn New York: Broude Brothers, 1967.

—, *Nobiltà di Dame*. Venice, 1600. Facs. edn Bologna: Forni, 1980. English: ed and trans. Julia Sutton, *Courtly Dance of the Renaissance: A New Translation and Edition of the* Nobiltà di Dame *1600. Fabritio Caroso*. New York: Dover, 1995.

Cornazano, Antonio, *Libro dell'arte del danzare*. Rome, Biblioteca Apostolica Vaticana, Codex Capponiano, 203. English: trans. Madeleine Inglehearn and Peggy Forsyth, *The Book on the Art of Dancing: Antonio Cornazano*. London: Dance Books, 1981.

Domenio da Piacenza, *De arte saltandj & choreas ducendj De la arte di ballare et danzare*. Paris, Bibliothèque Nationale, MS fonds it. 972. English trans. of choreographies David Wilson, *101 Italian Dances c. 1450–c. 1550: A Critical Translation*. Cambridge: Early Dance Circle, 1999.

Gresley of Drakelow papers. Derbyshire Record Office, D77 box 38, pp. 51–79. A transcription of this material is found in David Fallows, "The Gresley Dance Collection, *c*. 1500", *RMA Research Chronicle* 29 (1996).

Guglielmo Ebreo da Pesaro, *Guilielmi Hebraei pisauriensis de pratica seu arte tripudii vulgare opusculum incipit*. 1463. Paris, Bibliothèque Nationale, MS fonds it. 973. English: ed. and trans. Barbara Sparti, *De pratica seu arte tripudii: On the Practice or Art of Dancing*. Oxford: Clarendon Press, 1993.

Negri, Cesare, *Le Gratie d'Amore*. Milan, 1602. Facs. edn New York: Broude Brothers, 1969. English: G. Yvonne Kendall, "*Le Gratie d'Amore* 1602 by Cesare Negri: Translation and Commentary". D.M.A. Stanford University, 1985.

Santucci, Ercole, *Mastro da ballo*, 1614. Facs. edn, Hildesheim: Olms, 2004, with intro. by Barbara Sparti.

S'ensuit l'art et instruction de bien dancer. Paris, Michel Toulouze, n.d. Facs. edn, Geneva: Minkoff, 1985.

Renaissance

Arcangeli, Alessandro, *Davide o Salomè? Il dibattito europeo sulla danza nella prima età moderna*.Rome: Viella, 2000.

Brainard, Ingrid, *The Art of Courtly Dancing in the Early Renaissance*. West Newton, Mass.: Private Pub. 1989.

Carter, Françoise, "Number Symbolism and Renaissance Choreography". *Dance Research* 10/1 (1992), pp. 21–39.

Fermor, Sharon, "Studies in the Depiction of the Moving Figure in Italian Renaissance Art, Art Criticism, and Dance Theory". Ph.D. diss., Warburg Institute, University of London, 1990.

—, "Movement and Gender in Sixteenth-Century Italian Painting". In Kathleen Adler and Marcia Pointon (eds.), *The Body Imaged: The Human Form and Visual Cultures since the Renaissance*. Cambridge: Cambridge University Press, 1993, pp. 129–45.

Heartz, Daniel, "The Basse Danse: Its Evolution circa 1450 to 1550". *Annales musicologiques* 6 (1958–63), pp. 287–340.

Jones, Pamela, "Spectacle in Milan: Cesare Negri's Torch Dances". *Early Music* 14/2 (1986), pp. 182–96.

Kendall, G. Yvonne, "Dance, Music and Theatre in Late Cinquecento Milan". *Early Music* 32/1 (2004), pp. 75–95.

McGinnis, Katherine Tucker, "Moving in High Circles: Courts, Dance, and Dancing Masters in Italy in the Long Sixteenth Century". Ph.D. diss., University of North Carolina, 2001.

Marrocco, W. Thomas, *Inventory of 15th-Century Bassedanze, Balli, and Balletti*. New York: CORD, 1981.

Nevile, Jennifer, "Cavalieri's Theatrical *Ballo*: 'O che nuovo miracolo': A Reconstruction". *Dance Chronicle* 21/3 (1998), pp. 353–88.

—, "Cavalieri's Theatrical *Ballo* and the Social Dances of Caroso and Negri". *Dance Chronicle* 22/1 (1999), pp. 119–33.

—, "Dance and the Garden: Moving and Static Choreography in Renaissance Europe". *Renaissance Quarterly* 52/3 (1999), pp. 805–36.

—, *The Eloquent Body: Dance and Humanist Culture in Fifteenth-Century Italy*. Bloomington: Indiana University Press, 2004.

Padovan, Maurizio (ed.), *Guglielmo Ebreo da Pesaro e la danza nelle corti italiane del xv secolo*. Pisa: Pacini, 1990.

Sparti, Barbara, "Rôti Bouilli: Take Two 'el gioioso fiorito' ". *Studi Musicali* 24/2 (1995), pp. 231–61.

—, "Would You Like to Dance This Frottola? Choreographic Concordances in Two Early Sixteenth-Century Tuscan Sources". *Musica disciplina* 50 (1996), pp. 135–65.

Sutton, Julia, "Musical Forms and Dance Forms in the Dance Manuals of Sixteenth Century Italy: Plato and the Varieties of Variation". In *The Marriage of Music and Dance*. Papers from a conference at the Guildhall School of Music and Drama, London 1991. Cambridge: National Early Music Association, 1992.

Ballet de cour and baroque

Anthony, James R., *French Baroque Music from Beaujoyeulx to Rameau.* New York and London: Norton, 1974; rev. edn 1981.

Apostolidès, Jean-Marie, *Le Roi-machine: Spectacle et politique au temps de Louis XIV.* Paris: Editions de minuit, 1981.

Auld, Louis E., "Social Diversity in the *Ballet de Cour:* Le Château de Bicëtre". In A. Maynor Hardee (ed.), *Theater and Society in French Literature.* Columbia, S.C., 1988.

Bouquet-Boyer, Marie-Thérèse (ed.), *Les Noces de Pélée et de Thétis. Venise, 1639 – Paris, 1654,* Actes du colloque international de Chambéry et de Turin, 3–7 novembre 1999, Bern, New York, Oxford, and Vienna: Peter Lang, 2001.

Buch, David J., *Dance Music from the Ballets de Cour, 1575–1651: Historical Commentary, Source Study, and Transcriptions from the Philidor Manuscripts.* New York: Stuyvesant, 1994.

Christout, Marie Françoise, *Le Ballet de cour au XVII° siècle.* Geneva: Minkoff, 1987.

—, *Le Ballet de cour de Louis XIV. 1643–1672.* Paris: A. & J. Picard, 1967; new edn Paris: Centre national de la danse and Picard, 2005.

Coeyman, Barbara, "Theatres for Opera and Ballet during the Reigns of Louis XIV and Louis XV". *Early Music* (18 February 1990), pp. 22–37.

Debord, Guy, *Society of the Spectacle,* trans. Donald Nicholson-Smith. New York: Zone Books, 1994.

Feuillet, Raoul Auger, *Chorégraphie ou l'art de décrire la danse, par caractères, figures et signes démonstratifs.* Paris: Feuillet & Brunel, 1700.

Franko, Mark , *Dance as Text. Ideologies of the Baroque Body.* Cambridge: Cambridge University Press, 1993.

Gorce, Jerôme de la,"Un aspetto del mestiere teatrale di Torelli: la riutilizzazione delle scenografie dell' 'Andromède' per il 'Ballet de la nuit". In Francesco Milesi (ed.), *Giacomo Torelli. L'invenzione scenica nell'Europa barocca.* Fano: Fondazione Cassa di Risparmio di Fano, 2000.

Harris-Warrick, Rebecca, and Marsh, Carol G., *Musical Theatre at the Court of Louis XIV: Le Mariage de la Grosse Cathos.* Cambridge: Cambridge University Press, 1994.

Haskell, Harry, *The Early Music Revival: A History.* London: Thames & Hudson, 1988.

Hilton, Wendy, *Dance of Court and Theater: The French Noble Style, 1690–1725.* Princeton: Princeton Book Co., 1981.

Hourcade, Philippe, *Mascarades et ballets du Grand Siècle, 1643-1715.* Paris: Desjonquières et Centre National de la Danse, 2002.

Lacroix, Paul, *Ballet, et mascarades de cour sous Henri IV et Louis XIII (de 1581 à 1652).* Geneva: J. Gay & fils, 1868–70, repr. Geneva: Slatkine, 1968.

Laurenti, Jean Noel, "Feuillet's Thinking". In *Traces of Dance. Drawing and Notations of Choreographers,* ed. Laurence Louppe. Paris: Editions Dis Voir, n.d.

De Lauze, François, *Apologie de la danse et parfaite méthode de l'enseigner tant aux Cavaliers qu'aux dames.* n.p., 1623.

Lippe, Rudolf zur, *Naturbeherrschung am Menschen*. Frankfurt/M: Syndikat Reprise, 1979.

McGowan, Margaret M., *L'Art du ballet de cour en France 1581–1643*. Paris: Centre National de la Recherche Scientifique, 1965, repr. 1978.

Ménestrier, Claude-François, *Des représentations en musique anciennes et modernes*. Paris: René Guignard, 1687; repr. Geneva: Minkoff, 1992.

—, *Des ballets anciens et modernes selon les règles du théâtre*. Paris: René Guignard, 1682; repr. Geneva: Minkoff, 1972.

Orgel, Stephen, *The Illusion of Power. Political Theater in the English Renaissance*. Berkeley and Los Angeles: University of California Press, 1975.

Prunières, Henry, *Le Ballet de cour en France avant Benserade et Lully*. Paris: Henri Laurens, 1914; New York and London: Johnson Reprint, 1970.

Pure, Michel de, *Idée des spectacles anciens et nouveaux*. Paris 1668; facs. edn Geneva: Minkoff, 1972.

Rameau, Pierre, *Le Maître à danser*. Paris: Jean Villette, 1725. English: *The Dancing-Master*, trans. John Essex. London: J. Essex & J. Brotherton, 1728.

Rice, Paul F., *The Performing Arts at Fontainebleau from Louis XIV to Louis XVI*. Rochester: University of Rochester Press, 1989.

Saint-Hubert, M. de, *La Manière de composer et de faire réussir les ballets*. Paris: Targa, 1641; repr. Geneva: Minkoff, 1993.

Schlemmer, Oskar, *The Letters and Diaries of Oskar Schlemmer*. Middletown, Conn.: Wesleyan University Press, 1972.

Schwartz, Judith L., and Schlundt, Christena L., *French Court Dance and Dance Music: A Guide to Primary Source Writings, 1643–1789*. Stuyvesant, N.Y.: Pendragon Press, 1987.

Sparti, Barbara, "Dance and Historiography. Le Balet Comique de la Royne: An Italian Perspective", in Ann Buckley and Cynthis Cyrus (eds.), *Festschrift for Ingrid Brainard* (forthcoming).

Taruskin, Richard, *Text and Act: Essays on Music and Performance*. New York: Oxford University Press, 1995.

Tomko, Linda, "Reconstruction", in *International Encyclopedia of Dance*. New York: Oxford University Press, 1998.

Vallière, Louis César de la Baume le Blanc, duc de la, *Ballets, opéra, et autres ouvrages lyriques, par ordre chronologique depuis leur origine*. Paris, 1760.

For an exhaustive bibliography on *ballet de cour* cf. *Bibliographie de l'air de cour* compiled by Georgie Durosoir for the Centre de Musique Baroque de Versailles and available online at http://www.cmbv.com/images/banq/cp/cp014.pdf http://www.cmbv.com/images/banq/cp/cp014.pdf © Georgie Durosoir, CMBV, dépôt légal: novembre 2003.

On the *Balet comique de la Royne*

"Balthasar de Beaujoyeulx, Ballet Comique de la Reine Paris, 1582". In Selma Jeanne Cohen (ed.), *Dance as a Theatre Art: Source Readings in Dance History from 1581 to the Present*. New York: Harper & Row, 1974, pp. 19–31.

Bonniffet, Pierre, "Esquisses du ballet humaniste 1572–1581". In *Le Ballet aux XVIe et XVIIe siècles en France et à la cour de Savoie*. Geneva: Editions Slatkine, Cahiers de l'I.R.H.M.E.S., 1992, pp. 16–49.

Dellaborra, Mariateresa (ed.), *"Une Invention Moderne": Baldassarre da Belgioioso e il "Balet Comique de la Royne".* Lucca: Libreria Musicale Italiana, 1999.

Loret, Jean, *La Muze historique 1650–1665.* 4 vols., ed. C.-L. Livet. Paris, 1857–1878.

MacClintock, Carol and Lander (eds.), *Le Balet Comique de la Royne 1581.* New York: American Institute of Musicology, Musicological Studies and Documents 25, 1971.

McGowan, Margaret (ed.), *Le Balet Comique by Balthazar de Beaujoyeulx.* Binghamton, N.Y.: Center for Medieval and Early Renaissance Studies, 1982.

Prunières, Henry, *Le Ballet de cour en France avant Benserade et Lully.* Paris: Henri Laurens, 1914 ; New York and London: Johnson Reprint, 1970.

Ravelhofer, Barbara (ed.), *Terpsichore 1450-1900, Proceedings of the International Dance Conference.* Ghent, Belgium: The Institute for Historical Dance Practice, 2000.

Woodruff, Diane L., "The 'Balet Comique' in the Petit Bourbon: A Practical View", *Proceedings of the Society of Dance History Scholars.* Riverside: University of California Press, 1986.

Yates, Frances A., *The French Academies of the 16th Century.* London: The Warburg Institute, 1947; Nendeln, Liechtenstein: Kraus Reprint, 1968.

English masques

Sources

Ashbee, A., and Lasocki, D., *et al., A Biographical Dictionary of English Court Musicians, 1485–1714,* 2 vols. Aldershot: Ashgate, 1998.

Court Masques: Jacobean and Caroline Entertainments, 1605–1640, ed. David Lindley. Oxford: Oxford University Press, 1995.

Keller, Robert, database, *The English Dancing Master: An Illustrated Compendium, 1651–1728,* at www.izaak.unh.edu/nhltmd/indexes/dancingmaster/.

McGee, C. E., and Meagher, John, checklists on Tudor and Stuart entertainments, in *Research Opportunities in Renaissance Drama,* since 1982.

McManus, Clare, *Women on the Renaissance Stage: Anna of Denmark and Female Masquing in the Stuart Court 1590–1619.* Manchester: Manchester University Press, 2002.

Records of English Court Music, ed. A. Ashbee, 9 vols. Snodland, Aldershot: Ashbee/Scolar Press, 1986–96.

Tomlinson, Sophie, *Women on Stage in Stuart Drama.* Cambridge: Cambridge University Press, 2005.

General

Britland, Karen, *Drama at the Courts of Queen Henrietta Maria.* Cambridge: Cambridge University Press, 2006.

Daye, Anne, "Torchbearers in the English Masque", *Early Music* 26/2 (1998).

Holman, Peter, *Four and Twenty Fiddlers: The Violin at the English Court, 1540–1690.* Oxford: Clarendon Press, 1993.

Howard, Skiles, *The Politics of Courtly Dancing in Early Modern England.* Amherst: University of Massachusetts Press, 1998.

Inigo Jones: The Theatre of the Stuart Court, ed. S. Orgel and R. Strong, 2 vols. London: Sotheby Parke Bernet, 1973.

Peacock, John, *The Stage Designs of Inigo Jones: The European Context*. Cambridge: Cambridge University Press, 1995.

Ravelhofer, Barbara, *The Early Stuart Masque: Dance, Costume, and Music*. Oxford: Oxford University Press, 2006.

Walls, Peter, *Music in the English Courtly Masque, 1604–1640*. Oxford: Clarendon Press, 1996.

Part II

Adice, G. Léopold, *Théorie de la gymnastique de la danse théâtrale*. Paris: Chais, 1859.

Angiolini, Gasparo, *Dissertation sur les Ballets Pantomimes des anciens*. Vienne: Jean Th. de Trattnern,1765.

Astier, Régine, "In Search of L'Académie Royale de Danse". *York Dance Review* 7 (1978).

—, "La Vie quotidienne des danseurs sous l'Ancien Régime". *Les Goûts reunis*, 3rd series (1982).

Baxmann, Inge, *Die Feste der Französischen Revolution. Inszenierung von Gesellschaft als Natur*. Weinheim/Basel: Beltz 1989.

Blasis, Carlo, *The Code of Terpsichore*, trans. R. Barton. London: James Bullock, 1828.

—, *Notes Upon Dancing, Historical and Practical*, trans. R. Barton. London: M. Delaporte, 1847.

—, *Traité élémentaire, théorique et pratique de l'art de la danse*. Milan: Joseph Beati et Antoine Tenenti, 1820. English: *An Elementary Treatise upon the Theory and Practice of the Art of Dancing*, trans. Mary Stewart Evans. New York: Dover, 1968.

Bonin, Louis, *Die neueste Art zur galanten und theatralischen Tantz-Kunst*. Frankfurt: Joh. Christoff Lochner, 1712.

Beaumont, Cyril W., *Three French Dancers of the 18th Century: Camargo, Sallé, Guimard*. London: C. W. Beaumont, 1934.

Cahusac, Louis de, *La Danse ancienne et moderne ou Traité historique de la Danse*. 3 vols. Paris: Jean Neaulme, 1754.

Campardon, Emile, *L'Académie Royale de Musique au XVIIIe siècle*. Paris: Berger-Levrault & cie, 1884.

Carones, Laura, "Noverre and Angiolini: Polemical Letters". In *Dance Research* 5/I, New York: MacMillan, 1987, pp. 42ff.

Castil-Blaze, François Henri Joseph, *L'Académie Impériale de Musique. Histoire littéraire, musicale, chorégraphique, pittoresque, morale, critique, politique et galante de ce théâtre de 1645 à 1855*. 2 vols. Paris: Castil-Blaze, 1855.

Censer, Jack Richard and Hunt, Lynn, *Liberty, Equality, Fraternity: Exploring the French Revolution*. University Park, Pa.: Pennsylvania State University Press, c.2001.

Chants Révolutionnaires et patriotiques à l'usage des fêtes nationales et décadaires, Paris 1790.

Chapman, John V., "Auguste Vestris and the Expansion of Technique". *Dance Research Journal* 19/1 (1987).

—, "The Paris Opera Ballet School, 1798–1827". *Dance Chronicle* 12/2 (1989).

—, "August Vestris". *International Dictionary of Ballet*. vol. II, 1993.

Chazin-Bennahum, Judith, "Cahusac, Diderot, and Noverre: Three Revolutionary French Writers on Eighteenth-Century Dance". *Theatre Journal* (May 1983), pp. 169–78.

—, *Dance in the Shadow of the Guillotine*. Carbondale and Edwardsville: Southern Illinois University Press, 1988.

—, *The Lure of Perfection: Fashion and Ballet 1780–1830*. New York: Routledge, 2004.

Chéruzel, Maurice, *Jean-Georges Noverre: Levain de la Danse Moderne*. Conférence avec Projections. Paris: Saint-Germain-en-Laye, 1991.

Cohen, Sarah, *Art, Dance and the Body in French Culture of the Ancien Régime*. Cambridge: Cambridge University Press, 2000.

Craine, Debra, and Mackrell, Judith (eds.), *Oxford Dictionary of Dance*. Oxford: Oxford University Press, 2000.

Didelot, Charles Louis, *Three King's Theatre Ballets, 1796–1801*. London, 1796–1801; intro. Roland John Wiley, London: Stainer & Bell, 1994.

Diderot, Denis, *Troisième Entretien sur Le Fils Naturel, Oeuvres Complètes*, ed. J. Assézat and M. Tourneux. Paris: Garnier, 1875–7.

—, *Rameau's Nephew*, trans. L. W. Tancock. Harmondsworth, Midd: Penguin, 1966.

Dufort, Giambattista, *Trattato del ballo nobile*. Naples: Felice Mosca, 1728.

Editions d'Histoire Sociale (ed.), *Jean-Jacques Rousseau dans la Révolution Francaise*. Paris, 1977.

Fairfax, Edmund, *The Styles of Eighteenth-Century Ballet*. Lanham, Md.: Scarecrow Press, 2003.

Feuillet, Raoul Auger, *Chorégraphie ou l'art de décrire la danse, par caractères, figures et signes démonstratifs*. Paris: Feuillet & Brunel, 1700.

Franko, Mark, *Dance as Text. Ideologies of the Baroque Body*. Cambridge: Cambridge University Press, 1993.

Gallini, Giovanni-Andrea, *A Treatise on the Art of Dancing*. London: The author, 1762.

Gravelot et Cochin, *Iconologie ou Traité de la science des allégories à l'usage des artistes*. vol. I, Paris, 1791.

Guest, Ivor F., "Jason and Medea: A Noverre Ballet Reconstructed". *Dancing Times*. London (May 1992).

—, *The Ballet of the Enlightenment: The Establishment of the Ballet d'Action in France, 1770–1793*. London: Dance Books, 1996.

—, *Ballet under Napoleon*. Alton: Dance Books, 2002.

Habermas, Jürgen, *The Structural Transformation of the Public Sphere: An Inquiry into a Category of Bourgeois Society*, trans. Thomas Burger, with Frederick Lawrence. Cambridge, Mass.: MIT Press, 1989.

Halifax, George Savile, Marquess of, *Advice to a Daughter, chiefly with Regard to Religion*. Aberdeen: printed for and by Francis Douglass and William Murray in 1688.

Hammond, Sandra Noll, "Searching for the Sylph: Documentation of Early Developments in Pointe Technique". *Dance Research Journal* 19/2 (1987–8).

Hammond, Sandra N., and Hammond, Phillip E., "Technique and Autonomy in the Development of Art: A Case Study in Ballet". *Dance Research Journal* 21/2 (1989).

Harris-Warrick, Rebecca and Brown, Bruce Alan (eds.), *The Grotesque Dancer on the Eighteenth-Century Stage: Gennaro Magri and his World.* Madison: University of Wisconsin Press, 2004.

Hunt, Lynn Avery, *Politics, Culture, and Class in the French Revolution.* Berkeley : University of California Press, 1984.

Isaac, Mr., *A Collection of Ball-Dances Perform'd at Court: viz. The Richmond, the Rondeau, the Rigadoon, the Favorite, the Spanheim, and the Britannia.*1706.

Jenyns, Soame, *Poems by Soame Jenyns, containing Art of dancing, To Lord Lovelace, Essay on virtue, Written in Locke, Epitaph on Doctor Johnson; to which is prefixed a sketch of the author's life.* Manchester, 1797.

Kirstein, Lincoln, *Movement and Metaphor: Four Centuries of Ballet.* New York: Praeger, 1970.

Koegler, Horst, "The Northern Heirs of Noverre". *Dance and Dancers* (London) (February 1987).

Krüger, Manfred, *Jean-Georges Noverre und das Ballet d'Action.* Emsdetten: Lechte, 1963.

La Caffinière, Alex and Kanter, Katherine, "Why is Noverre not in the Curriculum?" *Dance Now* (London) 3/1 (Spring 1994).

Le Brun, Charles, *Méthode pour apprendre à dessiner les passions*, Amsterdam, 1702.

Lynham, Deryck, *The Chevalier Noverre: Father of Modern Ballet.* London, Sylvan Press, 1950; London: Dance Books, 1972.

McLeave, Sarah, "Marie Sallé: A Letter to the Duchess of Richmond". *Dance Research* 17/1 (Summer 1999), pp. 22–46.

Magri, Gennaro, *Trattato teorico-prattico di ballo.* Naples: Vicenzo Orsino, 1779. English: *Theoretical and Practical Treatise on Dancing*, trans. Mary Skeaping. London: Dance Books, 1988.

Malpied, *Traité sur l'art de la danse.* Paris: Bouïn, 1770.

Michel, Artur, "Le Ballet d'action avant Noverre". *Archives Internationales de la Danse* pt. I vol. 2 (April 1935), pt. 2 vol. 3/4 (October 1935).

Mori-Sugaya, Tatsuko, "Jean Georges Noverre's view on Dance Music". *Society of Dance History Scholars Proceedings.* Conference 2002: Philadelphia, Pa.

Moore, Lillian, "Noverre, First of the Moderns". *Dance Magazine* (September 1952).

North, Roger, *Memoirs of Musick being some historio-criticall collections of that subject* (1728), ed. Edward F. Rimbault. London, 1846.

Noverre, Jean-Georges, *Lettres sur la danse, et sur les ballets.* Lyons: Delaroche, 1760.

—, *Lettres sur la danse et les arts imitateurs.* Paris: Éditions Lieutier, 1952.

—, *Lettres sur la danse, sur les ballets et les arts*, revised and enlarged edition of 1760 *Lettres.* St Petersburg, 1803. English: *Letters on Dancing and on Ballets*, trans. Cyril Beaumont. New York: Dance Horizons, 1968.

Ozouf, Mona, *La Fête Révolutionnaire. 1789–1799.* Paris: Gallimard, 1976.

Pasch, Johann, *Beschreibung wahrer Tanz-Kunst.* Frankfurt: Wolffgang Michahelles & Johann Adolph, 1707.

Plan de Fête à l'Etre Suprême, qui sera célébré à Tours, le 20 Prairial en exécution du Décret du 18 Floréal, l'an second de la République, une et indivisible. Bibliothèque National, Paris.

Pruiksma, Rose A., "Generational Conflict and the Foundation of the Académie Royale de Danse: A Reexamination". *Dance Chronicle* 26/2 (2003).

Ralph, Richard, *The Life and Works of John Weaver. An Account of his Life, Writings and Theatrical Productions, with an Annotated Reprint of his Complete Publications.* London: Dance Books, 1985.

Rameau, Pierre, *Le Maître à danser.* Paris: Jean Villette, 1725. English: *The Dancing-Master*, trans. John Essex. London: J. Essex & J. Brotherton, 1728.

Reynolds, Sir Joshua, *Seven Discourses on Art* (delivered between 1769 and 1776), www.authorama.com/book/seven-discourses-on-art.html

Rice, Tamara, "The Evolution of Ballet". *Dancing Times* (London) December 1936.

Richardson, P. J. S., "Noverre's Parentage". *Dancing Times* (London) (November 1948).

—, "The First Noverre". *The Dancing Times* London February 1960.

Rosen, Charles, *The Classical Style: Haydn, Mozart, Beethoven.* New York, W. W. Norton, 1972; 1997.

Rousseau, Jean-Jacques. *Julie ou la Nouvelle Héloïse. Oeuvres Complètes.* Geneva: Gallimard, Bibliothèque de la Pléiade, 1964, vol. II.

Roy, Sanjoy, "Wrestling Noverre". *Dance Now* (London) 3/4 (Winter 1994).

Sieyès, Emmanuel Joseph, *Qu'est-ce que le tiers état?* Paris: Flammarion, 1988 (1788).

Sol, C., *Méthode très facile et fort nécessaire, pour montrer à la jeunesse de l'un et l'autre sexe la manière de bien dancer.* La Haye: l'Auteur, 1725.

Strässner, Matthias, *Tanzmeister und Dichter. Literaturgeschichte(n) im Umkreis von Jean Georges Noverre.* Berlin: Henschel, 1994.

Taubert, Gottfried, *Rechtschaffener Tantzmeister.* Leipzig: Friedrich Lanckischens Erben, 1717.

Touchard-Lafosse, Georges, *Chroniques secrètes et galantes de l'Opéra.* 4 vols. Paris: Schneider, 1846.

Voltaire (François-Marie Arouet). *Oeuvres Complètes.* 50 vols., ed. L. Moland. Paris: Garnier, 1877–85.

Weaver, John, *An Essay towards an History of Dancing.* London: J. Tonson, 1712.

—, *The Loves of Mars and Venus; A Dramatick Entertainment of Dancing, Attempted in Imitation of the Pantomimes of the Ancient Greeks and Romans.* London: W. Mears, J. Browne, 1717.

Wildeblood, Joan, *The Polite World.* London: Davis-Poynter, 1973.

Winter, Marian Hannah, *The Pre-Romantic Ballet.* London: Pitman, 1974.

Wycherly, William, *The Gentleman Dancing Master*, www3.shropshire-cc.gov.uk/etexts/E000294.htm.

Part III

Aschengreen, Erik, "The Beautiful Danger: Facets of Romantic Ballet", trans. Patricia N. McAndrew. *Dance Perspectives* 58 (Summer 1974), pp. 2–52.

—, *Der går dans*. Copenhagen: Gyldendal, 1998 (in Danish but with all important dates and names of the Royal Danish Ballet 1948–88).

Balanchine, George, *Balanchine's Complete Stories of the Great Ballets*, ed. Francis Mason. Garden City, N.Y. Doubleday, 1977.

Banes, Sally, *Dancing Women: Female Bodies on Stage*. London and New York: Routledge, 1998.

Baron, Auguste, *Lettres et entretiens sur la danse*. Paris: Donde-Dupré, 1824.

Barringer, Janice, and Schlesinger, Sarah, *The Point Book. Shoes, Training and Technique*. Hightstown N.J.: Princeton Book Co., 2004.

Beaumont, Cyril W., *Complete Book of Ballets: A Guide to the Principal Ballets of the Nineteenth and Twentieth Centuries*. London: Putnam, 1937, reprinted 1956; and *Supplement to Complete Book of Ballet*. London: C. W. Beaumont, 1942.

Beaumont, Cyril W., *The Ballet Called Giselle*. London: C. W. Beaumont, 1945.

Beaumont, Cyril W., and Idzikowski, Stanislas, *A Manual of the Theory and Practice of Classical Theatrical Dancing*. Mineola, N.Y.: Dover Publications, 1975–7.

Beaumont, Cyril W., and Sitwell, Sacheverell, *The Romantic Ballet in Lithographs of the Time*. London: Faber & Faber, 1938.

Benois, Alexandre, *Reminiscences of the Russian Ballet*, trans. Mary Britnieva. London: Putnam, 1941.

Bernstein, Susan, *Virtuosity of the Nineteenth Century: Performing Music and Language in Heine, Liszt, and Baudelaire*. Stanford, Calif.: Stanford University Press, 1998.

Binney, Edwin, III, *Glories of the Romantic Ballet*. London: Dance Books, 1985.

Bournonville, August, *My Theatre Life*, trans. Patricia N. McAndrew. London: A. & C. Black; Middletown, Conn.: Weslayan University Press, 1979.

Brown, David, *Tchaikovsky Remembered*. London: Faber & Faber, 1993.

Bruhn, Erik, and Moore, Lillian, *Bournonville and Ballet Technique: Studies and Comments on August Bournonville's Etudes Choregraphiques*. Hightstown, N.J.: Princeton Book Co., 1961, 2005.

Burt, Ramsay, *The Male Dancer*. London: Routledge, 1995.

Castil-Blaze, François-Henry-Joseph, *Dictionnaire de musique moderne*. 2 vols., Paris: Magasin de Musique de la Lyre Moderne, 1821.

—, *De l'opéra en France*. Paris: Chez l'auteur, 1826.

—, *La Danse et les ballets depuis Bacchus jusqu'à Mademoiselle Taglioni*. Paris: Castil-Blaze, 1832.

Chouquet, Gustave, *Histoire de la musique dramatique en France*. Paris: Librairie Firmin Didot Frères, 1873.

Clarke, Mary, and Crisp, Clement, *Ballet, An Illustrated History*. New York: Universe Books, 1973.

Clarke, Mary and Crisp, Clement, *Design for Ballet*. New York: Hawthorn Books, 1978.

Clarke, Mary, and Crisp, Clement, *Ballerina: The Art of Women in Classical Ballet*. London: BBC Books, 1987.

Christensen, Anne Middelboe, *Hvor danser Den Kgl. Ballet hen?* Interview med danserne om Bournonville-traditionen (Diversions of the Royal Danish Ballet) (English essay). Copenhagen: Schønberg, 2002.

Cohen, Selma Jeanne, *Dance as Theatre Art: Source Readings in Dance History from 1581 to the Present*. New York: Dodd & Mead, 1992.

Cordova, Sarah Davies, *Paris Dances. Textual Choreographies in the Nineteenth Century French Novel*. San Francisco: International Scholars Press, 1999.

Dahlhaus, Carl, *Nineteenth Century Music*, trans. J. Bradford. Berkeley: University of California Press, 1989.

Daly, Ann, *"Classical Ballet*: A Discourse of Difference", *Women and Performance* 3/2 (1987–8), pp. 57–66.

Delarue, Allison (ed.), *Fanny Elssler in America*. Brooklyn: Dance Horizons, 1976.

Deldevez, Edouard, *Mes Mémoires*. Le Puy: Marchessou Fils, 1890.

Dent, Edward, *The Rise of Romantic Opera*, ed. Winton Dean. Cambridge: Cambridge University Press, 1976.

Deshayes, André, *Idées générales sur l'Académie royale de Musique*. Paris: Mongie, 1822.

Dithmer, Monna (ed.), *Of Another World. Dancing between Dream and Reality*. Museum Tusculanum Press, Copenhagen, 2002.

Doolittle, Lisa and Flynn, Anne (eds.), *Dancing Bodies, Living Histories: New Writings about Dance and Culture*. Banff, Canada: The Banff Centre Press, 1999.

Fétis, François-Joseph, *Biographie universelle des musiciens*. 8 vols., Paris: Firmin-Didot & cie, 1875–83.

Fischer, Carlos, *Les Costumes de l'Opéra*. Paris: Librairie de France, 1931.

Foster, Susan Leigh, *Choreography and Narrative: Ballet's Staging of Story and Desire*. Bloomington and Indianapolis: Indiana University Press, 1996.

—, "The ballerina's phallic pointe", *Corporealities: Dancing Knowledge, Culture and Power*, ed. Susan Leigh Foster. London: Routledge, 1996, pp. 1–24.

Fulcher, Jane F., *The Nation's Image: French Grand Opera as Politics and Political Art*. Cambridge: Cambridge University Press, 1987.

Garafola, Lynn (ed.), *Rethinking the Sylph: New Perspectives on the Romantic Ballet*. Hanover, N. H., and London: Wesleyan University Press, 1997.

—, "The Travesty Dancer in Nineteenth Century Ballet", *Dance Research Journal* 17/2 (Fall–Spring 1985–6), pp. 35–40.

Gautier, Théophile, *Histoire de l'art dramatique en France depuis vingt-cinq ans*. 6 vols. Leipzig: Edition Hetzel, 1858–59; Geneva: Slatkine Reprints, 1968.

—, Théatres, Mystères, Comedies et Ballets. *OEuvres complètes*, Geneva: Slatkine Reprints, 1978.

—, *Gautier on Dance*, ed. and trans. Ivor Guest. London: Dance Books, 1986.

Gentil, Louis, *Les Cancans de l'Opéra: le journal d'une habilleuse 1836–1848*. Ed. Jean-Louis Tomvaco. Paris: CNRS Editions, 2000.

Gerhard, Anselm, *The Urbanization of Opera: Music Theater in Paris in the Nineteenth Century*. Chicago: University of Chicago Press, 1998.

Girard, René, *Deceit, Desire, and the Novel: Self and Other in Literary Structure*, trans. Yvonne Freccero. Baltimore: Johns Hopkins Press, 1965.

Guest, Ivor F., *Fanny Cerrito: The Life of a Romantic Ballerina*. London, Phoenix House, 1956.

—, *Victorian Ballet-Girl: The Tragic Story of Clara Webster*. London: A. & C. Black, 1957.

—, *Adeline Genée, a Lifetime of Ballet under Six Reigns; Based on the Personal Reminiscences of Dame Adeline Genée-Isitt*. London: A. & C. Black, 1958.

—, *The Romantic Ballet in Paris*. Middletown, Conn: Wesleyan University Press, 1966; London: Dance Books, 1980.

—, *Fanny Elssler*. Middletown, Conn.: Wesleyan University Press, 1970.

—, *The Romantic Ballet in England: Its Development, Fulfilment, and Decline*. Middletown, Conn.: Wesleyan University Press, 1972.

—, *The Ballet of the Second Empire*. London: Pitman and Middletown: Wesleyan University Press, 1974.

—, *Le Ballet de l'Opéra de Paris*. Paris: Flammarion, 1976.

—, *The Divine Virginia: A Biography of Virginia Zucchi*. New York: M. Dekker, 1977.

—, *Jules Perrot, Master of the Romantic Ballet*. New York: Dance Horizons, 1984.

—, *Ballet in Leicester Square: The Alhambra and the Empire, 1860–1915*. London: Dance Books and Princeton, N.J.: Princeton Book Co., 1992.

Hallar, Marianne, and Scavenius, Alette (eds.), *Bournonvilleana*. Copenhagen: Rhodos, 1992.

Hanna, Judith Lynne, *Dance, Sex and Gender: Signs of Identity, Dominance, Defiance, and Desire*. Chicago: University of Chicago Press, 1988.

Horosko, Marian, "If the Shoe Fits". *Dance Magazine* 60 (April 1986), pp. 80–1; 60 (May 1986), pp. 98–9.

Hutchinson, Ann, *Fanny Elssler's Cachucha*. Intro. Ivor F. Guest. New York: Theatre Arts Books, 1981.

Join-Diéterle, Catherine, *Les Décors de scène de l'Opéra de Paris à l'époque romantique*. Paris: Picard, 1988.

Jowitt, Deborah, *Time and the Dancing Image*. Los Angeles: University of California Press, 1988.

Jürgensen, Knud Arne, *The Ballet Tradition: The First Fifty Years, 1829–1879*. Vols. I–II. London: Dance Books, 1997.

Kahane, Martine, et al., *Le tutu*. Paris: Flammarion (Les petits guides de l'Opéra), 2000.

Karsavina, Tamara, *Theatre Street: The Reminiscences of Tamara Karsavina*. London: Heinemann, 1930.

Krasovskaya, Vera, "Marius Petipa and 'The Sleeping Beauty'", trans. Cynthia Read, *Dance Perspectives* 49 (Spring 1972).

—, *Vaganova: A Dance Journey from Petersburg to Leningrad*, trans. Vera M. Siegel, intro. Lynn Garafola. Gainesville: University Press of Florida, 2005.

Kschessinska, Mathilde (Kshesinska, Princess Romanovsky-Krassineky), *Dancing in Petersburg: The Memoirs of Kschessinska*, trans. Arnold Haskell. London: Gollancz, 1960.

Lawson, Joan, *A History of Ballet and its Makers*. London: Dance Books, 1923.

—, *A Ballet-Maker's Handbook: Sources, Vocabulary, Styles*. London: A. & C. Black and New York: Theatre Arts Books/Routledge, 1991.

Levinson, André, *Marie Taglioni*, trans. Cyril W. Beaumont. London: Dance Books, 1977.

—, *Ballet Old and New*, trans. from the Russian Susan Cook Summer. New York: Dance Horizons, 1982.

—, *Levinson on Dance. Writings from Paris in the Twenties.* Ed. Joan Acoccella and Lynn Garafola. Hanover N.H.: Wesleyan University Press, 1991.

Lifar, Serge, *Ballet, Traditional to Modern*, trans. Cyril W. Beaumont. London: Putnam, 1938.

—, *Giselle: Apothéose du ballet romantique.* Paris: Albin Michel, 1942.

—, *La Musique par la danse, de Lulli à Prokofiev.* Paris: R. Laffont, 1955.

Lynham, Derek, *Ballet Then and Now. A History of Ballet in Europe.* London: Sylvan Press, 1947.

McCarren, Felicia, *Dance Pathologies: Performance, Poetics, Medicine.* Stanford, Calif.: Stanford University Press, 1998.

Meglin, Joellen A., "Representations and Realities: Analyzing Gender Symbols in the Romantic Ballet", Ed.D. Diss. Temple University Philadelphia, 1995.

Mellor, Anne K. (ed.), *Romanticism and Feminism.* Bloomington: Indiana University Press, 1988.

Migel, Parmenia, *The Ballerinas. From the Court of Louis XIV to Pavlova.* New York: MacMillan, 1972.

Nettl, Paul, *The Story of Dance Music.* New York: Philosophical Library, 1947.

Nørlyng, Ole og Urup, Henning (ed.), *Bournonville. Tradition. Rekonstruktion.* (English summaries). Copenhagen: C.A. Reitzels Forlag, 1989.

Petipa, Marius, *Russian Ballet Master: The Memoirs of Marius Petipa.* Ed. Lillian Moore, trans. Helen Whittaker. London: A. & C. Black, 1958.

—,*The Diaries of Marius Petipa.* Ed., trans. and intro. Lynn Garafola. *Studies in Dance History* 3/1 (Spring 1992) Society of Dance History Scholar.

Pougin, Arthur, *Adolphe Adam: sa vie, sa carrière, ses mémoires artistiques.* Paris: Charpentier, 1877.

Reading Critics Reading: Opera and Ballet Criticism in France from the Revolution to 1848, ed. Roger Parker and Mary Ann Smart. Oxford: Oxford University Press, 2001.

Robin-Challan, Louise, *Danse et danseuses: l'envers du décor (1830–1850).* Thèse sociologie. Université de Paris VII, 1983.

Roslavleva, Natalia, *Era of the Russian Ballet.* Foreword Ninette de Valois. London: Gollancz, 1966.

Saint-Léon, Arthur, *La Sténochorégraphie: Ou, art d'écrire promptement la danse.* 1852.

—, *Letters from a Ballet-Master: The Correspondence of Arthur Saint-Léon.* Ed. Ivor F. Guest. New York: Dance Horizons, 1981.

Second, Albéric, *Les Petits Mystères de l'Opéra.* Paris: Kugelman 1844.

Slonimsky, Yuri, "Marius Petipa", trans. Anatole Chujoy, *Dance Index* 6/5–6 (May–June 1947).

Smith, Albert, *The Natural History of the Ballet Girl.* London: D. Bogue, 1847.

Smith, Marian, *Ballet and Opera in the Age of Giselle.* Princeton and Oxford: Princeton University Press, 2000.

—, "The Earliest *Giselle*? A Preliminary Report on a St Petersburg Manuscript". *Dance Chronicle: Studies in Dance and the Related Arts* 23/1 (2000), pp. 29–48.

Solomon-Godeau, Abigail, "The Other Side of Venus: The Visual Economy of Feminine Display", in Victoria de Grazia and Ellen Furlough (eds.), *The Sex of*

Things: Gender and Consumption in Historical Perspective. Berkeley: University of California Press 1996, pp. 113–150.

Sorell, Walter, *Looking back in Wonder: Diary of a Dance Critic.* New York: Columbia University Press, 1986.

—, *Dance in its Time.* New York: Columbia University Press 1986.

Souritz, Elizabeth, "Carlo Blasis in Russia (1861–1864)". *Studies in Dance History* 4/2 (Fall 1993).

Spilken, Terry, *The Dancers Foot Book: A Complete Guide to Foot Care.* Hightstown N.J.: Princeton Book Co., 1990.

Stepanov, Vladimir Ivanovich, *Alphabet of Movements of the Human Body: A Study in Recording the Movements of the Human Body by Means of Musical Signs.* Originally published in French 1892, New York: Princeton Book Publ. Dance Horizons, 1969.

Taruskin, Richard, *The Oxford History of Western Music,* New York: Oxford University Press, 2005.

Théleur, E. A., *Letters on Dancing.* Intro. Sandra N. Hammond. Society of Dance History Scholars: Pennington, N.J., 1990.

Terry, Walter, *On pointe! The Story of Dancing and Dancers on Toe.* New York: Dodd & Mead, 1962.

Verdy, Violette, *Giselle: A Role for a Lifetime.* New York: M. Dekker, 1977.

Véron, Louis-Désiré, *Mémoires d'un bourgeois de Paris.* Paris: Librairie nouvelle, 1856.

Wiley, Roland John, *Tchaikovsky's Ballets : Swan Lake, Sleeping Beauty, Nutcracker.* Oxford: Clarendon Press and New York: Oxford University Press, 1985.

—, (ed. and trans.), *A Century of Russian Ballet: Documents and Eyewitness Accounts 1810–1910.* Oxford: Clarenden Press, 1990.

—, *The Life and Ballets of Lev Ivanov: Choreographer of The Nutcracker and Swan Lake.* Oxford: Clarendon Press and New York: Oxford University Press, 1997.

Wolkonsky, Prince Serge, *My Reminiscences,* trans. A. E. Chamot. London: Hutchinson, n.d.

Newspapers
Journal des débats
Revue et gazette musicale de Paris

Part IV
Acocella, Joan, *Mark Morris.* New York: Noonday Press, 1995.

Acosta, Carlos, *Tocororo: A Cuban Tale.* London: Oberon Books, 2004.

Alfonso Rey, F., and Simón, P., *Alicia Alonso: Órbita de una Leyenda.* Madrid: SGAE, 1996.

Alonso, A., *Diálogos con la danza,* ed. P. Simón. La Habana: Letras Cubanas, 1986.

Amberg, George, *Ballet: The Emergence of an American Art.* New York: Duell, Sloan & Pearce, 1949.

Anderson, Jack, *The Nutcracker Ballet.* New York: Gallery Books, 1979.

—, *The One and Only: The Ballet Russe de Monte Carlo*. New York: Dance Horizons, 1981.

—, *Ballet and Modern Dance: A Concise History*. Hightstown, N.J.: Princeton Book Co., 1986.

—, *Art without Boundaries: The World of Modern Dance*. Iowa City: University of Iowa Press, 1997.

Anderson, Zoe, *The Royal Ballet: 75 Years*. London: Faber, 2006.

Baer, Nancy Van Norman (ed.), *Theatre in Revolution: Russian Avant-garde Stage Design, 1913–1935*. New York: Thames & Hudson; San Francisco: Fine Arts Museums of San Francisco, 1991.

—, (ed.), *Paris Modern: The Swedish Ballet 1920–1925*. San Francisco: Fine Arts Museums of San Francisco, 1995.

Banes, Sally, *Terpsichore in Sneakers: Post-Modern Dance*. Boston: Houghton Mifflin, 1979.

Beaumont, Cyril W., *The Monte Carlo Russian Ballet* (Les Ballets russes du Col. W. de Basil) London: C. W. Beaumont, 1934.

—, *The Sadler's Wells Ballet: A Detailed Account of Works in the Permanent Repertory*, with critical notes. London: C. W. Beaumont, 1947.

—, *Ballets of Today: Being a Second Supplement to the Complete Book of Ballets*. London: Putnam, 1954.

—, *Ballets Past and Present: Being a Third Supplement to the Complete Book of Ballets*. London: Putnam, 1954.

—, *Michel Fokine and his Ballets*. New York: Dance Horizons, 1981.

Beaumont, Cyril W., and Idzikowski, Stanislas, *A Manual of the Theory and Practice of Classical Theatrical Dancing: Cecchetti Method* (1922). Rev. edn, London, 1940. Reprints, New York: Dover Publications, 1975 and 2003.

Béjart, Maurice, *Béjart et la Danse de la symphonie pour un homme seul à la IX° Symphonie*. Brussels: Verbeeck, 1966.

—, *Le Ballet des mots*. Paris: Les Belles Lettres: Archimbaud, 1994.

—, *La Vie de qui?* Paris: Flammarion, 1996.

Bogdanov-Berezovskii, V. M., *Ulanova and the Development of the Soviet Ballet*, trans. Stephen Garry and Joan Lawson. London: 1952.

Bremser, Martha, *Fifty Contemporary Choreographers*. London: Routledge, 1999.

Brinson, Peter (ed.), *Ulanova, Moiseyev, and Zakharov on Soviet Ballet*, trans. E. Fox and D. Fry. London: Society for Cultural Relations, 1954.

—, *Background to European Ballet: A Notebook from its Archives*. Foreword by Mary Skeaping. Leyden: A. W. Sijthoff, 1966.

Buckle, Richard, *Nijinsky*. New York, Simon & Schuster, 1971.

—, *Diaghilev*. New York: Atheneum, 1979.

Buckle, Richard, in collaboration with John Taras, *George Balanchine: Ballet Master*. New York: Random House, 1988.

Chauviré, Yvette, and Mannoni, Gérard, *Yvette Chauviré – Autobiographie*. Paris: Le Quai 1997.

Choreography by George Balanchine: A Catalogue of Works, ed. Harvey Simmonds. New York: Viking, 1984.

Chujoy, Anatole, *The Symphonic Ballet*. New York: Kamin, 1937.

Clarke, Mary, *Dancers of Mercury*. London, 1961.

Cohen, Selma Jeanne, *Next Week, Swan Lake: Reflections on Dance and Dances*. Middletown, Conn.: Wesleyan University Press, 1982.

Copeland, Roger and Cohen, Marshall (eds.), *What is Dance?: Readings in Theory and Criticism*. New York: Oxford University Press, 1983.

Coton, A. V., *A Prejudice for Ballet*. London: Methuen, 1938.

—, *The New Ballet: Kurt Jooss and his Work*. London: D. Dobson, 1946.

Crisp, Clement, Sainsbury, Anya, and Williams, Peter (eds.), *Ballet Rambert: Fifty Years and On*. London: Ballet Rambert, 1981.

Daneman, Meredith, *Margot Fonteyn: A Life*. New York: Viking, 2004.

Danilova, Alexandra, *Choura: The Memoirs of Alexandra Danilova*. New York: Knopf/ Random House, 1986.

Denby, Edwin, *Looking at the Dance*. New York: Horizon Press, 1968.

—, *Dance Writings*, ed. Robert Cornfield and William MacKay. New York: Alfred A. Knopf, 1986, pp. 272–5, 445–50.

Duncan, Isadora, *My Life*. New York: H. Liveright, 1928.

Farrell, Suzanne, with Toni Bentley, *Holding on to the Air: An Autobiography*. New York : Summit Books, 1990.

Fisher, Jennifer, *Nutcracker Nation: How an Old World Ballet Became a Christmas Tradition in the New World*. New Haven and London: Yale, 2003.

Fokine, Michail, *Memoirs of a Ballet Master*, trans. Vitale Fokine, ed. Anatole Chujoy. Boston: Little, Brown, 1961

Franchi, Cristina (ed.), *Frederick Ashton. Founder Choreographer of the Royal Ballet*. London: Oberon Books, 2005.

—, (ed.), *Margot Fonteyn*. London: Oberon Books, 2005.

Frétard, Dominique and Tapie, Gilles (eds.), *Invitation: Sylvie Guillem*. London: Oberon Books 2006.

Garafola, Lynn, *Diaghilev's Ballets Russes*. New York: Oxford University Press, 1989.

García-Márquez, Vicente, *The Ballets Russes: Colonel de Basil's Ballets Russes de Monte Carlo, 1932–1952*. New York: Alfred A. Knopf, 1990.

—, *Massine. A Biography*. New York: Alfred A. Knopf, 1995.

García Victorica, Victoria, *El original Ballet Russe en América latina*. Buenos Aires: n.p., 1948.

Garis, R., *Following Balanchine*. New Haven: Yale University Press, 1995.

Giselle, film with Alicia Alonso and the National Ballet of Cuba, directed by E. Pineda Barnet (Havana: ICAIC, 1965).

Granet, Marcel, *Danses et legends de la Chine ancienne*. 2 vols. Paris: Presses Universitaires de France, 1959.

Grau, André, and Jordan, Stephanie (eds.), *Europe Dancing: Perspectives on Theatre Dance and Cultural Identity*. Eds. André Grau and Stephanie Jordan. London and New York: Routledge, 2000.

Häger, Bengt, *Ballets Suédois: The Swedish Ballet*, trans. Ruth Sherman. New York: H. N. Abrams, 1990.

Haskell, Arnold L., *Balletomania. New York*: Simon & Schuster: 1934.

—, *Diaghileff: His Artistic and Private Life*. New York: Simon & Schuster, 1935.

—, *Dancing Round the World*. New York: Dodge Comp., 1938.

—, *The National Ballet: A History and a Manifesto*. With an overture by Ninette de Valois. London: A. & C. Black, 1943.

Jeanmaire, Zizi, and Mannoni, Gérard, *Zizi Jeanmaire*. Paris: Assouline, 2002.

Jordan, Stephanie, *Moving Music : Dialogues with Music in Twentieth-Century Ballet* London: Dance Books, 2000.

Joseph, Charles M., *Stravinsky and Balanchine: A Journey of Invention*. New Haven : Yale University Press, 2002.

Jowitt, Deborah, "Celebrating the Solstice with Candycanes", in *Dance Beat: Selected Views and Reviews 1967–1976*. New York and Basel: Marcel Dekker, 1977.

Kahane, Martine, *Les Ballets russes de l'opéra*. Paris: Hazan, Bibliothèque Nationale, 1992.

—, *Nijinsky: 1889–1950*. Catalogue établi par Martine Kahane. Paris: Editions de la Réunion des musées nationaux, 2000.

Kavanagh, Julie, *Secret Muses: The Life of Frederick Ashton*. New York: Pantheon, 1996.

Kirstein, Lincoln., *Dance: A Short History of Classic Theatrical Dancing*. Westport, Conn.: Greenwood Press 1935/1970.

—, *Thirty Years: Lincoln Kirstein's The New York City Ballet, expanded to include the years 1973–1978*, in celebration of the company's thirtieth anniversary. New York: Knopf, 1978.

—, *Four Centuries of Ballet: Fifty Masterworks*. New York: Dover, 1984.

Laban, Rudolf von, *Modern Educational Dance*. London: Macdonald & Evans, 1948.

—, *A Life for Dance: Reminiscences*, trans. and annotated Lisa Ullmann. London: Macdonald & Evans, 1975.

Laws, Kenneth, *Physics and the Art of Dance: Understanding Movement*. Oxford and New York: Oxford University Press, 2002.

Lieven, Peter, *The Birth of Ballets-Russes*, trans. Leonide Zarine. London: George Allen & Unwin, 1936.

Lido, Serge, Lidova, Irène, and Béjart, Maurice, *Ballet dans le monde: Formes nouvelles*. Paris: Vilo, 1977.

Lidova, Irène, *Dix-sept visages de la danse française*. Paris: Art et Industrie, 1953.

—, *Roland Petit*. Paris: Vilo, 1956.

Lifar, Serge, *Serge Diaghilev, His Life, His Work, His Legend: An Intimate Biography*. New York: G. P. Putnam's Sons, 1940.

—, *The Three Graces: Anna Pavlova, Tamara Karsavina, Olga Spessivtzeva; the Legends and the Truth*, trans. Gerard Hopkins. London: Cassell, 1959.

Lopukhov, Fedor Vasilevich, *Writings on Ballet and Music*, ed. and intro. Stephanie Jordan; trans. Dorinda Offord. Madison: University of Wisconsin Press, 2002.

Mannoni, Gérard (ed.), *Roland Petit*. Paris: Avant-scène, 1984.

Mannoni, Gérard, *Roland Petit: Un chorégraphe et ses peintres*. Paris: Hatier, 1990.

Mannoni, Gérard, and Masson, Colette, *Maurice Béjart*. Paris: Plume 1991.

Maré, Rolf de (ed.), *Les Ballets Suédois dans l'art contemporain*. Paris: Editions du Trianon, 1931.

Massine, Léonide, *My Life in Ballet*. London: Macmillan, 1968.

Mazo, Joseph H., *Prime Movers: The Makers of Modern Dance in America*. Hightstown, N.J.: Princeton Book Co., 2000.

de Mille, Agnes, *America dances.* New York : Macmillan, 1980.

—, *Reprieve: A Memoir.* Garden City, N.Y.: Doubleday, 1981.

Morris, Mark, *Mark Morris's l'Allegro, il pensoroso ed il moderato: a celebration*, ed. Jeffrey Escoffier and Matthew Lore. New York: Marlowe & Co., 2001.

Nemenschousky, Leon, *A Day with Yvette Chauviré.* London: Cassell, 1960.

Nijinska, Bronislava, *Early Memoirs*, ed. and trans. Irina Nijinska and Jean Rawlinson New York: Holt, Rinehart & Winston, 1981.

Nijinsky, Romola. *Nijinsky.* New York: Simon & Schuster, 1934.

Nijinsky, Vaclav, *The Diary of Vaslav Nijinsky*, ed. Romola Nijinsky. Berkeley: University of California Press, 1968 (*c.*1936).

Norton, Leslie, *Leonide Massine and the 20th Century Ballet.* Jefferson, N.C.: McFarland & Co., 2004.

Perlmutter, Donna, *Shadowplay: The Life of Anthony Tudor.* Newark N.J.: Limelight Editions, 1995.

Petit, Roland, and Mannonni, Gérard, *Roland Petit, un choréographe et ses danseurs.* Paris: Plume 1992.

Plissetskaia, Maya M., *I, Maya Plisetskaya*, trans. Antonina W. Bouis, foreword by Tim Scholl. New Haven: Yale University Press, 2001.

Prevots, Naima, *Dance for Export: Cultural Diplomacy and the Cold War.* Intro. Eric Foner. Middletown, Conn.: Wesleyan University Press, 2001.

Propert, Walter Archibald, *The Russian Ballet 1909–1920.* London: John Lane The Bodley Head, 1921.

—, *The Russian Ballet 1921–1929.* London: John Lane The Bodley Head, 1931.

Rambert. A Celebration, comp. Jane Pritchard, intro. Mary Clarke and Clement Crisp. London: Rambert Dance Company, 1996.

Reynolds, Nancy and McCormick, Malcolm, *No Fixed Points.* New Haven: Yale University Press, 2003.

Sachs, Curt. *World History of the Dance*, trans. Bessie Schonberg. New York: Norton, 1965. (Originally published in German in 1933.)

Schneider, Marcel, and Michel, Marcelle, *Danse à Paris.* Paris: Grasset, 1983.

Scholl, T., *From Petipa to Balanchine: Classical Revival and the Modernization of Ballet.* London: Routledge, 1994.

Schorer, Suki, *Balanchine Pointework.* Studies in Dance History, no. 11. Madison: Wisconsin University Press, 1995.

Siegel, Marcia, "Decomposing Sugar Plums and Robot Mice". *Ballet Review* 19/1 (Spring 1991), pp. 58–62.

—, "Kingdom of the Sweet", *Hudson Review* 50/2 (Summer 1997), pp. 255–67.

Solomon, Ruth and John (eds.), *East Meets West in Dance: Voices in the Cross-Cultural Dialogue.* Chur, Switzerland: Harwood Academic Publishers, 1995.

Solway, Diane, *Nureyev: His Life.* New York: William Morrow, 1998.

Souritz, Elizabeth, *Soviet Choreographers in the 1920s*, trans. Lynn Visson. Durham, N.C.: Duke University Press, 1990.

Svenska baletten: Les Ballets Suédois, 1920–1925. Stockholm, 1969, 1995. Exhibition catalog, Dansmuseet.

Taper, Bernard, *Balanchine. A Biography. With a New Epilogue.* New York: Times Books, 1984; and Berkeley: University of California Press, 1996.

Teachout, Terry, *All in the Dances: A Brief Life of George Balanchine.* Orlando: Harcourt, 2004.

Terry, Walter, *Ballet Guide: Background, Listings, Credits, and Descriptions of More Than Five Hundred of the World's Major Ballets.* New York: Dodd, Mead, 1976.

—, *I Was There: Selected Dance Reviews and Articles, 1936–1976.* New York: Dekker, 1978.

—, *Alicia and her Ballet Nacional de Cuba.* Garden City, N.Y.: Anchor Books, 1981.

Vaganova, Agrippina, *Basic Principles of Classical Ballet: Russian Ballet Technique,* trans. Anatole Chujoy, ed. Peggy van Praagh. New York: Dover Publications, 1953/69.

Vaughan, David, *Frederick Ashton and his Ballets.* London: A. & C. Black, 1977.

Volkov, Solomon. *Balanchine's Tchaikovsky: Interviews with George Balanchine.* New York: Simon and Schuster, 1985.

Walker, Katherine Sorley, *Ninette de Valois: An Idealist without Illusions.* London: Hamish Hamilton, 1988.

Wiley, Roland John, "On Meaning in *Nutcracker*". *Dance Research* 3/1 (autumn 1984), pp. 3–28.

Encyclopedias and dictionaries

Balet Entsiklopediia. See *Soviet Ballet Encyclopedia.*

Concise Oxford Companion to the Theatre, The, ed. Phyllis Hartnoll and Peter Found. New York: Oxford University Press 1996/2003.

Concise Oxford Dictionary of Ballet, The, ed. *Horst Koegler.* Oxford, London, New York: Oxford University Press, 1982.

Concise Oxford Dictionary of Opera, The, ed. John Warrack and Ewan West. London, New York: Oxford University Press 1996/2003.

Dance Encyclopedia, The, ed. and comp. Anatole Chujoy and P.W. Manchester. New York: Simon & Schuster, 1967.

Dictionnaire des danses de la Renaissance, ed. Henri Jarrie. Arles: Harmonia Mundi, 1970.

Dictionnaire de la musique en France aux XVIIe et XVIIIe siècles, ed. Marcelle Benoit. Paris: Fayard, 1992.

Encyclopedia of Dance and Ballet, The, ed. Mary Clarke and David Vaughan. New York: Putnam, 1977.

Encyclopedia of Musical Theatre, The, ed. Kurt Ganzl. New York: Schirmer Books, 2001. 3 vols.

International Dictionary of Ballet, The, ed. Martha Bremser. Detroit: St James's Press, 1993.

International Encyclopedia of Dance, The, ed. Selma Jean Cohen and Dance Perspectives Foundation. Oxford: Oxford University Press, 1998, 2005.

Musik in Geschichte und Gegenwart: Allgemeine Enzyklopädie der Musik. Kassel: Bärenreiter, 1994.

New Grove Dictionary of Music and Musicians, The, ed. Stanley Sadie and John Tyrrell. London: Macmillan, 2001. 29 vols.

New Harvard Dictionary of Music, The, ed. Don Michael Randel. Cambridge, Mass.: Harvard University Press, 1986.

Oxford Dictionary of Dance, The, ed. Debra Craine and Judith Mackrell. New York: Oxford University Press, 2000.

Oxford Dictionary of Music, The, ed. Michael Kennedy, associate ed. Joyce Bourne. New York: Oxford University Press 1996/2003/4.

Oxford Encyclopedia of Theatre and Performance, ed. Dennis Kennedy. New York: Oxford University Press, 2003–5.

Pipers Enzyklopädie des Musiktheaters: Oper, Operette, Musical, Ballett, ed. Carl Dahlhaus and Sieghart Döhring. Munich: Piper, 1986–97.

Soviet Ballet Encyclopedia (Balet Entsiklopediia). Moscow: Sovetskaia Entsiklopediia, 1981.

Index of persons

Index of ballets

Subject index

The Cambridge Companion to Music

Topics

The Cambridge Companion to Ballet
Edited by Marion Kant

The Cambridge Companion to Blues and Gospel Music
Edited by Allan Moore

The Cambridge Companion to the Concerto
Edited by Simon P. Keefe

The Cambridge Companion to Conducting
Edited by José Antonio Bowen

The Cambridge Companion to Grand Opera
Edited by David Charlton

The Cambridge Companion to Jazz
Edited by Mervyn Cooke and David Horn

The Cambridge Companion to the Lied
Edited by James Parsons

The Cambridge Companion to the Musical
Edited by William Everett and Paul Laird

The Cambridge Companion to the Orchestra
Edited by Colin Lawson

The Cambridge Companion to Pop and Rock
Edited by Simon Frith, Will Straw and John Street

The Cambridge Companion to the String Quartet
Edited by Robin Stowell

The Cambridge Companion to Twentieth-Century Opera
Edited by Mervyn Cooke

Composers

The Cambridge Companion to Bach
Edited by John Butt

The Cambridge Companion to Bartók
Edited by Amanda Bayley

The Cambridge Companion to Beethoven
Edited by Glenn Stanley

The Cambridge Companion to Berg
Edited by Anthony Pople

The Cambridge Companion to Berlioz
Edited by Peter Bloom

The Cambridge Companion to Brahms
Edited by Michael Musgrave

The Cambridge Companion to Benjamin Britten
Edited by Mervyn Cooke

Edited by Richard Ingham

The Cambridge Companion to Singing
Edited by John Potter

The Cambridge Companion to the Violin
Edited by Robin Stowell